SARAH SIDDONS

SOME BOOKS BY
ROGER MANVELL

Non-fiction
Film
On the Air: A Study of Radio and Television
The Film and the Public
The Living Screen: A Study of Film and Television
This Age of Communication
New Cinema in Europe
New Cinema in the USA
New Cinema in Britain
Ellen Terry
Sarah Siddons

Novels
The Dreamers
The Passion

BOOKS BY
ROGER MANVELL and HEINRICH FRAENKEL

Doctor Goebbels
Hermann Göring
The July Plot
Heinrich Himmler
The Incomparable Crime
The Canaris Conspiracy
A History of the German Cinema

Roger Manvell

SARAH SIDDONS

Portrait of an Actress

Heinemann : London

William Heinemann Ltd

LONDON   MELBOURNE   TORONTO
JOHANNESBURG   AUCKLAND

First published 1970
© Roger Manvell, 1970

434 45026 X

Printed in Great Britain by
Morrison and Gibb Ltd, London and Edinburgh

To
Dame Sybil Thorndike, C.H.,
this book about her great
predecessor is affectionately
dedicated

Contents

Illustrations

Text Illustrations

s.s.—1*

Acknowledgements

IN NO BOOK I have written have I seemed to owe quite so much to the generous and enthusiastic help received from a wide range of people – sometimes because I asked for it and, sometimes, unexpectedly, because people I had not thought of approaching volunteered information or illustrations in the kindest possible manner. I must place at the head of the list of those who have helped me the late Richard Hubbard, formerly honorary librarian of the Authors' Club in London, whose private library was rich in eighteenth-century literature, and with whom I was in constant correspondence after his retirement to Wales up to the time of his sudden and unexpected death. Other helpers and advisers I name alphabetically merely to avoid the invidious situation of seeming to impose priorities on their work where none is intended. My special thanks, therefore, to:

Miss Jennifer Aylmer, Curator of the British Theatre Museum, for constant advice, and information about the Siddons material in the possession of the Museum;

Miss Kathleen Barker, author of *The Theatre Royal Bristol: the First Seventy Years*, for information connected with Mrs Siddons's links with that theatre, and for providing me with a list of contemporary Press references to her;

Miss Ann Brooke Barnett, Keeper of the Theatre Collection of the Department of Drama of the University of Bristol, for help in connexion with the illustrations;

Andrew Block, for his cheerful and thorough search for books and other material connected with the period;

Gerald Burden, for his expert help in connexion with tracing letters and other manuscripts of the period;

E. B. Cradel, Librarian of the University Library, Cambridge, for advice concerning the Lawrence-Siddons-Pennington correspondence now in the possession of the Library, and which forms the basis for Chapter 6 of this book;

Norman Cusden, for help in acquiring for me theatrical prints and drawings of the period;

Barry Duncan, for acquiring for me a copy of the rare Galindo letter to Mrs Siddons;

Miss Yvonne ffrench, my predecessor as a biographer of Mrs Siddons, for invaluable information and discussion, and for most generously allowing me the use of illustrations in her possession;

Mrs Enid M. Forster, Librarian of the British Drama League, for her unfailing help while I was using the rich resources of the B.D.L. Library for research;

Roland Gant, Editorial Director of William Heinemann Limited, for his constant encouragement during the preparation of this book, and advice with contacts;

J. W. Gardner, of Kingswood School, Bath, for advice in connexion with my researches in Bath;

Mrs Mary Gibson, for much personal help in Bath, and especially for compiling, with the help of Mrs Brackenbury, a list of references to Mrs Siddons in the contemporary Bath press;

Kenneth Garside, Librarian of King's College, for advice and help in obtaining elusive books;

Miss Norah C. Gillow, of the City of York Art Gallery, for help in connexion with Mrs Siddons's work at York;

Ronald Hall, Librarian of the John Rylands Library, Manchester, for constant help in connexion with the Siddons family correspondence in the possession of the Library;

Sir Julian Hall, Bt., of the Garrick Club, for his help in connexion with Siddons documentation preserved in the Library of the Garrick Club;

N. Higson, County Archivist to the East Riding of Yorkshire, for help in connexion with Siddons correspondence preserved in the County Record Office;

Mrs A. N. McKechnie of Bath, for giving me the splendid silhouettes of Mrs Siddons and John Philip Kemble which appear in this book;

Miss Dorothy E. Mason, Reference Librarian at the Folger Shakespeare Library, for checking the Siddons correspondence preserved in the Library, and providing photocopies;

Dr and Mrs N. C. Northmann, for tracing prints of the period of this book;

Peter Pagan, Director of the Municipal Libraries and Victoria Art Gallery, City of Bath, for help in connexion with the many Siddons documents preserved at the Library;

Sir John Summerson, Curator of the Sir John Soane Museum, for advice on architectural drawings of eighteenth-century theatres;

Miss Sybil Rosenfeld, Honorary Secretary of the Society for

Theatre Research, for advice and information;

Miss Helen D. Willard, Curator of the Harvard Theatre Collection at the Houghton Library of Harvard University, for help in connexion with the Siddons family correspondence preserved in the Collection, and for permission to quote from the original text of Mrs Siddons's biographical notes for Campbell.

I should also like to express my gratitude to Dr Levi Fox, Director of the Shakespeare Birthplace Trust, to J. F. W. Sherwood, Librarian of Hereford City Library, to Robert R. Wark, Director of the Henry E. Huntington Library and Art Gallery, to Mrs J. Perceval, of the Library of University College, London, and to Mrs Anderson of the Library of the Garrick Club, for the information they have given me, and to the staffs of the National Register of Archives, the National Portrait Gallery, the Print Room and Department of Manuscripts of the British Museum, the Victoria and Albert Museum, and at the following libraries – the British Drama League, the University of London, Bath Municipal Library, and the Rylands Library, Manchester.

Lastly, Mrs Enid Audus who helped me in putting together and typing the original manuscript. I also want to thank my wife for undertaking a considerable amount of difficult photocopying in connexion with the quotations from eighteenth-century sources which are a feature of this book.

January 1970.   ROGER MANVELL

I

Portrait of a Young Actress

==========◦⟡◦==========

O N THE NIGHT of 10 October 1782 Sarah Siddons stood
offstage in the wings of Drury Lane Theatre. She was
waiting to face the critical London public. Although she
had fifteen years' hard experience as an actress behind her, she
was feeling strained and nervous. The fact that she had been on
the stage since her childhood was of little use to her now. There
were particular reasons why she should be so tense. Earlier in her
career, seven years before, in 1775, David Garrick, in his final
season in this same theatre, had given her a great opportunity to
conquer this notoriously difficult and temperamental London
audience, and she had failed. Time and again through the months
of work at Drury Lane she had been given her chance to succeed.
She had failed then through sheer lack of resilience, working at
first too soon after the birth of her daughter Sally, and feeling
overshadowed by the older, jealous actresses who resented her
presence.

At that time she was only twenty-one years old, an immature
provincial player, unable to withstand the powerful rivalries of
these skilful and malicious women. Now, at twenty-eight,
following a prolonged and highly successful season at Bath,
England's most fashionable theatrical centre after London, she
felt far stronger. Her publicity – 'puffing', as it was then called –
had been carefully prepared in the London journals by William,
her husband and business manager. But no one, least of all Sarah,
who was shy and even diffident when it came to dealing with
people outside the theatre, could approach this moment of truth
on the open stage without experiencing great emotional strain.

As a young girl, she could be allowed to fail once; as a mature young woman, she must not fail. Her profession could not sustain a second collapse.

Above everything else she feared the loss of her voice. Every actor is familiar with this traumatic obsession that at the supreme moment his voice will disappear. Two days before, after the first of the two meagre rehearsals allowed her, she had found herself afflicted with a sudden hoarseness. She had recovered, but under the strain of performance she was afraid her throat might fail her again. But she knew after her prolonged successes in the provinces – in Birmingham, Liverpool, Manchester, York, and, above all, in Bristol and Bath – that once she stood firmly upon the stage and assumed her place as the character in the play, her fears would forsake her in the grand feat of actual performance. So, as she stood there waiting, she experienced what she used to call her state of 'desperate tranquillity'.

The play, Thomas Southerne's celebrated *Isabella, or, The Fatal Marriage*, had a part exactly suited to her powers. It also suited exactly the emotional susceptibilities of her audience, who went to the theatre to indulge themselves in the same emotions as those portrayed by the players. Actors and actresses were expected to cleave their way into the hearts of their audience, banishing all resistance, derision or would-be intellectual criticism by appealing directly and irresistibly to their emotional susceptibilities. Men would weep when moved to do so; fashionable women would fall into hysterics, fainting in the hot crush of the theatre pit. What audiences above all resented, and resented vociferously, was the inability of an actor or actress to stir them.

Isabella, or, The Fatal Marriage, though almost a century old, was written precisely to achieve these ends, and everyone knew it as well as they knew Shakespeare's more obvious plays. Isabella was a part Sarah had often played before, most notably in Bath. It called for a strong sense of pathos; it was the story of a devoted, single-minded, poverty-stricken woman who believes herself to be a widow and, against every inclination in her heart, remarries solely to give her child security and a better upbringing. The day following her marriage her first husband reappears and, driven distracted, she kills herself. Nothing was better calculated to conquer audiences in or out of London than the sub-Shakespearian rhetoric to which any actress of mettle could lay her tongue, as in this address to the sleeping Villeroy, the husband to whom she now realizes she has no real right:

Asleep so soon! O happy! happy thou!
Who thus can'st sleep: I never shall sleep more.
If then to sleep be to be happy, he
Who sleeps the longest, is the happiest;
Death is the longest Sleep. O! have a Care,
Mischief will thrive apace. Never wake more;
If thou didst ever love thy Isabella,
Tomorrow must be Dooms-day to thy Peace.
—The sight of him disarms ev'n Death it self.
—The starting Transport of new quick'ning Life
Gives just such Hopes; and Pleasure grows again
With looking on him—Let me look my last—
But is a Look enough for parting Love!
Sure I may take a Kiss—where am I going!
Help, help me, Villeroy!—Mountains, and Seas
Divide your Love never to meet my Shame.[1]

The moment she took the stage at the beginning of the play and spoke the first familiar lines, using all her skill to hush and then to move her audience, Sarah knew she was carrying her audience with her. The great climaxes lay ahead, when she would be able to take them by the throat through her grand displays of emotion. First of all she must win them, and after this gradually overwhelm them. Everything was in her favour: her voice had returned to her and she was using it with powerful effect; her mature but still youthful beauty was gaining their sympathy. Her very nervousness added strength to the performance; she knew how to draw on it to add sincerity and private feeling to the rhetoric and exhibitionism of the theatre. Before she finally left the stage that night, there was no doubt of her success. Acclamations had broken out long before the play was ended.

Quiet, absorbed still by the experiences of the night, triumphant certainly, but above all relieved at her overwhelming success, she retired exhausted to her new lodgings in the Strand to enjoy a 'frugal supper' with her husband, William, and her father, Roger Kemble. William was still overcome by his wife's success after the long years of labour and obscurity; Roger, an old actor who understood far better the turmoil of feeling his daughter had endured, wept silently for joy, brushing the tears from his cheeks. Now it would be all right. London was hers.

He and William, not so long ago a rather lumbering young actor in Roger Kemble's little troupe of strolling players, had seen Sarah's hidden talents grow through the prolonged period of her shy, unflowering immaturity. William would never understand his wife, whose mystery was that she concealed both genius and power under the guise of a tranquil and domesticated wife and mother. Her strength in the theatre was all the greater for the slowness with which it had developed. Only the tenacity with which she had lived through the hard adventures of her youth showed that this woman, in spite of her evident domesticity and her seven children, was entirely different, and would become the greatest name among tragic actresses in the history of the English theatre.

Sarah's father, Roger Kemble, had been an actor-manager of some note. Like Ben Terry, father of Kate, Ellen and Fred Terry, who were to 'stroll' almost a century later than Roger Kemble, he was to found one of the great dynasties of artists who have distinguished the English stage. Roger, like Ben, had no previous family connexions with the theatre; indeed, he was said to have worked as a barber, like his brother, before deserting this trade and becoming a player.[2] He was born in Hereford in 1721, and did not become an actor until he was thirty, drawn by some indefinable instinct to give up a safe trade for an insecure and socially disreputable life. He was a courteous man, handsome and well-bred. He was fortunate in 1752 to join one of those rarer travelling companies in the mid-eighteenth century which, under the actor-manager John Ward, who had appeared with Betterton as a child, were trying to bring respectability and social status to the actor's profession.[3] Ward, in fact, overdid it by becoming a Methodist and treating his players with the sternest discipline, so he was not amused when his strong-willed and beautiful daughter, Sally, fell in love with the fine figure and gentle manners of the actor who had recently joined her father's company. With Christian forbearance, Ward gave in: 'Well, my dear child,' tradition has it he said to Sally, 'you have not disobeyed me; the d-v-l himself could not make an actor of your husband.' Roger and Sally were married at Cirencester in 1753. Ward eventually passed on the goodwill of his company to his daughter and son-in-law, and retired from the profession, so deserving the addition of the word 'gentleman' after his name on his tombstone in Leominster, where he died twenty years later.

What the Kembles had inherited was the goodwill not only of Ward's company, but of the 'circuit' in which he had operated, in effect the English West Midlands stretching north to Lancashire and south to Warwickshire and Gloucestershire. Since strolling players were entirely subject to the whims of the various local authorities in whose districts they proposed to perform, to be known and even a little respected mattered considerably. Even so, respectable actors and actresses often had to seek local patrons among the gentry to 'protect' them, and cadge patronage from passers-by with handbills. However, only too frequently, groups of so-called 'actors' proved to be little better than drunken vagrants with whom the authorities could do what they liked under the vagrancy laws. The lowest kind of players were not actors at all, but travelling performers and showmen who, as often as not, indulged in petty thieving or slipped away in the night, leaving their debts behind them, and giving the whole profession of playing a bad name.

The theatre, in fact, existed only under sufferance, subject to the original licensing system introduced after the Restoration, and the subsequent Licensing Act of 1737. At the upper end of the scale existed the recognized London theatres, headed by Drury Lane and Covent Garden, which were licensed by royal patent, a system introduced in 1660 by Charles II in order to exercise control, both political and, from time to time, moral, over stage performances. The custom of touring or 'strolling' companies, originally at best carrying Letters Patent from the King or a licence from the Lord Chamberlain, grew up in the seventeenth century, and they played, as in Shakespeare's time, in any premises held to be suitable, from barns and inn yards to guildhalls if they were fortunate enough to win the favour of the authorities. During the eighteenth century companies working the provinces began to adopt circuits, and became in a fuller sense provincial, regional and local, with a touring system worked out to coincide with those weeks when the towns would be at their fullest and liveliest – for example during race weeks, or when fairs were taking place or the assizes were being held. The establishment of these circuits led to actual playhouses being built in the provinces in those towns which could be relied on to produce good audiences: some of the earliest eighteenth-century playhouses were built at Bath, Bristol and York.

The status of the players, however, was always in doubt, and

was controlled in the eighteenth century by the Act of 1713.[4]
The sterner religious elements in the community were staunchly
against letting them gain any sort of foothold, bringing sin and
damnation in their wake. It was this element who secured the
passing of the Licensing Act of 1737, which became an onerous
burden on the strolling players because, if invoked, it could
deprive them of the right to act plays for any kind of monetary
reward. The companies nevertheless continued to stroll, but they
had to circumvent the terms of the Licensing Act by charging
only for the musical part of the programme, and, nominally at
least, presenting the plays entirely free. Any local authority which
chose to be stiff-necked could invoke the Licensing Act against
the players and have them chased out of the town, and if the
authorities themselves were lax, that nuisance the common informer
could insist on a more rigorous application of the law. In the
eighteenth century Garrick, in particular, brought great social
distinction as well as genius to the London theatre, but working
under such strict limitations in the provinces the profession of
acting was always threatened by one form of persecution or
another. The actors and actresses, too, showed signs of strain and
temperament in their relations with one another; intense personal
rivalries and transference from one prominent London company
to the other were normal. Jealousy of fame afflicted actors and
actresses alike, nor were their personal lives entirely stable.
But the art of acting persisted in spite of all these difficulties and
certain cities outside London became centres where the theatre
was taken seriously; most of all, perhaps, Dublin, Edinburgh,
and cities with good stable managements such as Bath and
York.

Most players received their initial training in the provinces,
which turned them from youthful, stage-struck amateurs into
audience-hardened professionals. If they were to progress, it was
absolutely necessary to be accepted by one of the better stock
companies under a manager who respected his profession and
knew his public. Such managers certainly existed, more especially
in the later part of the eighteenth century. Among them, as we
shall see, were strong personalities like Tate Wilkinson, who
controlled the York 'circuit'. But the recruitment of actors was
often haphazard, while that of young actresses might well depend
more on their sexual than their acting abilities. Thomas Holcroft,
who was later to work for Roger Kemble, has left us a fascinating

a. The Façade of Drury Lane Theatre in 1777.

account, edited after his death by William Hazlitt, of how he was 'interviewed' first by the great actor Charles Macklin, who used talent scouts, one of whom picked up young Holcroft, and secondly by the equally famous Samuel Foote. Holcroft, son of a travelling salesman, had had a harsh upbringing of astonishing cruelty, and had been a stable-boy at Newmarket and a cobbler in London before trying his luck as an actor. Hazlitt takes up the story when the talent scout fancies the appearance of this likely-looking young man:

The next morning they proceeded to the place of appointment, when they found the great man seated on his couch, which stood by the fire; and on which, whenever he felt himself tired or drowsy, he went to rest, both day and night; so that he sometimes was not in bed for a fortnight together. As they went in, they were followed by his wife, who brought him a bason of tea and some toast, with each of which he found fifty faults in the rudest manner. He afterwards called to her several times, upon the most frivolous occasions, when she was dignified with the style and title of Bess. His countenance, as it appeared to Mr Holcroft at this interview, was the most forbidding he had ever beheld; and age, which had deprived him of his teeth, had not added to its softness. After desiring the young candidate to sit down, he eyed him very narrowly for some time, and then asked him, *What had put it into his head to turn actor?* The abruptness of the question disconcerted him; and it was some time before he could answer, in rather a confused manner, that he had *taken it into his head* to suppose it was genius, but that it was very possible he might be mistaken. 'Yes,' said he, 'that's possible enough; and by G—d, Sir, you are not the first that I have known so mistaken.' Holcroft smiled at his satire, and the other grinned ghastly with his leathern lips, for our tyro had not added to the beauty of his visage by repeating his words. While Macklin was drinking his tea, they talked on indifferent subjects; and as Holcroft did not happen to differ with him, but on the contrary had opportunities of saying several things which confirmed his opinions, he was pleased to allow that he had the appearance of an ingenious young man. When his beverage was finished, he desired him to speak a speech out of some play, which being done, he remarked that he had never in his life heard a young spouter speak naturally, and therefore he was not surprised that Holcroft did not: but, as he seemed tractable, and willing to learn, if he would call again on the morrow, he would hear and answer him further.

When they had descended into the street, Holcroft's companion assured him *it would do*, for that he had met with a very favourable reception; which was indeed the case, considering the character of the person to whom their visit had been paid. . . .

Holcroft, however, remained uncertain of Macklin and went on to see Foote:

He had the good fortune to find the manager at breakfast with a young man, whom he employed partly on the stage, and partly as an amanuensis. 'Well,' said he, 'young gentleman, I guess your business by the sheepishness of your manner; you have got the theatrical cacoethes, you have rubbed your shoulder against the scene: hey, is it not so?' Holcroft answered that it was. 'Well, and what great hero should you wish to personate? Hamlet, or Richard, or Othello, or who?' Holcroft replied, that he distrusted his capacity for performing any that he had mentioned. 'Indeed,' said he, 'that's a wonderful sign of grace. I have been teazed for these many years by all the spouters in London, of which honourable fraternity I dare say you are a member; for I can perceive no stage varnish, none of your true strolling brass lacker on your face.'—'No indeed, Sir.'—'I thought so. Well, Sir, I never saw a spouter before, that did not want to surprise the town in Pierre, or Lothario, or some character that demands all the address, and every requisite of a master in the art. But, come, give us a touch of your quality; a speech: here's a youngster,' pointing to his secretary, 'will roar Jaffier against Pierre, let the loudest take both.' Accordingly, he held the book, and at it they fell: the scene they chose, was that of the before-mentioned characters in Venice Preserved. For a little while after they began, it seems that Holcroft took the hint Foote had thrown out, and restrained his wrath: but this appeared so insipid, and the ideas of rant and excellence were so strongly connected in his mind, than when Jaffier began to exalt his voice, he could no longer contain himself; but, as Nic Bottom says, they both roared so, that it would have done your heart good to hear them. Foote smiled, and after enduring this vigorous attack upon his organs of hearing as long as he was able, interrupted them.

Far from discouraging our new beginner, he told him, that with respect to giving the meaning of the words, he spoke much more correctly than he had expected. 'But,' said he, 'like other novices, you seem to imagine that all excellence lies in the lungs: whereas such violent exertions should be used but very sparingly, and upon extraordinary occasions; for (besides that these two gentlemen, instead of straining their throats, are supposed to be in common conversation) if an actor make no reserve of his powers, how is he to rise according to the tone of the passion?' He then read the scene they had rehearsed, and with so much propriety and ease, as well as force, that Holcroft was surprised, having hitherto supposed the risible faculties to be the only ones over which he had any great power.[5]

Since Macklin offered Holcroft thirty shillings a week against Foote's twenty, Holcroft went with Macklin to Ireland.

Roger Kemble was too gentle a man to be an altogether effective theatrical manager in the tradition of Macklin and Foote. But what he lacked in ferocity was made up for by his wife, Sally; in addition to giving birth to twelve children, two of whom were to become famous, she ruled the Kemble company with the same iron discipline as her father had done before her. She put respectability above art, and was determined the Kemble company should have a good name with the public.

Her first child was born in 1755 while the company was on tour in Brecon. The Kembles, presenting such plays as Rowe's *Tamerlane* and Foote's *Englishmen at Paris*, had arrived in time for the May Fair and stayed two months, a sign that they were very welcome in Brecon and favoured by the authorities. Sally Kemble must have been glad of the rest, but the company had to move on to the spa at Llandrindod on 3 July to give a week's performances, leaving her behind at the Shoulder of Mutton Inn, where she gave birth to her daughter Sarah on 5 July.[6] On 14 July the child was baptized at the Church of St Mary, close by the inn; perhaps Roger Kemble's absence on tour led to a mistake being made in his name in the parish register: 'Sarah, d. of George Kemble, a comedian, and Sarah his wife.' Roger Kemble was, in fact, brought up a Catholic, while Sarah was a Protestant. The rule of the day in such mixed marriages was that while the male children were raised in their father's faith, the daughters should be raised in the mother's. Sarah was therefore christened a Protestant, and, a few days later, started with her mother the nomadic life of the provincial theatre, riding in the company's property cart, or perhaps, as a luxury, travelling by stagecoach.

Roger Kemble appears to have been reasonably prosperous. The accounts survive in his own handwriting for the year 1757, when his little daughter Sarah was two years old. In that year his 'shares' appear to have amounted to some £350, a reasonable sum for the period.[7] Whatever their fortunes, he and his wife were determined to give their family as good an education as was possible in the circumstances of constant travel. Roger Kemble is said to have opposed his daughter being trained for the stage, and his first son, John Philip, born at Prescott in Lancashire in 1757, was eventually to be sent at the age of ten to Sedgley Park, near Wolverhampton, a Catholic school for boys intended for the priesthood, and later to the English Benedictine College at Douai, to which his younger brother Stephen was also to be sent. Stephen, like John Philip, was to become an actor, but never the great artist his brother became.

Children followed at intervals for two decades. Sally Kemble took the pregnancies in her stride. Her son Stephen was born in the spring of 1758 in Kington, Herefordshire, shortly after his mother had left the stage where she had been playing Anne Boleyn (Bullen) in Shakespeare's *Henry VIII*. Anne Boleyn gave birth to her child during the period of the play, and so, almost, did Sally, whose confinement began the moment she got home from the theatre.

Sarah's upbringing, like that of the others when young, must be seen therefore as a life of movement from place to place, of appearance on the stage from early childhood for recitation and for child parts, of an education, particularly in elocution and singing, given by her mother, and, as she grew older, some schooling at the hands of others when her parents were, for a few weeks, settled in one place.

There are early glimpses of her during her childhood out of which her biographers have had to make as much as they could – even when the stories may be apocryphal, because Sarah herself and her parents spoke little of her earliest years. There is, for example, the story first told by Thomas Holcroft, who served for a while in Roger Kemble's company:

The company of which old Mr Kemble was the manager, was more respectable than many other companies of strolling players; but it was not in so flourishing a condition as to place the manager beyond the reach of the immediate smiles or frowns of fortune. Of this the following anecdote may be cited as an instance. A benefit had been fixed for some of the family, in which Miss Kemble, then a little girl, was to come forward in some part, as a juvenile prodigy. The taste of the audience was not, it seems, so accommodating as in the present day, and the extreme youth of the performer disposed the gallery to noise and uproar instead of admiration. Their turbulent dissatisfaction quite disconcerted the child, and she was retiring bashfully from the stage, when her mother, who was a woman of a high spirit, and alarmed for the success of her little actress, came forward, and leading the child to the front of the house, made her repeat the fable of the Boys and the Frogs, which entirely turned the tide of popular opinion in her favour.[8]

In a footnote to her voluminous memoirs, published post-humously as *Thraliana*, Mrs Piozzi adds another story from Sarah's childhood:

Mrs Siddons told me another odd Thing of her Childhood – She had read much in secret to divert herself – & all her little Books were filled with Stories of Reynard the Fox. – One day her Parents going up the Yard at some Inn – She saw an Animal wholly new to her, & ask'd what it was? a Fox my Dear says the Waiter, you must call it Renny. – She immediately went upstairs changed her Ribbons hasted down again, – & her Father found her a quarter of an hour afterwards curtseying respectfully before the Kennel door – What's ys for? said he. I am begging *Mr Reynard* replied Mrs Siddons – to *play me no Trick* while we remain in the Town.[9]

Other glimpses of Sarah as a child include the pretty story which her official biographer, Thomas Campbell, claims she told him herself:

One day, her mother had promised to take her out the following, to a pleasure party in the neighbourhood, and she was to wear a new pink dress, which became her exceedingly. But whether the party was to hold and the pink apparel to be worn, was to depend on the weather of tomorrow morning. On going to bed, she took with her her Prayer Book, opened, as she supposed, at the prayer for fine weather, and she fell asleep with the book folded in her little arms. At daybreak she found that she had been holding the prayer for rain to her breast, and that rain, as if Heaven had taken her at her word, was pelting at the windows. But she went to bed again, with the book opened at the right place, and she found the mistake quite remedied: for the morning was as pink and beautiful as the dress she was to wear.[10]

By the age of ten she was already responsive to the poetry of Milton, which was to prove a life-long devotion. Campbell writes:

I have heard her say that Milton's poetry was the object of her admiration earlier than Shakespeare's, and that when but ten years old she used to pore over *Paradise Lost* for hours together.

Perhaps Milton's curious combination of sensuality and austerity gave particular satisfaction to this girl who, as a woman, said that she feared to play Shakespeare's Cleopatra as she should be played, and realized, though she appears not to have interpreted it so on the stage, the intense femininity and sexuality of Lady Macbeth. Sarah Siddons was a singularly perceptive woman, though in the pursuit of respectability she did not always favour what she perceived. A taste for Milton, perhaps, provided one of the answers; his verse is as sensual as it is respectable. His strong dramatic sense and the grandeur of his rhetoric must have excited her.

Her earliest appearances on the stage are not recorded, nor did she even try to recollect them for Campbell. In February 1767, however, at the age of twelve she was appearing with the rest of the family at Worcester in an old wooden building in the yard at the back of the King's Head Inn. The playbill survives, carrying both in its layout and wording a host of implications about the local performances of the period:[11]

Worcester, 12th February, 1767.

MR. KEMBLE'S COMPANY OF COMEDIANS.

At the Theatre *at the King's Head*, this evening will be performed

A CONCERT OF MUSIC.

(To begin exactly at Six o'clock.)—Tickets to be had at the usual places.

Between the Parts of the Concert will be presented, *gratis*, a celebrated historical play (*never performed here*), called

CHARLES THE FIRST.

The Characters to be dressed in ancient habits, *according to the fashion of those times.*
The Part of King Charles, Mr. Jones;
Duke of Richmond, Mr. Siddons;
Marquis of Lindsay, Mr. Salisbury;
Bishop Juxon, Mr. Fowler; Gen. Fairfax, Mr. Kemble; Col.
Ireton, Mr. Crump; Col. Tomlinson, Mr. Hughes;
The Part of Oliver Cromwell, Mr. Vaughan;
Servant, Mr. Butler;

James, Duke of York (afterwards King of England),
Master J. Kemble;
Duke of Gloucester (King Charles's younger son),
Miss Fanny Kemble;
Sergeant Bradshaw (Judge of the pretended High Court of Justice),
Mr. Burton.
The Young Princess Elizabeth, Miss Kemble;
Lady Fairfax, Mrs. Kemble;
The Part of the Queen, Mrs. Vaughan.
Singing between the Acts by Mrs. Fowler and Miss Kemble.

_____

To which will be added, a Comedy called

THE MINOR.

And on Saturday next, the 14th instant, will be again presented
the above Tragedy, with a Farce that will be expressed in the bills
of the day.

_____

*** The days of Performances are Mondays, Thursdays, and
Saturdays.

First of all, the law, as we have seen, required that this
unlicensed company should not charge for dramatic as distinct
from musical performances. Roger Kemble was always on his
guard against possible prosecution. The play, therefore, had to
be presented 'gratis' between the 'parts' of the concert. Secondly,
the use of costume contemporary with the action of the play was
still a great rarity. Thirdly, the entire family appeared: Roger
Kemble (Fairfax), Sally (Lady Fairfax), John Philip (aged ten,
as the youthful James, Duke of York), Fanny Kemble (their
second daughter, aged eight) as King Charles's younger son, and
Miss Kemble (Sarah herself) as Princess Elizabeth. Sarah also
sang during the musical programme. Last, one must note that
Mr Siddons, Sarah's future husband, had already joined the
company. There are also records that Sarah played Ariel in *The
Tempest*, with other members of the family, and William, in the
cast.

Both Sarah and John Philip went to school in Worcester. It
says something for the repute of the Kembles that a certain
Mrs Harries, who ran a school for genteel young ladies called
Thornloe House, offered to teach Sarah for nothing. A letter

written in July 1767 shows how this player's daughter was at first received by her genteel companions:

My dear and honoured Mama,

I have received your letter and am truly sorry that you have had cause to complain of my remissness in keeping you informed of all our doings. . . .

A new pupil has been added to our number, a Miss Sarah Kemble. We had no expectation of her arrival, and at first felt her to be something of an interloper. She is very plain in her cloaths, and though[t] somewhat of a Brown Beauty, for her eyes and features, with the exception of a somewhat too long nose, merit much commendation. Her manner was not pleasing, withdrawing from our company, and holding herself aloof from our amusements.

But some of us, compassionating her isolation, and apparent melancholy, endeavoured to include her in our society, and I asked her what her parents were, and what was their position, as indeed dear Mama, you have advised me to do, to avoid the possibility of becoming intimate with an unsuitable or ungenteel acquaintance. But she answered without blush or confusion, that her father was Roger Kemble, the manager of a troupe of Strolling Players, who had arrived in the town travelling in a waggon.

You can imagine my embarrassment, my dear Mama, at having exhorted so damaging a confession, and I thought it best to make a curtsey and return to the other young ladies who were awaiting my report.[12]

Only when it came to the school theatricals was Sarah able to assume a proper place in the estimation of the other girls.

By now it was evident enough that Sarah was a girl of outstanding capacity. She could sing acceptably, accompanying herself on the harpsichord; she had a taste for literature; her elocution was as good as her parents could make it; she was beautiful and ladylike enough to be invited to the exclusive Thornloe House. Yet she was only twelve. Kemble, ambitious to give his daughter more than he was able to offer himself, was impressed, like others among the local people, by a scholar and soldier of fortune who was staying at the local inn, a man who could recite Horace as readily as he could tell extravagant tales and get through his money. This was William Combe, the celebrated eccentric who was later to create the character of Dr Syntax. He had been to Eton and Oxford, had studied law and been called to the bar, but his ambition to be a man of fashion had already led him to get through a fortune of £16,000. After squandering his money, he had enlisted as a private in the Army. Now he was destitute, and he prevailed on Roger to give him a benefit performance so that he might buy himself free of his uniform. He was also in the process of persuading him to let the beautiful young actress become his pupil, when Sally promptly scotched the idea. Combe's extraordinary later career before he became a hack writer was to include serving as a novitiate in a French monastery and as a waiter in Swansea.

Most unfairly, William Combe loathed the Kembles, and particularly Sarah, for the rest of his life, but in doing so he has provided us, through Samuel Rogers, with another telling glimpse of her as a young girl, which he intended to be malicious. He told Rogers how he remembered 'having seen Mrs Siddons when a very young woman, standing by the side of her father's stage, and knocking a pair of snuffers against a candlestick, to imitate the sound of a windmill, during the representation of some Harlequin-piece'.[13]

It was during 1770 or 1771 that the romance with William Siddons is said to have begun.[14] Sarah was about seventeen; he was eleven years older than she, and the fact that her parents solidly opposed the match merely convinced her that William was the only man for her. Under the strict eye of her mother, her experience of men had been negligible. William's sole qualification was that he was always there, and in love with her now that her womanhood was dawning under the maturing influence of the theatre. The Kembles did not want their talented daughter to marry an actor, least of all an actor as unqualified for success as William who, at twenty-seven, was still little more than a support-ing player. According to Campbell, he had been 'bred to business in Birmingham'; he came from Walsall, where his father kept a public-house. Born in 1744, he was first heard of theatrically as an amateur performer in Walsall in 1766. He had joined Kemble in 1767; James Boaden, Sarah's biographer, who knew him well in later life, claims he was 'a fair and very handsome man, sedate and graceful in his manners'. Moreover, says Boaden, he was a remarkably quick study, a useful talent in the constantly changing repertory of the day. He was also versatile – 'he could do anything from Hamlet to Harlequin,' Boaden claims. Certainly he was, at this age, sufficiently good-looking and gentlemanly in manner to enliven Sarah's youthful dreaming, and the opposition from her parents only served to reinforce their passion. Moreover, he was very popular with the public. The fact that he had no money other than his weekly earnings meant nothing to either of the lovers.

But it meant a great deal to the Kembles. As a result, they responded perhaps more readily than they should have done to the proposals of a minor member of the local squirearchy, a Mr Evans, Squire of Pennant – who had £300 a year with which to back his infatuation for Sarah. He became the suitor favoured by her parents. The whole affair was to develop into a *cause célèbre* in the eyes of the public in Brecon, where the situation reached its height as soon as William learned that an official proposal had been made for Sarah's hand. For a while William believed he had lost Sarah and that she had given in to her parents. He was so roused he charged Roger Kemble to his face with perfidy, and as a result was dismissed from the company. But Roger, soft-hearted as ever, allowed him a parting benefit. William used this occasion to sing some doggerel verses of his own composition which exposed to his audience's curiosity his jealousy and the wrongs he felt had been done him:

Ye ladies of Brecon, whose hearts ever feel
For wrongs like to this, I'm about to reveal,
Excuse the first product, nor pass unregarded,
The complaints of poor Colin, a lover discarded.

He even ventured to accuse Sarah of deserting him for the squire with the money:

Not easily turn'd, she her project pursued,
Each part of the shepherd was instantly viewed;
And the charms of three hundred a year, some say more,
Made her find out a thousand she ne'er saw before.[15]

The ladies of Brecon could not resist such pleading, and applauded him to the echo. Mrs Kemble, however, boxed his ears when he came off the stage.

Whether there was any truth in all this or not, Sarah refused to marry the squire and returned to the lover who had used the public stage to accuse her of faithlessness. A compromise was arranged; she was made to leave the stage and placed in an aristocratic household, the Greatheeds of Warwick. Thomas Campbell, who wrote from the authority of his position as Sarah's official biographer, describes her situation with discretion:

From a surviving member of that family, I learn that she came into it in a dependent capacity; and, though she was much liked, that her great latent genius was not even suspected. It was observed, however, that she passionately admired Milton; and I have seen a copy of his works which the Greatheeds presented to her at this period.[16]

Sarah Kemble, therefore, left both her lover and her profession. She went to live at Guy's Cliffe, in Warwick, the residence of a widow, Lady Mary Greatheed, becoming, in effect, at first a maid and later a 'companion' in that sympathetic and luxurious household for almost two years. It was a small price to pay; had she married the Welsh farmer she would never have returned to the stage. As it was, she was able to maintain a correspondence, now lost, with William, and he was even permitted to visit her. She maintained her talent for recitation by reading aloud. It was also said that she used to 'spout verse' in the servants' hall! Meanwhile, she had a new and aristocratic way of living to absorb, in extreme contrast to the harsh conditions she was used to. When, much later, she was to become the mistress of a succession of elegant residences in London, her initiation at the beautiful estate of Guy's Cliffe meant that she was already familiar with the graces of eighteenth-century life as well as its squalor.

According to Boaden, who knew her, she did not entirely retire from direct contact with the theatre. In his biography, originally published in her lifetime, he says that she approached Garrick himself for an audition, went to London and pleased him with her recitation of speeches from *Jane Shore*. Whether or not Boaden is right, and he is most probably wrong, there is no record that she denied it; however, she was almost always to keep silent about these earlier years. This hint of an initial encounter certainly does not tally with Garrick's reactions only four years later when his agents, recognizing her growing talent in the provincial theatre, recommended her to his notice.[17]

When, eventually, she was to leave Guy's Cliffe to marry, she left it as a friend of the family whom, in later years, she was to visit frequently as the great actress from London. Indeed, she had earned so much respect that Lady Greatheed admitted in later life, when her 'companion' had become famous, that even when Sarah was only a girl of seventeen, her mistress felt an irresistible inclination to rise from her chair when Sarah came in to attend her.

It was on 26 November 1773 that Sarah finally married William

Siddons whom she now affectionately called her 'Sid'. She was nineteen and he twenty-nine. Her parents recognized that the marriage was inevitable, and finally gave their consent to the match with a good enough grace. The ceremony took place at Holy Trinity Church, Coventry, and Roger Kemble was there to give away the bride. Now at last Sarah had become Mrs Siddons, and was announced as such on a playbill the following month when she was on tour with her husband on the Kemble circuit. By December, says the family's biographer, Fitzgerald, they were working at Wolverhampton, a city with a troublesome mayor who hated all players and tried to prevent any kind of theatrical performance.[18] But the patrons of the three companies present in the town prevailed, and the Kembles were able to announce that their daughter, Mrs Siddons, would play Charlotte in *The West Indian* and Leonora in *The Padlock* at a farewell 'bespeak' performance commanded by their local supporters. The final, complimentary verses spoken by Sarah have survived, and show something of the intimate nature of the relationship between the visiting players and their friends, who delighted in these final addresses to them from the stage, and would vociferously applaud each personal reference:

Ladies and Gentlemen, – My spouse and I,
Have had a squabble, and I'll tell you why –
He said I must appear; nay, vowed 'twas right,
To give you thanks for favours shown tonight. . . .

He still insisted; and to win consent,
Strove to o'ercome me with a compliment;
Told me that I the favourite here had reigned,
While he, but small, or no applause had gained. . . .

May th'All-good Power your every virtue nourish –
Health, wealth, and trade in Wolverhampton flourish![19]

The following year, 1774, Sarah and William decided to leave the family troupe and establish their independence by working in other companies. It was as leading members of a barnstorming group led by two actors, Chamberlain and Crump, that they finally found themselves in Cheltenham Spa during the summer. Cheltenham was just beginning to be a resort for the fashionable élite. It was here that the Siddons enjoyed a stroke of good fortune; Lord Bruce (later Lord Aylesbury) and his step-daughter,

the Honourable Henrietta Boyle, having nothing better to do
in the small town which was still little more than a village, decided
to risk taking a party to the only entertainment in the place, which
was Chamberlain and Crump's production of Otway's *Venice
Preserved*. They had decided to go, according to Campbell, in
order to 'enjoy a treat of the ludicrous, in the misrepresentation
of the piece', and a rumour concerning their attitude reached
Sarah before the performance. 'Our actress,' says Campbell,
'anticipated refined scorners, more pitiless than the rabble; and
the prospect was certainly calculated to prepare her more for the
madness than the dignity of her part. In spite of much agitation,
however, she got through it.' She heard 'suppressed noises' in
the audience, and went home after the play 'grievously mortified'.
But she need not have worried; the following day Lord Bruce
stopped William in the street and 'expressed not only his own
admiration for her last night's exquisite acting, but related its
effects on the ladies of his party. They had wept, he said, so
excessively, that they were unpresentable in the morning, and
were confined to their rooms with headaches.'

Sarah, in fact, had won the admiration of a new, aristocratic
patron in Henrietta Boyle, who was to become a lifelong friend.
Miss Boyle was beautiful, rich, fashionable, and by way of being
a poetess. She visited Sarah in her lodgings, praised her performance, and offered her every help, including the very practical
one of supervising her wardrobe and giving her the expensive
clothes an actress always needs but can seldom afford at the start
of her career. Lord Bruce went one better; on his return to
London he advised Garrick to consider her for his company.

Sarah's own account of this significant event in her life was
the first she wrote down in detail in the memoranda she prepared
in her old age for Campbell, the biographer she chose to write
her official biography:

About the middle of the Play, I heard some very unusual and apparently suppressed noises. I therefore concluded the fashionables
were now in the full enjoyment of thier anticipated amusement,
tittering and laughing as I thought most cruelly and without mercy.
The Play ended, and I returnd home grievously vexd and mortifyd.
The next day however, I recieved ample amends for M.ʳ Siddons
had met Lord Aylesbury in the street, who very politely hoped that
I had suffered less from my exquisite performance of Belvidera, that
[sic] the ladies of his family and thier whole Party had suffered from

my performance of it; assuring him at the same time that they had all wept so much and were so disfigured with red eyes and swoln faces, that they were this morning actually unpresentable being all confind to thier chambers with violent head-achs. M.ʳ Siddons hastend home with all speed to comfort me with this intelligence. Miss Boyle very shortly honord me with a visit at my Lodging; and that lovely, generous, sweet creature – then about 18 – encouraged and soothed me and indeed was unremitting in evry kind and delicate attention to my feelings and wishes, nay even condescended to make part of my Dresses with her own dear hand, and forgetting her high Rank, even to assume the character of directress of my Wardrobe.[20]

She adds nothing about the fact that she was pregnant. Her first child, Henry Siddons, was born at Wolverhampton on 4 October 1774, shortly after this fortunate season at Cheltenham.

Garrick, who was reaching the end of his long, outstandingly successful career in London, could not resist a lord; on the other hand, he had a sharp sense of standards in the profession he had done so much to raise, and he was in no hurry to introduce a young girl to his company, where he already had three leading actresses, Mrs Frances Abington, Mrs Mary Anne Yates and Miss Younge, with whose uneven and jealous temperaments he had to contend. However, it was quite normal to employ well-informed observers to attend performances by companies touring the provinces and report on any new talent they thought worth promotion to one of the London companies.

The first of these observers was the actor Tom King, an experienced member of Garrick's company.[21] According to Sarah's own recollections, he came to Cheltenham at Garrick's request and saw her act Calista in Rowe's play *The Fair Penitent*. 'I then knew neither himself nor his purpose,' she wrote. King apparently returned full of enthusiasm for the work of the young actress. But Garrick for the moment preferred to wait.

Sarah, always serious in her attitude to her profession, was studying at the age of twenty several of the greater roles for women. In her own small world she was already a leading actress. One of the parts she studied was Lady Macbeth, the character which years later became perhaps the greatest achievement of her career. Her own recollections show how she worked on her characters in her lodgings at night:

It was my custom to study my characters at night, when all the domestic cares and business of the day were over. On the night preceding that in which I was to appear in this part for the first time, I shut myself up as usual, when all the family were retired, and commenced my study of Lady Macbeth. As the character is very short, I thought I should soon accomplish it. Being then only twenty years of age, I believed, as many others do believe, that little more was necessary than to get the words into my head, for the necessity of discrimination, and the development of character, at that time of my life, had scarcely entered into my imagination. But to proceed. I went on with tolerable composure, in the silence of the night (a night I never can forget), till I came to the assassination scene, when the horrors of the scene rose to a degree that made it impossible for me to get farther. I snatched up my candle, and hurried out of the room in a paroxysm of terror. My dress was of silk, and the rustling of it, as I ascended the stairs to go to bed, seemed to my panic-struck fancy like the movement of a spectre pursuing me. At last I reached my chamber, where I found my husband fast asleep. I clapt my candlestick down upon the table, without the power of putting the candle out, and I threw myself on my bed, without daring to stay even to take off my clothes. At peep of day I rose to resume my task; but so little did I know of my part when I appeared in it at night, that my shame and confusion cured me of procrastinating my business for the remainder of my life.[22]

The following year, 1775, the Siddons were working in another, far better company: that of Joseph Younger. Garrick was prompted to make fresh inquiries about Sarah. First, he wrote to his friend the Reverend Henry Bate, that very energetic and socially-minded parson whom Boaden describes as 'lay in his manners', and who, as a Master of Fox Hounds, enjoyed sport, as a farmer had an interest in agriculture, and as proprietor of *The Morning Post* savoured all the gossip about affairs, including affairs of the theatre, which characterized the interest of every journalist in the eighteenth century. On 31 July Garrick wrote to Bate:

If you pass by Cheltenham in [sic] Your Way to Worcester, I wish you would see an Actress there, a Mrs Siddon's [sic]. She has a desire I hear to try her Fortune with Us; if she seems in Your Eyes worthy of being transplanted, pray desire to know upon what conditions she would make yᵉ Tryal, and I will write to her the post after I receive Your Letter.[23]

Bate went with his wife to see Sarah, and wrote to Garrick enthusiastically on 12 August:

After combatting the various difficulties of one of the cussedest cross-roads in this kingdom, we arrived safe at Cheltenham on Thursday last, and saw the theatrical heroine of that place in the character of *Rosalind*: tho' I beheld her from the side wings of the stage (a barn about three yards over and consequently under almost every disadvantage) I own she made so strong an impression upon me that I think she cannot fail to be a valuable acquisition to Drury Lane. Her figure must be remarkably fine, when she is happily delivered of a big belly, which entirely mars for the present her whole shape. – Her face (if I could judge from where I saw it) is one of the most strikingly beautiful for stage effect that ever I beheld: but I shall surprize you more, when I assure you that these are nothing to her action, and general stage deportment which are remarkably pleasing and characteristic; in short I know no woman who marks the different passages and transitions with so much variety and at the same time propriety of expression: in the latter 'humbug' scene with *Orlando* previous to her revealing herself she did more with it than any one I ever saw, not even your divine Mrs Barry excepted. It is necessary after this panegyric to inform you that her voice struck me at first as rather dissonant; and I fancy from the private conversation I had with her that in unimpassioned scenes it must be somewhat grating; however as I found it wear away as the business became more interesting, I am inclined to think it only an error of affectation, which may be corrected if not wholly emended. She informed me, she had been up on the stage from her cradle this tho' it surprized me gave me the highest opinion of her judgment, to find she had contracted no strolling habits, wch have so often been the tone of many a theatrical genius. She will most certainly be of great use to you at all parts on account of the great number of characters she plays, all of which I will venture to assert she fills with propriety tho' I have yet seen her but in one – She is as you have been informed a very good breeches figure, and plays the Widow Brady I am informed admirably: I should not wonder from her ease, figure and manner if she made the proudest she of either house tremble in genteel comedy: – nay beware yourself *Great Little* Man, for she plays Hamlet to the satisfaction of the Worcestershire Critics.

The moment the play was over I wrote a note to her husband (who is a damned rascally player tho' seemingly a very civil fellow) requesting an interview with him and his wife intimating at the same time the nature of my business. You will not blame me for making this forced march in your favour, as I learnt that some of the Covent Garden Mohawks were entrench'd near the place I intended carrying her by surprize. At the conclusion of the farce they waited upon me, and after I had opened my commission she expressed herself happy at the opportunity of being brought out under your eye, but declined proposing any term leaving it entirely with you to reward her as you think proper.

You will perceive that at present she has all that diffidence usually the first attendant on merit; how soon the force of Drury Lane examples added to the rising vanity of a stage heroine may transform her I cannot say. – It happens very luckily, that the company comes to Worcester for the race week, when I shall take every opportunity of seeing her, and if I find the least reason to alter my opinion, (perhaps too hastily formed,) you shall immediately have my recantation. – My wife whose judgments in theatrical matters I have a high opinion of, joins with me in these sentiments respecting her merit; – I should have wrote to you before, but no post went out from my place but this night's. – I shall expect to hear from you by return of the post, as Siddons will call upon me to know whether you look upon her as engaged. My wife joins me in respects to Mrs Garrick and yourself. I remain My Dᵣ Sir (after writing a damn'd jargon I suppose of unintelligible stuff in haste)

Ever Yours most truly
Henry Bate

P.S. Direct to me at the Hop Pole.[24]

Garrick, meanwhile, had written on 11 August to the comedian John Moody at the theatre in Liverpool to inquire '– have you ever heard of *Mrs Siddons* who is stroling [sic] about somewhere near You – ?' On 15 August he replied to Bate:

Dear Bate,

Ten thousand thanks for your very clear, agreeable, and friendly letter; it pleased me much, and whoever calls it *a jargon of unintelligible stuff*, should be knocked down if I were near him. I must desire you to secure the lady with my best compliments, and that she may depend upon every reasonable and friendly encouragement in my power; at the same time, you must intimate to the husband, that he must be satisfy'd with *the state of life in which it has pleased Heaven to call her*. You see how much I think myself obliged to your kind offices, by the flattering quotations I make from your *own* book. Your account of the *big belly* alarms me! – when shall we be in shapes again? how long does the lady count? when will she be able to appear? Pray compleat your good offices, and let me know all we are to trust. Should not you get some memorandum signed by her and her husband, and of which I will send a facsimile copy to them, under frank, if you will let me know their address.

I laughed at the military strategems of the Covent Garden Generals, whilst I had your genius to oppose them. If she has merit (and I am sure by your letter she must have) and will be wholly governed by me, I will make her theatrical fortune; if any lady begins to play at tricks, I will immediately play off my masked battery of Siddons against her. I should be glad to know her cast of parts, or rather what parts she has done, and in what she likes herself best – those I would have mark'd, and above all, my dear Farmer, let me know at what time she may reckon to lye-in, that we may reckon accordingly upon her appearance in Drury Lane. I repeat this to you because it is of the utmost consequence.

Pray let me hear from you again in answer to this. I make no compliments or excuses to you for the trouble I give you, because I feel by myself that you will take pleasure in obliging me.

I am, dear Farmer, most sincerely yours,

D. Garrick.[25]

Bate replied on 15 August: in this he outlined the parts Sarah preferred to play:

My Dear Friend,

I received your very friendly letter and take the first post from hence to answer it. I found it unnecessary to make the intimation you desired to the *husband*, since he requires only to be employ'd in any manner you shall think proper; and as he is much more tolerable than I thought him at first, it may be no very difficult matter to station him, so as to satisfy the man, without burdening the property. I saw him the other evening in *Young Marlow* in Goldsmith's comedy, and then he was far from despicable; neither his figure, nor face contemptible: – A jealousy prevailing thro' the theatre, upon a suspicion of their leaving them, the acting manager seems determined that I shall not see her again in any character, wherein she might give me a second display of her theatrical powers. I am resolved however to continue the siege till they give her something capital, knowing that must speedily be the case, or the garrison must fall by famine.

Now for the *Big Belly*: she has already gone *six months*, so that pretty early in December, she will be fit for service; as you certainly mean to open the ensuing campaign by charging in person at the head of your lines, I conceive she will come at a very favourable crisis to take a second command, when, your retreat from the field may be politically necessary. I am strongly for her 1st appearance in *Rosalind*; but you may judge better perhaps after a perusal of the list on the other side; the characters marked under are those which she prefers to others: –

Jane Shore	Monimia	Lady Townley
Alicia	Juliet	Portia
Roxana	Cordelia	Mrs Belville

Graec. Daughter	Horatia R. Falk	Violante
Matilda	Marianne	Rosalind
Belvidera	Imogen	Mrs Strickland
Calista	Charlotte	Clarinda
	Widow Brady	Miss Aubrey

You are certainly right respecting a memorandum between you; the moment therefore I receive one from you it shall be convey'd to them at Cheltenham where they return next week; and they have promised to return me an answer immediately at Birmingham, for which place I shall set off, the instant I have received your letter, on my way to town – In order to conclude this business finally and to the satisfaction of all parties, I am desired to request your answer to the three following particulars –

1. As they are ready to attend your summons at any time, 'whether they are not to be allowed something to subsist upon when they come to town, previous to her appearance'?
2. 'Whether you have any objection to employ *him* in any situation, in which you may think him likely to be useful'?
3. 'When you choose they should attend you'?

– As to the first, without you are inclined to have them at the opening of the house, perhaps her remaining in the country, in their own company, where they do very well, may ease you of some pence; but of this you must be the best judge. – With respect to him I think you can have no objection to take him upon the terms he proposes himself – I forgot to tell you that Mrs Siddons is about twenty years of age. It would be unjust not to remark one circumstance in favour of them both; I mean the universal good character they have presented here for many years, on account of their public as well as private conduct in life. – I beg you to be very particular in your answer to the 3 Quer^s, and likewise expressly to mention the time you wish to see them, that they may arrange their little matters accordingly. This I hope will enable me to effect everything you would expect from me, when you honour'd me with the commission, and if in the discharge of it I have been able to render you the least service, I shall reflect upon it as one of the most flattering circumstances of my life. Mrs Bate joins me in my respects to Mrs Garrick. I remain my dear friend, Ever Yours most truly,

Henry Bate.

N.B. She is the most extraordinary quick study I ever heard of: – this cannot be amiss, for if I recollect right we have a sufficient number of the *leaden-headed* ones at D. Lane already.[26]

A letter from William to Bate, dated 4 September and written from Cheltenham, survives, and reveals something of the anxiety he and his pregnant wife were enduring:

Revd Sir,

Your comm safe to hand this morning, I confess I was under some concern not hearing from you sooner for from the lines you showed me in Mr Garrick's letter at Worcester I had nearly assured myself of Mrs Siddons engagement, on which at my return to Cheltenham I gave my partners in management notice of my intention to part from them, and if anything had happened that we coud not have been engaged t'would have proved a very unlucky circumstance. However, Sir, your letter hath remov'd the apprehension I was under, and set me right again.

I am very agreeable Mrs Siddons shall be brought to bed in the Country and therefore shall continue here at Gloucester till she is able to remove to London meantime hope to be favoured by your correspondence with any advice you shall please to offer, or instructions Mr Garrick shall please to send me. Be so good, Sir, as to present my most respectfull compliments to him, and assure him he has confer'd an eternal obligation on me by his kind offer of the Cash but hope I shall not have occasion to trouble him for the pains you have taken and the services done me I shall ever retain the most gratefull sense, and am, with Mrs Siddons respects, your very hum. ser^t.

Wm. Siddons.[27]

Sarah's second child was expected, then, in November. From the point of view of her career, this was a great misfortune, for it meant that Garrick's interest in bringing the Siddons to Drury Lane had to be tempered by consideration of her pregnancy. Not only was Garrick seeking her out, but the managers of Covent Garden also. It must have been an anxious, frustrating time for both William and Sarah, who no doubt knew that Garrick had only one more full season to run before his retirement.

The correspondence between Garrick and William, who acted throughout the negotiations as his wife's manager, began on 7 October, the date Garrick wrote to William from his riverside house at Hampton:

Sir

This is one of the first letters I have written, since my recovery from a very Severe fit of the Gravel, which render'd me incapable of any business – As I am now much better, I flatter Myself that a letter from me will no[t] be disagreeable – I wish much to know how Mrs Siddons is, & about what time I may have the Pleasure of Seeing You in London – I beg that she will not make herself uneasy about coming, till she will run no risk by the journey – all I desire is that I may have the earliest information that can be had with any certainty, for I shall settle some business by that direction, which may be of immediate Service to Mrs Siddons & the Manager – if in the mean time you find it convenient to have any pecuniary Assistance from Me, I shall give it You with great pleasure – let me once more intreat that Mrs Siddons may have No Cares about me to disturb her, & that she may not be hurried to ye least prejudice of her health. I beg my Comp^{ts} & best Wishes to her in her present Situation, &

I am Sir Your most hu^{le} Servt

D. Garrick.

P.S. my hand shakes with weakness but I hope You will understand this Scrawl.[28]

William's reply does not survive, but the contents can be implied from Garrick's next letter, dated 19 October:

Sir

Whenever You please to draw upon Me for the fifteen pounds I shall pay it immediately – I am glad to hear that Mrs Siddons is so Well & Expect You will give me Notice when she is worse and better – if You find any difficulty in getting the Money on a draught upon Me, I will inquire & get the money paid in Gloucester.

I am Sir (with very best Wishes and Compliments to Mrs Siddons) Y^r Most Obed^t Ser^t

D. Garrick.[29]

Negotiations were concluded in a final letter from Garrick, addressed to 'Mr Siddons belonging to the Theatre at Gloucester', and written from Adelphi on 15 November:

Sir

I wish you joy of Mrs Siddons safe delivery, & I hope she continues Well –

I am oblig'd to Mr Dinwoody for his politeness, & shall return him the Money upon the first Notice of his return to Town: and now about Your coming to London – the Sooner I see you here, with convenience to Mrs Siddons, will be of more consequence to her & to me – she may have something to do, if I see her soon, which may not be in my power to give her if she comes later – nay indeed, if she cannot safely set out before the time you mention'd in a Former letter, it would (be better) for her not to appear this Season, but put off her joining Us till the next opening of our Theatre – but this I leave to your own determination – & now, let me desire You to give me the earliest Notice when you and Mrs Siddons can be here, & what part or parts she would rather chuse for her Onset, that I may prepare Accordingly – I should have no Objection to Rosalind, as Mr Bates thought it y^r favourite part, but that a Mrs King has made her first appearance in that Character – if You will set down 3 or 4 that You and She think her most capital parts, I will make the choice, in ye mean time.

I am Sr Your most hu^le Se^t

D. Garrick.[30]

The deal was safely concluded; Sarah had given birth to her second child, Sally, on 5 November. On 9 November William wrote to inform Garrick. Like her mother before her, at Kington in 1758, Sarah had been taken ill while acting in Gloucester:

Gloucester Nov 9 1775
From my former accounts of Mrs Siddon's time youl [sic] be surprized when I tell you she is brought to bed. She was unexpectedly taken ill when performing on the stage and early the next morning produced me a fine girl. They are both – thank heaven likely to do well, but I am afraid, Sir, notwithstanding this I shant be able to leave this much sooner than the time I last mentioned, for Mrs Siddons counting so much longer I had fixed the conclusion of some particular private concerns till that time. I hope, Sir, this will make no difference with you, if so woud endeavour to hasten my business if not I shall have time to conclude it and the satisfaction to think Mrs Siddons will be so much better to take her journey.

I am Sir your Ob^t Hum Ser^t

W. Siddons

P.S. I have just had the pleasure of seeing Mr Dinwoody whom you commissioned to supply me with the Cash. He told me I might have any sum I had occasion for so have made bold to take twenty pounds which I hope will meet with your approbation.[31]

William, it would seem, had not been entirely correct in his dealings with the London managers. His wife's sudden success may have gone a little to his head. It would appear he had agreed, or virtually agreed, at some time during the autumn that she should appear exclusively at Covent Garden.[32] A letter to him from John de la Bere, dated 13 December, expresses the anger of 'Mr Blackwell' and 'the gentlemen of Covent Garden' that

S.S.—2*

Mrs Siddons, after negotiating with them, should have in the
end agreed to go to Garrick at Drury Lane:

> They consider her subsequent engagement to Mr Garrick as an
> infringement of the agreement subsisting between them at Drury
> Lane. . . . I have only to recommend it to your consideration, whether
> you will not, on the footing of the agreement between the two houses,
> lose the chance of getting into either, and to add that Mr Blackwell
> has taken up this affair with great resolution, on the part of Covent
> Garden, and he says that Mrs Siddons absolutely promised him to
> drop all thoughts of connecting herself with Drury Lane.

It would seem that Garrick, through illness, had come into the
negotiations rather late in the day, and that once he had written
to them, Sarah and William were unable to resist the opportunity
of joining the greatest actor of the century in the final months of
his stage career.

Garrick's position in the English theatre was impregnable.
He had achieved for the status of the theatre in the eighteenth
century what Irving was to achieve the following century. In 1737
he and his tutor, Samuel Johnson, had left Lichfield to seek
wider opportunities in London. He was the son of an Army
captain, and when he had gone on the stage his family had
regarded it as a social disgrace. From childhood he had been
fascinated by acting; it was intended at first that he should study
for entrance to Lincoln's Inn, but he ended up with his brother
in the wine trade, and the death of his parents when he was in
London left him free to turn from amateur to professional
performances; he joined a company of players and made his
professional debut at Ipswich in 1741. He had a fine voice, and
this he cultivated because, for an actor, though his movements
were good, he lacked a commanding height. His genius lay in the
direction of originality – the substitution of sharply observed
characterization for the strutting and fretting of the average actor;
and intelligent, well-articulated speech for the bombast he
despised. He had made his mark initially in London in *Richard III*
in October 1741, after his return from Ipswich.

Garrick astonished his audiences by what a contemporary
biographer calls 'his easy and familiar, yet forcible style in
speaking and acting'. His expression, too, grew out of the needs
of the character he was playing; he had 'good mobile features,
and flashing expressive eyes'. The older actors, traditionalists

such as James Quin, Garrick's principal rival until Quin's retirement to Bath in 1751, had declaimed rather than acted; only
Charles Macklin's famous impersonation of Shylock as a tragic
character instead of a buffoon (also first seen in 1741, the year of
Garrick's great success), was at all like Garrick's own serious
approach to characterization.

Garrick's reforms had extended into presentation, which aimed
at inducing audiences to take the play seriously as art, and not
treat it as a mere spectacle and social occasion into which they
could intrude. Although his earlier career lay outside the royal
theatres – at Lincoln's Inn Fields, and in his partnership with
Thomas Sheridan in Dublin – his fame as a stage director had
started with his management of Drury Lane, which began in 1747.
At Drury Lane he presented carefully planned seasons, working
assiduously himself on the preparation and revision of scripts of
plays, both new and old, including those of Shakespeare; in a
period when preparation was usually scanty and rehearsals of the
more familiar plays reduced to a bare walk-through, Garrick
took his time with everything that engaged his attention. He did
not favour the fixed interpretation of established characters, and
he enjoyed astonishing his public with startling new interpretations. He introduced new, more elaborate forms of scenery,
lighting by candles, and costumes. To be invited to join his
company and appear with him was, therefore, as near to the top
in the English theatre as any provincial actress could attain, even
though at the age of only fifty-seven he was a tired and to some
extent a sick man, who had only four years to live. Also, he was
bad-tempered, vain, reputed to be mean, and proud of the social
position his success had brought him. He had married a dancer,
Eva Marie Violetti, who was five years younger than he, but who
was to survive him by almost half a century.

A whole generation of talented, difficult actresses had worked
with him. He did not believe in appearing with nonentities,
whether actor or actress, and his company normally contained a
number of famous players. His leading ladies had included the
beautiful and even-tempered Peg Woffington (who had been for
a while his mistress), Mrs Cibber, Mrs Bellamy, and Mrs
Abington. When Sarah arrived in London to join him, there were,
as we have seen, three notable actresses in his company: Mrs
Yates, aged forty-eight, Mrs Abington, who was almost forty,
and Miss Younge, who was still youthful. There seemed to them

little need for this chit from the countryside. Mrs Yates and Miss Younge even felt disposed to be difficult.

Garrick did not care; he could be difficult too, if only by introducing another woman to flout them. Whatever his motives for pursuing Sarah, he appears to have used her somewhat capriciously, perhaps to score off the other women, who were constantly quarrelling and complaining. Sarah arrived in London in mid-December, exhausted from childbirth, accompanied by her husband, her baby and her infant son Henry, aged two. Garrick, perusing her list of favourite parts, had decided she should open on the Friday after Christmas, 29 December, in the part of Portia, one she preferred. She was to appear with Tom King, who had helped 'discover' her; he was to play Shylock. The playbills went out announcing her, not by name, but as 'a Young Lady (being her first appearance)'.

From the beginning, Garrick seemed to favour her, and so she earned the nickname of 'Garrick's Venus' because, in addition to the major parts she played, she appeared as Venus in *Jubilee*, a pageant originally devised by Garrick for presentation at Stratford-upon-Avon in honour of Shakespeare, but revived during the season as an 'after-piece' to *The Merchant of Venice*. Garrick treated Sarah as a *protégée*, but whether because he genuinely admired her or merely because he wanted to spite the viragos in the company is not clear; she eventually came to see it as the latter. The situation, combined with her strained physical condition and her nervousness, preyed on her, and when *The Merchant of Venice* opened a couple of weeks after her arrival in London, she collapsed in the face of a 'numerous and splendid' audience. Her voice failed her and she spoke hoarsely and inaudibly; her gait and movements were uncertain; her dress (a salmon-coloured 'sack-back' from the Drury Lane wardrobe) was ugly and faded. The press, except for Bate's *Morning Post*, was uniformly hostile – there was a 'vulgarity in her tones'. In Woodfall's *Morning Chronicle* she was told to 'throw more fire and spirit into her performance', but was praised for her fine figure.

Her actual situation must be imagined to understand what happened. She had very little money, and a husband and two young children to care for. She had arrived, for the very first time as far as we know, in the capital city, which after the comparatively small towns to which she was used must have appeared overwhelmingly large and intimidating. She was now, suddenly, with almost no time for preparation, made to star in one of London's two most prominent theatres, far grander and larger than anything she had experienced before; she was to appear as a member of His Majesty's Company, in which, from the female side, she met with nothing but hostility and jealousy. Although Garrick made much of her, and Tom King remained a good friend, she must have felt very much alone. In her debilitated condition she was unable to rise to the great opportunity which had been offered to her. She also suffered, on her own admission, from timidity. William, if we are to go by his behaviour later, was probably no less nervous than she, and would be likely to offer poor support in so severe a test as this. There were only two things she could do – sweep on to the stage with spirit and conquer the dragons of London, or go through the performance competently and professionally. Unfortunately, she did neither. Although an experienced actress, she was untrained, and accustomed only to small provincial theatres. She miscalculated the scale of Drury Lane and its audience, and she quite simply underplayed.

There are arguments as to why Garrick chose Portia for her début instead of some tragic or melodramatically pathetic part in which she might have risen to the occasion through sheer feminine emotional appeal. Garrick, it must be remembered, was normally an expert judge of actors. He probably chose a part in which he felt she could not altogether fail through the nervousness which he knew would affect her; he also knew he could rely on Tom King to sustain the play as Shylock, which in effect was what happened. On 3 January she repeated the part, and did better, to judge from a letter published in the *Morning Chronicle*. Her next appearance, on 13 January 1776, in an abridgement of Ben Jonson's *Epicoene*, was also a failure, but scarcely through her fault, since she had to pretend, as one of the Ladies Collegiate, to be a boy disguised as a woman! On 1 February she played a conventional heroine in Bate's new opera, *The Blackamoor Washed White*, a piece which ended in uproar and a riot caused by Bate's innumerable enemies, with whom he had the habit of fighting duels. She came off badly in the *Morning Chronicle*, which said: 'All played well except Mrs Siddons who, having no comedy in her nature, rendered that ridiculous which the author evidently intended to be pleasant'. In the next play, presented on 15 February, she was given an *ingénue* part in Hannah Cowley's first play, a comedy called *The Runaway*; then she appeared in a farce called *Love's Vagaries*. After this, on 23 May, she appeared with Garrick and Miss Younge in *The Suspicious Husband*, and apparently made something of the part of the young wife, Mrs Strickland, since she was rewarded in the *Post* with the praise that she 'was by no means inferior' to Garrick and Miss Younge. The next play put on in the summer was one of Garrick's favourites, *Richard III*. In this he gave her the part of Lady Anne; the only notice she received for this was 'lamentable', though the other ladies, Mrs Hopkins and Mrs Johnston, did not fare any better. Garrick, in entrusting her with this part in his last season, was in fact paying her a considerable compliment. But again she failed, and it was the last part she was given. Garrick, nervous himself, was straining to give a tremendous performance in which he seemed to surpass himself. After repeating the play on 5 June, and a few days later on 10 June, he retired, leaving the management of the theatre largely in the hands of Sheridan, the dramatist.

Much later, Sarah was to recall to the actor John Taylor the effect it had on her to play opposite Garrick:

> I told her that Mr Sheridan had declared Garrick's Richard to be very fine, but did not think it terrible enough. 'God bless me!' said she, 'what could be more terrible?' She then informed me, that when she was rehearsing the part of Lady Anne to his Richard, he desired her, as he drew her from the couch, to follow him step by step, for otherwise he should be obliged to turn his face from the audience, and he acted much with his features. Mrs Siddons promised to attend to his desire, but assured me there was such an expression in his acting, that it entirely overcame her, and she was obliged to pause, when he gave her such a look of reprehension as she never could recollect without terror. She expressed her regret that she had only seen him in two characters, except when she acted Lady Anne with him, – and those characters were Lear and Ranger; that his Lear was tremendous, and his Ranger delightful.[33]

Sarah had her own view of what happened; she never really forgave Garrick for what she regarded as his cruelty to her:

> I was at that time well-looking and certainly, independantly of any other claim, well worth my poor five pounds a week. His praises were most liberally and flatteringly conferrd upon me. But his attentions great and unremitting as they were all ended in worse than nothing: but how was all this admiration consistently with his subsequent conduct to be accounted for? Why thus I believe: He was retiring

By His **M A J E S T Y's C O M P A N Y**,
At the Theatre Royal in Drury-Lane
This prefent **M O N D A Y**, May 27, 1776,
Will be prefented a **T R A G E D Y**, call'd
KINGRICHARDtheThird.
King Richard by **Mr. G A R R I C K**,
(Being his Firft Appearance in that Charaƈter thefe 4 Years).
Richmond by Mr. **P A L M E R**,
Buckingham by Mr. **J E F F E R S O N**,
Treffel by Mr. **D A V I E S**,
Lord Stanley by Mr. **B R A N S B Y**,
Norfolk by Mr. **H U R S T**,
Catefby by Mr. **P A C K E R**,
Prince Edward by Mifs **P. H O P K I N S**,
Duke of York MafterPULLEY, Lord Mayor Mr **GRIFFITHS**,
Ratcliffe by Mr. WRIGHT, Lieutenant by Mr. FAWCETT,
King Henry by Mr. **R E D D I S H**,
Lady Anne (Firft Time) Mrs. **SIDDONS**,
Dutchefs of York by Mrs. **J O H N S T O N**,
Queen by Mrs. **H O P K I N S**.
To which will be added
The D E V I L to P A Y.
Sir John Loverule by Mr. **V E R N O N**,
Jobfon by Mr. **M O O D Y**,
Lady Loverule by Mrs. **J O H N S T O N**,
Nell by Mrs. **W R I G H T E N**.
Ladies are defired to fend their Servants a little after 5 to keep Places, to prevent Confufion.
The Doors will be opened at Half after **F I V E** o'Clock
To begin exaƈtly at Half after **S I X** o'Clock.   Vivant Rex & Regina.

To-morrow, (by particular Defire) BRAGANZA, with Bon Ton, or High Life above Stair
(Being the laft Time of performing them this Seafon.)
And Dancing by **Mr. SLINGSBY** and Signora **PACINI**.

b. Playbill: Garrick and Sarah Siddons in *Richard III* at Drury Lane,
27 May 1776.

from the management of Drury Lane and I suppose chose at that time to wash his hands upon all its concerns and details. I, moreover, had served what I believe was his chief object in his exaltation of poor me, and that was the mortification and irritation of Mrs Yates and Miss Younge, whose consequential and troublesome airs were it must be confessed enough to try his patience. As he had now almost with[drawn from] it, the interests of the Theatre grew I suppose rather indifferent to him, for he always objected to my appearing in any very prominent character, telling me that the fore namd ladies would poison me if I did. I of course thought him not only an Oracle but *my friend,* and in consequence of his advice, Portia in the M^t of Venice was fixd upon for my debut, a Character in which it was not likely that I should excite any great sensation. I was therefore meerly *tolerated.* The fulsome adulation that courted him in the Theatre cannot be imagined, and whosoever was the luckless wight who should be honord with his distinguished and envyd smiles of course became an object of spite and malevolence. Little did I guess that I myself was now that wretched victim; for some times He would hand me from my own seat in the Green-room to place me next to his own. He also selected me to personate Venus at the revival of The Jubilee. This gained me the malicious apellation of *Garrick's Venus* and the ladies who so kindly bestowed it on me, so determinedly rushed before me in the last scene, that had he not broken through them all, and brought us forward with his own hand, my little Cupid and my self, whose appointed situations were in the very front of the stage, might as well have been in the Island of Paphos at that moment. He would even flatter me by sending me into the Boxes when he acted any of his great Characters – Oh! It was enough to turn an older and a wiser head, cruel cruel treatment! He promised Mr Siddons to procure me a good Engagement with the new Managers des[i]rd him to give himself no trouble about it but to put my cause entirely into *his* hands. He let me down however after all these protestations, in the most humiliating manner and instead of doing me common justice with those Gentlemen rather depreciated my talents. This Sheridan afterwards told me and said that Mrs Abington when she heard of it, told them they were all fools for dismissing me.[34]

Mrs Abington was evidently alone in recognizing the great talent and passion lying hidden beneath the nervous timidity which seems to have muted everything Sarah did during those painful six months, a period she was never to forget throughout her life. She had to earn the living, with William a poor second. Before they had set off on their summer tour of the provinces,

Garrick, so soon to leave the theatre, had assured them all would be well for them at Drury Lane the following winter. As early as 9 February, William had written to Garrick expressing his hope for re-engagement:

Sir

I make bold to trouble you with an epistle in which I have presumed to solicit your friendship and endeavour for our continuance in Drury Lane; I account we have been doubly unfortunate at our onset in the Theatre, first, that particular circumstances prevented us from joining it at the proper time, and thereby rendered it impossible for us to be mingled in the business of the Season where our utility might have been more observed, second, that we are going to be deprived of you as a manager, and left to those who, perhaps, may not have an opportunity this winter of observing us at all: These considerations, Sir, have occaisond [sic] this address with hope you will lay them before Mr Lucy, and the gentlemen your successors; and, as there has been no agreement with regard to Salary between you and us, it may here be necessary to propose that article, thereby to acquaint them with what we shall expect which (as we are so young in the Theatre) is no more than what I think we may decently subsist on and appear with some credit to the profession. That is for Mrs Siddons three pound a week, for myself two, this I flatter myself we shall both be found worthy of for the first year, after that (as it may be presumed we shall be more experienced in our business) shall wish to rise as our merits may demand. I am, Sir, with many apologies for this freedom, your most obedient and very humble Ser^t

Wm Siddons. Saturday morn. Feby 9 1776[35]

Whatever assurances Garrick may have given them proved vain. No sooner had they reached Birmingham than the blow fell. The pain of it can be felt still in Sarah's recollections written half a century later:

When the London Season was over, I made an Engagement at Birmingham for the ensueing Summer little doubting of my return to Drury Lane for the next Winter but while I was fulfiling my engagement at Birm, to my utter astonishment and dismay, I rec^d an official letter from the Prompter of Drury Lane acquainting me, that my services were no longer necessary. Who can concieve the size of this cruel disappointment, this dreadful reverse of all my ambitious hopes in which too was involved the subsistence of two helpless infants! It was very near destroying me. My blighted prospects indeed induced a state of mind, which preyed upon my health, and for a Year and an half, I was supposed to be hastning to a decline. For the sake of my poor babies however, I exerted myself to shake off this despondency, and my endeavours were blessed with success, in spite of the degradation I had suffer'd from being banishd Drury Lane as a worthless candidate for fame and fortune.[36]

c. Actresses in Performance.

2

Bath

==========================⊂୬⋙୨==========================

HE BLOW HAD fallen, unexpected and mortifying. Sarah
was bitterly humiliated, by what appeared to be the heartless
treatment she had received from the new management in
London. Whatever favours she had received from Garrick, and
whatever the motive behind them, the hard fact remains that she
had made no mark during her six months at Drury Lane. But the
six years which followed in the provinces were by no means
wasted. Sarah broadened and strengthened her art, and at the
same time learned how to gain complete control over her audiences;
she became a true star actress. She worked for prolonged periods
with managements she trusted, culminating in her great period
of success in the theatres of Bath and Bristol. In her private life,
though her painful shyness and reticence remained, she began to
acquire a much wider range of friends both inside and outside
the profession, and to acquire greater social assurance, especially
during the years spent in Bath. Throughout the whole period,
however, she was forced to live in very restricted circumstances;
her wage was normally only three pounds a week while she was
working, supplemented by whatever William was able to earn
playing supporting parts, and the all-important benefit performances. During this time she became pregnant three times;
her second daughter, Maria, was born in 1779, her third, Frances
Emilia, in 1781, and her fourth, Eliza Ann, in 1782. Frances
Emilia was to die in infancy.

Apart from Bath and Bristol, the principal cities in which she
appeared were Birmingham, Liverpool, Manchester and York.
All were places of importance, well capable of supporting theatres.

Birmingham at mid-century was a sizable town of small industries; the population by the end of the century exceeded 70,000. Liverpool was beginning to rival Bristol as a great port, serving the growing trade with America, including the all-important slave trade; the population of Liverpool had reached 80,000 in 1801, exceeding Bristol's 63,000. Manchester became second only to London, with a population in 1801 of almost 100,000: London with its suburbs stood at 864,000. In contrast, Bath and York were market towns, their social importance out of proportion to their size. In 1801 Bath's population was 30,000; York's 24,000.

There are, of course, a number of contemporary accounts of the provincial theatre at this time, and the relative position of the theatres in these lively and thriving centres. Outstanding for the vigour of his writing and the reliability of his information is the manager Tate Wilkinson, who was to do much to help Sarah in her career.

Tate Wilkinson, whatever his quirks and vanities, achieved as much in his own way for the status of the actor in the provinces as Garrick had achieved in London.[1] Before becoming a provincial manager, he had been a well-established actor, playing in London. It raised his wrath to see the men and women in his companies treated like beggars when they should at the very least be received as craftsmen, and at best as artists of some distinction. His principal centres of activity became York and Hull. He believed in the importance of the provinces for the development of the drama, maintaining direct links with the London theatre. During the period in which Sarah was maturing her art, in effect between 1776 and 1782, there were already established theatres with royal patents at Norwich, York, Hull, Liverpool, Manchester and Bristol.[2] Tate Wilkinson was responsible for building theatres in Leeds and Wakefield, as well as in York and Hull.

Wilkinson is a vigorous writer with a great deal to say about Sarah. In about 1790, he wrote his *Memoirs* (published in 1791), surveying the achievements of the past half-century, and his later, more famous book *The Wandering Patentee* was published in 1795, and covered his experiences in Yorkshire during the period 1770–95. He wrote, he said, in a style 'entirely my own, and will not be pilfered from me by any writer whatsoever', adding, 'I pay and keep myself warm with self-compliments, else I should freeze.' His writing is discursive, gossipy, full of amusing anecdotes and self-puffing mixed with a nice frankness: 'My wine', he writes in *The Wandering Patentee*, 'is often rebellious . . . I am not by any means a drunken man, but from accident (almost now and then unavoidable) I live more freely than my stomach and health would permit, were strict prudence the guide.' He spent, he claims, 'no less than 500 l. by obtaining an act of Parliament in my own name for two royal patents, for twenty-one years, for York and Hull theatres.' Nevertheless, he is a realist as far as the business of the theatre is concerned:

> Not that the bad success of a Theatre ever much affected my philoso-
> phy, for I never knew a bad house disconcert my spirits, nor a good
> one raise them . . . if the sum total of the year produces a tolerable
> granary for the supply of homely board, I have all the sing-song of
> a Frenchman.[3]

He opened his new theatre in Leeds in July 1771, and describes it enthusiastically:

> The Theatre was built very neat – aye, and very splendid, compara-
> tively speaking to the mean places, such as the barns, warehouses,
> etc., to which they had been accustomed. However, with the help
> of good scenery, wardrobe, and in truth, a very excellent company,
> with a various and strong catalogue of plays, the houses were well
> attended.[4]

Well-known local patrons were very necessary to get such ventures off to a good start, and at Leeds the town clerk, together with an alderman and his wife, proved extremely helpful.

By the 1780s, the best theatres in the provinces, in his view, compared favourably with those in London:

> The Little Theatre in the Hay Market, as it was called twenty-six
> years ago, till it was beautified and put into its present form by
> Mr Foote and Mr Colman, would *now* cut a very *contemptible figure*
> in most towns of England, and not fit to enter, after seeing Bath,
> Edinburgh, Bristol, Liverpool, York, and many other theatres. By
> this progress and embellishment of regular, handsome, well orna-
> mented theatres, with good scenery, wardrobe, and band, (at York
> in particular the latter) we may be assured that these theatres are
> superior to those wherein Booth, Betterton, and Cibber acted; for
> though Drury Lane was larger than the most of our present country
> theatres, yet forty years ago the audience part of those London
> theatres were very crazy, inconvenient, and not pleasing to the eye-
> . . . Drury Lane, like London Bridge, has been much frittered and

patched at very great expence; and, after all, the only way to repair will be to pull it down, and erect a new one: – which I understand is to be done, and I wish for health to see it finished. In proper built convenient theatres, I am told, Paris has within these few years taken the lead, though some time ago it was greatly inferior.[5]

Tate Wilkinson believed in maintaining a two-way relationship with the London theatre, developing new talent in the provinces and bringing the great stars of Drury Lane and Covent Garden to be seen for short summer seasons by his regional audiences. He wrote: 'Tho' London improves and matures, and is the most enviable theatrical situation, yet genius will be found in every rank, soil and station.' He thought the prejudices among the more distinguished players in the capital against working in the provinces merely stupid, and he was glad that he, for one, managed to change this. Writing from the vantage point of 1790, he said:

> . . . the Londoners will be astonished to be truly informed, that *now* Mrs Siddons, Mrs Jordan, and others, make their true golden harvest on their summer excursions out of the metropolis. Bath, from its great fashionable resort and consequence, has of course an improving theatre; and though only one hundred miles distant from London, causes in the Londoners many a wishful look to honour Bath with five or six nights in the course of a season, and thereby secure a couple of hundred pounds. . . . Dublin and Edinburgh are equal to reward their labours, by holding out a lucrative and happy asylum. Great theatrical personages, who formerly used to look upon a city or town as a *bore*, now, on the contrary, in the summer grant they are commodious, respectable, and even alluring; and with great good manners, compliance, and condescension, will consent to trifle away a few nights at such insignificant places: Even the Jordan herself, who at present reigns as our modern Thalia, has deigned to visit Cheltenham, Reading, Margate, Richmond, and Harrowgate, which places yielded great profits, silver medals, and subscriptions falling at her feet in plentiful showers.[6]

The greatly improved condition of the roads and transport in the latter part of the eighteenth century helped, 'the roads being so excellent to what they were formerly', as Wilkinson says. Not that this helped uniformly – audiences could get to London much more readily and acquire London affectations and prejudices! This was reflected in their reaction now and counter-reaction later to Sarah, as he observed:

Mrs Siddons was thought a good actress at York when in her prime
of life, but not so great an actress, nor followed in the rage of the
times when she was dismissed the theatre as incapable of her engagement, till the Londoners recanted their former ill-judged decisions;
and as a contrary effect, when most deservedly sanctioned, they
fainted, screamed, and expired whenever that lady acted a few years
afterwards. And for the honour of country judgment, be it remembered, that had they in that instance followed London example
(often the case) why that said London had lost the pleasure of seeing
(take her all in all) the finest actress within memory.[7]

During his period in the theatre he had seen the great changes
which took place in audience behaviour. Once again, Garrick had
been influential in this matter as far as London was concerned.
He had, first of all, begun to establish the principle that the
audience should not sit on, around and above the stage, a practice
normal until he abolished it, and indeed encouraged by the
actors on their benefit nights. Tate Wilkinson is especially ironic
about this:

> But, my kind reader, suppose an audience behind the curtain up
> to the clouds, with persons of a menial cast on the ground, beaux
> and no beaux crowding the only entrance, what a play it must have
> been whenever Romeo was breaking open the supposed tomb, which
> was no more than a screen on those nights set up, and Mrs Cibber
> prostrating herself on an old couch, covered with black cloth, as
> the tomb of the Capulets, with at least (on a great benefit night) two
> hundred persons behind her, which formed the back ground, as an
> unfrequented hallowed place of *chapless* skulls, which was to convey
> the idea of where the heads of all her buried ancestors were packed.
> . . . Mr Garrick was a doctor, but too late to cure this evil at his
> setting forth, – better however late than never: but he *only* remedied
> the disease for the advantage of the train of actors that followed him.[8]

He gives a marvellous description of Holland's first appearance
in *Hamlet* and Quin's final appearance in 1753 as Falstaff:

> The Stage was at 5s. – Pit and Boxes all joined together at 5s. There
> was only one entrance on each side the stage, which was always
> particularly crowded. First, they sported their own figures to gratify
> self consequence, and impede and interfere with the performers,
> who had to come on and go off the stage. Affronting the audience
> was another darling delight – particularly, offending the galleries,
> and thereby incurring the displeasure of the gods, who shewed
> their resentment by dispersing golden showers of oranges and half-

eaten pippins, to the infinite terror of the ladies of fashion seated in the pit on such public nights, where they were so closely wedged as to preclude all possibility of securing a retreat, or obtaining relief till the *finale*, when they all moved from their situation by general consent. . . . The first time Holland acted Hamlet it was for his own benefit, when the stage was in the situation here described. On seeing the Ghost he was much frightened, and felt the sensation and terror usual on that thrilling occasion, and his hat flew *a-la mode* off his head. An inoffensive woman in a red cloak, (a friend of Holland's) hearing Hamlet complain the air bit shrewdly, and was very cold, with infinite composure crossed the stage, took up the hat, and with the greatest care placed it fast on Hamlet's head, who on the occasion was as much alarmed in *reality* as he had just then been feigning. But the audience burst into such incessant peals of laughter, that the Ghost moved off without any ceremony, and Hamlet, scorning to be outdone in courtesy, immediately followed with roars of applause: The poor woman stood astonished, which increased the roar, &c. It was some time before the laughter subsided; and they could not resist a repetition (that merry tragedy night) on the re-appearance of the Ghost and Hamlet.

Mr Quin, aged sixty-five, with the heavy dress of Falstaff, (notwithstanding the impatience of the audience to see their old acquaintance) was several minutes before he could pass through the numbers that wedged and hemmed him in, he was so cruelly encompassed around.[9]

It is eye-witness descriptions such as these which give us a true feeling of the stage at this time, and of the kind of conditions Sarah herself only too often had to face in the less developed provincial centres.

Respect for the actor, respect for the play, and respect for the institution of the theatre, these were Tate Wilkinson's objectives, and the objectives of all responsible managements inside and outside London. If the players behaved like mountebanks, they would be treated as such, but Wilkinson would not tolerate that the responsible kind of players he employed should be treated without proper respect. He had seen this too often, as late even as the 1770s:

When the public take an ill-natured turn, no persons suffer the lash more severely than players, for they look on them as their servants and lawful game; and as such think they have a greater privilege over performers than any other set of dependents or clan of persons whatever.[10]

The royal patents gave status to a company:

> Patents have not only been a security for theatrical property, but
> have put the country actors on a more decent level, which was highly
> necessary. . . . An actor in London is very differently respected to
> what he is in the country.[11]

While in London, audiences had acquired by custom a measure
of self-discipline, this was not yet always so in the provinces:

> The good government that prevails in general at Drury Lane and
> Covent Garden theatre is owing to conformity: decorum begets
> decorum. Consequently the strict order to be found in the London
> audiences does not owe its happy preservation entirely to three or
> four constables in waiting, or to ten or twelve of the King's guards.
> . . . When the propriety of London is singled out, let it be well
> recollected that *the audiences there preserve their own respect*; for the
> instant the curtain draws up all noise subsides, and every person
> sits down; nor will they suffer the actors to proceed if a hat remains
> on a head: but in most country theatres, when the performance
> begins, the gazers in the galleries stand up, and with their hats on;
> nay hats are too often seen on in the pit.
> If at London a rioter is vociferous in the gallery, they are from
> custom and good regulation so habituated to order and necessary
> attention, that the offender is by universal consent delivered over to
> the constables, who not only conduct the culprit out of the gallery,
> but if guilty of throwing bottles, etc., on the stage, or into the pit or
> boxes, he is conveyed before a justice to be properly punished. A
> disturbance there, even of a short duration, seldom happens in the
> pit; for the instant of interruption the person is removed by force,
> and turned out with disgrace and ignominy.[12]

Tate Wilkinson abolished the unnecessary extension of the
performance caused by introducing additional entertainment
during the intervals:

> There is one superiority which the Bath and Yorkshire Theatres
> can boast, which is not having interludes, etc., between the acts . . .
> at the established Theatre it is sometimes unpardonable and dis-
> graceful, and must be attended with great inconvenience to all
> sober families to have their servants out till past twelve o'clock at
> a playhouse.[13]

This not only shortened the performance (which in many theatres
dragged on from 6.00 until midnight), but concentrated attention
on the play and its presentation.

Since actors were paid for each working week on about the scale of artisans (a mere labouring family might earn collectively during this period of the century as little as one pound a week), their benefit nights, occurring usually once a season for leading players, were of the greatest importance in bringing a substantial addition to their income.[14] These benefits depended on the goodwill individual actors and actresses could raise in the community where the performance took place. Tate Wilkinson did not, naturally, abolish this incentive to good work and good public relations in his company, but in 1766, when he took over management in York, he did abolish the humiliating practice of letting actors tout for patronage and then give public thanks for the support they had received from the stage after the performance – 'The custom of the man and his wife returning thanks on the stage – and what was truly dreadful, the draggle-tailed Andromache in frost, rain, hail, and snow, delivering her benefit playbills from door to door.' So accustomed were the actors to this practice that they protested, and he told them of

> ... the discredit they appeared in when compared with the performers in London, Dublin, Edinburgh, Liverpool, Bath and every other theatre under regular and gentleman-like establishment. . . . Therefore I, against all remonstrances . . . confirmed as a law, that the manner of returning thanks, and parading the streets with playbills, should be utterly abolished. . . . Good God! – what a fight! to actually behold Mr Frodsham, bred as a gentleman, with fine natural talents, and esteemed in York as a Garrick, the Hamlet of the age, running after, or stopping a gentleman on horseback to deliver his benefit bill, and beg half-a-crown [then the price of the boxes].

The standard of acting, thought Tate Wilkinson, had improved out of all recognition; there was 'decent acting in general throughout the kingdom', and 'five to one actors of merit now to what there were in 1747'. However, both wages and production costs were rising during the latter part of the century. In 1766 a player in York could get as little as 13/6d a week, ('however little that may now seem'), though he could lodge with board for 4/– a week. Even though he had to pay them, Wilkinson approved of higher salaries for actors. He had known them to be near starving in his youth, and considered by the local townsfolk as contrivers of bad debts. He was enlightened enough to advocate the establishment of a theatrical fund to help needy, sick or aged players of repute.

The Siddons' £5 a week in London, and her £3 in the Midland and Northern companies (plus a benefit) must be judged in the light of this background. On these benefit nights the actors often only received a part of their takings, the management deducting costs. In London, the scale was altogether different, and star players automatically charged fees to their less distinguished colleagues if their appearance might greatly increase the takings. Tate Wilkinson had experienced this himself: 'When I had a benefit at Covent Garden, 1760, I only paid 60 l; now I believe performers pay 120 l; and if Mrs Jordan acts in that benefit, it is ten guineas more.' As for rising production costs, he writes: 'One play got up now will cost more than three would fifty years ago.' But the prices of seats were rising proportionately, and so were the takings of capacity houses: 'In 1750, two hundred pounds before the curtain, at Covent Garden, was judged an amazing sum. Now, we hear of upwards of four hundred pounds; but the people of the season, I dare pronounce, are not equal to Mr Garrick's reign, the expenses are grown so enormous.'[15]

He gives the prices of seats in the 1790s: in London 6/– for box seats in the winter theatres; in the provinces 4/- at York, Bristol, Liverpool, 'and even little Windsor', 5/- at Bath. The prices at York would be raised to 5/– when a great London star paid a brief seasonal visit.

This, broadly speaking, was the kind of provincial theatre into which Sarah, accompanied by William as a poor second, had to earn her living for the next six years. From the point of view of the provincial managements, any actress who could be billed as fresh from Drury Lane was at a reasonable advantage, though sophisticated audiences would, at this stage at least, want to know why she had not stayed there. With Richard Yates and Joseph Younger as their managers, the Siddons were in reasonably good hands for their first engagement. They opened in a theatre in New Street, Birmingham, where Sarah's voice was still considered to be weak. When she learned that she was no longer wanted at Drury Lane, she stayed with the Northern management and was sent on with William to Liverpool and Manchester, where she added the part of Hamlet to her standard repertoire, which included the leading parts in Murphy's play *The Grecian Daughter*, Rowe's *The Fair Penitent*, and Home's *Douglas*. She kept Hamlet in her repertoire, though she was never to play the Prince in London. At Birmingham she played opposite an actor of real

quality, John Henderson, who, had he not died in 1785 at the age
of only thirty-eight, would probably have become one of the
great stars of the English stage. It was acting with Henderson
which was eventually to bring her to Bath, where Henderson was
highly regarded as a leading actor. To him more than anyone
she owed not only her eventual transference to Bath, but her final
return to London. He was tireless in promoting her. However,
she was not yet to be invited to Bath, which ranked as the principal
theatrical centre outside London; the invitation finally arrived in
October 1778.

After she had enjoyed a spring holiday on the moors in 1777
with some new friends, the actress Elizabeth Inchbald and her
husband, whom she had met in Liverpool, Tate Wilkinson
managed to secure her in April 1777 for a month's appearances
at his theatre in Blake Street, York; there she appeared from
Easter to Whitsuntide. After this, a highly successful month's
work which excited Tate Wilkinson's abounding admiration,
though he always had fears that her health would give way, she
returned to her former managers, Yates and Younger, for whom
she appeared in further seasons in Manchester and Birmingham.
She also spent one of the intervening summers, that of 1777, in
Liverpool.

In spite of her ill-health, which she claimed lasted for about
eighteen months after the shock of her rejection by Drury Lane,
the two years and more she spent in the North before settling in
Bath were, to say the least, encouraging. She was in theatres of
repute and in favour both with her managements and her audiences.
At York, Tate Wilkinson actually appeared with her, playing
Evander to her Euphrasia in *The Grecian Daughter*; Wilkinson
has recorded his own engaging story of this period:

Miss GLASSINGTON made her appearance at York, in Jane Shore,
Saturday, April 26, 1777, but very unfortunately for Miss Glassington,
Mrs SIDDONS was then the leader of theatrical fashion at Manchester,
from whence intelligence moves quick to York. For though she had
not obtained the London public voice, being rejected at Drury-Lane,
(not very much to the credit of Mr. Garrick's judgment,) yet that
truly intrinsic merit, that unquenchable flame of soul and spirit,
prevented even London prejudice to hurt her in the opinion of
country audiences: And London critics should consider that in
large towns and cities, or places of public resort, men of learning,
science, and discernment, must not only reside, but have perpetually

the assistance of people of the great lead, who sanction in London, – as at Bath and York, during the public races and assizes, where the first people of the law, and of every rank, honour us with their company.

Now this said Mrs Siddons (at the time Miss Glassington was to play on trial for an engagement at York) had engaged for the vacation from Easter to the races at Whitsuntide: Mr Siddons was also retained for the said intermediate weeks. Mrs Siddons's first appearance on the York stage, was on Tuesday, April 15, 1777, in the Grecian Daughter. I had the honour of being her old father, as *Evander*. Her state of health appeared to me so injured, (though I perceived every other requisite) that I actually trembled from her apparent weakness, fearing she would never be able to sustain that fatiguing character with proper energy and spirit; and I must add, that the friends of Mrs Hudson and others wished her not to succeed, – merely because she had *not* bore the bell in London. Our great critic, Mr Swan, was one who took the lead; but she had no sooner performed Rosalind, Matilda, Alicia, Lady Townly, and Lady Alton, but all bowed to her shrine; and Mr Swan was the foremost then in lavish praise: He indeed was ever guided by fashion and consequence. She also acted Indiana, the Irish Widow, Arpasia, and Horatia in the Roman Father; and likewise Semiramis for her own benefit on Saturday, May 17, when the York season finished.

I never remember so great a favourite, as a York actress, as Mrs Siddons was in that short period: – Every one lifted their eyes with astonishment, that such a face, judgment, &c. could have been neglected by the London audience, and by the first actor in the world, (Mr Garrick) as if not of sterling worth.

In her Arpasia, I recollect her fall and figure after the dying scene was noticed, as most elegant; nor indeed do I recognise such a mode of disposing the body in so picturesque and striking a manner as Mrs Siddons does on such prostrate occasions. Great wishes were entertained at York of her coming again as a resident actress; but her stars had ordained better for her; – she had only lowered a little, but was soon raised to the topmost height, as we all see and acknowledge. My best hopes of her return were founded on the finery I had promised – What lady likes it not? Mr Younger's wardrobe was not very good or various, and by no means equal to mine at York; and indeed in that point I still vaunt that I am the tippy: For be it known to all men, that for Lady Alton, I decked Mrs Siddons in a most elegant full sack, with a large hoop, (as then worn, and I am partial too for the stage) and that sack was really elegantly adorned with silver trimmings, &c. This struck her fancy so much, that she declared herself delighted, and laughingly used to repeat, she wished she could convey it with her to Manchester, it made her feel so happy.

Were I to mention this to Mrs Siddons, probably such a trifling matter may have escaped her volume of memory. I should *not* have ventured to have inserted it, had not Mrs Wilkinson assured me that I am perfectly right. Indeed I am not deranged in that respect, however I may be failing in other insignificant points. At that time I can with truth boast, we had the pleasure of Mrs Siddons's company almost constantly at my house, much to the satisfaction of Mrs Wilkinson, myself, and my friends.

Mrs Siddons *then said* she liked her country excursions, and the civilities she met with so well, and thought her treatment in London had been so cruel and unjust, she never wished to play there again. Her state of health did not, by any means, at that time, promise the power of such renovation, strength, and execution, as she now is so happy to possess: But her acting was well imagined then, though not attended to in London by any means as it ought to have been. Mr Woodfall, who is certainly a good critic, and super-excellent observer, advised her not to think of a London Theatre, to which her powers were very inadequate, but keep to such little Theatres as she had been accustomed to, and where she might be heard. But O what a change did there happen! as Mrs Siddons certainly for four or five years drew more money, not only in London, but in many distant Theatres in England, Ireland, and Scotland, than any actor or actress ever did, or perhaps ever will do, and at higher prices (Mr Garrick not excepted).[16]

A first glimpse of Mrs Siddons as a letter-writer comes at this period, in a letter to her new friend Mrs Inchbald, referring to a recent, over-expensive visit to Liverpool of Miss Younge (or Yonge, as Sarah spells her name) of Drury Lane, whom she refers to as 'exotic': 'I played Hamlet in Liverpool', Sarah Siddons wrote,

to near a hundred pounds, and wish I had taken it to myself; but the fear of charges, which, you know, are most tremendous circumstances, persuaded me to take part of a benefit with Barry, for which I have since been very much blamed; but he, I believe, was very much satisfied, and in short so am I. Strange resolutions are formed in our theatrical ministry: one of them I think very prudent – (this little rogue Harry is chattering to such a degree I scarce know what I am about) – but to proceed: our managers have determined to employ no more exotics; they have found that Miss Yonge's late visit to us (which you must have heard of) has rather hurt than done them service; so that Liverpool must from this time forth be content with such homely fare as we small folk can furnish to its delicate sense. . . . Present our kind compliments to Mr and Mrs Wilkinson,

and tell the former I never mention his name but I wish to be
regaling with him over a pinch of his most excellent Irish snuff,
which I have never had a snift of, but in idea, since I left York.[17]

It is pleasant to imagine Sarah, at the age of twenty-two, enjoying
her snuff with the thirty-eight-year-old Tate Wilkinson, like any
old trouper.[18]

It was early in this period of her work in the provinces that
Sarah was joined by her brother, John Philip Kemble, then a
youth of nineteen who at Christmas 1775 (just before Sarah's first
appearance at Drury Lane) had abandoned his studies for the
priesthood at Douai. After six years' residence at the College,
the urge to become an actor had proved too strong for him; he
had discovered he had no vocation, though he had been a successful
student, admired for his declamation. He left Douai a good scholar
in Latin and Greek and, like his sister, he was a very quick study.
He was admitted to the company at Manchester during the winter
season of 1776–7, having made an indifferent début on the stage
in January 1776 at Wolverhampton. It was said that Roger
Kemble had refused to have anything to do with him. However,
by October 1778 he was a good enough actor, in spite of a somewhat weak voice, to become one of Tate Wilkinson's leading men
for a period of three years. He was a serious, intellectual young
man, dedicated to his profession, and anxious to succeed as a
dramatist. He also gave lectures on oratory; the records show
that he appeared as Macbeth in Hull, that he ventured into
comedy as Captain Plume in Farquhar's *The Recruiting Officer*,
and even took a benefit in December 1778 in *Belisarius*, a tragedy
he had written himself. He was, according to his contemporary
biographer Boaden, 'becoming speedily an object of great importance to the manager'.

He was also in love with Sarah's friend, the actress Elizabeth
Inchbald. He met her in Liverpool for the first time, as Sarah
had done. In 1777 Elizabeth was a young woman of twenty-four,
tall and golden-haired, and with a figure Boaden describes as
'striking'; she was highly intelligent and well-read, and had a
witty tongue as well as a nice taste in clothes. She was eventually
to leave the stage and become a successful dramatist. As a young
girl she had always wanted to leave her country home in Essex
and 'see the world', as she put it; this led her finally to run away
to London at the age of nineteen. Her brother, George Simpson,
was on the stage, and the idea of acting appealed to her. She

endured all the usual familiar trials of a young girl living virtually unprotected in eighteenth-century London, and in June 1772, when still only nineteen, she had married an actor, Joseph Inchbald, a man very much older than herself who was not particularly successful, but kindly enough and devoted to his hobby of painting. By 1777 their relationship had considerably cooled, and Sarah's handsome young brother was encouraged to become a constant visitor at the Inchbalds' lodgings. Elizabeth was of just the right age to entrance the serious, scholarly young man, so intellectually passionate and so eager to win a rapid success in a profession which he soon found offered him a social freedom unknown at Douai. As a Catholic filled with doubts and unhappily married to a Protestant, Elizabeth could understand his recent problems, as well as his troubles with his father. Theirs was to become a celebrated friendship, lasting the whole of their lives. 'His countenance', writes Boaden, 'was remarkably striking, his figure, though muscular, slender; he greatly exceeded the usual measure of learning among young men, was very domestic in his habits, and fond of a friendly friend.' Elizabeth soon saw that he had one. 'She seems to have paid him the homage', says Boaden tactfully, 'of a very particular study as a character out of the common road, and consequently in some danger of losing his way.'

Elizabeth was by now an experienced actress, with some five years in the provincial and Scottish theatre behind her, in which she had known privation as well as some modest success. Like many actors, including John Philip himself, she is said to have been reduced to going into the fields to eat raw turnips, the legendary food of out-of-work or impoverished actors in debt.

It is from Elizabeth Inchbald's diaries, edited by that tireless and enthusiastic biographer Boaden, that we get a direct portrait of Sarah. 'Mrs Siddons', writes Boaden, echoing Elizabeth Inchbald, 'was indefatigable in her domestic concerns, for her husband and child; that she neither felt degraded nor unhappy, but cheerfully lightened her task by *singing* away the time.' She 'almost threw away ambition, and, buckling to her hard lot, passed many a day washing and ironing for her family; and, at the conclusion of her labours, regaled the society with a song, and lured her brother to join her in a duet.'[19]

There followed, in the spring of 1778, the holiday on the moors. According to Boaden, there had been severe differences between

Elizabeth and her husband over Kemble. Now, however, the dust
appears to have settled sufficiently for William and Sarah, Elizabeth
and her husband, Kemble and two other members of the company,
Lane and Jefferson, to hire a chaise and

> . . . pass a few days at Northwick; after which, through Appledore-
> combe, they arrived at country lodgings on Russell Moor, there
> living together and in much harmony. . . . While her husband paints,
> Mrs Inchbald reads with Mr Kemble. In the afternoon they all
> walk out, and in the evening play cards, and sometimes get more
> infantine in their sports: these clever people go out upon the moor
> to play at 'blind man's buff' or 'puss in the corner'.

Boaden's polite wording conceals the fact that Elizabeth
Inchbald was in a nervous state, frequently ill, and, as acknowledged by Boaden, at loggerheads with her relatively mild husband.
She was reading widely, and beginning to edge her way into
writing. She was, says Boaden, 'remarkably unsettled', and
suffering grave religious doubts. She even threatened to go
home to the family farm in Essex. Kemble, however, became her
constant companion; his presence alleviated her 'melancholy'.
She affirms in her memoirs that he never became her lover,
though this might have been from her resolve, not his, since he
was to prove very susceptible to women. But Elizabeth, says
Boaden, 'had always a very teasing love of admiration and
attention'. At one stage she even let an actor called Davis lodge
with them and dress her hair for the stage. Mr Inchbald did not
favour this relationship either.

After a period of separation while Sarah and William were
working in York, the friends met again in Manchester. Elizabeth's
journal continues:

> On the 26th of May I rose at three in the morning, and left Man-
> chester in a post-chaise with Mrs Siddons and her maid. The
> gentlemen rode on the stage-coach. They breakfasted at Maccles-
> field; after which they proceeded on their journey to Birmingham;
> Mr Inchbald on horseback – Mr Kemble was taken into the chaise
> by the ladies; till very late in life he was an indifferent horseman.
> At Birmingham, in their usual style, the Siddons and the Inchbald
> families lived together; and sometimes Mr Inchbald painted in the
> apartment of Mrs Siddons, whose exertion had given her a fit of
> illness. His wife went through her parts with Mr Kemble, and, there
> will be little doubt, benefited much by his critical remarks. . . . Here,
> in the old style, these amusing people, as rogues and vagabonds,

were informed against; and their worships the magistrates, in their sagacity, not wiser than the laws, though perhaps wishing they had alike been permitted to sleep together, stopped the performances. Something was now, of necessity, to be done. The society, so delightful to them, was broken up; the Siddonses and their brother Kemble went for a few days, first to Warwick, and then to Wolverhampton.[20]

Sarah's final performance at Liverpool in June proved something of a disaster, though through no fault of hers. The story is told in an amusing letter written by John Kemble to Elizabeth on 18 June, and sent from Liverpool:

On Monday night we opened our theatre. Before the play began, Mr Younger advanced before the curtain, if possible to prevent any riot, with which he had publicly been threatened for presuming to bring any company to Liverpool who had not played before the King. In vain did he attempt to oratorize; the remorseless villains threw up their hats, hissed, kicked, stamped, bawled, and did everything to prevent his being heard. After two or three fruitless entrances, and being saluted with volleys of potatoes and broken bottles, he thought proper to depute Siddons as his advocate, who entered bearing a board large enough to secure his person, inscribed with Mr Younger's petition to be heard. The rogues would hear nothing, and Siddons may thank his wooden protector that his bones were whole. Mrs Siddons entered from P.S. and Mrs Kniveton O.P. – *mais aussi infortunées – hé bien!* Madame Kniveton *a la mauvaise fortune de tomber dans une convulsion sur les plancs*: the wretches laughed, and would willingly have sent a peal of shouts after her into the next world loud enough to have burst the gates of her destination.[21]

The autumn of 1778 saw Sarah and the family in Bath for the first of her seasons in John Palmer the Younger's Theatre Royal. Palmer had invited her to join his company, initially at least, on Henderson's enthusiastic recommendation.[22] Henderson had joined Palmer's company in 1772, but by 1778 he had left Bath and moved up to London. Sarah had consented to go to Bath virtually in a secondary position in the company as far as comedy was concerned, because Palmer's theatre, the first in the provinces to receive a royal patent by special Act of Parliament in 1768, was recognized as the leading theatre outside London by virtue of the city's unique social reputation.

The best and the worst which England could produce in the way of an élite had chosen to make Bath a fashionable centre.

As a spa, its reputation dated from Roman times, and it had the good fortune, for those with carriages or bath-chairs to transport them, to be built on seven hills, some of them very steep, and to have become, by the time Sarah arrived, one of the handsomest small cities in the world. It was, in effect, England's second capital in the late-eighteenth century. Its streets, circuses, squares, terraces and crescents had been the creation of a brilliant succession of mid-century architects, city designers and social dictators – Beau Nash, creator of and ruler over the Assembly Rooms, Ralph Allen, Mayor of Bath, builder of Prior Park and organizer of the posting system which brought the élite from London to Bath along the Great West Road, and John Wood and his son, the inspired architects who laid out Bath. Line after line of beautiful limestone buildings spread over the valley and hills, giving the city a panoramic setting which still delights the eye. In the 1770s Bath was a thriving, elegant community of some 30,000, including its population of visitors, most of whom had come for their pleasure rather than their health. Sheridan's *The Rivals*, written three years earlier, represented the Bath atmosphere to perfection, at least as the city liked to see itself portrayed.

John Palmer the Younger was a man of great enterprise.[23] His father, Palmer the Elder, a wealthy brewer and tallow-chandler, had organized the building of the old Orchard Street Theatre in 1750, during the period of Beau Nash's ascendancy. In 1775, Palmer the Younger had spent around £1,000 in renovating the theatre under the supervision of his namesake, John Palmer the architect, and in 1779 he was to take out a further twenty-year lease on the theatre at £200 a year, though the proprietors (made up of the original subscribers to the building) excused him three years' rent (that is, £600) because of the money he had spent on renovations. The building, in which Sarah was to make so great a reputation, was essentially a simple one, not to be compared with the far more celebrated Theatre Royal in Beaufort Square, built under John Palmer the architect's supervision in 1805, when the Orchard Street Theatre was closed as no longer adequate for the purpose. The renovated theatre in Orchard Street in which Sarah appeared was an easy building in which to work, with a new proscenium arch decorated with doric and ionic columns, and what Fitzgerald was to describe as a 'handsome crushroom'; it also enjoyed, and needed, a ventilated ceiling. However, it had no grand façade, merely a door into the street.

Sarah's work was not to be confined to Bath. John Palmer the manager had acquired in April 1779 a twenty-year lease of the newly-patented Theatre Royal in Bristol – it had received its royal licence in February 1778 – on terms very similar to those in Bath: £200 a year plus ground rent and taxes, but with three years' payment of the £200 rent excused if he undertook renovations in the theatre. This led to the company commuting between Bath and Bristol, which Sarah, pregnant again in the winter of 1778–9, found so trying. Palmer, of course, had this closely organized, using his own pioneering post-chaises from which he was soon to develop another enterprise, express mail-coaches for passenger transport and postal service on the new, fast roads.

Sarah herself describes the situation she was in as a member of the joint Bath-Bristol company from September 1778:

> I now made an Engagement at Bath. Here my talents and industry were encouraged by the gre[a]test indulgence and I may say with some admiration. Tragedies which had been almost banished again resumed thier proper interest, but I had the mortification of being obliged to Personate many subordinate characters in Comedy, the first being in the possession of another Lady. This I was obliged to submit to, or forfiet part of my week's salary, too serious a diminution of my very small Income which was only three pounds a week. Tragedies now became more and more fashionable. While I laboured hard, I however earned a reputation. Hard labour indeed it was; for after the Rehearsal at Bath on a Monday morning, I had to go and act at Bristol in the evening of the same day, and reaching Bath again after a drive of twelve miles, long after midnight, I was obliged to represent some fatigueing part there on the Tuesday evening. Mean time I was gaining private friends and publick reputation. My industry and persevereance were indefatigueable. That I had strength and courage to get through all this labour of mind and body, interrupted too, by the cares and childish sports of my poor children who were (most unwillingly often) hushd to silence for interrupting my studies, I look back with wonder.[24]

In fact, she made her first appearance in Bath as Lady Townley in *The Provoked Husband* on 24 October 1778 and did not have to play in Bristol until 15 March, when she acted as the Countess in Hartson's *The Countess of Salisbury*. Her somewhat secondary position in the company as far as the highly-regarded comedy parts were concerned meant that she was expected to play on Thursday evenings, which were notorious for bad attendance owing to the Cotillion Balls which took place in Bath each week on that night. She did not have to wait long, however, before a favourable notice appeared in the *Bath Chronicle*, which said of her performance as Elwina in Hannah More's *Percy*, a tragedy, that 'in the judgement of the town' she was 'the most capital actress that had performed here these many years'. After Garrick's death in 1779, on 29 April, while still in her first season, she was chosen to read Sheridan's *Monody on Garrick*.

Her extraordinary energy and resilience during this first winter in Bath, and spring in Bath and Bristol, have to be appreciated. From October to May, a period of eight months at the close of which she was within a few weeks of giving birth to her second daughter, Maria, in July 1779, she rehearsed and performed nearly thirty different characters (including the Queen in *Hamlet*, Portia, Juliet and Imogen), and from March to the end of May she had to travel to and from Bristol several times a week to do so.[25] When the dual system was in full operation, she would rehearse in Bath on Monday morning, play in Bristol that night, return by coach overnight or early the next day to appear in Bath on Tuesday evening. Wednesdays and Fridays were allocated to Bristol, and Tuesdays, Thursdays and Saturdays to Bath. Thursday was the day at first given over to tragedy, since this was likely to appeal to the more serious audiences less likely to be involved in the Cotillion Balls; Palmer appears to have relied on her to build up an audience for tragedy, though she persisted in sharing the taste of the Bath audiences for comedy, in which she sometimes, as she says, had to play subordinate roles, or forfeit her money. She relied on William to help with the children, drill her in her parts, which changed from night to night, and earn a little extra much-needed money by appearing in small parts, such as the five-line part of Derby in Rowe's *Jane Shore*, in which his wife played the lead, and Guildenstern in *Hamlet*, in which she played the Queen. But it was recorded by the actress Mrs Summers, who worked with Sarah in Bath, that he 'was sometimes very cross with her when she did not act to please him'.

Boaden, pleasantly verbose, describes the manner in which she gradually won approval in her Thursday evening appearances:

Undoubtedly Bath was a desirable station to Mrs Siddons. Till the fashion follows the performer the performer must follow the fashion. Bath is a more select London. But the theatre for some time was sufficiently cool on the nights of its greatest ornament. Tragedy, although the most exalted delight of a refined nature, is seldom sought by those who are merely in search of amusement; when a rage is once excited it is followed, not for its object but its vogue. Palmer for a considerable time troubled Mrs Siddons only on his Thursday nights, when the cotillion balls carried off everything that could move to the Rooms; and that eye was frequently bent on vacancy that ere long was to fascinate all ranks and ages of life. . . . Old Mr Sheridan distinguished himself early in the host of admirers, and asserted, I have no doubt with exact truth, that Mrs Siddons was more pathetic even than Mrs Cibber. . . . The Thursday nights, from a vacuum, soon became a plenum; the charms of the cotillion itself were resisted, and no nights at all in the Bath Theatre were attended by the fashionable world but those on which Mrs Siddons acted.[26]

The principal actor with whom she appeared was William Wyatt Dimond, a sound if somewhat old-fashioned player who was popular as a personality; he became a joint acting-manager to the company and stayed as a principal resident actor until his retirement in 1801.

The birth of Sarah's third child, her daughter Maria, on 1 July 1779 came during the summer recess.[27] She was to start work again in her second Bath season on 27 September, appearing then as Lady Macbeth. She stayed in Bath for four seasons in all, until June 1782, when she was almost twenty-eight, and considered herself, like Dimond, wholly settled in the district. She left for London only because the salary she earned, even with the growing benefits accorded her and William's little extras, did not bring in enough to provide them all with a reasonable standard of living. She had to employ help to look after the children, and the family's average earnings over the years could not have exceeded much more than £6 or £7 a week until the end of her period in Bath, though her benefits rose steadily – £124 in 1780–1, and, from three successive benefits in 1781–2, a total of £398. 11. od.

The Siddons eventually went to live in Axford's Buildings (now 33 The Paragon), a handsome line of new houses recently built on the east side of the London Road, and about half a mile from the Orchard Street Theatre.[28] In January 1780 Sarah introduced her younger sister, Fanny Kemble, into the company. Sarah's fourth child was born in April the following year and

baptized Frances Emilia on 26 April 1781, according to an
entry in the register of Bath Abbey. This child was to die in
infancy.

Bath, then, became her first experience of a place she could
regard as home, and she lived there until she left for London in
1782. She acquired many useful patrons and friends, and she was
seen by many fashionable and influential people as well as by
those prepared to gush over her growing powers as an actress,
especially in dramas of sentiment, suffering and tragedy. We
begin from this time to find her referred to increasingly in the
great mass of correspondence, diaries and memoranda which so
wonderfully preserve the spirit and humour of the English
eighteenth century, like a vast, composite and well-informed
self-portrait.

Fanny Burney, Madame d'Arblay, was among the first of the
more distinguished people to note down her reactions to Sarah.[29]
She was, she said, taken by a friend 'to see an actress she is
dotingly fond of, Mrs Siddons in *Belvidera*; but instead of falling
in love with her, we fell in love with Mr Lee, who played Pierre –
and so well!' She refers to this visit again when she was asked
later to see Sarah in the same part in London, but refused: 'I had,
however, seen and been, half killed by Mrs Siddons in *Belvidera*,
or I would not have been so heroic in my domesticity.' However,
she admitted that she 'admired her very much'. Other admirers
of this period were Thomas Sheridan, father of Richard Brinsley
Sheridan; Thomas Linley, father of Elizabeth Linley, the
celebrated singer with whom Richard Brinsley eloped; Mrs
Thrale, later to become an intimate friend; and Hannah More.
Above all, perhaps, in terms of social influence, she was warmly
accepted by one of the great beauties of the age, Georgiana,
Duchess of Devonshire, who was loud in her praises of Sarah
wherever she went. A further lifelong friend was another lay-
minded parson, the Reverend Sedgewick Whalley, who had
bought a house in the centre of the Royal Crescent soon after it
was built, and was one of Bath's many pleasant and well-known
eccentrics. He was happy to leave his living in Lincolnshire in the
hands of a permanent curate, who was paid a fraction of Whalley's
stipend for his pains. Whalley, who was eleven years older than
Sarah, was left free to indulge his fancies for literature and the
arts, for society, gossip and travel, drawing confidently on the
accumulated resources of the succession of wealthy women whom

he married. He attempted to write verses and plays, and was a true 'man of feeling', who wept even at a military band. He adored lap-dogs, and had his portrait painted by Reynolds. A kindly, self-indulgent dilettante, he befriended Sarah and her husband, and afforded her a sympathetic outlet for conversation and letter-writing which neither his wife nor her husband seemed at all to resent. Her letters to him, many of which have been preserved, give us a continuous, first-hand impression of her as a woman, and her feelings about her work and her domestic life. Whalley became for her a valued male confidant.

The surviving letters to Whalley date from the autumn of 1781, by which time she already counted him and his wife as friends. He had recently married Elizabeth Sherwood, a widow with a handsome estate in Somerset. Writing to him on 16 July from Bristol, Sarah said:

I cannot express how much I am honoured by your friendship, therefore you must not expect words, but as much gratitude as can inhabit the bosom of a human being. I hope, with a fervency unusual upon such occasions, that you will not be disappointed in your expectations of me tonight; but sorry am I to say I have often observed, that I have performed worst when I most ardently wished to do better than ever. Strange perverseness! And this leads me to observe (as I believe I may have done before), that those who act mechanically are sure to be in some sort right, while we who trust to nature (if we do not happen to be in the humour, which, however, Heaven be praised, seldom happens) are dull as anything can be imagined, because we cannot feign. But I hope Mrs Whalley will remember that it was your commendations which she heard, and judge of your praises by the benevolent heart from which they proceed, more than as standards of my deserving. Luckily I have been able to procure places in the front row of the next to the stage-box, on the left hand of you as you go in. These I hope will please you.[30]

In another, undated letter, but written sometime in 1782 while she was still in Bath, she tells him she was studying one of her parts till three in the morning after returning from Bristol at midnight.

While Sarah was in Bath, she met for the first time, as a boy, the person who as a man was to bring so much trouble to both her and her daughters. This was Thomas Lawrence, the artist who in childhood became a prodigy in portraiture. Lawrence was

still only a boy when his parents brought him to Bath.[31] He had
been born in Bristol on 13 April 1769, the fourteenth child of an
innkeeper who had made a runaway match with a girl both younger
and of better family than himself. Thomas Lawrence the father
was an ambitious man of great cultural as well as social pretensions,
and usually elaborately overdressed. He was always overreaching
himself, miscalculating his business capacities. He was, in fact,
more than slightly absurd, but also very ruthless. His behaviour
was to have a lifelong effect on his son's character.

After failing in his attempt to develop the White Lion and the
American Coffee House in Broad Street, Bristol, into a profitable
inn and social centre, in 1773 he took over the Black Bear at
Devizes, Wiltshire, advertising it to 'the nobility, gentry and
others' as a place of high-class resort. Devizes was a recognized
staging-post between London and the West Country. Young
Thomas, then aged four, was described by Mrs Nalder, a woman
who worked for Lawrence at the Black Bear, as 'a very beautiful
and engaging child . . . of remarkably fascinating manners'
who drew her portrait, producing 'an excellent likeness'. Lawrence
senior was much excited by his son's gift and saw in it opportunities for ingratiating himself with the great people, such as Garrick,
who is described by the same woman as visiting the inn frequently,
'staying sometimes a week or a fortnight at a time'. Lawrence
senior was 'remarkably fond of politics, theatricals and recitations,
and prided himself on his readings of Milton and Shakespeare'.
Looking at his infant son's drawings, Lawrence was convinced
of the child's genius, but instead of conserving and developing
these talents he set out to exploit them; not content with this,
he taught his son to declaim the works of his favourite poets for
the benefit of the guests, who were not always entertained by this
or by the familiarity with which they were treated by their
landlord. Nevertheless, the child won a certain amount of well-
meaning patronage from the local gentry. Even Sir Joshua
Reynolds, staying at the inn, expressed himself surprised at the
excellence of the boy's work. Other visitors of note included
Fanny Burney and Mrs Thrale, who stayed there together in
April 1780; in her diary Fanny Burney described the family at
some length, noting that young Thomas was 'a most lovely boy
of ten years of age, who seems to be not merely the wonder of the
family, but of the times, for his astonishing skill in drawing'.
That same year Thomas's father took him to London as the guest

for several weeks of Hugh Boyd, who showed off the child's
talents in London society.

Lawrence senior was so preoccupied with poetry and art that
he became bankrupt once again. He then decided that the only
secure way of making money was to exploit the growing fame of
his eleven-year-old son, whose portrait by William Hoare of Bath
was already selling well as a print. By now the child's earnings
were beginning to be considerable; he worked fast under pressure
from his father, and the charges for his portraits in crayon rapidly
rose from their initial price of a guinea. While Sarah was earning
£3 a week in Bath, young Lawrence, completing four commissions
a week, was soon to be earning three or four times as much.

In 1780 Lawrence took his family on tour, first of all to Oxford
and then to Salisbury and Weymouth, ending up in Bath, where
they were to stay for six years. The actual date of the first meeting
of Sarah and the boy is not known. It is thought that she stayed at
some time at the Black Bear on her way to Bath, and that the child
made his first drawing of her then. Once he was settled in Bath and
become the cynosure of the fashion there, he came to see her
frequently and drew several portraits of her – from this period
date his drawings of Sarah as Euphrasia in *The Grecian Daughter*
and as Zara in *The Mourning Bride*; both were engraved and sold
widely as prints. These were completed before he was thirteen,
the age he had reached when she left Bath in 1782.[32]

Young Thomas Lawrence's life, though hard, was by no means
inactive. During his adolescence in Bath he became very athletic,
and was to become both a good shot and a good fencer; from
childhood he had been an exceptionally adept pugilist. He appears
to have begun to experience an idealized kind of love for Sarah
when he was twelve or thirteen, and to have told his horrified
father that he wanted to go on the stage himself. Lawrence senior
saw to it at once that, whatever his son's talents might be, Palmer
should do everything he could to dissuade him. He even refused
a most generous offer from Lady Frances Harpier, sister of the
Earl of Warwick, to give £1,000 so that the boy, who had had no
time for the schooling his brothers and sisters received, should be
educated in Rome; she had even offered to adopt him. This, too,
was firmly refused. The Lawrence family were almost entirely
dependent on the boy for their living.

When, finally, in 1786, Thomas Lawrence set up as a painter in
London, it was his father who took him there and hired apartments

for him in Leicester Square at the high rent of four guineas a week. He was still only seventeen. He had recently taken to oils, and before he left Bath he painted the portrait of Sarah's mother which still hangs in Bath at the Victoria Art Gallery. It is thought to be the first portrait of her to be executed in oils.

It can be imagined that there was growing pressure on all sides to persuade Sarah to make a second attempt in London. The praises of Henderson and the Duchess of Devonshire, who were, perhaps, the prime movers, put the first pressures upon her to change her mind. Henderson paid a brief professional visit to Bath in November 1778, when she played the Queen to his Hamlet, Portia to his Shylock, and Beatrice to his Benedick, and the effect of the renewal of their friendship Sarah has described herself:

> I remained at Bath about three years, during which time Mr Henderson came there to act for a few nights. He was most kindly encourageing to me, and on his return to London, spoke favourably of me. I acted Beatrice with his Benedick and he said my Comedy was equal to my Tragedy. He was a fine Actor without the advantage of person, countenance, or voice, but he was the soul of feeling and intelligence.[33]

The first approach to her from Drury Lane was apparently undertaken on Sheridan's behalf as early as July 1780: a letter of Sheridan's dated 12 July survives, in which he says: 'I am at present endeavouring to engage Mrs Siddons, of the Bath Theatre.' She must have wavered when approached again in 1781, for her friend Whalley rushed into print prematurely with verses on her departure to Drury Lane. She was finally won over at the end of the 1781–2 season:

> And in the Autumn I received an invitation to revisit Drury Lane. After my former dismissal thence it may be imagined this was a triumphant moment. The aimiable and lovely Dss. of D(e)vonshire to whom I had the honour of being introduced during her visit to Bath, was present at many Tragedies. I had the pleasure of recieving her unqualified approbation and she spoke highly of me on her return to London.
>
> I was truly grieved to leave my kind Bath friends, and was also fearful that the power (of) my voice was not equal to filling a London Theatre. My friends too were also doubtful; but I soon had reson to think that the ill construction of the Bath Theatre, and not the weakness of my voice, was the real cause of our mutual fears.[34]

What really forced her to give way was, in the end, money. Although she was doing exceptionally well from her increased number of benefits, Palmer was adamant against increasing her salary.[35] 'What a pity this man did not sooner become sensible to Mrs Siddons's value and his own interest,' wrote another Bath friend, Penelope Sophia Weston, a relative of the Whalleys, who much later, as Mrs William Pennington of Bristol, was to play a most dramatic part in Sarah's life. It appears from her letter that Palmer repented of his parsimony, and offered Sarah an increase too late for her to accept it. 'The terms he has now offered,' continued Miss Weston, 'were she at liberty to accept them, would be such a security to her ease and happiness (which, with all her merit, I am afraid is not so certain in town), that one cannot help lamenting such perverse infatuation.'[36]

Sarah was determined to retire gracefully, and made her well-known bow from the Bath stage by advertising that at her benefit on 21 May she would 'produce to the Audience THREE REASONS for her quitting this Theatre.' The secret was kept until the night itself, and, after appearing in *The Distressed Mother* (a version of *Andromaque*), she addressed the audience in verses of her own composition. First she thanked them for their support, and then continued:

> The time draws nigh when I must bid adieu
> To this delightful spot – nay even to you –
> To you, whose fost'ring kindness rear'd my name,
> O'erlooked my faults, but magnified my fame.

Then she posed herself the question so many were asking:

> Why don't I here, you'll say, content remain,
> Nor seek uncertainties for certain gain?
> What can compensate for the risks you run;
> And what your reasons? Surely you have none.

She left the stage and returned immediately with Henry and Sally trailing beside her, and Maria in her arms. She went on:

> These are the moles that bear me from your side;
> Where I was rooted – where I could have died. . . .
> Have I been hasty? Am I then to blame;
> Answer, all ye who own a parent's name?[37]

Since Sarah was eight months pregnant, she might well have

made her plea to the audience as Four Reasons. She was delivered of another daughter, her fourth, Eliza Ann, on 2 June 1782, while she was still at Bath.[38] When she was recovered, she and William, with over £400 in their pockets from benefits and gifts after her final appearances in both Bath and Bristol, set off on holiday to Weymouth. Already sheer dread of appearing in London was settling upon her.

3

Drury Lane Regained

<hr>

BEFORE FINALLY deciding whether or not she should face
the greatest test in her career, Sarah felt entitled to a short
holiday. She had sent William and the family to Weymouth
whilst, apparently, undertaking some further professional engagement in the West Country. On 20 August 1782 she wrote a letter
to the Whalleys which describes in graphic, entertaining detail her
journey by coach, which she calls the 'machine', from the West
Country to Weymouth; it is one of the most descriptive and
characteristically observant of her letters to have survived, and
it is notable that she still seems to be against finally committing
herself to London, a hesitancy no doubt due to having, for the
first time in her life, some hundreds of pounds in hand. She
writes:

> We were five of us in the machine, all females but one, a youth of
> about sixteen, and the most civilized being you can conceive, a
> native of Bristol too.
>
> One of the ladies was, I believe, verily, a little insane, her dress
> was most peculiar, and manner the most offensive, I ever remember
> to have met with; her person was taller and more thin than you can
> imagine, her hair raven black, drawn as tight as possible over her
> cushion before and behind, and at the top of her head was placed a
> solitary fly-cap of the last century, composed of materials of about
> twenty sorts, and as dirty as the ground; her neck, which was a thin
> scrag of a quarter of a yard long, and the colour of a walnut, she
> wore uncovered for the solace of all beholders; her Circassian was
> an olive-coloured cotton of three several sorts, about two breadths
> wide in the skirt, and tied up exactly in the middle in one place only.
> She had a black petticoat, spotted with red, and over that a very

thin white muslin one, with a long black gauze apron, and without the least hoop. I never in my life saw so odd an appearance, and my opinion was not singular, for wherever we stopped, she inspired either mirth or amazement, but was quite innocent of it herself. On taking her seat amongst us at Bristol, she flew into a violent passion on seeing one of the windows down. I said I would put it up if she pleased; 'To be sure,' said she, 'I have no ambition to catch my death.' No sooner had she done with me, but she began to scold the woman who sat opposite to her for touching her foot: 'You have not been used to riding in a *coach*, I fancy, good woman.' She met in this lady a little more spirit than she had found in me, and we were obliged to her for keeping this unhappy woman in tolerable order the remainder of the day. Bless me! I had almost forgot to tell you that I was desired to make tea at breakfast. Vain were my endeavours to please this strange creature; she had desired to have her tea in a basin, and I followed her directions as near as it was possible in the making her tea, but she had no sooner tasted it than she bounced to the window and threw it out, declaring she had never met with such a set of awkward, ill-bred people; what could be expected in a stage-coach, indeed? She snatched the canister from me, poured a great quantity into the basin, with sugar, cream, and water, and drank it all together.

Did you ever hear of anything so strange? When we sat down to dinner, she seemed terrified to death lest anybody should eat but herself. The remaining part of our journey was made almost intolerable by her fretfulness; one minute she was screaming out lest the coachman should overturn us; she was sure he would, because she would not give him anything for neglecting to keep her trunk dry; and, though it was immoderately hot, we were obliged very often to sit with the windows up, for she had been told that the air was pestilential after sunset, and that, however other people liked it, she did not choose to hazard her life by sitting with the windows open. All were disposed, for the sake of peace, to let her have her own way, except the person whom we were really obliged to for quieting her every now and then. She had been handsome, but was now, I suppose, sixty years old. I pity her temper, and am sorry for her situation, which I have set down as that of a disappointed old maid.

At about seven o'clock we arrived at Dorchester; on my stepping out of the coach a gentleman very civilly gave me his hand – who should it be but Mr Siddons, who was come on purpose to meet me? He was very well, and the same night I had the pleasure of seeing my dear boy more benefited by the sea than can be conceived. He desires me to thank Mr Whalley for the fruit, which he enjoyed very much. We have got a most deplorable lodging, and the water and the bread are intolerable, 'but travellers must be content'. Mr Whalley was so good as to be interested about my bathing – is there anything I could refuse to do at his or your request? I intend to bathe to-morrow morning, cost what pain it will. I expected to have found more company here.[1]

But there could in the end be no doubt what she must do. To London she went in September, and matters became sufficiently settled for announcements to appear from Drury Lane that 'Mrs Siddons (From the Theatre Royal, Bath) will shortly make her appearance at this Theatre in a Capital Character in Tragedy'. The salary agreed was ten guineas a week. After careful thought, and advice from Thomas Sheridan, it was decided she should appear for the first time as Isabella, a part in which she had enjoyed a sustained success during countless revivals in Bath. The part drew on her powers for pathos, and she never failed to reduce susceptible audiences to tears. Sheridan believed she could not fail to have the same effect in London. Further, her own son Henry, now aged eight, could appear with her. So it was announced that she would appear in *Isabella, or, The Fatal Marriage* on 10 October 1782.

The whole of the preceding fortnight, during which she appears to have rehearsed with the company only twice, filled her with apprehension.[2] The memory of this time never left her, and she recalled it most painfully in her notes for Thomas Campbell, written some fifty years later:

For a whole Fortnight before this memorable day, I suffered from nervous agitation more than can be imagined. No wonder, for my own fate and that of my little family hung upon it. I had quitted Bath, where all my efforts had been successful, and I feared lest a second failure in London might influence the publick mind greatly to my disadvantage in the event of my return thither from Drury Lane disgraced as I formerly had been. In due time, I was summoned to a Rehearsal of Isabella. Who can imagine my terror? I fear'd to utter a sound above an audible whisper [for] some minutes, but by degrees enthusiasm cheated me into forgetfulness of my fears, and I unconsciously threw out my voice, which faild not to be heard in the remotest part of the House by a friend who kindly undertook to ascertain the happy circumstances. The countenences, no less than tears and flattering encouragements of my companions in this affecting Drama, emboldened me more and more, and the second Rehearsal was even more affective than the first. Mr King, who was then Acting Manager, was loud in his applauses. This second Rehearsal took place upon the Eighth of Novr 82, and on the evening

1. Sarah Kemble. By Sir Thomas Lawrence. Probably painted about 1785 in Bath. (*By courtesy of the Victoria Art Gallery, Bath*)

2. Roger Kemble. By Thomas Beach. Exhibited in the Royal Academy 1787. (*By courtesy of the Victoria Art Gallery, Bath*)

3. Sarah Siddons as Zara. From a mezzotint after a drawing by Lawrence executed at the age of thirteen. (*Burney Collection, British Museum*)

4. Thomas Lawrence at the age of thirteen. Engraving from a self-portrait. (*British Museum*)

5. Sarah Siddons at the age of twenty-one. By Gilbert Stuart. (*National Portrait Gallery, London*)

6. Sarah Siddons in the character of Isabella, with her son Henry as Biron's child. From an engraving after a picture by William Hamilton.

7.   William Siddons. By John Opie. (*The Tate Gallery, London*)

8.   David Garrick. Attributed to G. Dance 1771.
    (*National Portrait Gallery, London*)

9. Interior of the old Theatre Royal, Orchard Street, Bath. From Mowbray Green's *Eighteenth Century Bath Architecture*. (*Photograph by courtesy of the Theatre Collection, Department of Drama, University of Bristol*)

10. Interior of the old Theatre Royal, Drury Lane, 1792. (*Photograph by courtesy of the Theatre Collection, Department of Drama, University of Bristol*)

11. John Henderson.
By Gilbert Stuart.
(*Victoria and Albert
Museum, Crown
Copyright*)

12. Tate Wilkinson.
Attributed to Stephen
Hewson. (*York City
Art Gallery*)

13. Sarah Siddons as Jane Shore. After the portrait by William Hamilton. (*Victoria and Albert Museum, Crown Copyright*)

14. Sarah Siddons rehearsing in the Green Room with her father and John Henderson. From a drawing by Thomas Rowlandson. (*Victoria and Albert Museum, Crown Copyright*)

15.   Sarah Siddons as Euphrasia. By William Hamilton.
(*Victoria and Albert Museum, Crown Copyright*)

16.   John Philip Kemble. By Gilbert Stuart.
(*National Portrait Gallery, London*)

of that day, I was siezed with a nervous hoarseness, which made me extremely wretched; for I dreaded being obliged to defer my appearance on the Tenth, longing as I most ardently [did] at least to know the worst. I went to Bed therefore in a state of dreadful suspense. Awaking the next morning however out of that restless unrefreshing sleep, which had so long pursued me, I found upon speaking to my husband that my voice was very much clearer. This of course was a great comfort to me, and *moreover* the Sun which for many days had been completely obscured, shone brightly through my curtains. I hailed it though tearfully, yet thankfully, as a happy omen and even now am not ashamed of this (as it may perhaps be calld) childish superstition. On the morning of the Tenth, my voice was most happily perfectly restored, and again the *blessed Sun shone brightly on me.*[3]

She was thus encouraged and supported by men of great experience in the theatre; Thomas Sheridan, who knew her best work well, and Thomas King, her old admirer who had seen her act in Cheltenham and advised Garrick to bring her to London six years before, and had played Shylock to her Portia. Then her father, now aged sixty-one, came up to town to be with her in the theatre on the night:

On this eventful day my Father arrived to comfort me and to be a witness of my trial. He accompanyd me to my Dressing-room at the Theatre, there left me, and I, in one of what I call my desperate tranquilities (which usually possess me under terrifick circumstances) completed my dress, to the astonishment of my attendants, without uttering one word, though frequently sighing most profoundly. At length I was calld to my fierey trial. I found my venerable Father behind the scenes, little less agitated than myself. The awful consciousness that one is the sole object of attention to that imense space, lined as it were with human intellect from top to bottom, and on all sides round, may perhaps be imagined but can not be described, and never never to be forgotten – my dear dear Father too, embracing me from time to time with joyful tears.[4]

10 October 1782 has become one of the celebrated nights in the English theatre, comparable only with the night Garrick took the town by storm in *Richard III* in October 1741, or when Edmund Kean presented himself as Shylock at Drury Lane in January 1814, and made his name overnight. For Sarah, still aged only twenty-eight, it had been a long, hard, uphill struggle against the memory of what she still held to be a total disgrace

six years before. But she took her fabulous success quietly, though
she was too overcome to speak the special epilogue written for
the occasion:

> Of the general effect of this nights performance I need not speak.
> It has already publickly been recorded. I reached my own quiet
> fire side after the, till this night unheard, reitterated shouts and
> plaudits. I was half dead, and my joy, my thankfulness, were of too
> solemn and overpowering nature to admit of words or even tears.
> My Father my husband and myself sat down to a frugal, neat supper
> in a silence uninterrupted except by joyful exclamations from Mᴿ
> Siddons. My Father enjoyd his refreshments, but occasionlly stop'd
> short, and laying down his knife and fork, and lifting up his beutiful
> and venerable face, which was partly shaded by his silvered hairs
> hanging about it in luxuriant curls, let fall such abundant showers
> of delicious tears, that they actually poured down into his plate.
> We soon parted for the night, and I, worn out with continued
> broken rest, anxiety, and laborious exertion, after an hour's intro-
> spection (who can concieve the intenseness of that reverie), fell into
> a sweet and profound sleep; which continued to the middle of the
> next day. I arose alert in mind and body.[5]

After it was all over she wrote with eagerness and relief to
Whalley in Bath:

> My dear, dear friend, the trying moment is passed, and I am crowned
> with a success which far exceeds even my hopes. God be praised!
> I am extremely hurried, being obliged to dine at Linley's; have
> been at the rehearsal of a new tragedy in prose, a most affecting
> play, in which I have a part I like very much. I believe my next
> character will be Zara in the *Mourning Bride*. My friend Pratt was,
> I believe in my soul, as much agitated, and is as much rejoiced as
> myself. As I know it will give you pleasure, I venture to assure you
> I never in my life heard such peals of applause. I thought they would
> not have suffered Mr Packer to end the play. Oh, how I wished for
> you last night, to share a joy which was too much for me to bear
> alone! My poor husband was so agitated that he durst not venture
> near the house. I enclose an epilogue which my good friend wrote
> for me, but which I could not, from excessive fatigue of mind and
> body, speak. Never, never let me forget his goodness to me. I have
> suffered tortures for the unblest these three days and nights past,
> and believe I am not in perfect possession of myself at present;
> therefore excuse, my dear Mr Whalley, the incorrectness of this
> scrawl, and accept it as the first tribute of love (after the decisive
> moment) from your ever grateful and truly affectionate, S. SIDDONS.[6]

Sarah appeared as Isabella eight times during the three weeks which followed, and the piece was then kept in repertory and revived sixteen times during the rest of the season, between November and June 1783. Her nervousness disappeared, and she began to respond more easily and assuredly both to the play and the audience. By the second performance the élite among the theatre-goers were competing to obtain seats: among those mentioned as being there were Lord North, Lady Shelbourne, and Lady Essex; Sheridan himself sat in a box surrounded by the Linley family, his eyes streaming tears at Isabella's fate. According to Boaden, 'literally the greater part of the spectators were too ill to use their hands in her applause'. After such a feat, the concluding farce played as a curtain-dropper for the night seemed more and more out of place – 'Mrs Siddons having so absolutely depressed the spirits of the audience', as Tom Davies was to write a year or so later.

Everyone competed to pay her compliments; even the veteran Macklin was heard to grunt, 'I think she performs well.' Commemorative verses were written and published. The press this time was more than kind. The *Morning Chronicle* recorded that applause was repeated again and again during the later acts of the play: 'She wore her sorrows and agonies with such a natural simplicity that she arrested all attention.' The *Morning Post* claimed she was greater than Mrs Cibber, praising the 'minute beauties' of her performance, though criticizing her on certain points, her exhibition of grief tending to monotony, her passion sometimes too 'brisk and fluttering', her voice raised sometimes too harshly and inharmoniously. This suggests the symptoms of nervousness. The *Post* ended, however: 'A late hour prevents us from dwelling on the merits of this accomplished woman who beyond all comparison is the first tragic actress now on the English stage.'

An extensive season lay before her, combining hard work with the consolidation of her fame. On 30 October she appeared as Euphrasia in *The Grecian Daughter*, which she was to repeat eleven times during the season. On 8 November followed *Jane Shore*, which she repeated fourteen times causing, says Boaden, sobs and shrieks

. . . among the tenderer part of her audiences; or those tears, which manhood at first struggled to suppress, but at length grew proud of indulging. We then, indeed, knew all the luxury of grief; but the nerves of many a gentle being gave way before the intensity of such appeals, and fainting fits long and frequently alarmed the decorum of the house, filled almost to suffocation.[7]

The management made an error of judgement in letting her play in the actor Thomas Hull's prose tragedy, *The Fatal Interview*, which was coolly received and withdrawn after three performances. According to Genest, Sheridan 'damned the play to save the actress'. However, in November a hundred barristers made her a collective present of one hundred guineas in appreciation of her work. On 29 November came *The Fair Penitent*, in which she played Calista.

For her first benefit on 14 December she chose to appear in the familiar part of Belvidera in *Venice Preserved*; including the hundred-guinea presentation, the benefit brought her around £800; *Venice Preserved* was to be repeated thirteen times. The management, in gratitude to her, gave her a 'clear' benefit, free of all theatre charges. They had already given her Garrick's former dressing-room, situated at stage-level. In the midst of so much admiration and reward, which, it must be remembered, had come upon her in a matter of weeks, she felt it necessary to publish some sort of statement of gratitude:

Mrs Siddons would not have remained so long without expressing the high sense she had of the great honours done her at her late benefit, but that after repeated trials she could not find words adequate to her feelings, and she must at present be content with the plain language of a grateful mind – that her heart thanks all her · benefactors for the distinguished, and she fears, too partial encouragement which they bestowed on this occasion. She is told that the splendid appearance on that night, and the emoluments arising from it, exceed anything ever recorded on a similar account in the annals of the English stage; but she has not the vanity to imagine that this arose from any superiority over many of her predecessors, or some of her contemporaries. She attributes it wholly to that liberality of sentiment which distinguishes the inhabitants of this great metropolis from those of any other in the world. They know her story – they know that for many years, by a strange fatality, she was confined to move in a narrow sphere, in which the rewards attendant on her labours were proportionally small. With a generosity unexampled, they proposed at once to balance the account, and pay off the arrears due, according to the rate, the too partial rate, at which they valued her talents. She knows the danger arising from extraordinary and unmerited favours, and will carefully guard against any approach of pride, too often their attendant. Happy shall she esteem herself, if by the utmost assiduity, and constant exertion of her poor abilities, she shall be able to lessen, though hopeless ever to discharge, the vast debt she owes the public.[8]

The repertoire for the first season was now virtually complete, but for her second benefit on 18 March she played Zara in *The Mourning Bride*. This brought her a further £650. In her turn, Sarah played for the benefit of her fellow-actors. During the season, from 10 October to the end of June 1783, she gave eighty major performances.

There was some element of rivalry in the choice of certain of these plays. The leading ladies at Covent Garden were no other than Mrs Yates and Miss Younge, with Henderson as their leading man. The management tried unsuccessfully to counteract the rush to Drury Lane by presenting Mrs Yates as Euphrasia and Henderson as Evander in *The Grecian Daughter* on 21 October, a week before Sarah's opening in the same play. Mrs Yates played opposite Henderson in *Macbeth*, a part in which she was acknowledged to be excellent. Later in the season, Miss Younge ventured to rival Sarah as Zara, with Mrs Yates also in the cast. But nothing could detract from Sarah. London society was determined she should become the fashion.

Anna Seward, the 'Swan of Lichfield', friend of Thomas Whalley whom she addressed as Edwy ever since his poem *Edwy and Edilda* had been published, gives us the mood of the town.[9] She loved to think of herself, isolated in Lichfield, as one of the *ton* of Bath and London, and she had her link with Dr Johnson to bring her to the capital. She sent her gushing, affected letters to Whalley, and hastened up to London in the spring to see his friend (and, she hoped, her own) and enjoy her triumph. 'Edwy, my dear Edwy,' she had written, 'teach . . . thy Siddons to love me.' She reached London on 25 March, but failed to get in the theatre that evening:

> I arrived here at five. Think of my mortification! Mrs Siddons in *Belvidera* tonight, as is supposed for the last time before she lies in. I asked Mrs Barrow if it would be impossible to get into the pit. 'O heaven!' said she, 'impossible in any part of the house.'[10]

She wrote again from London on 10 March. She was, she said:

. . . transfixed by the consciousness how poor and inadequate are all words to paint my Siddonian idolatry. Every attempt fruitless to procure boxes. I saw her for the first time, at the hazard of my life, by struggling through the terrible, fierce, maddening crowd into the pit. . . . I have seen her in *Jane Shore* and *Calista*. . . . I am as devoted to her as yourself, and my affection keeps pace with my astonishment and delight; for I have conversed with her, hung upon every word which fell from that charming lip; but I have never felt so awed in my life. The most awkward embarrassment was the consequence.

Her determination to see all the plays in Sarah's repertoire gave her infinite trouble:

A gentleman of Mrs B.'s train accidentally popped us, before the play began, into places a man was keeping in the fifth row of the front boxes, on our promise of retiring if they were claimed before the first act was over, after which we should, by the rule of the house, have a right to keep them. Oh! even when the siren spoke, with all her graces and melting tones, I wished to have the speech over, so ardently did I long for the moment when possession for the night might become secure. Our stars fought for us, the act was over, the box-keeper retired with a shilling reward for not bustling us, and in a second the people who had taken the places claimed them! Vain was their claim; our beaux asserted our right to keep them, and keep them we did.[11]

Not everyone, however, was so eager to be bowled over. Sir Horace Walpole voiced his initial criticisms of Sarah's performances in *Isabella* in his celebrated letter to the Countess of Ossory, written from Strawberry Hill on 3 November 1782:

. . . have been for two days in town, and seen Mrs Siddons. She pleased me beyond my expectation, but not up to the admiration of the *ton*, two or three of whom were in the same box with me; particularly Mr Boothby, who, as if to disclaim the stoic apathy of Mr Meadows in 'Cecilia', was all bravissimo. Mr Crawfurd, too, asked me if I did not think her the best actress I ever saw? I said, 'By no means; we old folks were apt to be prejudiced in favour of our first impressions.' She is a good figure, handsome enough, though neither nose nor chin according to the Greek standard beyond which both advance a good deal. Her hair is either red, or she has no objection to its being thought so, and had used red powder. Her voice is clear and good; but I thought she did not vary its modulations enough, nor ever approach enough to the familiar – but this may come when more habituated to the awe of the audience of the capital. Her action is proper, but with little variety; when without motion, her arms are not genteel. Thus you see, Madam, all my objections are very trifling; but what I really wanted, but did not find, was originality, which announces genius, and without both which I am never intrinsically pleased. All Mrs Siddons did, good sense or good instruction might give. I dare to say, that were I one-and-twenty, I should have thought her marvellous.[12]

His further comments appear in letters written in December. The first was to William Mason:

I cannot think Mrs Siddons the greatest prodigy that ever appeared nor go to see her act the same part every week and cry my eyes out every time. Were I five-and-twenty I suppose I should weep myself blind, for she is a fine actress, and fashion would make me think a brilliant which seems to me only a very good rare diamond.

The second letter he wrote on Christmas night to the Countess of Ossory, and shows an increasing inclination towards her:

Mrs Siddons continues to be the mode, and to be modest and sensible. She declines great dinners, and says her business and the cares of her family take up her whole time. When Lord Carlisle carried her the tribute money from Brook's, he said she was not *manièrée* enough. 'I suppose she was grateful,' said my niece, Lady Maria. Mrs Siddons was desired to play 'Medea' and 'Lady Macbeth' – 'No,' she replied, 'She did not look on them as female characters.' She was questioned about her transactions with Garrick: she said [he did] nothing but put her out; that he told her she moved her right hand when it should have been her left. – 'In short,' said she, 'I found I must not shade the tip of his nose.'

Sarah herself looks back on the period with solace and gratitude in her notes for Campbell:

I should be afraid to say how many times Isabella was successively repeated with still encreasing favour. I was now highly gratified by a removal from my very indifferent and inconvenient Dressing room to one on the stage floor, instead of climbing a long stair case; and this room (oh unexpected happiness) had been Garrick's Dressing room. It is impossible to imagine my gratification when I saw my own figure in the self same Glass which had so often reflected the face and form of that unequalled Genius, not perhaps without some vague, fanciful hope of a little degree of inspiration from it. About this time I was honored by the Whole Body of the Law with a Purse of a hundred Guineas.

I cannot now remember the regular succession of my various

characters during this season; I think Belvidera came soon after Isabella who almost precluded the appearance of all others for a very long time. But I well remember my fears and ready tears on each subsequent effort, lest I should fall from my high exaltation. The crowds collected about my Carriage at my outgoings and incomings, and the gratifying and sometimes commical remarks I heard on those occasions were sometimes extremely diverting.[13]

In her letters to the Whalleys we get much closer to her in her period of success, when everything still appeared a novelty to her. She was living very near the theatre in lodgings at 149 Strand, and wrote on 20 November 1782 to Whalley and his friends who were anxious about their local friend Samuel Pratt's play, which they, like he, hoped Sarah would promote:

Your letter to poor Pratty is lying on the table by me, and I am selfish enough to grudge it him from the bottom of my heart, and yet I will not; for just now, poor soul, he wants much comfort, therefore let him take it, and God bless him with it! You have heard of the laurel which the gentlemen of the bar have adorned my brows with, no doubt. It is indeed an honour I could not have hoped to arrive at; but (in the sincerity of truth I speak it) not half so grateful to my soul as that sweet wreath with which your friendly hand encircled my humble head. I wish, for your honour more than my own, the subject was more worthy of your commendations; but indeed your esteem confers a value wherever it is placed. I hope you don't forget, my dear sir, that you are to give me your picture.

I did receive all your letters, and thank you for them a thousand times: one line of them is worth all the acclamations of ten thousand shouting theatres. *The Fatal Interview* has been played three times, and is quite done with: it was the dullest of all representations. Pratty's Epilogue was vastly applauded indeed. I shall take care how I get into such another play; but I fancy the managers will take care of that too. *They wont let me play in Pratty's comedy.* How cruel! I am sadly grieved about it.[14]

In her desire to do the right thing now that she was in a position of influence, Sarah made the mistake of introducing her younger sister Frances into the Drury Lane company; she first appeared in January 1783, and supported Sarah in *Jane Shore* and *The Mourning Bride*. She was to stay at Drury Lane for some seasons, though she was much criticized in comparison with her sister, whom she to some extent resembled in looks. She later married Francis Twiss, a dramatic critic, and eventually, much later, set up a school for young ladies in Bath, charging high fees on the strength of her connexion with the great Mrs Siddons.

The final accolade of artistic and social approval for Sarah came with royal patronage early in 1783. Boaden writes:

> Their Majesties, when visiting the theatres, hardly ever ventured upon tragedy. The King himself enjoyed a hearty laugh at his favourite comedian.

But in January His Majesty decided it was time he saw the new phenomenon at Drury Lane for himself; again in the words of Boaden:

> There was an ardour in this patronage that showed the deep impression she had made. On the 2nd her Euphrasia was graced by majesty; on the 9th her Belvidera; on the 20th her Calista; on the 23rd her Shore; and on the 28th her Isabella.[15]

It was almost as if the King, a kindly and sentimental man who took his position so much to heart that it drove him at times right out of his mind, found in the grand pathos of Sarah's acting a free outlet for his emotions. She was summoned to Buckingham House. Her recollections of this are precise:

> The Royal family very frequently honoured me with thier presence. The King was often moved to tears which he as often vainly endeavoured to conceal behind his eye-glass, and her Majesty the Queen, at one time told me in her gracious broken English that her only refuge from me was actually turning her back upon the stage at the same time protesting 'It is indeed too disagreeable'. In short all went on most gloriously at the Theatre, and to complete my triumph, I had the honour of recieving the commands of Thier Majesties to go and read to them, which I frequently did both at Buckingham House and at Windsor. Thier Majestys (independantly of the honour and glory) were the most gratifying, because the most unremittingly attentive, of auditors. The King was a most judicious and tasteful critick both in acting and Dramatick composition. He told me he had endeavourd vainly to detect me in a false emphasis, and very humourously repeated many of Mr Smith's, who was then the principal Actor. He graciously commended the propriety of my action particularly my total repose in certain situations. 'This is,' he said, 'a quality in which Garrick faild. He never could stand still; he was a great fidget.' . . . One could not appear in the presence of the Queen except in a Dress, not elsewhere worn, called a Saque, or Negligeé, with a hoop, treble ruffles and Lappets, in which costume

I felt not at all my ease. When I arrivd at B^m House for the first time, I was conducted into an anti-chamber, where I found some ladies of my acquaintance, and in a short time the King enterd from the Drawing room, in the aimiable occupation of drawing the Princess Amelia, then scarce three years old, in a little Cane Chair. He graciously said something to one of the ladies, and left the lovely baby to run about the room. She happened to be much pleasd with some flowers in my bosom, and as I stoopd down, that she might take them if so disposd, I could not help exclaiming to a lady near us, 'What a beautiful baby! How I do long to kiss her!' When she instantly held her little Royal *hand* to my mouth to be kissed; so early had she learnd this lesson of Royalty. Her Majesty was extremely gracious and more than once during the reading desired me to take some refreshment in the next room. I declined the honour, however, altho' I had stood reading till I was ready to drop, rather than run the risk of falling down by walking backwards out of the room (a ceremony not to be dispensed with), the floor, too, being rubbed bright. I therefore remaind where I was, till Thier Majestys retired. I afterwards learned from one of the ladies who was present at the time, that Her Majesty had expressed herself surprised to find me so collected in so new a position, and that I had conducted myself as if I had been used to a Court. At any rate, I had frequently personated Queens.[16]

Royal patronage earned to this extent within four months of her arrival in London only increased the demand to see her in the theatre, and, if possible, to make social contact with her. She herself had to make adjustments; within nine months she had moved up in the social scale from the level of a provincial actress earning £3 a week with modest, if satisfactory, benefits bringing her an overall income of around £8 a working week, to that of a London 'society' actress whose income in the first nine months, with two substantial benefits, represented some £50 a working week. This money, by the laws of the time, belonged to her husband, who was naturally quite unused to handling such sums and was to prove, in the long run, quite inadequate to managing the family's affairs. The pressure on Sarah to become a figure in London society was now very great, but her shyness, which amounted almost to timidity, made her shrink from contact with this rout of overdressed, tattling women and profligate men, as they might well appear to her after the effete gentility which passed for 'society' and 'culture' in Thomas Whalley's circle in Bath's Royal Crescent. Fanny Burney (later, in 1793, to become

Madame d'Arblay, when she married a refugee general from France), reveals how overcome with shyness she was at an 'assembly' given by the Honourable Mary Monckton (later the Countess of Cork), a society woman with a somewhat grotesque, squat figure, plenty of rouge, diamonds and lofty headgear, and, according to Fanny Burney, with 'an easy levity in her air, manner, voice and discourse'. She enjoyed giving parties which mingled the famous and fashionable with people of rank, and she liked to be thought one of the new women intellectuals, a 'Blue' in fact.[17] Fanny Burney, who was thirty, had been herself much in the public eye since it was discovered she was the anonymous author of the successful society novel, *Evelina*, which had appeared in 1778; her second novel, *Cecilia*, had just been published, and was equally successful. She was an intelligent, observant, but somewhat gossipy woman, and one of Dr Johnson's favourites. She records first of all Dr Johnson's reactions to Sarah's sudden fame; he was over seventy, and not the least prepared to respond to fashion with good grace:

'How the people talk of Mrs Siddons!' said the Doctor, 'I came hither in full expectation of hearing no name but the name I love and pant to hear, – when from one corner to another they are talking of that jade Mrs Siddons! till, at last wearied out, I went yonder into a corner, and repeated to myself Burney! Burney! Burney! Burney!' ... 'But, indeed, Dr Johnson,' said Miss Monckton, 'you must see Mrs Siddons. Won't you see her in some fine part?' 'Why, if I *must*, madam, I have no choice.' 'She says, sir, she shall be very very much afraid of you ... she said so to me; I heard her say it myself.' ... 'Well, madam, if you so desire it, I will go. See her I shall not, nor hear her; but I'll go, and that will do. The last time I was at a play, I was ordered there by Mrs Abington, or Mrs Somebody, I do not remember who, but I placed myself in the middle of the first row of the front boxes, to show that when I was called I came.'[18]

Fanny met Sarah socially for the first time at Mary Monckton's assembly, and was favourably impressed:

She is a woman of excellent character, and therefore I am very glad she is thus patronised, since Mrs Abington, and so many frail fair ones, have been thus noticed by the great. She behaved with great propriety; very calm, modest, quiet, and unaffected. She has a very fine countenance, and her eyes look both intelligent and soft. She has, however, a steadiness in her manner and deportment by no means engaging. Mrs Thrale, who was there, said: 'Why, this is a leaden goddess we are all worshipping! However, we shall soon gild it.'

A lady who sat near me then began a dialogue with Mr Erskine, who had placed himself exactly opposite to Mrs Siddons; and they debated together upon her manner of studying her parts, disputing upon the point with great warmth, yet not only forbearing to ask Mrs Siddons herself which was right, but quite overpowering her with their loquacity, when she attempted, unasked, to explain the matter. Most vehement praise of all she did followed.[19]

Sarah gave Campbell her own version of Mary Monckton's technique of acquiring her more celebrated guests:

I was inviegled into this Snare by Miss Monckton, now Lady Cork. This Lady had given me her word of honour that I should meet only Half a dozen of our mutual friends, for I had often told her very seriously that it suited niether my studys or my inclinations to be engaged in *Parties*, from which I begged most earnestly to be excused; for to say the truth, I had been forwarned how eagerly any new and notorious person was pursued for exhibition. Miss Monckton solemnly promised me to keep her word, and assured me that I need never fear meeting a crowd at *her house*. The appointed Sunday Evening came. I went to her very much in undress at the early hour of Eight, on account of my little boy, whom she desired me to bring with me (more for *effect* I suspect, than for his beaux yeux). I found with her, as I had been taught to expect, three or four ladies of my acquaintance, and the time pass'd in agreeable chat had been much longer than I apprehended. I was of course preparing speedily to return home, when successive and incessantly repeated thunderings at the door, and the sudden influx of such a throng of people as I had never before seen collected in any private room, counteracted evry attempt which I could make for escape. I was therefore obligd in a state of indiscribable mortifycation to sit quietly down till I know not what in the morning, but for hours before my departure the room I sat in was so painfully crowded that the people actually stood upon the chairs round the walls, that they might look over thier nieghbour's heads to stare at me, and if it had not been for the benevolent politeness of Mr. Erskine, who had been acquainted with my arrangement, I know not what weakness I might have been surprisd into, especially being tormented as I was, by the ridiculous interrogations of some learned ladies who were called Blues, the meaning of which title I did not at that time appreciate, much less did I comprehend the meaning of much of thier learned talk. These profound ladies, however, furnished much amusement to the Town many weeks, nay, I believe I might say, for the whole of the winter. Glad enough was I at length to find myself at peace in my own bed-chamber.

I was, as I have confess'd, an ambitious candidate for fame, and my professional avocations alone, independently of domestic arrangements, were of course incompatible with habitual observances of Parties and Concerts, &c. I therefore often declind the honour of such invitations.[20]

Mrs Hester Lynch Thrale was considered by the London gossips to be Dr Johnson's most intimate woman friend, an intimacy which had lasted almost twenty years, though she was over thirty years younger than he. He may even have been, in his own way, in love with her, and she certainly forfeited his friendship when, after her husband's death in 1781, she eventually married an Italian music-master, Gabriel Piozzi, in 1784 – after endless self-debate, and, says Boswell, correspondence with Johnson himself, who died the same year. Later she was to become one of Sarah's closest friends, and indeed shared something of the same temperament; she was a very knowledgeable, shrewd woman, but reserved and retiring in general company, and she only became animated when at ease with people she recognized as her friends. Dr Johnson was to have his celebrated first meeting with Mrs Siddons in the autumn of 1783, during her second season at Drury Lane.

A satirical version of the Monckton episode, which became a *cause célèbre*, was published afterwards in *The Observer*, with real names disguised under the kind of pseudonyms fashionable at the time:

I now joined a cluster of people, who had crowded round an actress, who sat upon a sofa, leaning on her elbow in a pensive attitude, and seemed to be counting the sticks of her fan, whilst they were vieing with each other in the most extravagant encomiums. 'You was adorable last night in Belvidera,' says a pert young parson with a high toupée. 'I sat in Lady Blubber's box; and I can assure you she, and her daughters too, wept most bitterly. But then that charming mad scene – but, by my soul, it was a *chef d'œuvre!* Pray, madam, give me leave to ask you, was you really in your senses?' 'I strove to do it as well as I could,' answered the actress. 'Do you intend to play comedy next season?' says a lady, stepping up to her with great eagerness. 'I shall do as the manager bids me,' she replied. 'I should be curious to know,' says an elderly lady, 'which part, madam, you yourself esteem the best you play?' 'I shall always endeavour to make that which I am about the best.' An elegant and enchanting young woman of fashion now took her turn of interrogating, and with many apologies begged to be informed by her if she studied those enchanting looks and attitudes before a glass. 'I never study anything but my author.' 'Then you practise them at rehearsals,' rejoined the questioner. 'I seldom rehearse at all!'[21]

Sarah's appearance was, very naturally, the subject of constant comment and exact description in the press. Boaden quotes one which appears singularly careful, and was published, he says, soon after she began her performances at Drury Lane in 1782:

There never, perhaps, was a better stage figure than that of Mrs Siddons. Her height was above the middle size, but not at all inclined to the *embonpoint*. There is, notwithstanding, nothing sharp or angular in the frame; there is sufficient muscle to bestow a roundness upon the limbs, and her attitudes are, therefore, distinguished equally by energy and grace. The symmetry of her person is exact and captivating. Her face is peculiarly happy, the features being finely formed, though strong, and never for an instant seeming over-charged, like the Italian faces, nor coarse and unfeminine under whatever impulse. On the contrary, it is so thoroughly harmonised when quiescent, and so expressive when impassioned, that most people think her more beautiful than she is. So great, too, is the flexibility of her countenance, that the rapid transitions of passion are given with a variety and effect that never tire upon the eye. Her voice is naturally plaintive, and a tender melancholy in her level speaking denotes a being devoted to tragedy; yet this seemingly settled quality of voice becomes at will sonorous or piercing, over-whelms with rage, or, in its wild shriek, absolutely harrows up the soul. Her sorrow, too, is never childish; her lamentation has a dignity which belongs, I think, to no other woman; it claims your respect along with your tears. Her eye is brilliant and varying like the diamond; it is singularly well placed; 'it pries,' in Shakespeare's language, 'through the portal of the head,' and has every aid from brows flexible beyond all female parallel, contracting to disdain, or dilating with the emotions of sympathy or pity or anguish. Her memory is tenacious and exact, her articulation clear and distinct, her pronunciation systematic and refined.

Nor has Nature been partially bountiful – she has endowed her with a quickness of conception and a strength of understanding equal to the proper use of such extraordinary gifts. So entirely is she mistress of herself, so collected, and so determined in gestures, tone, and manner, that she seldom errs, like other actors, because she doubts her power of comprehension. She studies her author attentively, conceives justly, and describes with a firm consciousness of propriety. She is sparing in her action, because English nature does not act much; but it is always proper, picturesque, graceful, and dignified; it arises immediately from the sentiments and feeling, and is not seen to prepare itself before it begins. No studied trick or start can be predicted; no forced tremulation of the figure, where the vacancy of the eye declares the absence of passion, can be seen; no laborious strainings at false climax, in which the tired voice reiterates one high tone beyond which it cannot reach, is ever heard; no artificial heaving of the breasts, so disgusting when the affectation is perceptible; none of those arts by which the actress is seen, and not the character, can be found in Mrs Siddons. So natural are her gradations and transitions, so classical and correct her speech and deportment, and so intensely interesting her voice, form, and features, that there is no conveying an idea of the pleasure she communicates by words. She must be seen to be known. What is still more delightful, she is an original; she copies no one, living or dead, but acts from Nature and herself.[22]

At the end of her first season, when she was approaching twenty-nine, Thomas Holcroft wrote, in the course of a lengthy study in the *English Review*: 'Her eye is large and marking and her brow capable of contracting to disdain, or dilating with the emotions of sympathy or pity; her memory is tenacious, and her articulation clear, distinct and penetrating.' In the papers of Lord Palmerston, the second viscount, the following note appears: 'When Mrs Siddons first acted, the people fainted away so frequently that somebody said the orange women now cry nothing but "Hartshorn" and "Lavender drops".'

Garrick was, perhaps, the first of the great English actors to reveal something of a modern attitude to publicity, especially favouring portraits, which could be reproduced in the form of cheaply-priced engravings. Garrick encouraged painters to take an interest in the theatre and paint theatrical portraits, especially of himself, and for a while he gave a home to Johan Zoffany. Theatrical and offstage portraits grew in numbers, together with 'conversation pieces' showing successful actors and actresses at leisure in society. Descriptive 'likenesses' of the famous had become the stock-in-trade of fashionable artists at all levels, led by Reynolds, Gainsborough, Lely, Romney, de Wilde and Zoffany.

After her début, Sarah was naturally sought after by eminent portrait painters, though the most celebrated portraits, those by

Reynolds (1784), Gainsborough (1785) and the paintings and drawings by Lawrence in his maturity (1796 and after), were to come later. In 1782 she sat to the Scottish painter William Hamilton, at his studio in 63 Dean Street; this portrait (he was to paint others of her) was in the character of Isabella. According to Campbell:

> One day, after her sitting, Mr Hamilton and his wife were bidding good morning to the great actress, and accompanying her down stairs, when they pointed out to her her own resemblance to an antique sculpture of Ariadne, that stood on the staircase. Mrs Siddons was taken by surprise, and her honesty was here a traitor to her vanity. She clasped her hands in delight, and said, 'Yes, it is very – ' but, immediately recollecting herself, before she got out the word *like*, substituted the word, beautiful. 'It is so very beautiful, that you must be flattering me'. She then sat down on the staircase to contemplate the sculpture, frequently exclaiming, 'It is so very beautiful, that you must be flattering me.' She departed, however, evidently well pleased to believe in the likeness: but it would require one to be as handsome as herself to have a right to blame her self-complacency.[23]

Another portrait completed in 1783 was that by George Romney. In this year, too, engravings of Lawrence's early portraits were published, including that of Sarah in the part of Zara in *The Mourning Bride*.

Drury Lane was to be Sarah's principal theatre for the next twenty years, though she was frequently to tour in England, Scotland and Ireland during the summer recesses. The theatre which was to become the centre of her professional life, was over a century old. It had been designed and built originally by Wren in 1674 as an intimate house seating probably less than a thousand spectators; it had then a stage some forty-five feet wide, while the apron stage projected forward seventeen feet and the acting area behind the proscenium extended back fifteen feet.

After 1700 the theatre was constantly being refurbished, redecorated and re-gilded. In Garrick's time the capacity of its small auditorium soon proved to be inadequate. Not only did it hold too few people (especially after Garrick had banished them from the stage area), it was also unable to match Garrick's ambitions for scenic presentation, and the need for more money at the box-office. So in 1762 it underwent considerable enlargement, with its seating increased to hold 2,200; after this, a capacity house could bring in over £350. But this was only a temporary improvement; a major conversion was undertaken in 1775 by the Adam brothers, not so much to increase audience capacity as to improve the comfort and elegance of the building. Boxes were enlarged and augmented, new passages and entrances were installed, the façade outside was made more imposing, all at a cost of some 4,000 guineas. This was the theatre in which Sarah worked in 1776 and again from 1782 to 1792, when the theatre was entirely rebuilt, and made to hold an audience of 3,600. George Colman the Elder comments rather unfavourably on the Adam renovations in his memoirs:

> The Messrs. Adam contrived to give the interior of an old gloomy theatre a new, a gayer and even a gaudy appearance; but when the first feelings of surprise were passed, men began to reflect a little on the propriety of style adopted in the alteration, and it was generally agreed, that though the whole was creditable to the skill and taste of the architect, the decorations were but ill adopted, since the audience part of a play house should by no means divert the eye of the spectator from the scenic effect of the stage, and distract it by an assemblage of unnatural objects, displayed in all the glare of no-meaning painting.

He preferred, he said, Covent Garden, and the Haymarket (of which he was to become manager in 1776) which he described as 'lightly elegant, and not too extravagantly gay'.

Under Garrick's management presentation was improved out of all recognition. Before then, Drury Lane productions took little account of scenery, since most of the action was played on the apron, flanked by the deep proscenium structure, which had on each side the doors used for the entrance and exit of actors as well as the first line of the boxes holding the spectators. The scenery used consisted of stock sets, unless the scale of pantomime or opera called for more. The scenic artists were little better than stage-hands. By the late 1750s Garrick had begun to change this; costs in scenery, including wages, rose to as high as £1,674 during the final season, when Sarah was a member of the company; the bills for lighting (always extremely expensive) rose to £2,000. Costumes, too, though largely contemporary (except, to some extent, in Roman or classical plays), were mostly provided by the actors themselves, but even so the cost to the theatre was considerable, amounting to over £1,000 a season even in the earlier years of Garrick's management.

Lighting the theatre was something of a problem. Up to 1765, the whole theatre, both on stage and off, was lit by candles, at an average annual cost of some £400. The stage itself was illuminated beautifully if not brilliantly by six movable chandeliers hung over the stage, each bearing twelve candles. Footlights made up of candles supplemented these. After 1765, the chandeliers were abolished, the footlights improved, and side-wing lights were introduced, after the French style, adjustable to raise or lower the lighting for special effects and their power augmented by reflectors. Multi-wick oil lamps were used to improve on the candles, which were nevertheless also retained. The lighting was a great source of danger, and theatres frequently burnt down. Drury Lane was a notable exception.

When Sarah came on the stage, therefore, she would be far more aware of the physical presence of her audience than is the case in the normal theatre of today. The lighting which illuminated her would be insufficient to obscure them, and in any case when she came downstage to the front of the apron, the audience in their boxes would be on either side, as well as in front of her. She would use the proscenium doors as the main means of entrance and exit, and treat both the apron stage and the back stage as equal areas for the deployment of action and movement. Garrick's tendency, with his romantic but much more representational scenery, had been to put the action somewhat further back into the picture area of the stage in comparison with Restoration production, which had always emphasized the use of the forestage. The scenery, as Richard Southern so brilliantly discovered, consisted largely of what he terms the 'groove-sliding, wing-and-shutter' systems, solid parallel wings set in successive grooves on each side of the stage and capable of being pulled back offstage to reveal other wings for other sets.[24] Gates, archways, and even doors could be constructed in these movable wings, while the stage would be backed by a single, painted scene. Enclosed box-sets did not come into use in England until the nineteenth century, nor did the lowering of the proscenium curtain during the course of the play either to divide the acts or hide the change of scenery. After the initial rise of the curtain at the beginning of the play, the visible change of scene was accepted as a convention until well into the nineteenth century, even until the time of Irving, though the curtain might be lowered during the play for exceptional reasons. The act divisions, however, were marked by the playing of music, Garrick insisting by the 1770s that the musicians, to save disturbance, should stay in their places throughout the play.

The audience did not behave with much ceremony. Only the most exceptional cases, such as the Royal Family, could enjoy individual seats. In the normal way the audience sat crushed together on long benching, even in the boxes which flanked the auditorium and extended on three levels into the proscenium itself. At the back of the auditorium the boxes gave way to three circles set successively above the pit and accommodating in receding rows a considerable body of people. Places in the boxes were, of course, reserved in advance. The most notorious crush was that which took place in the pit, the queue outside pressing forward the moment the doors were opened, ruthlessly rushing in to claim the best of the unreserved places. Late-comers caused pandemonium.

Covent Garden was near by, and Tate Wilkinson gives a vivid idea of what it was like on a bad night in winter to be caught without transport between the two houses after the plays were over:

> When I got into the Piazza, the alarm for coach and chair was wonderful; I was terribly drove by the distressed crowd. . . . I had no notion that Drury-Lane theatre had finished 'The Twelfth Night,' &c. earlier than Covent Garden, therefore determined to post away for that theatre, thinking I might luckily get a coach on that spot, but the getting there, though so short a distance, cost me many a sigh and sob, though I cannot say tear, but was near paying that tribute to my sorrows from the accumulated distresses I felt: Indeed my situation must be allowed disagreeable, no great coat, but wind, rain, and tempest; pushed on all sides by the link-boys, coach-men, chair-men, and crowd; hustled by the pick-pockets; and dreading every moment to be thrown down by the slippery inter-mixture of snow and rain, which nothing could have prevented but some friendly wet puddle, which received my sliding slippery feet. . . . With much difficulty, and my mind suggesting, fever, cold, additional broken limbs, robbery, and the being run over, I at length by the help of Providence, or perchance of 'The divinity that doth hedge a motley king,' arrived at the box-lobby of Drury-Lane theatre, where I was informed the performance had closed near an hour, but to my sight the appearance of the box company was just as when the curtain might have been supposed to have dropped. The universal outcry for 'coach' and 'chair', was inconceivable, and

at *any price*, 'half-a-guinea to the city'; 'half-a-guinea to Grosvenor-Square', &c. . . . In the box-lobby I gave many marks of uneasiness, and expressions of sorrow and distress that I could not engage a coach for Gray's-Inn Lane: The box-keepers then in waiting all knew me, and gave every consolation in their power, not only in words of comfort, but the more pleasing promised assurance of relief the first opportunity; for one or two of them whispered me to be quiet, and I should not be left unlike a gentleman without my carriage. . . . At length in loud words I heard, 'Mr Wilkinson's carriage is waiting!' On the first sound of such welcome and un-expected tidings, I was at a loss how to act, supposing a Mr Wilkin-son's real carriage was waiting, as there are many rich Wilkinsons as well as poor; but my stupor was relieved by the box-keeper advancing and bowing to me to attend me to my carriage. He readily explained the quick mode he had taken to relieve my impatience and anxiety, as many in waiting would suppose it was my own vehicle. I judged all my cares were over, but at the bottom of the box steps I was saluted by my Cockney coachman as follows, '*Lookye, my master*, I knows not whomsomdever you may be, but the night is so bad it vill be the death of me and my cattle, and I don't ax you for my fare, for I was not on any stand, and you can't oblige me as how to take you, so minds I tells you, that I von't take you into my coach, for as how to carry you to Graves-Inn Lane, without that you will give me eight shillings; and I vont because I vont, and so I tells you; but if you will give me that there price, vy I will drive you as vell as I can.' I stopped his harangue, and assured him I would on my honour give him eight shillings, which silenced his oration, and into the coach I got, and felt myself in a paradise, and with the utmost difficulty I was slowly dragged to my hotel, where I cheerfully paid the sum stipulated, with a bumper of brandy into the bargain; and the Jehu was so faithful on his part of assurance, that when at the hotel there were three or four gentlemen in great distress for a coach, but contrary to that part of the town where his home was destined for the night, that he would not accept any bribe whatever, but made his exit, exulting in the favour he had bestowed in bringing the *gemman* to his lodgings on so dismal a night.[25]

Sarah was appearing with a competent rather than a brilliant company. Henderson, probably the greatest actor in England during the interim period between Garrick and Kemble, was appearing at Covent Garden. Until Sarah was joined in her second season in 1783–4 by her brother John Philip, the leading parts at Drury Lane were being played by such actors as William Smith, John Palmer, William Brereton and Robert Bensley. William

Smith was 'accomplished, gentlemanly' but with 'a healthy, hunting countenance' and a smooth, powerful, but monotonous voice; he had studied at Oxford during the early 1750s, and he was to be Sarah's first Macbeth at Drury Lane. John Palmer had a towering figure, a fair complexion, and an explosive manner; as an actor he had been familiar to the public from Garrick's time, and had been the original Joseph Surface for Sheridan; he also played such parts as Sir Toby Belch, Falstaff or Anthony Absolute.[26] Robert Bensley, with what Boaden calls his 'nasal solemnity' and ungainliness of body, could be 'terrible and even sublime', and Boaden claims that his 'understanding . . . rendered him always respectable, and sometimes nearly excellent'; he played such parts as Pierre in *Venice Preserved* and Evander in *The Grecian Daughter*. As for William Brereton, who had made his name by the manner in which he had risen to Sarah when playing Jaffier in *Venice Preserved*, his mind was unstable and he was to die in 1787. Sarah had to wait until her brother John Philip Kemble joined the company before gaining an actor approaching her own stature.

Sarah did not rest a moment after the great labour of the season. She seemed to need to prove herself over and over again, and having conquered London she determined to conquer an entirely new audience, the Irish. She was no doubt drawn to Dublin because her brother John Philip had been playing there with some success since November 1781. Sarah travelled with her husband and sister, and with William Brereton and Francis Aickin, a supporting actor in 'manly, polite' roles.

Except for the money she earned (and she amassed about £1,000 in Dublin and Cork), the visit could not be regarded as a success.[27] First of all, the voyage across the Irish Sea was bad, and she felt her reception on the other side was far colder than it should have been. One of the best of her letters to Whalley survived to describe what happened: she wrote on 14 July 1783 from Cork, about a month after she had left England:

> We got very safe to Holyhead, and then I felt as if some great event was going to take place, having never been on sea. I was awed, but not terrified; feeling myself in the hands of a great and powerful God, 'whose mercy is over all His works'. The sea was particularly rough; we were lifted mountains high, and sank again as low in an instant. Good God! how tremendous, how wonderful! A pleasing terror took hold on me, which it is impossible to describe . . . and

here, my dear friend, let me give you a little wholesome advice; allways (you see I have forgot to spell) go to bed the instant you go on board, for by lying horizontally, and keeping very quiet, you cheat the sea of half its influence. We arrived in Dublin the 16th of June, half-past twelve at night. There is not a tavern or a house of any kind in this capital city of a rising kingdom, as they call themselves, that will take a woman in; and do you know I was obliged, after being shut up in the Custom-house officer's room, to have the things examined, which room was more like a dungeon than anything else – after staying here above an hour and a half, I tell you I was obliged, sick and weary as I was, to wander about the streets on foot (for the coaches and chairs were all gone off the stands) till almost two o'clock in the morning, raining too as if heaven and earth were falling together. A pretty beginning! thought I; but these people are a thousand years behind us in every respect. At length Mr Brereton, whose father had provided a bed for him on his arrival, ventured to say he would insist on having a bed for us at the house where he was to sleep. Well, we got to this place, and the lady of the house vouchsafed, after many times telling us that she never took in ladies, to say we should sleep there that night. I never was so weary and so disgusted in my life.

The city of Dublin is a sink of filthiness; the noisome smells, and the multitudes of shocking and most miserable objects, made me resolve never to stir out but to my business. I like not the people either; they are all ostentation and insincerity, and in their ideas of finery very like the French, but not so cleanly; and they not only speak but think coarsely. This is in confidence; therefore, your fingers on your lips, I pray. . . . I have got a thousand pounds among them this summer. I always acknowledge myself obliged to them, but I cannot love them. . . . Some people place the whole happiness of life in the pleasures of imagination, in building castles; for my part, I am not one that build very magnificent ones – nay, I don't build any castles, but cottages without end. May the great Disposer of all events but permit me to spend the evening of my toilsome bustling day in a cottage.[28]

She appeared on 21 June 1783 in *Isabella* at the famous Smock Alley Theatre, Thomas Sheridan's Smock Alley,[29] now managed by Richard Daly, formerly a student of Trinity College, a handsome, vain, excitable, quarrelsome man with a squint who paid Kemble five pounds a week to appear as his leading man in a prodigious series of parts including Hamlet, Othello, Iago, King Charles, Richard III, Shylock, Biron, Mark Antony, Romeo, Macbeth, and Henry V – thirty-eight, in fact, within a

single season. Kemble's beloved Elizabeth Inchbald was also in
the company, and so was the vivacious Miss Francis, later to
become the celebrated Mrs Jordan. Kemble was also to pay
romantic attention to another pretty actress, Miss Philips. He was
as happy in Ireland as his sister was unhappy, though Daly, who
had travelled to London to put her under contract, disliked him
just as much as he disliked Sarah. Daly was determined, however,
to present a fashionable actress from London, and build up the
quality of his audience, especially as he was losing Kemble to
Drury Lane the following season. Sarah's brother had secured
a good three-year contract to appear in London.

Although Sarah was on the whole well received in Dublin – she
could scarcely be otherwise – there was some opposition in the air.
Inspired perhaps by Mrs Crawford, the rival actress at the Crow
Street Theatre, and her followers, certain malicious reports
began to appear in the press of which this, attributed to West
Digges, who disliked Sarah, was typical:

> On Saturday Mrs Siddons, about whom all the world has been
> talking, exposed her beautiful adamantine, soft, and comely person,
> for the first time, in the Theatre Royal, Smock Alley. The house was
> crowded with hundreds more than it could hold, with thousands of
> admiring spectators that went away without a sight. . . . She was
> nature itself – she was the most exquisite work of art. . . . Several
> fainted, even before the curtain drew up. . . . The fiddlers in the
> orchestra blubbered like hungry children crying for their bread and
> butter; and when the bell rang for music between the acts, the tears
> ran from the bassoon player's eyes in such showers that they choked
> the finger stops, and, making a spout of the instrument, poured in
> such a torrent upon the first fiddler's book; but not seeing the
> overture was in two sharps, the leader of the band actually played
> in two flats; but the sobs and sighs of the groaning audience, and
> the noise of the corks drawn from the smelling-bottles, prevented
> the mistake being discovered. . . . The briny pond in the pit was
> three feet deep, and the people that were obliged to stand upon the
> benches, were in that position up to their ankles in tears. An Act of
> Parliament against her playing will certainly pass, for she has infected
> the volunteers, and they sit reading *The Fatal Marriage*, crying and
> roaring all the time. May the curses of an insulted nation pursue
> the gentlemen of the College, the gentlemen of the Bar, and the
> Peers and Peeresses that hissed her on the second night. True it is
> that Mr Garrick never could make anything of her, and pronounced
> her below mediocrity; true it is the London audience did not like her.
> But what of that?[30]

Sarah found that some members of the Irish audiences tended to be familiar – 'Sally, me jewel, how are you?' cried a man in Cork, at which she merely froze into tragic *hauteur*. But she was prepared to weather these difficulties for the sake of the fortune she was earning within a mere ten weeks, and she enjoyed meeting again Henrietta Boyle, now the Honourable Henrietta O'Neill of Shanes Castle, where she was to stay on her return visit the following year. She was delighted, too, when John Jackson, manager of the theatre in Edinburgh, came to Ireland especially to negotiate for her to appear in Edinburgh during the summer of 1784.

Sarah reached London in September 1783, after an appearance in Liverpool; on 8 October, when she had returned to her house in the Strand, she had to prepare for her new season at Drury Lane, her first appearance being in a 'Command Performance' of *Isabella*. The Royal Family attended, making the presentation a splendid social occasion, though the King sat under his great state canopy of crimson velvet mounted in a structure of gold, clothed only in a plain suit with gold buttons; the Queen, however, was splendid in her white satin and diamonds. Sarah wrote to the Whalleys on 7 October: 'The King commands *Isabella* tomorrow, and I play Jane Shore on Saturday. . . . Is it not a little alarming? I fear I shall be superannuated in a few years.'

John Philip Kemble had made his London début a week or so earlier, on 30 September, in *Hamlet*. This initial appearance was, in its own way, as successful as Sarah's the year before. Kemble presented a new Hamlet, quite unlike Garrick's; the playing was not only intellectual, deliberate and completely self-possessed, but the twenty-six-year-old actor gave the character a softness and tenderness hitherto unknown. This was a new Hamlet for the romantic age. The performance became an immediate topic for discussion; his voice, like his sister's, though beautiful in enunciation, could lack resonance in a large theatre, and he had minor affectations of movement and pronunciation: 'leetle' for little, 'fastijjus' for fastidious, 'varchue' for virtue. But whatever his faults, Kemble's Hamlet was unquestionably the performance of a scholar-actor of a new order in the theatre, serious, dedicated, sure of himself, able to progress in power and command with each repetition. He was an imposing man, built, as Sir Walter Scott was to say much later, 'on a scale suited for the stage, and almost too large for a private apartment', though Elizabeth Inchbald did not think so. On the stage he looked his best as

Coriolanus, wrapped in a Roman toga, or what passed for one. With Garrick gone and Henderson declining, there was to be no one to equal Kemble until Edmund Kean emerged twenty years later. During the season he was to play, in addition to twelve repetitions of Hamlet, Richard III, Sir Giles Overreach, King John and Shylock, among other parts. He played with his sister in *The Gamester* (Beverley to her Mrs Beverley), and at royal request in *King John* (King John to her Constance). It is curious that John Philip's younger brother, Stephen, made his début the same month at Covent Garden, playing Othello on 24 September. The family went to support him, as the *Morning Herald* reported:

> The Siddons and the Kembles were seated over the stage-box . . . to see their brother Stephen Kemble's first appearance. Nature, whose effusions have in public secured to the former an universal admiration, operated very powerfully and frequently on this occasion. The tears of sensibility stole down her cheek, and with a sister's sympathy, spoke all the brother felt.[31]

Kemble's fee at Drury Lane was only five guineas a week, far less, for example, than was paid to Smith, who received the 'top' weekly rate for men of £15, and took his choice of key parts until his retirement in 1788, when he left the stage, and stage management, in the hands of Kemble. Sarah was now drawing £20 a week, and, like the rest, handsome benefits, in addition to the prospects of earning inflated fees during her summer tours: these represented, in the 1783–4 season, some £2,000 in all from Drury Lane, and a further £1,000 at least from the summer tour of Edinburgh and the Irish cities. She began to acquire the reputation of a hard bargainer – or William, her business manager, acquired it on her behalf.[32] John Philip was soon to learn equally well how to feather the Kemble nest. There was to be trouble soon for Sarah as her reputation for being close-fisted grew, and indeed flourished quite unreasonably amongst those anxious to find fault with her. She appeared on average three nights a week only at Drury Lane; she played twelve parts on fifty-three occasions during the eight months of the London season. Some of these parts, of course, were in revivals of old plays; as far as her Drury Lane public were concerned they had the opportunity of seeing her in six new characters, among them two from Shakespeare – Constance in *King John* and Isabella in *Measure for Measure*, which opened on 3 November, with Palmer as Angelo, Smith as the Duke, and Brereton as Claudio.

In October 1783 Sarah had her first encounter with Dr Johnson, a meeting second only in honour to her audiences at Buckingham House. When she wrote her own account of this occasion, she had the advantage of being able to look up Boswell. Johnson was a very sick man aged seventy-four. There are two versions of this celebrated meeting, that given to Boswell by Kemble, who was apparently present at the time, and that written many years later by Sarah herself for Campbell. Since they differ considerably in the parts of the conversation they record, they supplement each other. According to Kemble's recollection:

When Mrs Siddons came into the room, there happened to be no chair ready for her, which he observing, said with a smile, 'Madam, you who so often occasion a want of seats to other people, will the more easily excuse the want of one yourself.'

Having placed himself by her, he with great good humour entered upon a consideration of the English drama; and, among other enquiries, particularly asked her which of Shakspeare's characters she was most pleased with. Upon her answering that she thought the character of Queen Catharine, in Henry the Eighth, the most natural: – 'I think so too, Madam, (said he;) and whenever you perform it, I will once more hobble out to the theatre myself.' Mrs Siddons promised she would do herself the honour of acting his favourite part for him; but many circumstances happened to prevent the representation of King Henry the Eighth during the Doctor's life.

In the course of the evening he thus gave his opinion upon the merits of some of the principal performers whom he remembered to have seen upon the stage. 'Mrs Porter, in the vehemence of rage, and Mrs Clive, in the sprightliness of humour, I have never seen equalled. What Clive did best, she did better than Garrick; but could not do half so many things well; she was a better romp than any I ever saw in nature. – Pritchard, in common life, was a vulgar ideot; she would talk of her *gownd*; but, when she appeared upon the stage, seemed to be inspired by gentility and understanding. – I once talked with Colley Cibber, and thought him ignorant of the principles of his art. – Garrick, Madam, was no declaimer; there was not one of his own scene-shifters who could not have spoken *To be, or not to be*, better than he did; yet he was the only actor I ever saw, whom I could call a master both in tragedy and comedy; though I liked him best in comedy. A true conception of character, and natural expression of it, were his distinguished excellencies.' Having expatiated, with his usual force and eloquence, on Mr Garrick's extraordinary eminence as an actor, he concluded with this compliment to his social talents; 'And after all, Madam, I thought him less to be envied on the stage than at the head of a table.'[33]

Sarah herself stresses Johnson's great courtesy to her on this and during their subsequent meetings, which continued up to within a few weeks of his death in December 1784:

I do not exactly remember the Time but it was not long before I was honoured by an invitation from Dr Johnson. He was then a wretched invalid, and had requested my friend Mr Windham, of whom he was very fond, to persuade me to favour him by drinking tea with him in Bolt Court. An account of this evening may be found in Boswel's memoirs of Dr J.^n. When I beggd to know his opinion of Mrs Pritchard's acting, whom I had never seen, he said, 'Madam, she was a vulgar idiot. She never read any part of the Play, except her own part, and she said *gownd*.' Is it possible, thought I, that Mrs Pritchard, the greatest of all the Lady Macbeths should never have read the Play? I concluded that he must have been misinformed, but I was afterwards told by a gentleman, an accquaintance of Mrs P., that he had sup[p]ed with her one night after acting that Part and that he then heard her say she never had read that Play. I cannot believe it.

The D.^r spoke highly of Garricks various Talents, & when Mr Windham and myself were discussing some point respecting him, he said, 'Madam, do [not] trouble yourself to endeavour to convince Windham. He is the very Bull-dog of an argument and will never loose his hold.' His favourite female character was Katherine in Henry the Eighth. He was very desirous of seeing me in that Play but, said he, 'I am too deaf, and too blind, to see or hear at a greater distance than the stage Box, and I have little taste for making myself a Public gaze in so distinguishd a situation.' I assured him that nothing could gratify me so much, and that I would procure for him an easy Chair at the stage door behind the Scenes, where he would both see and hear, and be perfectly concealed. He appeared greatly pleased with this arrangement, but, unhappily for me, he did not live to fulfil our mutual wishes. Some weeks before he died I made him some morning visits at the request of Mr Windham. He was extremely, though formally, polite; always apologised for being unable to attend me to my Carriage; conducted me to the head of the stairs, kissed my hand, and bowing, said, 'Dear Madam, I am your most humble Servant'. This ceremony and these words were always repeated without the smallest deviation.[34]

Johnson himself, in a letter written on 27 October 1783 to Mrs Thrale, expressed his own pleasure in Sarah's visits:

Mrs Siddons, in her visit to me, behaved with great modesty and propriety, and left nothing behind her to be censured or despised. Neither praise nor money, the two powerful corrupters of mankind, seemed to have depraved her. I shall be glad to see her again. Her brother Kemble calls on me, and pleases me very well.[35]

The fact that Sarah was now beginning to appear in Shakespeare at Drury Lane revealed her growing confidence in her powers. Her choice of Isabella, with her fiercely painful stand for morality above the calls of kinship, seemed to suit the moral temper of the time. The heroics of sublimated virtue had a special appeal to eighteenth-century audiences. Sarah knew she was good in such concentrated, defiant speeches, the 'moral energy' (as Boaden put it) which the part of Isabella required; but the Isabella of *Measure for Measure* lacked the more obvious sentiment of Southerne's Isabella, which the King liked so much. Nevertheless, he decided to see this other, harsher Isabella, and apparently succumbed to the brilliance of Sarah's performance. But she appeared in *Measure for Measure* only five times during the season.

Her second Shakespearean part was the brief but impassioned one of Constance in *King John*, opening on 10 November 1783. It was put on, according to Campbell, at the request of King George, who wanted to see her act in the play with her brother.[36] The press reception was, to use Campbell's phrase, 'truculent', but although the play was only presented four times during the season, Constance was to become one of Sarah's finest parts, and one which she developed greatly with experience. The press was possibly beginning to be affected by a gathering movement against her, inspired perhaps by the partisans of the actresses at Covent Garden. 1783 and 1784 were to be in any case difficult years for Sarah, in which the great swing of public favour in her direction was to be challenged by others in the profession. Perhaps the most bitter campaign was that waged by Mrs Anne Crawford, formerly the wife of the Irish actor Spranger Barry, and aged now fifty and unhappily re-married. Her nose had been put out of joint by Sarah's success in Ireland; she had come storming back to London to 'attack' Sarah, as the partisan press put it, on her home ground. In November she reappeared at Covent

Garden after an absence of five years in her favourite part of
Lady Randolph in Home's play *Douglas*, a part in which Sarah
was also due to appear the following month; it was noticed, in
the words of Fitzgerald, that the rival actresses

> ... represented quite a different school of interpretation, the 'level'
> portions of the play being hurried over, or given in neutral tones,
> by Mrs Crawford, who reserved herself for sudden bursts, as the
> occasion demanded; whereas Mrs Siddons adopted the favourite
> Kemble principle of elaborating the utmost effect, whether of
> elocution or feeling, out of almost every line.

Mrs Crawford proved utterly unequal to the struggle with her
far younger rival, who was still under thirty. As Boaden put it,
Sarah 'had many advantages in the competition – youth, beauty,
a finer figure, more power of eye, a voice in its whole compass
sound and unbreaking. Her declamation, too, was more studied,
finished, and accurate.'

Sarah also appeared during the 1783–4 season in three other
new parts, Mrs Beverley in Moore's *The Gamester*, the title role
in *The Countess of Salisbury* by Hartson, and Sigismunda in
Tancred and Sigismunda by Thomson, neither of the last two
being of much merit. Of the three, *The Gamester* was the most
popular, and it was presented as often as the revival of *Isabella*
from the first season. She appeared in this sentimental melodrama
with her brother, and excited 'tears and acclamations' in both
the Prince of Wales and the Duke of Cumberland. The season
finished on 13 May. In spite of the very variable popularity of the
plays that had been chosen, there could be no doubt of Sarah's
continued success in the eyes of her fashionable audience.

During the season, Sarah was painted by Reynolds as 'The
Tragic Muse', and she has left her own account of this. There is
more than a little complacency in her description of herself,
though it must be remembered that when she wrote this she was
old and in retirement, thinking back over the triumphs of the
past:

> As much of my time as could now be 'stoln from imperious affairs',
> was employ'd in sitting for various Pictures. I had frequently the
> honour of Dining with Sir Joshua Reynolds in Leicester Square. At
> his house were assembled all the good, the wise, the talented, the
> rank and fashion of the age. About this time he produced what is
> reported to be the finest female Picture in the world, his glorious

Tragedy. In tribute to his triumphant Genius I cannot but remark his instantaneus decission on the attitude and expression. In short, it was in the twinkling of an eye.

When I attended him for the first sitting, after many more gratifying encomiums than I dare repeat, he took me by the hand, saying, 'Ascend your undisputed throne, and graciously bestow upon me some grand Idea of The Tragick Muse'. I walkd up the steps & seated myself instantly in the attitude in which She now appears. This idea satisfyd him so well that he, without one moments hesitation, determined not to alter it. When I attended on him for the last sitting, he appeared to be afraid of touching it, and, after pausingly contemplating his unequald glorious work, he said, 'No, I will meerly add a little more colour to the face'. I then beged him to pardon my presumption in hoping that he would not hieghten that tone of complexion so exquisitely accordant with the chilling and deeply concentered musing of Pale Melancholy. He most graciously complyd with my petition; and some time afterwards, when he invited me to go and see the Picture finished and in the Frame, he did me the honour to thank me for persuading him to pause upon hieghtening the colour, being now perfectly convinced that it would have impaired the effect, adding that he had been inexpressibly gratifyd by observing many persons weep in contemplating this favourite effort of his Pencil, and adding with his own benevolent smile, 'You yourself, you know, can do no more than bring forth tears which, tho' you do not see, and sighs and sobs which, tho' you do not hear, you make us all so severely feel'. I was delighted when he assured me that he was certain that the colours would remain unfaded as long as the Canvass would hold them together, which unhappily had not been the case with all his works. He then most gallantly and most flatteringly added, 'And to confirm my opinion, here is my name, for I have resolved to go down to posterity upon the hem of *your* Garment'. Accordingly, it appears upon the border of the drapery. Here ended this charming visit, and, shortly afterwards, his precious Life. . . . Sir Joshua often honourd me by his presence at The Theatre. He approved very much of my costumes and my hair *without powder*, which at that time was used in great profusion, with a reddish-brown tint and a great quantity of pomatum, which, well kneaded together, modeled the fair ladies tresses into large curls like demy-cannon. My locks were generally braided into a small compass so as to ascertain the size and shape of my head, which to a Painter's eye was of course an agreeable departure from the mode. My short waist too was to him a pleasing contrast to the long stiff stays and hoop petticoats which were then the fashion even on the stage, [and] obtain his unqualified approbation. He always sat in the Orchestra, and in that place were to be seen (O glorious constellation!) Burke, Gibbon, Sheridan, Windham, and, 'though last not least', the illustrious Fox of whom it was frequently observed that 'Iron tears were drawn down Plutos cheek'; and these great men would often visit my Dressing Room after the Play, to make thier bows and honour me with thier applauses. I must repeat, O glorious days! Niether did H.R.H. The Prince of Wales withold this gracious approbation. Garrick's conduct toward me was by these Gentlemen attributed to Jealousy, and Mr. G. A. Steevens was heard to say (in referrance to the clamorous applause of my first night), 'If Garrick could hear this, it would turn him upon his face in his Coffin'. For my own part, I never could give credit to this notion, for it is utterly inconcievable that he should have seen anything in an untaught unpractised Girl to excite such a feeling, and as I have already observed I really think it was meerly for the pleasure of mortifying others that he distinguished me – cruel cruel pleasure![37]

There can be no doubt that the young actress and her husband were flattered by the attention paid to them by the greatest men of the age, such as Dr Johnson and Sir Joshua Reynolds, who on occasion asked them to dine with him and his friends. Here Sarah might meet Burke and William Windham, through whom she came to meet Johnson. She was a frequent visitor to Buckingham House, where, as we have seen, she became a kind of Court reciter. The Queen took such a kindly interest in her that through royal influence she procured a place for her son at Charterhouse, while the King showed his concern by urging her not to use white paint on her skin lest it harm her. 'I cannot imagine how I could be suspected of this disgusting practice,' she complained.

She was becoming adjusted to the social life which accorded with her position in the theatre, but she was pestered with unwanted attention. As she wrote in her reminiscences for Campbell:

My door was soon beset by various persons quite unknown to me, whose curiosity was on the alert to see the new Actress, some [of] whom actually forced thier way into my Drawing-room in spite of remonstrance or opposition. This was as inconvenient as offensive, for, as I acted usually thrice a week and had besides to attend Rehearsals, it may be imagind I had but little time to spend unnecessarily. One morning, although I had previously given orders not to be interrupted, my servant enters the room in a great hurry, saying, 'Ma'am I am very sorry to tell you there are some ladies below who say they must see you, and it is impossible for me to prevent it. I have told them over and over again that you are particularly engaged, but all in vain, and now Ma'am you may acctually hear them on the stairs.' I felt extremely indignant at such unparalelld impertinence, and before the servant had done speaking to me, a tall, elegant, invalide-looking person presented herself at the door (whom I am afraid I did not recieve very graciously), and after her, four more, in slow succession. A very awkward silence took place; when presently, the first Lady began to accost me in a most inveterate Scotch accent, which was scarcely intelligible to me in those days. She was a person of very high rank. Her curiosity had been, however, too powerful for her good breeding. 'You must think it strange,' said she, 'to see a person entirely unknown to you intrude in this manner upon your privacy; but you must know I am in a very delicate state of health, and my Physician won't let me go to the Theatre to see you, so I am come to look at you here.' So *she* sat down to look, and *I* to be looked at, for a few painful moments, when she arose and apologised; but I was in no humour to overlook such insolence, and so let her depart in silence.[38]

The strain of the season, ending in May, had told on Sarah's health. She was not well, as a note in Palmerston's *Memoirs* for April 1784 records: 'I have just been to see Mrs Siddons play, *Belvedere* which she did with her usual excellence, though she looks ill. If I stay next week I shall be in town at her benefit.'[39] He was to see her again, later in the year, in Ireland. This is the first reference to the recurrent ill-health which was to plague her, and which was no doubt partly due to nervous strain. She took every difficulty to heart. However, she was still only thirty, and always prepared to work hard. She and William wanted to collect as much money as they could, but she also wanted the challenge and the excitement of working in the theatre. Like many people who have known extreme poverty, she wanted to feel the comforting presence of considerable sums standing to her credit, and the only way to secure herself and her family and her other dependents was to continue earning while the sun shone. And this meant accepting the rigours of summer tours in the English provinces, in Scotland and in Ireland. It brought her large sums of money but did her health little good.

She opened in Edinburgh on 22 May, at the Theatre Royal, Shakespeare Square, less than a fortnight after the last night at Drury Lane. She was to be received in a manner which finally endeared Edinburgh to her so that it became, with Bath, a city of the happiest recollections. But she (or perhaps more properly

William) was becoming over-sharp in affairs of money, either through inexperience, lack of tact, or a nervous tendency to be over-grasping.

She and William, who acted throughout her career as her business manager almost until his death, acquired a reputation for hard dealing over contracts, and this gave Sarah's enemies considerable openings for attack through exaggeration and misrepresentation. William's methods of negotiation with John Jackson, the manager in Edinburgh, who (as we have seen) had taken the trouble to cross the sea to Dublin the previous summer to secure her services, offer a case in point. The original terms arranged were £400 for nine appearances, plus a 'clear' benefit. In the meantime, the Siddons had heard that Jackson was to receive a donation of £200 from the Scottish gentry to help him sustain the visit. William took the matter up at once, and not only insisted, in his wife's name, on revising the terms to half the clear receipts on what promised to be overflowing houses, but in the end pocketed the £200 as well. Jackson had, in effect, been blackmailed into accepting these new demands, or losing his star at the last moment. Sarah and William were to clear almost £1,000 in receipts and gifts of gold and silver from what became ten normal performances, one benefit for herself, and a further charity benefit for the Edinburgh workhouse.

Perhaps these difficulties made Sarah apprehensive of her reception by audiences in a country traditionally hostile to the theatre; less than forty years before, mobs of religious fanatics had burnt a playhouse to the ground. Play-acting was held by such people to be 'louping against the Lord', while the Scottish author of *Douglas* had been forced to flee his native land and seek refuge and sustenance in London. But those days of persecution were past. Now Sarah was to present *Douglas* in Edinburgh in the presence of the author, together with Congreve's *The Mourning Bride* and *The Gamester*. With the crush, the heat inside the theatre became so overpowering that doctors profited from the large numbers of women who fainted away and caught what was called 'Siddons fever'.

The Edinburgh audiences had to be understood, as Sarah herself acknowledges:

On the first night of my appearance I was surprised and not a little mortifyd at that profound silence which was indeed an awful contrast to the bursts of applause I had been used to hear in London. No, not a hand moved till the end of the scene, but then indeed I was most amply remunerated. Yet, while I admire the fine taste and judgment of this measure, I am free to confess it renders the task of an Actor almost too laborious, because customary interruptions are not only gratifying and cheering, but they are also really necessary in order to gain breath and voice to carry one on through some violent exertions; though after all it must be confessd that *Silence* is the most *flattering* applause an Actor can recieve.[40]

In conversation with Campbell, she gave more details about that celebrated opening night:

At last, as I well remember, she told me she coiled up her powers to the most emphatic possible utterance of one passage, having previously vowed in her heart, that if *this* could not touch the Scotch, she would never again cross the Tweed. When it was finished, she paused, and looked to the audience. The deep silence was broken only by a single voice exclaiming, 'That's no bad!' This ludicrous parsimony of praise convulsed the Edinburgh audience with laughter. But the laugh was followed by such thunders of applause, that, amidst her stunned and nervous agitation, she was not without fears of the galleries coming down.[41]

Whether the audiences remained slow to give applause or not, on the evening she played Isabella Sarah was so carried away she had to be helped from the stage, while in the audience one particular young lady became hysterical and was carried from the theatre screaming the line from the play: 'Oh, my Biron! My Biron!'; she was the heiress Miss Gordon of Gight in Aberdeenshire, who later married the Honourable John Biron and became the mother of Lord Byron.

Throughout the season, the demand for seats remained unabated.[42] Queues formed at midday to get into the theatre at the specially early hour of three o'clock, and it is well known that the General Assembly of the Church of Scotland had to rearrange their hour of meeting because some of the younger element among them 'flocked to the playhouse to get lessons in elocution'. People came to Edinburgh by coach from as far away as Newcastle, and in a single day, according to Dibden, historian of the Scottish theatre, there were recorded 2,557 applications for 630 places in the theatre. The door to the gallery had to be guarded by soldiers, and it was said that their bayonets were sometimes dyed a suspicious hue after the crush; the story goes that one young lady on her way out to tea found herself swept into the theatre pit, and was only rescued from the press by being lifted bodily on to the stage. It was also claimed that thieves came up from London and exercised their specialized skills in purloining wigs, hats, canes and snuff-boxes, as well as the usual bag of purses and watches.

Sarah enjoyed her visit to 'dear Edinburgh', and valued especially the reception she received from the intellectuals, artists and poets: 'never never can I forget the private no less than public marks of their most gratifying suffrages', she wrote for Campbell. 'Here I became acquainted with the venerable author of *Douglas*, Dr Blair, Mr D. Hume, Dr Beattie, Mr Mackenzie etc etc, and passed with them a succession of happy fleeting days, which never failed to enlighten and delight.'

Sarah's last performance in Edinburgh was on 11 June. Before she left, she published an open statement of thanks in the Edinburgh *Courant*:

> Mrs Siddons confesses she has not words enough to express the feelings she entertains of her reception in this city; but humbly hopes she may be understood by this brief but sincere silence, that she is grateful for all favours, and will ever hold them dear in her remembrance.

She now had to face a long sea voyage to Dublin. She left Scotland like a queen, and an extraordinary account of her departure was written by the Reverend Dr Mackenzie, minister of Portpatrick:

> I shall give you an instance of her (Mrs S's) amazing sensibility. . . . Our village consists of a natural crescent facing the sea, bounded by rocks, and a range of hills in the background. When she came to the shore to embark, and raised her eyes to throw a parting look, I suppose, at Scotland, the wildness of the scene about her, – the rocks, the seas, and perhaps the primitive appearance of the natives, – rushed upon her so powerfully that she heaved a deep sigh, and, looking terrified for a moment, to our utter astonishment, she emitted all at once one of her wild cries. The effect was powerful beyond description; the rocks, the shore, and the concave conveyed the echoes. There was a general rush from the houses scattered along the beach. Seeing men, women and children so alarmed, she herself apparently became more terrified; she repeated the cry, and actually screamed aloud. It was melancholy, and was mournful, and was piercingly loud. In a moment, as if by a sudden shock, or through the influence of some supernatural agency, the whole of the people

lamented and sobbed aloud. Such a scene I have never witnessed. There happened, singular to say, at that instant to pass a burial; the village bell tolled. . . . When she repeated these words, I then saw the scene she had in view:

> Methinks I stand upon some naked beach,
> Sighing to winds, and to the seas complaining,
> While afar off the vessel sails away
> In which my treasure and my soul's embarked.

. . . One vessel actually sailed off, and the other would have followed if her husband had not interfered. 'Come,' says he, 'my dear, what is all this for? You don't propose to swim to Ireland – Egad, if you don't make haste, the vessel will sail absolutely.'

Then Dr Mackenzie adds:

The husband of the great actress seems to be a good, plain sort of a man. One thing with regard to him is rather remarkable. I asked him, when his wife was in one of her tragic fits, whether he was affected equally with the rest of the audience. 'Why, really,' says he, 'I have often wondered at myself in this particular. When she cries, I laugh. I cannot for the soul of me help it. And when she or her audience are grave, I am always near crying. I remark this of myself invariably. Besides,' says he, 'do you know that small beer is good for crying. The day that my wife drinks small beer, she cries amazingly: she is really pitiful. But if I was to give her porter, or any stronger liquor, she would not be worth a farthing.'[43]

On 21 June 1784 Sarah wrote to the Whalleys from Dublin, owing them a letter and worried as to where she should address it, for they were away on their travels. Of her Scottish season she wrote: 'They treated me most nobly.' But she had not a moment to call her own:

I pant for retirement and leisure, but am doomed to inexpressible and almost unsupportable hurry. You guessed, as you generally do of me, rightly, generously, like yourself. . . . To say the truth, I have been more and longer ill this last winter than I ever was in my life. . . . If you can, do let me know particularly where I can address you in August, as I hope I shall then be able to call a few hours my own.[44]

She then continues with a matter which was to become most troublesome to her, and throws some further light on her attitude, and that of William, to money. It concerned the bad relations which had developed between herself and Whalley's eccentric friend, Samuel Pratt of Bath.

I have offended him, and I am sorry he should see cause for offence. I fear he thinks unworthily of me. All I can say is, that I do not deserve it; that I should be most happy to render him any service; though I cannot stoop to a vindication of myself to one, who ought to know me better than to accuse me of a vice which is of all others the least excusable, and I hope the least likely to find a place in my bosom. The matter is this. He asked for a little money, which I was so happy as to be able to furnish him with, some time ago; and he very civilly tells me he knows that I am getting a vast deal of money, and wonders I can be so unfeeling as ask him for the trifling sum he owes me. In short, he says as plainly as possible, that not necessity but avarice prompts me to this request. Mr Siddons was very happy to be able to lend him five hundred pounds last winter, and I thought my little modicum, lent a year before, and which I was to be paid in a few weeks after it was lent, might be spared from that. I have said thus much, that you may not think it strange in future to find no exact account of him from me, for I never see him now. Poor man! I respect his talents and pity his imprudence. . . . Be satisfied, my dearest friends, that I am not yet forsaken by the public; they are very, very kind to me. I stay here till the end of July, and then return to London. God Almighty bless you both! and I only desire you to love me as I do you.[45]

Her stay in Ireland was to be a troubled one; for one thing, she was not well. She was fortunate, however, in being invited to stay with her old friend, Henrietta O'Neill. The Honourable Mrs O'Neill lived in a mansion of great beauty which made a great impression on Sarah. Shanes Castle was on the Antrim shore of Lough Neagh, and she described for Campbell the extreme luxury she found there:

I made a visit to Shanes Castle, the magnificent residence of M[rs] O'Niel, and oh!, that I could describe the beauty and splendour of this scene of enchantment, which, alas, is now leveled to the earth by a tremendous Fire. Here were assembled all the talent and rank and beauty of Ireland. Among the persons of the Lienster family was poor Lord Edward Fitzgerald, the most aimiable, honourable, though misguided and unfortunate youth I ever knew. It is scarce possible to concieve the splendour of this almost Royal Establishment, except by recollecting the circumstances of an Arabian Nights entertainment. Six or eight carriages with a numerous throng of Lords and ladies and gentlemen on Horseback began the day by making excursions about this terrestrial paradise, returning home but just in time to dress for dinner. The table was servd with a profusion and elegance to which I have never known anything comparable. The side-boards [were] decorated with adequate magnificence, at which appeared several immense silver Flagons containing Claret. A fine band of musicians played during the whole of the repast. They were stationed in the Corridor which led from the dining room into a fine Conservatory, where we pluckd our desert from numerous trees of the most exquisite fruits, and where the waves of a superb Lake washd its feet while its cool delicious murmurs were accompanyd with strains of celestial harmony from the Corridor.[46]

At the end of her tour, which included Belfast, Cork and Limerick, she was received 'on a visit of some length' by the Dowager Duchess of Leinster, the mother of Lord Edward Fitzgerald.

But Sarah Siddons was never happy in the Irish theatres. From the outset things began to go wrong, though her contract in Dublin was good – £50 a night for twenty appearances. First of all, she had trouble again with Daly, who seemed to resent her stardom while at the same time wishing to exploit it for the sake of his theatre. In her own words:

The Manager of the Theatre very soon chose to adopt ev[er]y means of vexation for me that he could possibly devise, meerly because I venturd to suggest at Rehearsal that his proper situation as Falconbridge in King John was at the right hand of the Kings. During the scene between Constance and Austria, he thought it necessary that he should (tho he did it most ungraciously) adopt this arrangement; but his malevolence pursued me unremittingly from that moment, absurdly fancying that he was of less importance placed at so great a distance from the front of the Stage, the Kings being seated at the end of the stage. He had little or nothing to say and being in the front, would have greatly interrupted and diminished the effect of Constances best scene. He was a very handsome man and, I believe, was mortifyd that his personal attractions had faild to pervert my judgment in the grouping of this Scene. He however made me suffer sufficiently for my pertinacity, by employing all the Newspapers to abuse and annoy me the whole time I remained in Dublin, and even to pursue me to England with malignant abuse (but of that, hereafter). The Theatre meantime was attended to his hearts content. Indeed, the whole of this Engagement was all that my most sanguine [hopes] could have inspired.[47]

To make matters worse, she fell ill with a fever, and the season had to be interrupted for two weeks while she was confined to her bed. Lord Palmerston was in Dublin, and noted on 13 August:

'Dublin is emptier and duller than any place in the world. . . . Mrs Siddons is still here, she has been ill but is recovered, and is to act two or three nights more.' Even this enforced absence from the theatre became the subject for malicious rumour, that she was not ill at all, but malingering. Lord Palmerston wrote again on 19 August 1784:

> Mrs Siddons has performed three or four times since my being here. I have taken the opportunity of seeing her much at my ease for I am ashamed to say that the houses have not been near full. She seems to have many enemies here and is constantly abused in some of the papers, so that I guess her expeditions to Ireland may probably not be very frequent in future. I have seen her in some new parts and among them in the Fine Lady in *Lethe* in which I think she succeeded very well, though it is the fashion to say not. Her singing is certainly bad and had better be omitted.[48]

On 26 July William himself had written of Sarah's illness to their friend Sir Charles Hotham Thompson:

> Mrs Siddons got last week a very bad cold attended with a sore Throat and Fever. The day it first came upon her, she got through with great difficulty; but it so inflamed her disorder that she has since been in great danger, though with care and attendance she is getting up again a-pace. Certain of your esteem and concern for her I was induced to send this, fearing you might meet with any of the Irish papers and guess from them things were worse than they now are.
>
> P.S. A terrible riot at the theatre, with the Lord Lieutenant etc. Poor Mrs Siddons went through the part of Lady Randolph without being heard a single line, and now and then an apple, potatoe or something else going very near her; indeed Sir Charles, I am no politician, but this country is in a strange ferment. However I hope they'l suffer me to bring my precious property safe out of it, and then '*to it boys, if you please!*'[49]

Then followed the two most unfortunate events of all, which became so far twisted from the truth that the repercussions were to cause Sarah great distress when she returned to London. The first concerned her fellow actor from Drury Lane, William Brereton, who had been so far lifted from mediocrity by acting Jaffier to her Belvidera that, although married to an actress who worked at Drury Lane, he was rumoured to be in love with her. It was at his desire that he was invited to join the Dublin company without any salary, though he was to receive a 'clear' benefit with Sarah appearing on his behalf. Brereton, who, it will be remembered, suffered from mental instability, fell ill in Dublin; since he had taken no part in her benefit, she considered herself within her rights not to play entirely free in his. When playing for benefits, she was prepared to reduce her fee from £50 a night to £30; for Brereton, she proposed to lower this still further, to £20. Then she had fallen ill herself, and his benefit performance was cancelled altogether. Immediately the rumour began to circulate that she had refused to appear for his benefit. Brereton may even have started the rumour himself; he was unstable enough at this time to attempt suicide.

The second distressing event concerned the veteran actor West Digges who, it will be remembered, Sarah had suspected the previous year of satirizing her successes in the press. The story has perhaps been most clearly and simply put by Lee Lewis, an actor of the period, who was to a minor degree involved:

As she was rehearsing the part of *Belvidera*, one morning, Digges, as he was standing for the part of *Pierre*, suddenly sank down. It was no less than a paralytic stroke, which deprived him of the use of one side. He was taken from the theatre, and, I believe, never returned to where he had fretted and strutted so many hours. Mrs Siddons's engagement was coming to a conclusion; and she was advertised for Cork a few days after. In the meantime, a person came to her, and told her that it would be a charitable action if she would perform in a benefit play for poor Digges. Her answer was, that she was sorry she had but one night to spare, and for that she thought she was engaged in honour to play for the Marshalsea prisoners, as she had intended, in the year before. This, to be sure, was a denial to Digges, though not an uncharitable refusal: and yet, what an artful and fiend-like use was made of it! As will appear. The messenger had not been long gone, when it struck her that it would be more humane to assist this old unfortunate; and immediately she dispatched a person to Drumcondra, where Digges then was, to say that Mrs Siddons had reconsidered the matter, and would be glad to perform for him. He was thankful, and the night and play were fixed. There was a good house. The next day, while preparing for her journey for Cork, she received a note from Digges, expressing his gratitude. It will be proper to inform my reader, that while she was at Dublin there was a little sparring between her and the Manager. At Cork the misunderstanding was renewed, and I there made my own observations. These little bickerings brought down many paragraphs upon her from the party; and, directly after, a

paper war ensued. She was accused of having charged Digges fifty
pounds for playing at his benefit. A very artful letter, written by a
Mr F—y, upon that subject, appeared in a Morning print; and, as
it was inserted with a more mischievous intent than any of the rest,
so it had a greater effect. It was now predicted, that she was to be
driven from the London stage whenever she should appear on it:
and, among the rest, appeared a paragraph, calling on any of her
profession to come forth, and say if she had ever done a kind action.
This was rather an unlucky challenge: for, a few weeks before, even
in the city of York, it was a fact, that she had performed three times
without any emolument to herself: once for my benefit; once for
that of Mr Aickin, of Covent Garden; and once for the benefit of a
poor-house. I should have thought myself base indeed to have
remained neutral at such a time; and I immediately published this
circumstance in several of the Morning prints. Should not Mr
Digges have done the same? But, though called upon, and urged by
many of Mrs Siddons's friends, he, for reasons best known to
himself, kept an obstinate silence, and even suffered a rumour to
prevail that she had taken money from him. But, at last, being
closely pressed, he sent a letter, in which he owned that she had
played for him gratis. He died soon after: and peace be to his manes!
Mrs Siddons appeared on the London boards; and, though this
confession of her having performed gratis was made public, there
were persons determined not to believe it, and who absolutely
insulted her: but, as I have said before, they were but few in comparison of her powerful and numerous friends, and the vipers were
soon crushed.[50]

Sarah wrote her own version for Campbell, adding new
circumstances:

By indefatiguable labour and cruel annoyances, we got together
(Mͬ S[iddons] and myself) from all the little country Theatres, as
many as would enable us to attempt Venice Preservd. Oh such a
scene of disgust and confusion, it is impossible to concieve. The
motive, however, procured us indulgence, and I acted Belvidera
without ever having seen the face of any one of the Actors, as there
was no time for even one Rehearsal. But poor Mͬ Diggs was very
considerably assisted by this most ludicrous performance, and I put
my disgust into my pocket.

Thus ended my Irish engagements, but not so the persecution of
the Manager, by whose malignity the Newspapers were filled with
the most unjust unqualifyd abuse of me, and all the time I was on
a visit of some length to the Dowͬ Dss. of Lienster, unconscious of
the gathering Storm, the public mind was thus poisoned against me.[51]

After the troubled tour of Ireland, the Siddons hurried back
to London in September, where Sarah was due to appear early
the following month. Her shock on returning to London and
finding her dearly-won reputation being undeservedly destroyed
by her enemies so preyed upon her mind that she induced her
husband (or was persuaded by him) to publish a letter in the
principal journals on 30 September, the day the 1784–5 season
at Drury Lane opened. William signed the letter on her behalf:

The following is an answer to the scandalous stories lately circulated to the prejudice of Mrs Siddons's private character.

TO THE PRINTER.

SIR, – I am unused to write for public inspection, but I will not
hesitate to state the truth, and I think the generous and candid will
excuse the rest. I therefore declare that Mrs Siddons never wished,
asked, nor accepted a single farthing from Mr Digges; and that, a
few days after his benefit, that gentleman acknowledged his obligations to her by a very polite note, which Mrs Siddons (not expecting
so malignant an attack) destroyed.

With regard to Mr Brereton, so far from refusing to perform for
him, she agreed to do it for a much smaller sum than she was to
receive from any other comedian, though every performer for whom
she played gave her considerably less than the manager paid her
nightly, for twenty nights together; but just as the benefits were
commencing she was taken ill, and confined to her bed nearly a
fortnight. When she recovered, her strength would not permit her
to perform immediately more than three nights a week: and as the
manager expected his engagement fulfilled, and was to leave Dublin
at a particular time, she was obliged to forego the performing for
Mr Brereton; she, after that, made another attempt to serve him;
why it failed, Mr Brereton can truly tell; but, I will be bold to assert,
without affording the smallest ground for any charge against Mrs
Siddons. These are solemn facts on which I leave the public to judge.
Animadversions on her public performance and the questioning of
her professional talents I shall ever submit to, feeling that those who
so liberally reward her exertions have the best right to judge of their
degree of merit, and to praise or censure them as they think proper;
but all attacks upon her private conduct that, if unnoticed, would
deservedly lower her in the estimation of the public, and render her
less worthy of their favour and kindness, I hold myself bound to
answer.   W. SIDDONS.

Thursday, September 30.[52]

On the night this letter was published, 30 September, Tom King spoke a Prologue opening the season at Drury Lane. Sarah was not appearing, but King had loyally included a line on her behalf which referred to her 'living worth'. The fact that this was ill-received showed that the public was by no means satisfied that their former idol had been exonerated. It has to be remembered that theatre society in London, and the press they read, with circulations at best of three or four thousand, belonged to a very small, enclosed, gossip-ridden world, in which everyone, the good and the bad, the enlightened and the prejudiced, knew everyone else, and where reputations could be made and unmade overnight as a result of unscrupulous or jealous pressures. The ladies of the theatre, in particular, were vulnerable to these sudden changes of feeling, and the less reputable journals enjoyed rubbing salt into any wounds by inserting unpleasant paragraphs of direct comment or sly innuendo, which had happened in Sarah's case in both the Irish and the English press.

On Sunday 3 October, William was able to publish a formal letter from Brereton, supporting Sarah's case:

> SIR, – I am concerned to find Mrs Siddons has suffered in the public opinion on my account. I have told you before, and I again repeat it, that to the friends I have seen I have taken pains to exculpate her from the least unkindness to me in Dublin. I acknowledge she did agree to perform at my benefit for a less sum than for any other performer, but her illness prevented it; and that she would have played for me after that had not the night been appointed after she had played three times in the same week – and that the week after her illness – and I am very willing you shall publish this letter, if you think it will be of the least service to Mrs Siddons, to whom I am proud to own many obligations of friendship. – I am, Sir, your very humble servant.   W. BRERETON.

> Mr Siddons cannot withhold his public thanks from Mr Brereton for his obliging letter, and he has no doubt but that Mr Digges will in a little time furnish Mrs Siddons with another written testimony, that will entirely confound the artful schemes of her detractors.[53]

People remarked on the apparent coldness of this letter, which had evidently been written to order. Boaden, for example, remarks on its 'churlishness', and he thinks that Brereton was jealous of Kemble's supplanting him in younger roles opposite Sarah. We must, however, take account of Brereton's state of mind. His final mental collapse was now imminent.

On 5 October, a second letter appeared, which only made the position worse. One suspects the clumsy, tactless hand of William behind the composition of this second letter, which is just as formal in tone as the first.

> SIR, – Having been informed that the letter signed by me in the several morning papers of yesterday, respecting Mrs Siddons's conduct to me while in Ireland, has not been so clearly understood as it was both the intention on my part and justice to her that it should, I think it necessary again to repeat that it was in no respect owing to Mrs Siddons that I had no benefit in Ireland; but, on the contrary, that in the course of a long and dangerous illness I received proofs of friendship from her which I shall ever recollect with gratitude, and avow now with sincere satisfaction.   W. BRERETON.[54]

Brereton was to appear with her and Kemble that night in *The Gamester*. Sarah would therefore face the first night of her new season in London with her nerves laid bare, her sensitivity and her timidity uppermost.

The evening was catastrophic. The pain can still be felt in her recollections written some forty years later for Campbell:

Alas! How wretched is the being who depends on the stability of public favour! I left London the object of universal approbation, and on my return, but a very few weeks afterwards, was recieved on my first nights appearance with universal oprobium, – accus'd of hardness of heart, of the most sordid avarice, and total insensibility to evry thing and evry body, except my own interest. Unhappily, contrary winds had for some days precluded the possibility of recieving such letters from Dublin as would have saved me from these atrocious calumnies [and] from the horrors of this dreadful night, when I was hurled from the exaltation which I had attaind, to the degradation of hissing and hooting and all the humiliating circumstances of public scorn. What sad reverse of fortune!

During this horrible clamour, I made several vain attempts to be heard when at length a Gentleman stood forth in the middle of the front row of the pit, impelled by benevolence and manly feeling for the oppressed, who, as I advancd to make my last attempt at being heard, accosted me in these words: 'For heavens sake, madam, do not degrade yourself by an apology, for there is nothing necessary to be said' (Like Abdiel, 'faithful found among the faithless, faithful only he'). His admonition was followed by reiterated clamour, when my dear brother appeard and hurried me away from this Scene of savage persecution and insult. The instant I quitted it, I fainted in his arms, and on my recovery I was thankful that my persecutors had not had the gratification of beholding this weakness. Alas, why had I enemies, but because to be prosperous is sufficient cause for enmity. After I was tolerably restord to myself again, I was besought by my husband, my brother, and Mr. Sheridan to present myself again before that audience by whom I had been so cruelly and unjustly degraded, and where, but in consideration of my children, I never would have appeared again.[55]

In case of trouble Sarah had come to the theatre with a speech prepared. It was this that Sheridan and the others behind the scenes were inducing her to try to deliver. Summoning all the courage she had gained from long experience in dealing with troublesome, if not actually hostile audiences, she reappeared alone on the stage and said:

> Ladies and Gentlemen, – The kind and flattering partiality which I have uniformly experienced in this place would make the present interruption distressing to me indeed, were I in the slightest degree conscious of having deserved your censure. I feel no such consciousness. The stories which have been circulated against me are calumnies. When they shall be proved to be true my aspersers will be justified; but, till then, my respect for the public leads me to be confident that I shall be protected from unmerited insult.[56]

This was far better, and had greater restraint and dignity than the over-argumentative letters of the week before, in which people might detect too great a note of concern about money. The benefits system created an awkward relationship between the stars of the theatre and their principal supporting players, as well as with the management and even the public. The offer of benefits (whether 'clear' or subject to deductions of various sorts, including fees to stars whose presence could make the occasion far more profitable) enabled penurious managers to cut back on the regular wages of their players; they could argue that it was up to each individual player to prove his popularity with the public by inducing them to crowd in on his benefit night and so support him with their money. But since it was the stars the public really wanted to see, anyone in Sarah's position was under constant pressure to appear in benefit performances. This was quite easy at Drury Lane, where the season extended to several weeks; but during the intensive summer tours, when the seasons lasted from one to three weeks, and her fees were very high for each performance, the benefits system was difficult to manage and could cost the star considerable sums in lost earnings, though the public tended to feel she could well afford it. Here lay the essential danger to Sarah of the Digges and Brereton affairs.

Boaden was present on the occasion and gives his own account of how she behaved:

> Mr Kemble had long been studied in these popular exhibitions, and, finding that for the present nothing was likely to be done, he wisely concluded that her absence was most likely to decide the house in her favour; and, repeating their respects in the usual manner, he led her off the stage, and left her noisy assailants to consider. After some interval the calls for her became less mixed with opposition than before, and she came again on the stage, but alone; and deliberately advancing to the very inimitable grace which always attended her . . . addressed the audience. . . . There was a male dignity in the understanding of Mrs Siddons that raised her above the helpless timidity of other women.[57]

Lord Archibald Hamilton wrote on 10 October to the Siddons's friend, Sir Charles Hotham:

> The howling storm was quite subsided, I hope never more to shock her sensibility, which alas! has been too often the butt of malice. I thought her rather pale and thin; probably owing to the late agitation of her mind; for I hear she is in perfect good health, and feels herself on ground so firm that she is not to be shaken by these late ill-founded imputations . . . surely she is made of mould too refined and precious for that Society of Barbarians, who, I am told, *would actually have tarr'd & feathered Her*, had she not been protected by the Duchess of Leinster – God reward them as they deserve!
>
> Last night I was charmed as much as ever. She is always new and wonderful.[58]

William himself wrote on 15 October:

> I have the happiness to inform you that Mrs Siddons stood the rude shock with greater firmness than could have been expected, and is now pretty well, but says, though for her children's sake she shall be obliged to continue in her profession, it will never have those pleasing charms it had before.[59]

Here, then, were the divergencies in Sarah's nature. At heart she conformed to the conventional view of women as 'timid' and 'helpless' creatures, who depended on men for strength and support; yet at the same time, she could, when she wished, draw on a strength which a romantically conventional admirer such as Boaden can only describe as 'male'. Offstage, her timidity made her seem to be dependent on her menfolk, but experienced men such as Sheridan, King and her brother John Philip (though he was still only twenty-seven), recognized the innate strength on which she could draw, and sometimes forced her to do so. They made an all-powerful, regnant actress out of a woman who, once she was offstage, seemed conventional, vulnerable, quietly domesticated and almost exaggeratedly virtuous.[60] This was the mask she preferred to wear to cover the great, theatric passions which were present inside her, and which she nurtured and disciplined for the stage. And she could not give up, as she sometimes claimed she wanted to do, because of her children.

Although she had in fact survived this further test at Drury Lane, insulting paragraphs continued to appear in the press, many, perhaps, inspired by that friend-turned-enemy, Pratt. But Sarah knew now that she could survive the remnants of opposition. She wrote in the third person on 30 October to Lord Hardwicke to thank him 'for his congratulations supposing his Lordship had heard of the attack made upon her by her enemies of which no Prime Minister had ever more'.[61] By this time a brief letter from West Digges to William Woodfall, a respected journalist, had reached *The Morning Chronicle*:

> Sir, – I empower you to declare to the publick, that I did not pay Mrs Siddons for playing for my benefit. I thanked the lady by letter for her politeness, which I am informed she has mislaid. I think it is but justice to inform you of this. West Digges.[62]

Better late than never, the public thought, and the worst was over. However, Sarah was to bear permanently the reputation of stinginess. From now on she was 'Lady Sarah Save-all'. This was unfair. The worst that might be said of her is that she was seldom warmly, spontaneously generous; rather, like many people who have known poverty, she was calculatingly so. Like Shakespeare, she believed in money, in the perquisites of social position, and in securing her family, of whom she was now the sole means of support. She had had certain bad experiences with money, like the very generous loan made to Pratt, who had become, partly because of it, her enemy and detractor. She had no rich lovers, whose money she could have thrown around in careless abundance as long as it lasted. She had considerable domestic responsibilities, and she was determined to honour these so long as her health, strength, and popular acclaim lasted. Further, she had no means of knowing when she might become pregnant once again.

Some months after her troubles in the theatre were dissipated, Sarah wrote on 13 March 1785 to the Whalleys:

> I have been very unhappy; now 'tis over I will venture to tell you so. . . . I have been charged with almost everything bad, except incontinence; and it is attributed to me as thinking a woman may be guilty of every crime in the catalogue of crimes, provided she retain her chastity. God help them and forgive them; they know but little of me . . . what makes the wound rankle deeper is, that ingratitude, hypocrisy, and perfidy have barbed the darts. But it is over, and I am happy. Good God! what would I give to see you both, but for an hour! how many thousand thousand times do I wish myself with you, and long to unburthen my heart to you. I can't bear the idea of your being so long absent. I know you will expect to hear what I have been doing; and I wish I could do this to your satisfaction. Suffice it to say, that I have acted Lady Macbeth, Desdemona, and several other things this season, with the most unbounded approbation; and you have no idea how the innocence and playful simplicity of the latter have laid hold on the hearts of the people. I am very much flattered by this, as nobody ever has done anything with that character before. My brother is charming in Othello; indeed, I must do the public the justice to say that they have been extremely indulgent, if not partial, to every character I have performed.[63]

'I have paid severely for my eminence,' she wrote to them two days later.

> . . . I knew you too well to suppose you could hear of my distresses without feeling them too poignantly. I resolved to write when I had overcome my enemies: you shall always share my joys, but suffer me to keep my griefs from your knowledge. Now I am triumphant, the favourite of the public again; and now you hear from me.
>
> A strange capricious master is the public; however, one consolation greater than any other, except one's own approbation, has been, that those whose suffrages I esteemed most have, through all my troubles, clasped me closer to their hearts; they have been the touchstone to prove who were really my friends.[64]

But she was now very well-off indeed. Her salary for the season of 1784–5 was £24.10s weekly, while Kemble's fee was ten guineas. For this she was expected to appear not less than three times a week. In addition, there were the substantial earnings of her benefits, and the very high fees she earned during her summer tours. Her earnings reached between £4,000 and £5,000 a year. Her level of income did not make her popular with her sisters; as she told Samuel Rogers: 'Alas, after I became celebrated none of my sisters ever loved me as they did before.' She did her best for them, but, as Genest put it, 'she could not make them actresses'. Frances Kemble, the eldest after Sarah, sustained by her great beauty and undoubted intelligence, became a modestly successful actress at Drury Lane, staying with the company from 1783 to 1786, when she married Francis Twiss. Elizabeth Kemble, who was two years younger than Frances, had also appeared on occasion at Drury Lane from 1783; in 1785 she married an actor and dentist, Charles Edward Whitlock, and eventually went to America, where she appeared as a tragic actress with some success. Sarah was later to describe her as 'a noble, glorious creature, very wild and eccentric'. Campbell, who met her only later in her life, said she was 'just what Mrs Siddons would have been if she had swallowed a bottle of champagne'. What with her brother Stephen at Covent Garden and her brother John Philip at Drury Lane, there was no shortage of Kembles on the London stage.

A far more troublesome sister than either Frances or Elizabeth was Julia Anne Kemble, who was nine years Sarah's junior. She was also the greatest failure. She, too, aspired to be an actress, but ended a debased sort of exhibitionist of the kind Sarah would have been the first to resent. She was large, she was lame, and she squinted. She married a provincial actor called Curtis, who turned out to be a bigamist, but apparently she preferred living a free life in London from which, every so often, she would emerge in the pursuit of money, proclaiming loudly that she was sister of the great Mrs Siddons. During the 1783 season at Drury Lane she gave a lecture on chastity at Dr Graham's Temple of Hymen, and associated with Dr Graham in a manner likely to bring further discredit to the word. She published both novels and poetry. To draw further attention to herself, she even attempted to commit suicide by taking poison in Westminster Abbey. None of this was calculated to help Sarah during the difficult period of the Digges affair. The Kembles were labelled 'marble-hearted' and none more so than 'mighty Mrs Siddons'. In 1792 Julia married a man called Hatton and went to America, only to return a few years later and settle in London. Sarah allowed her £20 a year, provided she kept 150 miles from the capital.

Having settled her affairs to the best of her ability, Sarah steeled herself to face another arduous season, with revivals of old work sandwiched between the presentations of new productions – eight new characters and nine old ones, with a total of seventy-one appearances before the end of the season early in May. One can understand when calculating the work involved in all this, Henderson's remark to Palmer of Bath, 'Let me assure you, upon the credit of experience, that to keep over fifty characters of great magnitude, importance and variety, distinct and strong upon the mind and memory, is no trifling business.'

With *The Gamester* launched afresh, Sarah Siddons appeared on 3 November as Margaret of Anjou in *The Earl of Warwick*, an adaptation of a French play by La Harpe; in spite of her acknowledged excellence in the past, she played it only three times. Then on 7 November she played a second character called Zara, this time in another adaptation from the French, Voltaire's *Zaïre*; in this she played opposite Smith and Brereton. It had little attraction and after only two performances was not revived. On 2 December another new play was far more popular: this was Cumberland's *The Carmelite*, in which she appeared as Matilda. This was the most successful new production of the season and was performed twelve times; both Smith and Kemble played with her. One other new play in the repertoire, Massinger's *Maid of Honour*, survived only three performances before Sarah prepared herself for what was to be the finest achievement of her career, Lady Macbeth. This was due to open on 2 February 1785.

4

'Charming Siddons'

———————⌒⋀⋀⋀⌒———————

O F ALL THE CHARACTERS she interpreted, the one
representing her highest achievement was probably Lady
Macbeth. She was to play the part repeatedly until her
retirement in 1812, and even after this she revived the performance
several times. Neither she nor her public seemed able to part
with it. And yet, most strangely, she always played Lady Macbeth
against her own inner conception of how it should be done.

Lady Macbeth is one of Shakespeare's more ambivalent
characters. It was not until the twentieth century that ambivalence
became valued for its dramatical and psychological potentialities
in characterization on the stage. Until the present time, the
history of Shakespearian interpretation has consisted of each
generation of actors imposing their own particular style upon the
ambivalences which bring such added value to many of Shakespeare's greatest, most rewarding characters. Each generation,
responsive to the taste of its time, performs these characters as
it thinks it must, or as it thinks it can. This accounts for the
drastic revision to which Shakespeare's text has been subject
from the seventeenth to the nineteenth centuries, though from the
period of Garrick to that of Irving the movement was gradually
in the direction of restoring the original text to its proper place,
and facing, as a result, the ambiguities in performance which the
full and balanced realization of Shakespearean characterization
demands.

Garrick, for example, played Shylock for sentiment, discarding
the traditionally villainous Jew, which formed only a part of
Shakespeare's original conception. Irving, in his production of

119

1888, re-established a more just balance in the relationship of Macbeth and Lady Macbeth, establishing Lady Macbeth's essential weakness, though she is wrought-up by ambition; he emphasized the evil inherent in Macbeth himself, who had previously been played as a weak man preyed upon by a virago of tragic strength and stature.

The Kembles, both John Philip amd his sister Sarah, were very conscious of the need to re-examine Shakespeare in as scholarly a way as possible. This was, in any case, in keeping with the spirit of the age, during which Shakespeare's text was being subject to close examination by a new generation of scholars, many of them known personally to Sarah and her brother. Even in her strolling days, Sarah as a young girl had been fascinated by the character of Lady Macbeth, as actresses mostly are, sensing the feminine, unresolved complexity – the strength, the weakness of woman – which Shakespeare, obviously understanding women, gave her. Now, at the age of thirty, and nearing the height of her powers, Sarah determined to appear in *Macbeth* at Drury Lane, with Smith, not Kemble at this juncture, as Macbeth.

Somewhere around 1815, after her retirement, she determined to put on paper what she believed to be the correct interpretation of the part. She may have sensed that another actress in a later age might feel more free to emphasize the complexities in the character than she was able to in the eighteenth century. It is a tribute to her intellectual honesty that she wrote as she did, and almost a century later Ellen Terry was to attempt to give the part the ambivalence which Shakespeare conceived and which Sarah was the first to expound. She began by emphasizing that this 'astonishing creature' should be regarded afresh, 'disengaged' from 'that idea of the person of her representative which you have been so long accustomed to contemplate'. Far from being meat for some dire tragedy queen, Lady Macbeth, says Sarah, should be:

> most captivating to the other sex, – fair, feminine, nay, perhaps, even fragile – . . . captivating in feminine loveliness . . . a charm of such potency as to fascinate the mind of a hero so dauntless, a character so amiable, so honorable as Macbeth, to seduce him to brave all the dangers of the present and all the terrors of a future world . . . every fascination of mind and person . . . yet of a temper so irresolute and fluctuating, as to require all the efforts, all the

excitement, which her uncontrollable spirit, and her unbounded influence over him, can perform. . . .

It is very remarkable that Macbeth is frequent in expressions of tenderness to his wife, while she never betrays one symptom of affection towards him, till, in the fiery furnace of affliction, her iron heart is melted down to softness.[1]

There seems no doubt that Sarah accepted the traditional interpretation of Macbeth as a potentially good man led astray – though in her notes on the play, taken act by act, she is forced to admit that it was Macbeth who 'in the first instance suggested his design of assassinating the King'. However, as she sees it, it is Lady Macbeth's 'remorseless ambition' which enables her to 'taint' and 'revile' him until he is 'abashed', 'humbled before this unimaginable instance of female fortitude'. The promptings of his better nature are once more suppressed, and he undertakes the murder, the final stages of which she is forced to complete when he proves unfit to do so.

Thereafter, Sarah stresses, the actress should play for remorse; she emphasizes what was absent in previous interpretations – Lady Macbeth's protective love for her husband:

. . . we behold for the first time striking indications of sensibility, nay, tenderness and sympathy; and I think this conduct is nobly followed up by her during the whole of their subsequent eventful intercourse. . . . Yes; smothering her sufferings in the deepest recesses of her own wretched bosom; we cannot but perceive that she devotes herself entirely to the effort of supporting him.

She plays the scenes in which we see Lady Macbeth as Queen, she says, with 'dejection of countenance and manner'. During the banquet scene she should be 'dying with fear', and in her interpretation she claims that she allows Lady Macbeth to see Banquo's ghost when Macbeth does. In conclusion, she says of Lady Macbeth that:

Her feminine nature, her delicate structure, it is too evident, are soon overwhelmed by the enormous pressure of her crimes. Yet it will be granted, that she gives proofs of a naturally higher toned mind than that of Macbeth. . . . Her frailer frame, and keener feelings, have now sunk under the struggle – his robust and less sensitive constitution has not only resisted it, but bears him on to deeper wickedness, and to experience the fatal fecundity of crime.

This interpretation of Lady Macbeth was admittedly written with hindsight, after performing the part at Drury Lane and elsewhere over a period of more than a quarter-century.[2] Yet from the first the impression she created in the audience was far from this – she inspired sheer awe and terror. Her audience on 2 February 1785 – her benefit night – included Reynolds, Gibbon, Fox, Windham and Burke (who, in his *Reflections on the French Revolution*, was to speak of 'the tears that Garrick formerly, or that Siddons not long since, have extorted from me'). The tears were not for Lady Macbeth, but for the line in characterization Sarah and her audiences most favoured: pathos, moral sentiment, and rhetorical fervour and disdain. The whole of wronged womanhood spoke through her voice. In her heart, she still fancied herself in comedy, because she had in private a certain quiet sense of humour. But on the whole it would appear she was unable to project humour, and relied, as so many other and lesser actresses have done, on her beauty and her charm to get her through the lighter kind of play successfully. Few comedies stayed in her permanent repertoire.[3]

Up to the period her brother became acting manager for Sheridan at Drury Lane in 1788, six years after her own successful return to the London stage, the range of her successful parts lay in tragedy and melodrama. In Shakespeare she had featured in London in *Measure for Measure* (Isabella), *King John* (Constance), *Macbeth* (Lady Macbeth), *Othello* (Desdemona), *The Merchant of Venice* (Portia), *Hamlet* (as Ophelia, though she was later to play the Queen), *Cymbeline* (Imogen), and *King Lear* (Cordelia). Apart from Shakespeare, whom she did not attempt at all during her first London season of 1782–3, and only introduced more extensively after her brother, John Philip Kemble, had arrived to support her, she relied for the most part on the favourite heroines of the period – in particular those in Southerne's *Isabella* (Isabella), Otway's *Venice Preserved* (Belvidera), Rowe's *Jane Shore* (Jane Shore) and *The Fair Penitent* (Calista), Home's *Douglas* (Lady Randolph), Murphy's *The Grecian Daughter* (Euphrasia), Moore's *The Gamester* (Mrs Beverley), and Cumberland's *The Carmelite* (Matilda). Of these only *The Carmelite* was a new play; the rest were all well-tried theatre pieces from an earlier period.

A glance at these characters is sufficient to establish the common threads of characterization which run through them. All are in one way or another wronged wives, except Jane Shore, who is a wronged mistress. Only one play permits a happy end, *The Carmelite*. Of the others, there is one death by starvation (Jane Shore), three by suicide, one by murder, while one ends in despair for a dead husband. In three of the plays desperate complications arise from a situation involving a long-lost husband or son. In two others, the heroine becomes involved in dire circumstances through the faults of a husband – one gambles and is imprisoned for debt, another is imprisoned for conspiring against the state. Three nights a week Sarah paraded her despair, her pleadings, her resentment against the wrongs done her and stilled the house into frozen silence with her emotional rhetoric. She became the embodiment of all women who had been wronged, and the consciences of her self-willed, violent and sentimental audiences were stirred. Women had few enough legal rights at this time, but they had tongues in their heads and used them. Off the stage, Sarah was as submissive a wife as she could be, but on the stage she spoke with an impassioned energy felt by many to have never before been equalled in the English theatre.

Fitzgerald tries to divide the kind of parts in which she appeared during her London career into categories, 'those in which she overwhelmed her hearers with the grandeur and majesty of her impersonating' and those 'when she excited, pleased, and interested them'. In comedy, in which she tried so hard to shine, he admits her to have been 'mediocre, or, at most, intelligent'. Her tragic characters, apart from Shakespeare, he claims were either purely melodramatic, like Mrs Haller, or presented a 'classical dignity' with 'the modern shapes of emotion', like *The Grecian Daughter* and Jane Shore. He believes her outstanding characterizations were Lady Macbeth, Queen Katherine, Constance, and Volumnia, in all of which 'grandeur . . . almost breathed from every motion'. Her concept of Lady Macbeth as comprised in her afterthoughts in retirement he believes to have been wrong, that of a 'tender, beautiful, interesting lady who poisoned her husband's love, who was urged on by ambition and who, after the deed was done, was filled with . . . as much remorse as he was'. In this interpretation, Sarah was evidently ahead not only of her own time, but of Fitzgerald a century later. Yet it was a conception which influenced greatly the manner in which Ellen Terry was to approach the part in Henry Irving's production of 1888.

Her attitude to other, potentially rival, actresses seems to have been as generous as that of Ellen Terry herself; while staying at Shanes Castle in Ireland, she wrote to the Duchess of Leinster on 1 July 1785 about another actress, a Miss Ogilvie:

As I am (unluckily for me) *forced* to believe that *Envy* is the prevalent passion in human nature, there is some cause to doubt, wether the good understanding which has so long subsisted between Miss Ogilvie and myself will not shortly be at an end, for I hear such encomiums on her Dramatic Talents as make me a little uneasy and I beg your Grace will inform her, if she persists in her rivalship we *must* break tho' I rather think it is more likely that I shall love her more and more – perhaps this is having too good an opinion of oneself and there is no answering for what feelings a *powerful rival* might create; this however I am sure of, that people of Genius I cannot help *loving* in any *other* instance.[4]

Like any highly creative actress, she developed the parts she retained in her repertoire as she matured. They grew with her, and until the end of her career she was in the habit of studying them carefully, turn by turn, immediately before each performance. She left nothing to chance, realizing, as her repertoire grew, the truth of Henderson's remark about the great burden on the memory which such varied work demands. Though she did not normally appear more than three times a week in London, the pace increased in the height of the summer tours. But in London during the 1784–5 season at Drury Lane, she appeared in no less than seventeen parts, eight of which were new to her in London. Moving from one long part to another so rapidly, development was correspondingly slow, spread over the seasons and the years.

Description of her as a performer naturally varies. There are the more detailed reactions in the London press which have already been quoted. Though these may reflect prejudice, they spring from some comparative knowledge of the theatre of the time and were meant to excite discussion among the more sophisticated theatregoers. But, like press notices today, they reflect the performance of a single, first night. And there are the recollections, for what they are worth (which is variable) of those who saw her and hastened to record in diaries and correspondence what their reactions were. The longer-term recollections of those biographers who knew her, such as Boaden or Campbell, or of students of the theatre, such as Hazlitt, who saw her in her later maturity, tend to reflect the accumulated image which her performances in particular parts created over the years, the result usually of performances of her middle and later life rather than those of her twenties or early thirties. Then there are the surviving recollections of her professional colleagues, such as Tate Wilkinson, Holcroft or Taylor. They see her as a co-worker, a presence beside them on the stage. All of them bear witness, in one way or another, to the fact that, once she was on the stage, she had the effect of an emotional tornado. She became possessed, and in consequence came to possess her audience.

It is not easy for us today to understand how this was possible when the greater part of what she was playing, apart from Shakespeare, was fustian melodrama which could not survive for more than a few minutes in our contemporary theatre. Neither actors nor audiences were looking for naturalism in the theatre; the nearest they came to this was in the comedies of Sheridan and Goldsmith, or in the better novels of the period. But in the tragedies and melodramas in which Sarah starred so prominently, naturalism was as foreign as it is in 'grand' opera. When Sarah said that what she was looking for in plays, whether new or old, was 'truth to nature', she did not mean naturalism; she meant that the situations and the emotions expressed by the characters should be credible ones which both she and her audiences could accept as true to human nature, however extravagantly they might be expressed. Once she was sure that this was so, she took absolute control of the part, using whatever words were provided to project the passions of the character as an opera singer uses the often inferior words of a libretto as a stepping-stone to the higher emotional levels represented by the music. In other words, she orchestrated the part by means of her high talent in the use of voice and gesture. The fustian verse, so inadequate or even ludicrous when set down in cold print, became unaccountably enriched when she gave her impassioned expression to it. It was sufficient if the play gave her a 'natural' vehicle for such expression. The rest she did herself, supported by her fellow actors, whose responsibility was at least not to let her down, and at best to rise as far as they could to the occasion she inspired. Brereton, judged usually an indifferent actor, apparently caught something of the fire from her lips when he played Jaffier, and was suddenly accounted magnificent.

It is the nature of this wonderful verbal orchestration which we try to discover through the descriptions left us by writers who responded to the conventions of this kind of theatre with as little question as opera-goers apply to the conventions of opera. Performance was measured against performance, traced back in living memory to the work of great players earlier in the century. Garrick's orchestration had been in the direction of a 'closeness to nature' – which does not mean naturalism in the modern sense, but an increase of human credibility in the ways he made his characters speak and the way he invented business for them. They become intensified, sublimated human beings, still rhetorical by our standards, since every passion had to be given its outward, visible sign through the art of 'pantomime', the constant deployment of face and body to reflect and, when necessary, heighten, the expression of the voice. This meant that the whole performance became a conscious, highly wrought work of art, to every phase of which a responsive audience should react with a shared emotion. Only plays of an extraordinary, positive quality, such as Shakespeare's, remained consciously appreciated while the great actors and actresses of those times performed in them. For the most part, the plays became a kind of familiar crutch which an actor and audience kicked aside once the performance had entered upon its inspired way.

It is interesting to look at the way Sarah discussed new plays which she felt to be inadequate. Plays were constantly being submitted to her by amateur writers, especially among her friends and acquaintances, who could think of nothing more glorious than to write a play which she could be induced to sponsor with the management at Drury Lane. Sarah's natural shyness and hatred of embarrassing or hurting her friends became a torture to her when she was forced to consider these inadequate scripts, which she knew she could not bring herself to promote. One of her worst experiences was telling her dear friend Dr Whalley that his play *Astarte* simply would not do. Having read it, she wrote to him on 28 September 1785:

MY DEAR FRIEND, – I feel at this moment in the most painful situation I ever experienced. I tremble to offend you, to disappoint your expectations. But have you not conjured me to be sincere? and shall I not obey you? Yet, was that conjuration necessary? No; for to you I ever have, and always will, lay open my whole heart. I am aware what danger I should incur in the present instance with any living creature but yourself; but you are noble-minded, and will not love me less for my honesty, and the agonising proof I now give you of my at present torturing affection for you. It is impossible

for you to conceive, though you may a little guess, by the length of
this (to me) dreadful preface, how difficult it is to say – how shall I
say it? – 'Astarte' will not do as you and I would have it do! Thank
God! 'tis over. This has been so bitter a sentence for me to pronounce,
that it has wrung drops of sorrow from the very bottom of my heart.
This has been one of the severest trials that friendship and affection
ever experienced. You have already rejected all praise, but such as
should follow every effort of yours, therefore I am silent. Yet, let
me entreat, if you have an idea that I am too tenacious of your
honour, that you will suffer me to ask the opinions of others, which
may be done without naming the author. I must however premise,
that what is charming in the closet often ceases to be so when it
comes into consideration for the stage. Surely, surely, my ever dear
Mr Whalley will not be angry with me. I shall be the most miserable
of women till I hear from you. You have not an idea of what I have
suffered for these three days past, and the very painful struggles I
have sustained between my affection and my delicacy. Let me dismiss
the grievous subject with conjuring you to speak your wishes, and
to rely on my performing them with all the powers of my soul and
body.[5]

In 1787 she had a similar unpleasant task in telling Whalley
that another new play, by Bertie Greatheed, the son of her great
friend and early patron Lady Mary Greatheed, would not do
either. Here her specific criticisms are very clearly expressed:

Your friend, Mrs Piozzi, may be an excellent judge of a poem
possibly, but it is certain that she is not of a tragedy, if she has
really an opinion of this. It certainly has some beautiful poetry, but
it strikes me that the plot is very lame, and the characters very, very
ill-sustained in general, but more particularly the lady, for whom
the author had me in his eye. This woman is one of those monsters
(I think them) of perfection, who is an angel before her time, and is
so entirely resigned to the will of heaven, that (to a very mortal
like myself) she appears to be the most provoking piece of still life
one ever had the misfortune to meet. Her struggles and conflicts
are so weakly expressed, that we conclude they do not cost her much
pain, and she is so pious that we are satisfied she looks upon her
afflictions as so many convoys to heaven, and wish her there, or
anywhere else but in the tragedy. I have said all this, and ten times
more, to them both, with as much delicacy as I am mistress of; but
Mr G. says that it would give him no great trouble to alter it, so that
he seems determined to endeavour to bring it on the stage, provided
I will undertake this milksop lady. I am in a very distressed situation,

for unless he makes her a totally different character, I cannot possibly have anything to do with her.

I beg that you will not, on any account, give the least hint of my having read, or had anything to do with it, for it is impossible to make you conceive the danger of it; and that you will, if you ever write to Mr G—d, enforce this as much as possible. Mrs Piozzi is not to know it. Mr Siddons, who is a much better judge of the conduct of a tragedy than myself, says it will not do at all for the stage in its present state, for the poetry seems to be all its merit; and if it is to be stripped of that – which it must be, for all the people in it forget their feelings to talk metaphor instead of passion – what is there to support it? I wish, for his own sake, poor young man, that he would publish it as it is. I pity him, because I find he has been very much flattered about it, and I can conceive that a conviction of so pleasing an error, must bring with it almost insufferable pain in so unexperienced and unpractised a man, who perhaps knows not at present what disappointment means; it is really pitiable. Adieu, my best beloved. Pray put this letter into the fire directly lest some unlucky chance should bring it to observation.[6]

Campbell, writing for a succeeding generation, is equally emphatic that the literary values of a play were nothing compared with its potential dramatic values – an old enough point, but one usually overlooked when judging the theatrical effectiveness of the bad plays of the eighteenth century:

No performer was destined oftener than Mrs Siddons to expend superlative genius on the acting of indifferent dramas. It is true that she sometimes turned this misfortune into the means of creating additional astonishment. Where there was little or no poetry, she made it for herself; and might be said to have become at once both the dramatist and the actress. Where but a hint of a fine situation was given, she caught up the vague conception, and produced it in a shape that was at once ample and defined; and, with the sorriest text to justify the outpouring of her own radiant and fervid spirit, she turned into a glowing picture what she had found but a comparative blank.[7]

There exists still a copy of *Venice Preserved* which Sarah used, marking up the lines in blue pencil which she felt should be brought out, turning their sickening over-statement into some form of theatrical splendour:

Oh! give me daggers, fire, or water:
How I could bleed, how burn, how drown, the waves

Huzzing and foaming round my sinking head,
Till I descended to the peaceful bottom
Oh! there's all quiet, *here* all rage and fury:
The air's too thin and pierces my weak brain;
I long for thick substantial sleep: *Hell! hell!*
Burst from the centre, rage and roar aloud
If thou art half so hot, so mad as I am.[8]

Boaden, who saw her so frequently in the theatre, gives many examples of how she handled the speeches in her plays.[9] In *The Grecian Daughter*, for instance, when she threatens Dionysus:

> The commanding height and powerful action of her figure, though always feminine, seemed to tower beyond her sex. Till this night we had not heard the full extent, nor much of the quality of her voice. An opportunity occurred, even in the first act, to throw out some of its most striking tones. . . . The audience trembled when, in a voice that never broke nor faltered in its climax, she thus to earth and heaven denounced the tyrant—

> Shall he not tremble when a daughter comes,
> Wild with her griefs, and terrible with wrongs?
> The man of blood shall hear me! – Yes, my voice
> Shall mount aloft upon the whirlwind's wing. . . .

But in this character she had an opportunity to throw out that collected and dignified contempt. . . . It is of all our emotions that I think the most suited to her countenance—

> Think'st thou then
> So meanly of my Phocion? Dost thou deem him
> Poorly wound up to a mere fit of valour,
> To melt away in a weak woman's tear?
> Oh, thou dost little know him!

At the last line there is a triumphant hurry and enjoyment in her scorn, which the audience caught as electrical, and applauded in rapture for at least a minute.

Or in *Jane Shore*:

> Why should I think that man will do for me,
> What yet he never did for wretches like me?

The hopeless sweetness that lingered on to the conclusive rhymes still comes occasionally upon my ear, and I think, if the sub-divisions of our musical scale were more numerous, that I could note down its tune.

Or when Jaffier leaves Belvidera in the care of the conspirators she does not trust, in *Venice Preserved*:

> As she is rising from her knees . . . the alarmed yet searching survey which she took of them was one of those expressions in which the actress writes with characters of fire. . . . The agony of astonishment in which she listens to Jaffier's bequest of her, with the accompanying dagger – the sob of melting reproach upon the words –

> O, thou unkind one!

and the insupportable pathos with which she uttered –

> Don't, pry'thee don't, in poverty foresake me!

prepared the house for the repetition of the word 'Jaffier!' as she is borne off.

Or these moments from *Macbeth*, starting with the reading of Macbeth's letter to his wife:

> She read the whole letter with the greatest skill, and, after an instant of reflection, exclaimed –

> Glamis thou art, and Cawdor – and shalt be
> What thou art promised.

> The amazing burst of energy upon the words 'shalt be' perfectly electrified the house. . . . When the actress, invoking the destroying ministers, came to the passage –

> Wherever in your sightless substances
> You wait on nature's mischief,

> the elevation of her brows . . . the raised shoulders, and the hollowed hands, seemed all to endeavour to explore what yet were pronounced no possible objects of vision.

And the sleepwalking scene:

> all her actions had the wakeful vigour; she laded the water from the imaginary ewer over her hands – bent her body to listen to the sounds presented by her fancy, and hurried to resume the taper where she had left it, that she might with all speed drag her pallid husband to their chamber.

As for her manner in other kinds of play, it is important to realize that while she was still young Sarah was, as Boaden puts it in describing her performance as Mrs Lovemore in *The Way to Keep Him*, 'to the full as lovely' as, in later years, she was impressive in the 'terrible', and as in Ophelia she was 'exquisitely simple'.

Individual reaction to her performances gives us further clues to her style and personality on the stage. It is best, perhaps, to start with the King himself, talking to Fanny Burney, Madame d'Arblay, in 1785:

> 'I am an enthusiast for her,' cried the King, 'quite an enthusiast. I think there was never any player in my time so excellent – not Garrick himself; I own it!' Then coming close to me, who was silent, he said, 'What? what?' – meaning, what say you? But I still said nothing, I could not concur where I thought so differently.[10]

Although initially critical, Fanny Burney had come to admire Sarah's work. She wrote in her diary on 1 February 1788:

> Mrs Siddons played Portia; and charmingly, though not, I think, with so perfect an entrance into the character as I have observed in her performance of some other parts.[11]

Women, however, were not normally as reticent as Fanny Burney, who was later to become much more enthusiastic herself in her appreciation of Sarah. For example, in 1788 she wrote:

> I do think that Mrs Siddons for Vigour of Action, pathetic Tone of Voice, and a sort of Radiance which comes round her in Scenes where strong heroic Virtues are displayed, *never had her Equal*. For Versatility of Genius, or Comprehension of various Characters, Pritchard was greatly her Superior: Add to this that our present Idol is eminently handsome – dear Pritchard's *Person* came against her perpetually – but what a *Mind* she had![12]

Delighting in her enthusiasm, Anna Seward describes Sarah's Rosalind when she writes to Sophia Weston from Lichfield on 20 July 1786:

> . . . the playful scintillation of colloquial wit, which most strongly mark that character, suit not the dignity of the Siddonian form and countenance. Her dress was injudicious . . . an ambiguous vestment, that seemed neither male nor female. [But when she says to Orlando, 'To *you* I give myself – for I am *yours*, she becomes] the whole soul of enamoured transport . . . that mistress of the passions.[13]

An extreme case of enthusiasm was, as we have seen, that of Miss Gordon of Gight, the future mother of Lord Byron, when she saw Sarah perform in *Isabella* during her first visit to Edinburgh in the summer of 1784. Nor, according to Dibden, were the ladies of Glasgow less backward in fainting than those of London when Sarah appeared in their city in August 1785. Genest says of her Isabella:

> Like a torrent she bore down all before her – her person was greatly in her favour, rising above the middle stature, but not too much so – she looked, walked and moved like a woman of a superiour rank – her countenance was most expressive – her eyes so full of information, that the passion was told from her look before she spoke – her voice, tho' not so harmonious as Mrs Cibber's, was strong and pleasing – not a word was lost for want of due articulation . . . she excelled all performers in paying attention to the business of the scene; her eye never wandered from the persons she was speaking to, or at whom she ought to look when she was silent.[14]

Genest, like so many others, records 'the many accidents of persons falling into fits in (sic) the time of her acting'.

Perhaps Mrs Thrale's notes are better calculated to give a sober appreciation of her work. Like Fanny Burney, she refuses to be entirely overcome; in 1789 she wrote:

> Kemble is an agreable Actor, and very sensible and pleasing Man; I love him and his charming Sister sincerely, but have more Sense than to take them for Garrick and Pritchard. – 'Tis a shame even to hear them compared. Mrs Pritchard was *incomparable*, her Merit overbore the want of Figure, her Intelligence pervaded every Sense. . . . Dear Siddons represents only a Lover distress'd or a Woman of Virtue afflicted, with peculiar Happiness . . . her powers are strong and sweet, vigorous and tasteful; but limited and confined.[15]

Of Sarah's Juliet she wrote:

> Mrs Siddons acted Juliet last night. – She does it so *naturally* says someone, so artifically rather said I; but she is a great Performer. . . . The pouting Scene with the old Nurse was the cleverest thing I ever saw – so pretty, so Babyish, *so* charming. Her coaxing Scene in Othello where poor Desdemona innocently pleads for Cassio is of the same kind – prodigiously fine indeed.[16]

Mrs Thrale quotes a friend who wrote the following illuminating description of Sarah's appearance on the stage, especially in *Macbeth*:

> . . . though somewhat large of bone, [she] was thin, and surprisingly graceful. Her countenance might, with strict justice, be called

17. Sarah Siddons. Painter unknown.
(*Victoria and Albert Museum, Crown Copyright*)

18. Elizabeth Inchbald. From an engraving, frontispiece to Boaden's *Memoirs of Mrs Inchbald*, 1833.

19. John Philip Kemble as Vincentio in *Measure for Measure*. Artist unknown. (*Victoria and Albert Musum, Crown Copyright*)

20.   Sarah Siddons. From *The Tragic Muse*, by Sir Joshua Reynolds.
Engraving by W. Holl.

21. John Philip Kemble as Richard III. After William Hamilton.
(*Victoria and Albert Museum, Crown Copyright*)

22. Sarah Siddons. Engraving from the painting by Thomas Gainsborough.
(*The National Gallery, London*)

23. Sarah Siddons. A sketch by George Romney, in oils.

24. Sarah Siddons. By John Downman. (*National Portrait Gallery, London*)

25. Sarah Siddons as Lady Macbeth. (*Photograph by courtesy of the Theatre Collection, Department of Drama, University of Bristol*)

26. Sarah Siddons as Lady Macbeth, by Henry Fuseli.

27.   Sarah Siddons as Mrs
Beverley in *The Gamester*, 1783,
with John Philip Kemble as
Mr Beverley. (*British Museum*)

28.   Sarah Siddons in the character of the Tragic Muse, 1783.
(*British Theatre Museum*)

beautiful. It was composed of the finest proportion imaginable; her mouth was wonderfully expressive of good sense, sweetness, and scorn. Her eyes were brilliant and piercing, and could be seen to sparkle or glare at an incredible distance on the stage: as all must recollect, who saw her as Lady Macbeth, when She rose from her throne at the solemn supper, and was descending to chide her terrified husband. Or when, with swathed jaws, and corpse-like aspect, she stalked in her sleep from the back of the scene. The effect of her eyes was greatly assisted by a power she had of moving her eyebrows, and the muscles of her forehead. By her countenance alone, she could signify anger, revenge, sarcasm, sorrow, pride, and joy, so perfectly, that it was impossible to misunderstand her, though she had not spoken a word. She so constantly acted the character of great personages in affliction, that, on a whole, she had a mournful visage, and an awful tone of voice, very detrimental to the success of her comic attempts; and indeed unfriendly to her effects in the less impassioned scenes of tragedy; or when she played merely genteel women in middle life. At times, in private company, she gave one a notion of a wicked, unhappy Queen, rather than of a purely well-bred gentlewoman.

When I made some such remarks as these to Mrs Piozzi, she said I was partly right; but that her friend, Mrs Siddons, could be infinitely comic when she pleased, and was among her intimates; though anything but a comedian on the boards. She then added a very amusing description of her having a family party, ordering the parlour-door to be made fast, and proceeding to perform most of the part of Sir Anthony Absolute, with astonishing spirit and pleasantry.[17]

Another distinguished writer was Madame de Staël, who expressed through the heroine of *Corinne* her views of Sarah's performance as Isabella:

La noble figure et la profonde sensibilité de l'actrice captivèrent telle-ment l'attention de Corinne, que pendant les premiers actes ses yeux ne se détournèrent pas du théâtre. La déclamation anglaise est plus propre qu'aucune autre à remuer l'âme, quand un beau talent en fait sentir la force et l'originalité. Il y a moins d'art, moins de convenu qu'en France; l'impression qu'elle produit est plus immédiate; le désespoir veritable s'exprimerait ainsi; et la nature des pièces et le genre de la versification plaçant l'art dramatique à moins de distance de la vie réelle, l'effet qu'il produit est plus déchirant.

En Angleterre on peut tout risquer, si la nature l'inspire. Ces longs gémissements, qui paraissent ridicules quand on les raconte, font tressaillir quand on les entend. L'actrice la plus noble dans ses manières, Madame Siddons, ne perd rien de sa dignité quand elle se prosterne contre terre. Il n'y a rien qui ne puisse être admirable, quand une émotion intime y entraîne.

*   *   *   *   *

    Enfin il arriva ce moment terrible où Isabelle, s'étant échappée des mains des femmes qui veulent l'empêcher de se tuer, rit, en se donnant un coup de poignard, de l'inutilité de leurs efforts. Ce rire du désespoir est l'effet le plus difficile et le plus remarquable que le jeu dramatique puisse produire; il émeut bien plus que les larmes; cette amère ironie du malheur est son expression la plus déchirante. Qu'elle est terrible, la souffrance du cœur, quand elle inspire une si barbare joie, quand elle donne, à l'aspect de son propre sang, le contentement féroce d'un sauvage ennemi qui se serait vengé![18]

It is, however, the professionals who give us the greatest accuracy of detail in their descriptions of her at work in the theatre. Charles Mathews describes what she had to put up with when she was in Leeds during a summer season. A rough section of the audience, the croppers from the mills, treated the star actress from London as if she still belonged to some low-class strolling company:

> ... at Leeds, 'Bonny Leids', as John Winter with *bitter irony* termed it, she encountered much annoyance and interruption from that part of the spectators whom it was not possible to exclude. The gentry who came from the surrounding neighbourhood, shared with the performers the drawback of whatever conduct the respective humours of the frequenters of pit and gallery chose to exhibit. These parts of the theatre were generally occupied with what were called 'croppers', and their wives and sweethearts, (namely, the working people in the cloth manufactories of the town,) who were at this time semi-barbarous in their manners and habits, and who moreover held in the most supreme contempt, if not abhorrence, the professors of the art they willingly paid to be amused by. The men would not hesitate, like the Irish, to make their comments audibly, though *un*like the Irish, they were destitute of humour to compensate for their interruptions. It was very painful to the admirers of Mrs Siddons to witness her involuntary submission to such brutal treatment. It was not surprising that the majestic and refined style of her performances should not be appreciated by such people; they would have prized far higher the efforts of a good wear-and-tear pair of lungs, that could 'split the ears of the ground-lings', than the beautiful subdued tones, for which this accomplished

mistress of her art was so celebrated in particular scenes, and which reached the heart by their tenderness.

One night when she had been acting Jane Shore, Mr Mathews, who had been rooted to the spot watching her every look and word, until the curtain fell, was quitting the front of the house, when a man hurrying towards the gallery-door, rather late for the half-price, was accosted by another who was leaving it. 'Eh, Tommy, where beest thou ganging?' – 'I'se ganging to t' play,' replied the comer. 'Well, then, thou may'st ha' my place if thou can'st get it, for I'se ganging hame again.' – 'Why,' asked "Tommy", with anxiety; 'is t' play over?' (meaning the whole night's performance.) 'Nay,' said the other, 'I know not; but I'se tired o't all.' – 'Well,' said his friend; 'but thou'st seed the great Lunnon laker, Missis Siddons, I reckon?' – 'Eh, I know not,' quoth the malcontent; 'I've been there this half-hour, and I seed nought but a fond woman ligging o' top o' t' fleer.' [A foolish woman lying upon the floor; in other words, Jane Shore in her dying scene.]

. . . On one memorable night, however, during her engagement, a *contretems* of a ludicrous nature occurred, for which no part of the audience was answerable. The evening was excessively hot, and Mrs Siddons was tempted by a torturing thirst to consent to avail herself of the only obtainable relief proposed to her at the moment. Her dresser, therefore, despatched a boy in great haste to 'fetch a pint of beer for Mrs Siddons,' at the same time charging him to be quick, as Mrs Siddons was in a hurry for it. Mean while the play proceeded, and on the boy's return with the frothed pitcher, he looked about for the person who had sent him on his errand; and not seeing her, inquired 'Where is Mrs Siddons?' The scene-shifter whom he questioned, pointing his finger to the stage where she was performing the sleeping scene of Lady Macbeth, replied – 'There she is.' To the surprise and horror of all the performers, the boy promptly walked on the stage close up to Mrs Siddons, and with a total unconsciousness of the impropriety he was committing, presented the porter! Her distress may be imagined; she waved the boy away in her grand manner several times, without effect; at last the people behind the scenes, by dint of beckoning, stamping, and calling in half-audible whispers, succeeded in getting him off with the beer, part of which in his exit he spilled on the stage; while the audience were in an uproar of laughter, which the dignity of the actress was unable to quell for several minutes.

When the night's performance had closed, the boy was taken aside and severely lectured by the prompter, upon his stupid conduct. Winter, who was a sort of patron to him, was present during his correction, and when it was over, patted the boy upon the shoulder mildly, saying in mock solemnity of tone, – 'Eh, Moses, ma bairn, let me gi' thee a piece of advice, and be sure ye recollect it all the days o' thy life. Niver go upon t' stage, Moses, ma lad, without thy name's i' t' bill.'[19]

Tate Wilkinson, however, gives the most complete description of these provincial tours. Sarah appeared in his principal theatres during the summer of 1786, when she was acknowledged to be the greatest lady of the London stage. Those towns with theatres belonging to Wilkinson's circuit in Yorkshire which she was not to visit took the manager to task most severely, while Sarah made a small fortune out of those towns where she did appear. Wilkinson began by contrasting the professionalism of her behaviour with the angry whims of Mrs Crawford, who had been performing recently in Leeds and York; Mrs Crawford, he writes:

. . . loves money, and would, I am assured, have obtained a great deal more, but for her plaguing herself as well as other people, and fretting and fuming at every trifle. How different in a theatre is Mrs Siddons! – she never heeds trouble – if truly indisposed, and possible to rise from her bed, she is certain in her duty to the public. And, as I suppose I am not singular in receiving such kind behaviour, she is a treasure to enter into an engagement with, without adhering to the golden advantages she brings: For in her behaviour she is truly a nonpareil. As a proof – she has not known until she arrived at York, what play she was first to appear in, or what characters she was to act during a course of six plays. If a dress has not arrived in time by the carriers, she sometimes has asked what was to play such a night; never saying such a play will do better than another, or such a part would be too fatiguing, but is always ready to oblige. A good lesson for many great as well as little ladies to attend to.[20]

The actor Charles Young, who normally played the old retainer, Jarvis, in *The Gamester*, told Campbell a story of the effect upon him of Sarah's intensity of performance:

He was acting Beverley with her on the Edinburgh stage, and they had proceeded as far as the fourth scene in the fifth act, when Beverley has swallowed the poison, and when Bates comes in, and says to the dying sufferer, 'Jarvis found you quarrelling with Lewson in the streets last night', Mrs Beverley says, 'No! I am sure he did not!' to which Jarvis replies, 'Or if I did?'' – meaning, it may be supposed, to add, 'the fault was not with my master:' – but the moment he utters the words 'Or if I did?' Mrs Beverley exclaims, 'This false, old man! – they had no quarrel – there was no cause for quarrel!' In uttering this, Mrs Siddons caught hold of Jarvis, and gave the exclamation such piercing grief, that Mr Young said his throat swelled, and his utterance was choked. He stood unable to speak the few words which, as Beverley, he ought to have immediately delivered: the pause lasted long enough to make the prompter several times repeat Beverley's speech, till Mrs Siddons, coming up to her fellow actor, put the tips of her fingers on his shoulders, and said, in a low voice, 'Mr Young, recollect yourself.'[21]

During the 1780s Sarah sat almost continually to a succession of painters. In addition to her portrait as Isabella by William Hamilton undertaken for the 1782–3 season at Drury Lane, and Reynold's *The Tragic Muse* (1784), she was the subject of a fine sketch by Romney in 1783, while in 1785 Gainsborough painted his celebrated portrait, perhaps the most beautiful 'public' representation of her, just as Lawrence's numerous drawings and paintings (fourteen are known to exist) are the best 'private' studies. For Gainsborough she is the *grande dame*, severely beautiful, composed and magnificent in her fashionable clothes. It is well known that he had trouble with her long, Kemble nose, altering and refashioning it to suit his needs. 'Confound the nose,' he exclaimed, 'there's no end to it!' For Lawrence she was the woman at home, and as seen by a man evidently fond of her and who recognized the depth of feeling behind the repose of her face. Hamilton alone was to complete at least five portraits of her, four in theatrical characters – as Isabella, Euphrasia, Jane Shore, and Lady Randolph. But there were many others who painted her, including John Downman, J. K. Sherwin (another Euphrasia), and Thomas Stothard. A sketch verging towards caricature is Rowlandson's celebrated picture of her 'being instructed by her father', whereas outright caricature can be seen in the gross manner of the period by W. Mansell ('Queen Rant') and Gillray ('Blowing up the Pic Nic's'). In that curious instance of genre painting she crouches at the feet of the Devil in Lawrence's notorious *Satan*, while Romney posed her as 'Tragedy' in *The Infant Shakespeare instructed by the Passions*. From many of these works, as well as from other portraits by such artists as Sherwin, Repton, Shireff, Westall, Hone, Shelley, Chinnery, and Collins came a flood of engravings, many of them atrocious, at least to modern eyes, so that every admirer might possess a portrait, from the commissioned painting down to the crudest print. Noted engravers competed with one another to secure the reproduction rights of the best works, and even Sarah herself was drawn into

the tussle over who should engrave *The Tragic Muse* – she wanted
Haward to have the rights, which were however claimed by
Valentine Green, who ended up by calling Reynolds a liar and
so losing the day.[22]

Even if she had wanted it, Sarah had little time left to herself
in which to enjoy any private life. Already there began to be
some doubt, now that her marriage was on the second decade,
that she was altogether happy with her husband, who in 1784 had
entered his forties, and was almost eleven years her senior. It is
customary to denigrate him, but his position was difficult. The
law of the period made him head of the household and master
of his wife's earnings. From a reasonably competent supporting
actor who might have remained acceptable in one or any other
of the better provincial companies, he had declined into the
unexciting and unwanted husband of a woman of genius, who
was proclaimed throughout the land and capable of earning
several thousand pounds a year. It would have required a man of
some imagination, unusual sympathy and generous good humour
to rise graciously with his wife, become her unselfish support in
both public and private, learning meanwhile to become the
skilful administrator of her career and fortune, and at the same
time ready to take her place in some part as an understanding
parent of their growing family of young children. But both
socially and domestically, William Siddons appears to have
been if not exactly a nonentity, at least a man who was out of
his depth. He conducted his wife's business, adequately perhaps,
but without much discretion; from the somewhat cringing and
fussy man revealed in his early letters to Bate and Garrick,
written when he had already turned thirty, he had changed now
to the peremptory and over-sharp bargainer with the provincial
managers. He appears to have been a very nervous man, fond in
his own limited way of his wife and children, relatively good-
humoured, but arbitrary and at times ill-tempered. No doubt
as he grew older and more used to his wife's fame, he felt that he
must assert whatever authority he had left, since he had little
else to do but manage the family affairs. He gave his wife an
allowance out of her earnings, and handled the rest of the money
himself.

The first hint of any domestic trouble between William and
Sarah comes in a significant passage in the reminiscences of the
actor, John Taylor:

I called on her one morning, when I found her in the act of burning some letters of her own which had been returned to her by the executor of the gentleman to whom they had been addressed. As I sat nearer to the fire, she handed them to me as she read them in succession to throw into it. As I was going to dispose of one in this manner, a printed paper dropped out of it, which she must have overlooked. I took it up, and found that it consisted of some verses which had appeared in 'The St James's Chronicle', and which contained some very severe strictures on her character. The name of the subject of this satire was not printed, but appeared in manuscript on the top of the lines in the handwriting of her deceased correspondent. As no real friend of Mrs Siddons could thus invidiously point out the object, it struck me, as I had heard the departed person was a poet, that he had attacked her at one time for the purpose of insidiously defending her at another. She seemed to be surprised and shocked at this discovery, and I then ventured to ask her if her departed friend had ever, like Stukely in the play, endeavoured to excite her jealousy against Mr Siddons. After a short pause, she said she remembered he had once hinted to her that Mr Siddons had a mistress at Chelsea. The mystery then seemed to be revealed, and the design of the writer developed, as Mrs Siddons was at that time in the fulness of her personal beauty. I left her in a state of consternation, and called on her in the evening, when I found her father and mother, to whom the matter had been communicated; but they testified no surprise, and said they had never liked the man, and thought that he had some wicked purpose in view. This anecdote cannot be uninteresting, as it illustrates human nature, and relates to a distinguished and meritorious individual.

I must here pay a short tribute to the memory of Mr Siddons, whose character I always held in high respect. He was a handsome, gentlemanly-looking man, with a good understanding and pleasing and affable manners. . . . Mr Siddons had been overshadowed by the great talents of his wife; but if she had only adorned the domestic circle by her virtues and good sense, he would then have appeared fully upon an equality with such a partner, to all who might have had the pleasure of being acquainted with him. Many cheerful hours I have passed with him and the family. I was for many years in the habit of dining with Mr John Kemble on Christmas-day, and on old Christmas-day with Mr Siddons and his family.[23]

Sarah herself alludes in a letter written to the Whalleys on 13 March 1785 to some troublesome rumours stirred up by a servant who had been dismissed:

Our old Mary, whom you must remember, has proved a very viper.

She has lately taken to drinking, has defrauded us of a great deal of money given her to pay the tradespeople, and in her cups has abused Mr Siddons and me beyond all bounds; and I believe in my soul that all the scandalous reports of Mr Siddons' ill-treatment of me originated entirely in her.[24]

During the autumn of 1784 the family had moved to a pleasant house, No. 14 (later 28) Gower Street, Bloomsbury, of which William eventually acquired the lease until 1814. In March 1785 she wrote to the Whalleys: 'We have bought a house in Gower Street, Bedford Square; the back of it is most effectually in the country, and delightfully pleasant.' The family were to live in Gower Street until 1790, when they sold their lease and moved to 49 Great Marlborough Street in Soho. Two children were to be born to Sarah at Gower Street; one was stillborn. Sarah was pregnant at regular intervals until 1785, when she was thirty-one. After this, she had only one other daughter, Cecilia, born in 1794. When the family moved to Gower Street Henry was already ten, Sarah nine, Maria five, and Eliza Ann two; little Frances Emilia, it will be remembered, had died soon after birth in 1781. After her return to London, there is an allusion in Anna Seward's correspondence to Sarah facing another confinement, of which there is no other known record. It is difficult to see how, in the crowded year of 1783, when she was ceaselessly employed, she could have had a miscarriage without some public reference being made to it. However, on 27 December 1785 her second son, George, was born, and she did not reappear on the stage until 26 February 1786, when she played Belvidera at a benefit performance at Covent Garden for the family of her old friend Henderson, who had died the previous November. On 12 January 1786 she wrote to Whalley:

All is well over, my dear Mr Whalley. I have another son, healthy and lovely as an angel, born the 26th of December; so you see I take the earliest opportunity of relieving the anxiety, which I know you and my dear Mrs Whalley will feel till you hear of me. My sweet boy is so like a person of the Royal Family, that I'm rather afraid he'll bring me to disgrace; my sister jokingly tells him she's sure 'my lady his mother has played false with the Prince', and I must own he's more like him than anybody else. I will just hint to you that my father was at one time very like the King, which a little saves my credit. I rejoice that you are well, and have such pleasant society, but I wish to God you would return![25]

In 1788, however, she suffered not only a miscarriage, but the loss of her youngest daughter, Eliza Ann. The miscarriage occurred whilst she was appearing at Drury Lane in *The Regent*, the play by Bertie Greatheed she had so much criticized in her letter to Whalley. The play, which opened on 20 March, seems, according to some reports, to have been quite well received; according to Campbell it ran twelve nights, though not with Sarah as the too-virtuous heroine Dianora. She was taken ill on the second night. The full text of Mrs Thrale's diary, published only in 1951, throws a little more light on what happened. First of all, Mrs Thrale claims in her notes of 4 April that the play was highly successful – 'everybody agreed,' she writes, 'that such a first Tragedy has never been presented to an English Audience since Shakespeare's *Romeo and Juliet*.' Bertie Greatheed, who Mrs Thrale describes as 'good, flexible, and kind-hearted', suffered a grave disappointment – 'Siddons suddenly taken ill had miscarried on the very day that should have brought him his first Benefit – and now God knows when she may be up again. . . . Mean Time Siddons has lost a live Child, besides that to whom life had never been given.'

The mystery which so much puzzled Sarah's later biographer, Mrs Parsons, concerned the birth and even the existence of Sarah's third daughter, Elizabeth Ann Siddons, who died at the age of six about the same time as her mother suffered this miscarriage. No record of her birth survives in Bath or anywhere else. Sarah alludes to her death in a letter written on 18 April to a Mrs Soame in which she refers to 'the loss I have sustained'.[26]

A few rare references to this child occur in the various letters kept by Whalley; for example:

> Your little Eliza is as fair as wax, with very blue eyes, and the sweetest tuneful little voice you ever heard. (28 September 1785)
> My children are all well, clever, and lovely. . . . I want sadly to find a genteel, accomplished woman to superintend my three girls under my own roof. (11 August 1786)
> My family is well, God be praised! . . . At Christmas I bring my dear girls from Miss Eames, or rather, she brings them to me. Eliza is the most entertaining creature in the world; Sally is vastly clever; Maria and George are beautiful; and Harry is a boy with very good parts, but not disposed to learning. My husband is well. . . . (1 October 1786)

The children's education, as the correspondence with the

Whalleys already quoted shows, was in the hands of a Miss Eames. On 28 September 1787 she rushed off a letter to Whalley which began:

> Though I have but a moment of my own, being just in the middle of the hurry of placing my children at a fresh school, I cannot prevail upon myself to defer giving you the pleasure of hearing that Mr Siddons is entirely out of danger, though still so weak as to be unable to see any living soul. I have been a little feverish with watching and anxiety, but a few saline draughts have restored me. . . . Miss Weston is in town, but Mr Siddons' illness has deprived me of the pleasure of seeing her. It is now I think a full month since I have seen the face of any body out of my own family, and Mr Siddons' progress is so very slow, that at present I have little prospect of living any other life.[27]

Eventually, in 1790, she placed Sally and Maria in a 'finishing' school in Calais.

It is from this period that we have a much more intimate picture of Sarah's life through those letters which have been preserved, together with the diaries and correspondence of her friends, in particular Mrs Thrale. She was frequently in demand by the Royal Family, to whom she had, as we have seen, been appointed a kind of official 'reader'. She received no payment for her performances. Lady Harcourt undertook certain of the arrangements for these visits to Court; Lord and Lady Harcourt were among the more aristocratic of her patrons, whom she soon came to regard as respected friends. They had a fine estate at Nuneham, near Oxford, where from 1785 she and her family were frequent guests. She wrote to Lord Harcourt from Gower Street in 1785:

> My dear Lord, – I do myself the pleasure to inform you that I shall have the happiness – no, that's not expressive of what I mean – I mean to say the honour and glory of obeying the commands of our good and gracious Queen next Wednesday, for which triumph I can never enough thank my charming Lady Harcourt; and if you would both do me the honour to drink your tea in Gower Street next Sunday, you would greatly add to the favours you have already conferred.[28]

In the notes she wrote for Campbell, Sarah gives more details of this act of patronage, and of a royal visit to Nuneham:

> Afterwards I had the honour of attending thier Majesties at

Windsor also. The Readings there were arranged in the appartments of my dear and honoured friend, Lady Harcourt, whom I had lately seen as the noble and majestic Hostess of Nuneham, doing the honours of her splendid mansion when the King and Queen and several of the younger branches of the Royal family came while I was on a visit there. They were so delighted with their loyal and noble Hosts, and so charmd with all they saw, that thier attendants were sent back to Windsor for what was necessary for three days, and even *then* they were loth to depart. One may imagine the usual style of Magnificence in which they livd, which was but little deranged by the unexpected arrival and continuance of such illustrious guests.

I was then on my anual visit to this beauteous place.[29]

Sarah also hastened to describe the visit in a letter to Whalley dated 28 September 1785:

The Queen has been graciously pleased to admit me to her presence twice, at her house in town; and the other day, when I was on a visit to Lady Harcourt, they came there and stayed all night. They saw me twice in the course of the day, and the whole of the family who were present overpowered me with their condescension and goodness. It is impossible for words to express their goodness. I have read to them three times, and the other day her Majesty very graciously sent me a box of powders, which she thought might be of use to me, and which she said I need not be afraid of, as she always took them herself when in my situation. These very superior honours, as you may suppose, create me many enemies; but it was always so, and I must bear their malignity with the best grace I can.[30]

Fanny Burney, Madame d'Arblay, found herself, when she was in attendance to the Queen, responsible on August 15 1787 for looking after Sarah when on a Court visit to Windsor. She describes it in her diary; the Queen, she wrote:

. . . told me Mrs Siddons had been ordered to the Lodge to read a play, and desired I would receive her in my room.

I felt a little queer in the office; I had only seen her twice or thrice, in large assemblies, at Miss Monckton's, and at Sir Joshua Reynolds's, and never had been introduced to her, nor spoken with her. However, in this dead and tame life I now lead, such an interview was by no means undesirable. I had just got to the bottom of the stairs, when she entered the passage gallery. I took her into the tea-room, and endeavoured to make amends for former distance and taciturnity, by an open and cheerful reception. I had heard from sundry people (in old days) that she wished to make the acquaintance, but I thought it, then, one of too conspicuous a sort for the quietness I had so much difficulty to preserve in my ever-increasing connections.

Here all was changed; I received her by the Queen's commands, and was perfectly well inclined to reap some pleasure from the meeting. . . .

I found her the heroine of a Tragedy, – sublime, elevated and solemn. In face and person, truly noble and commanding; in manner, quiet and stiff; in voice, deep and dragging; and in conversation, formal, sententious, calm, and dry. I expected her to have been all that is interesting; the delicacy and sweetness with which she seizes every opportunity to strike and to captivate upon the stage had persuaded me that her mind was formed with that peculiar suscepti-bility which, in different modes, must give equal powers to attract and to delight in common life. But I was very much mistaken. . . .

Whether fame and success have spoiled her, or whether she only possesses the skill of representing and embellishing materials with which she is furnished by others, I know not; but still I remain disappointed. . . . She appeared neither alarmed nor elated by her summons, but calmly to look upon it as a thing of course, from her celebrity.[31]

Sarah read from the play *The Provoked Husband*, and then left to spend a week with the Harcourts at St Leonards.

Sarah's friendly relations with the Harcourts began at least as early as 1784; on 26 September of that year, Sarah sent Lady Harcourt one of her most delightful, informal letters about nothing in particular:

Was there ever such stupidity? Good God! if I had but called at the lodge – well, I deserve my disappointment; but I knew, my dear Lady Harcourt, the occasion that *must* call you away, and was not certain how long the etiquette of Court might detain you; so that, after some vexation, and then comfort, in the hope of catching you for a moment in town. . . . I called at Harcourt House the next day, but think on my disappointment when the porter told me his lord and lady were gone out of town. I lifted up my hands and eyes, you know how; my lord too can guess, who does not disdain a little fidget any more than myself, you know. . . . Presently your very dear and kind letter was put into my hand, which did me infinitely more good than all the salts, sal volatile, &c., in London could have done.[32]

An undated letter survives from 1787 addressed to Lord Harcourt, in which she invites them both to dine at Gower Street and hopes that they may exchange portraits. The summer visits to

Nuneham were sandwiched in between her numerous provincial tours. After one of these, in an undated letter to Lord Harcourt, she writes that she has taken to modelling portrait-heads in clay:

I cannot tell you how sorry I am to leave Nuneham, or rather to leave you and Lady Harcourt, for though I think the situation as beautiful as it can be, I feel that *place* has less to do with my happiness than I could imagine, for since you and Mr Siddons have left me to contemplate its beauties accompanied only by Maria, I heartily wish myself even in London, which I should at all times detest but for the friends I see there; my spirits are not equal to, or my internal resources are too few, for a life of solitude. . . . I have employed all this dismal day in devising little comforts for my next summer's residence here, and in finishing my model; and will you, my dear lord, allow it the honour of your protection till I can find some means of having it conveyed to town? In all events, you will find the poor little head standing on your table. . . . I can never be sufficiently thankful for the large share I have enjoyed this summer.[33]

Only one thing seems to trouble her about the Royal Family – the relationship of the Prince to Mrs Fitzherbert. About this she wrote to Whalley on 12 January 1786, shortly after the birth of her son George:

I have no news for you, except that the Prince is going to devote himself entirely to a Mrs Fitzherbert, and the whole world is in an uproar about it. I know very little of her history, more than that it is agreed on all hands that she is a very ambitious and clever woman, and that 'all good seeming by her revolt will be thought put on for villany', for she was thought an example of propriety. I hear, too, that the Duchess of Devonshire is to take her by the hand, and to give her the first dinner when the preliminaries are settled; for it seems everything goes on with the utmost formality; provision made for children, and so on. Some people rejoice and some mourn at this event. I have not heard what his mother says to it. The Royal Family have been nearly all ill, but are now recovering, and they graciously intend to command me to play in *The Way to Keep Him*, the first night I perform. They are gracious to me beyond measure on all occasions, and take all opportunities to show the world that they are so.[34]

Her closest friendship was undoubtedly with the Whalleys, whom she had known since her days in Bath. She writes primarily to Whalley, rather than to his wife, no doubt because of the link his artistic dilettantism represented. No one would worry about their wholly literary friendship; Sarah was as above suspicion as Caesar's wife, and Whalley in his forties was very much a platonic ladies' man. For Sarah he was a confidant who understood her, she felt, probably far better than her husband. She addressed him (and his wife, when she remembered) with an extravagant affection which goes far beyond the flamboyant courtesies of the period. Indeed, it reveals a deep-seated need in her for friendship and understanding, as in her letter of 15 March 1785:

If you could look into the hearts of people, trust me, my beloved and ever-lamented friends, you would be convinced that mine yearns after you with increasing and unalterable affection. See there now – how have I expressed myself? That is always the way with me: when I speak or write to you, it is always so inadequately, that I don't do justice to myself; for I thank God that I have a soul capable of loving you, and trust I shall find an advocate in your bosoms to assist my inability and simpleness. You know me of old for a matter-of-fact woman.[35]

She begs Whalley on 11 August 1786 to talk more about himself and his wife, and not to make his letters, as it seems he often did, exercises in literary description of the places he was visiting:

Your last was indeed a very scrambling letter, and I hope you will make amends in your next. I beseech you not to give me descriptions of the country, for I am totally uninterested in such accounts, and I grudge the room they take up in some of your letters, which might be so much more satisfactorily filled up with the most trifling accounts of your dear selves: all that relates to you is interesting, but I don't care sixpence about situation, vegetation, or any of the ations.[36]

But the Whalleys were not the easiest correspondents to keep track of in their movements both on the Continent and in England; the postal service of the day was not calculated to keep pace with such ardent tourists. Sometimes letters became lost, and Sarah, in a panic that she had done something to offend them, seems driven almost to distraction for fear she might be losing contact with the friends she valued so much. She writes on 11 November 1785:

My hand ceases to tremble, and my heart to sink and palpitate, but your goodness still blinds my eyes with tears. My happiness at this moment overpays me for long, long sufferings, and the most agonising suspense. In short, I am in such a tumult of joy, that I shall almost literally obey your injunction, my best, my noblest friend; for these appellations can belong to no one so properly as to your glorious self. My heart is so full, I cannot give vent to my feelings in anything like coherent language; but may the happiness you have given to it be returned a thousand and ten thousandfold to your own breast! My dearest Mrs Whalley, why did you not write a word of comfort to your unhappy friend? Oh, tell her she must set my heart entirely at rest, – yet are you not one soul? You are, and I will be happy. Did you, or did you not, my most honoured, receive two letters from me when I was in Edinburgh this summer? for you have never mentioned them, and I cannot bear that you should think me guilty of the wretched indolence that I know you do a little suspect me of.[37]

It is in these letters to the Whalleys that her essential simplicity, even her domesticity can be found. The woman who dominated the London stage appears to have worried herself to death over trifles in her private relationships. She wrote to Whalley on 24 August 1787:

Though I have not a moment's time just now, I cannot forbear conjuring you to believe, that I have written to you three times since the receipt of your last dear letter, and have been miserable at not hearing from you. I was posting off this very morning (had not the sight of your precious writing prevented me) to enquire for you of our dear Mrs Jackson. I perceive that I was misled, and that my letters, written in the warmth and sincerity of affection, may at this moment be exposed to the gaze of the vulgar in some post-office in Glo'stershire, for they were addressed to you at Winscombe, Glo'stershire. I wish I could get them again, with all my heart, for I am afraid that you will by some chance recover them, and I own I am vindictive enough to withhold such a gratification from you as long as possible. Will you never know me? Don't you remember the injustice you did me two years ago, when I had written twice in the space of six weeks from Edinburgh? For heaven's sake, impute anything to me rather than suppose that any earthly circumstance of wealth, or honour, or grandeur, or any other nonsense of the kind, can abate my esteem and love for you. I have had a thousand horrible fancies about you and my dear Mrs Whalley, and, in short, you can no otherwise make me amends but by promising me faithfully to date your letters in future. Had you done so now, you would have saved yourself the crime of unjust suspicion, and me the torture of anxiety and the woundings of your reproaches. Here are letters and parcels for you; what shall I do with them?

Give a thousand loves to Mrs Whalley for me.[38]

As for herself, Sarah gives some news of the family, such as
the children's health and education, and a little gossip about the
love affairs and marriages of her sisters, which usually come as a
relief to her; for example, on 15 March 1785: 'My sister Frances
is not married,' she wrote to Whalley,

> . . . and I believe there is very little reason to suppose she will be
> soon. In point of circumstances I believe the gentleman you mention
> would be a desirable husband; but I hear so much of his ill-temper,
> and I know so much of his caprice, that though my sister, I believe,
> likes him, I cannot wish her gentle spirit linked with his.

This refers to George Steevens, the dramatic critic and
Shakespearean commentator, who thought Frances had a mind
'in every way stronger and more cultivated than her sister's', and
took what opportunities he could of celebrating her at the expense
of Sarah.[39] Again, on 28 September the same year, Sarah wrote:
'My sister Elizabeth is married very well to a Mr Whitlock, a
very worthy actor.' Whitlock was one of the managers of the
company in Chester. On 11 August 1786 she wrote again of
Frances:

> Yes, my sister is married, and I have lost one of the sweetest com-
> panions in the world. However, I am not so selfish as to wish it
> otherwise. She has married a most respectable man, though of but
> small fortune, and I thank God that she is off the stage; this is a
> younger brother of the traveller, and as unlike him in every particular
> as it is possible.[40]

The respectable man was, of course, Francis Twiss, another and
far better-tempered dramatic critic, a profession for which
Frances obviously showed great partiality. On 1 October 1786
Sarah wrote: 'My family is well, God be praised! My two sisters
are married and happy. Mrs Twiss will present us with a new
relation towards February.' Frances Twiss was later to establish
a fashionable school in Bath. Sarah was evidently thankful her
sisters were safely bestowed and away from the stage to which she
had herself brought them, a kindness which, as Boaden points out,
was an error in tactics:

> I must think it injudicious in the branches of the Kemble family to
> croud as they did to London. It was unlikely that any very strong
> dissimilarities should exist in their persons: as far as they resembled
> each other, in the same play they defeated the purposes of exhibition.[41]

Sarah opened her heart to the Whalleys about her personal ambitions which accounts to some extent for the hard bargaining she and William conducted over her fees in the provincial theatres. Her desire was to win some kind of permanent security for her family in as short a time as possible, since like many people who achieve sudden fame, she did not at first believe that it could last. She was in constant fear that some other young actress might displace her with the public, or that she would for some other reason fall from favour. This explains her panic when she suffered unpopularity over the Digges and Brereton affairs. Her sole objective, she claimed, was to amass £10,000 in savings, and acquire a country cottage. This cottage became a kind of symbol to her, alternately rising and receding with her hopes, her castle in the air:

> Now, I'll begin my cottage again: it has been lying in heaps a great while, and I have shed many tears over the ruins; but we will build it up again in joy. You know the spot that I have fixed upon, and I trust I have not forgotten the plan! Oh! what a reward for all that I have suffered, to retire to the blessings of your society. (To the Whalleys, 15 March 1785)[42]

> With what transport do I look forward to the time when we three meet again in the dear, dear cottage! I have three winters' servitude, and then, with the blessing of God, I hope to sit down tolerably easy, for you know I am not ambitious in my desires. (To the Whalleys, 11 November 1785)[43]

Finally, she writes in triumph on 1 October 1786:

> I have at last, my friend, attained the *ten thousand pounds* which I set my heart upon, and am now perfectly at ease with respect to fortune. I thank God, who has enabled me to procure to myself so comfortable an income. I am sure, my dear Mrs Whalley and you will be pleased to hear this from myself.[44]

It is evident that, when their various wanderings brought them together, the two families, or some of their members, met and even stayed together whenever they could, either in London or the countryside. Mrs Thrale, for instance, notes in her diary on 1 May 1787 that the Whalleys had come over from Brussels: 'They live with Mrs Siddons whilst in London,' she says, and then adds, finally succumbing to the universal opinion, 'How charming that dear Mrs Siddons is! off the Stage as well as on.'[45]
But Sarah's many friends created some difficulties for her.

For instance, there was Mrs Thrale herself insisting upon writing
an unwanted epilogue for Bertie Greatheed's unwanted tragedy,
The Regent, which he so dutifully kept revising in his earnest
endeavour to meet Sarah's rather embarrassed criticisms. Sarah
was a fairly regular guest of the Greatheeds at Guy's Cliffe,
where Bertie, now married, still lived. She writes of one of these
visits in a letter to Whalley on 18 October 1787:

> I do not think it is likely that we shall meet in Bath next spring;
> but do you know that I am grown to love Mr and Mrs Greatheed
> very much, and perhaps not a little the more than I otherwise should,
> because they seem so entirely sensible of the worth of my best-
> beloved friends. We parted on Saturday with the most fervent
> wishes that we might altogether meet one day at Guy's Cliffe,
> whither they have so kindly and earnestly invited Mr Siddons to
> recover himself, and he will be at that truly charming, and to me
> uncommonly interesting, place next Wednesday. I think he is a
> great-minded man, and she, though not quite so charming in point
> of mind, yet equal perhaps in more essential points.[46]

Bertie Greatheed's play, *The Regent*, was, as we have seen,
finally produced at Drury Lane in March 1788, but six months
before this Mrs Thrale had slipped her Epilogue into Sarah's
unwilling hands. Mrs Thrale wrote in September:

> I have written an Epilogue for Mr Greatheed's Tragedy, but it
> won't do for Mrs Siddons she says, so it must be changed I trow.
> Let nothing ever tempt me to write for the Stage, no Patience can
> hold out against their Objections and their Criticisms and their
> Mock-Importance – they teize Mr Greatheed to Frenzy.[47]

Nevertheless, Sarah went to dine with Mrs Thrale on 11 October,
though the Epilogue was still in doubt.

Her reputation now permanently assured, even in her own
eyes, Sarah had come to hate any kind of worry or trouble.
This accounts for her continual, lengthy explanations of her side
in the bad relations she had with Whalley's friend Pratt, the
importunate bookseller from Bath who fancied himself as a
dramatist and writer of telling Epilogues.[48] Her success had led
him to try to make use of her as a channel for getting his plays
produced, and, as we have seen, he had borrowed money from
her and William. The trouble with Pratt developed, his vicious
small-mindedness matched by her obstinacy, though contact

between them was never entirely severed. Why, she reasoned, should she be the first person to make the move towards a reconciliation when, as she firmly believed, he was wholly in the wrong? But the affair troubled her, and she wrote many revealing pages defending her position to Whalley:

I have never seen Mr Pratt since I heard from you, but he discovers his unworthiness to my own family; he abuses me, it seems, to one of my sisters in the most complete manner. How distressing is it to be so deceived! . . . I must beg you will not mention (I believe I am giving an unnecessary caution) anything I have told you concerning Mr Pratt. I would not wish him to know, by any means, that I have been informed of his last unkindness, because it might prevent his asking me to do him a favour, which I shall be at all times ready to grant, when in my power. I must tell you that after the very unkind letter he sent me, in answer to mine requesting the ten pounds, I never wrote to or heard from him until about three months ago, when he wrote to me as if he had never offered such an indignity, recommending a work which he had just finished to my attention. He did not tell me what this work was, but I had heard it was a tragedy. To be made a convenient acquaintance only, did not much gratify me; but, however, I wrote to say he knew the resolution I had been obliged to make (having made many enemies by reading some, and not being able to give time to read all tragedies), to read nobody's tragedy, and then no one could take offence; but that if it was accepted by the managers, and there was anything that I could be of service to him in (doing justice to myself), that I should be very happy to serve him. I have heard nothing of him since that time till within these few days, when he wrote to my sister Fanny, accusing me of ingratitude, and calling himself the ladder upon which I have mounted to fame, and which I am kicking down.

What he means by ingratitude I am at a loss to guess, and I fancy he would be puzzled to explain; our obligations were always, I believe, pretty mutual. However, in this letter to Fanny, he says he is going to publish a poem called 'Gratitude', in which he means to show my avarice and meanness, and all the rest of my amiable qualities, to the world, for having dropped him, as he calls it, so injuriously, and banishing him my house. Now, as I hope for mercy, I permitted his visits at my house, after having discovered that he was taking every possible method to attach my sister to him, which you may be sure he took pains to conceal from us, and I had him to my parties long after I made this discovery. In short, till he chose to write this letter, which I disdained to reply to, he called us usual. He had the modesty to desist from calling on us from that time, and

now has the goodness to throw this unmerited obloquy on me. I am
so well convinced that a very plain tale will put him down, that his
intention gives me very little concern. I am only grieved to see such
daily instances of folly and wickedness in human nature. It is worth
observing, too, that at the very time he chose to write this agreeable
letter, I was using my best influences with Mr Siddons to lend him
the money I told you of before. I find he thinks it is not very prudent
to quarrel with me, but has the effrontery to think that I should
make advances toward our reconcilement; but I will die first. 'My
tow'ring virtue, from the assurance of my merit, scorns to stoop so
low.' If he should come round of himself (for I have learnt that best
of knowledge, to forgive), I will, out of respect of what I believe he
once was, be of what service I can to him; for I believe he meant
well at one time, when I knew him first, and the noblest vengeance
is the most complete. Once more, your fingers on your lips, I pray![49]

Considering the great strain placed upon her, both as an actress
and as the mother of a growing family, she seems to have maintained a fair measure of correspondence, particularly with the
Whalleys. Although the general standards of public health
improved greatly during the latter part of the eighteenth century,
and London was reputed to have become one of the cleanest
cities in Europe, most people were subject to ill-health, especially
to colds and influenza in the winter, while the delicate suffered
from tuberculosis. From the age of thirty, Sarah herself, strong
though she must have been in her youth, began to become
subject to occasional illness; she wrote to the Whalleys on 23
March 1787: 'I am quite well after an illness of ten months. It
was not the malady you suspected, but a miserable nervous
disorder.' According to Boaden, 'it became apparent that her health
could not sustain any long continuance of such prodigious efforts
as she had made during her first season. She frequently fainted
away at the close of her performances, and it was long before she
was sufficiently recovered to be supported into her dressing-room.'
Such failure in health and strength, together with sickness in other
members of the family, inevitably disrupted her professional life,
as had happened in Dublin in 1784. On 20 July 1787 she wrote
from Edinburgh to her friend, Sir Charles Hotham:

My poor Harry was seiz'd the very night before we had proposed
setting out for Edinburgh with a violent scarlet fever the Symptoms
for some time very alarming (but thank God they soon subsided)
which detained us in Town for a week. . . . I hope and trust it is

over, for the present we are all well. I am the better for Sea-bathing.
. . . We go on very successfully here, and in a fortnight we shall be
at Glasgow; from thence, as I find myself pretty well and as there
is little likelihood of my going there afterwards . . . I shall go to
Norwich and play a few nights where I shall probably put two
hundred pounds in my pocket. This is at present a secret, and you
my dear Sir Charles are well enough acquainted with the *Theatric
politics* to know the necessity of being a little mysterious sometimes.[50]

Postponements in the appearance of a star actress would cause
considerable dislocation in the provincial theatres, since the
boxes were usually booked in advance, as Sarah's letter to
Whalley of 11 August 1786 shows:

I leave this place for York next Tuesday, where I shall be about
a month. . . . It has been impossible to get a place in the boxes for
these six months past at York; they were all taken on the supposition
of my playing there long before the affair was settled.[51]

William's health, too, was declining. John Kemble wrote to
Sir Charles Hotham from London on 19 September 1787:
'Mr Siddons has been confin'd to his bed with a violent though
slow fever for some time; he begins however to improve and we
think him out of all danger.'

Sarah was staying with the Greatheeds at Guy's Cliffe in
September 1788 when, with a suppressed excitement most
unusual in her, she was able to send momentous news to Sir
Charles Hotham in a letter dated 22 September:

Tho' I have nothing to do I find myself more busy than ever. I
returned to Guy's Cliff last Friday, found my children and my
friends as well as possible and of course myself in good spirits, and
not the worse for having put fifteen hundred pounds into my pocket
this Summer.

Now let me tell you, my dear Sir, that nothing could be more
flattering than the honours done to me by your noble brother and
Sister at Norwich, for which I am infinitely oblig'd tho' so unfortunate as to be unable to profit by their goodness.

And what do *you think* and you my dear Lady *Dorothy*, aye and
you Miss Hotham, if you are at charming Dalton, where I wish I
could fly to tell you this Secret with which I am ready to burst,
and which fills me with joy and fear and agitations of all sorts and
kinds, for God knows, how he will be able to go thro' such a fag as
it will be, you are all crying '*the deuce take her what can she mean?*'

Why then this I mean, John Kemble is Deputy Manager at Drury Lane this Winter – now the murder's out!

I snatched up my pen the instant I rec'd his letter to tell you these agreeable news, and with kindness and best wishes I this instant take my leave, for dinner is going in and my appetite is keen.[52]

The great quarter-century of the Kemble family partnership at Drury Lane, which was to continue later at Covent Garden, was about to begin.

d. John Philip Kemble.

5

The Kemble Partnership

===========⟨∾∽∾⟩===========

JOHN PHILIP KEMBLE'S succession to executive management at Drury Lane represented an extraordinary measure of success. He was thirty-one. He had come to Drury Lane from the provinces only five years earlier, in 1783, at the age of twenty-six, after his season in Dublin. At Drury Lane there were, as we have seen, a number of actors of some status and favour with the town – Smith, Palmer and King among them – while Henderson, the greatest actor of the period, remained at Covent Garden until his death in 1786. There was little to oppose the rise of a new, young actor with the appearance, manner, intelligence and authority which Kemble so rapidly assumed once he had the stage at Drury Lane at his disposal. He was, however, unable to take over the established parts of the older actors; he was forced to strike out on his own, playing apart from his sister, as he did in *Hamlet*, the play in which he first appeared in an interpretation which caused much discussion. John Taylor, as an old and experienced actor, gives his own, frank reaction to Kemble's initial performance:

I was, at first, so little an admirer of John Kemble's performance of 'Hamlet', that considering it stiff, conceited, and unnatural, I wrote four epigrams in ironical commendation of it, and inserted them together in a public print which I then conducted. The late Mr Francis Twiss, who took a strong interest in the welfare of Mr Kemble, introduced me to him in the lobby of Drury Lane Theatre. I had just before seen him point Kemble's notice to me, and heard him whisper the word epigrams: I was, therefore, not prepared for the unaffected civility with which he addressed me. We immediately fell into conversation, and I remember that Mr Kemble very soon began a defence of declamation, stating it as originally constituting one of the chief features of theatrical excellence on the Grecian stage; whence, on reflection, I inferred that he thought I was disposed to require too much of the manners of familiar life in dramatic representations. From that time we often met in company, became well acquainted, and, judging from myself, our intercourse gradually ripened into what is commonly denominated friendship. I am convinced that if he had been born to affluence, and in a higher station, he would have been a distinguished character in political life. He had suffered the privations naturally incidental to a connexion with a provincial theatre; but when he rose to reputation and fortune in the metropolis, he acted with a spirit and liberality that seemed as if he were 'to the manner born'.[1]

Boaden was also there, excited by the prospect of seeing this new production of *Hamlet* – 'the play as originally written by Shakespeare; by which was to be understood no more, than that it was not the miserable alteration of the play, which had so discredited the taste and judgement of Garrick'. Boaden claims that Sarah went out of her way to ensure that all her friends gave him their support:

On Mr Kemble's first appearance before the spectators, the general exclamation was, 'How very like his sister!' and there was a very striking resemblance. His person seemed to be finely formed, and his manners princely . . . there struck me to be in him a peculiar and personal fitness for tragedy. The first great point of remark was, that his Hamlet was decidedly original. He had seen no great actor whom he could have copied. His style was formed by his own taste or judgment, or rather grew out of the peculiar properties of his person and his intellectual habits. He was of a solemn and deliberate temperament – his walk was always slow, and his expression of countenance contemplative – his utterance rather tardy for the most part, but always finely articulate, and in common parlance seemed to proceed rather from organization than voice.[2]

Indeed, some critics complained he was 'too scrupulously graceful'.

Kemble's parts before he took over management in 1788 included Gloucester in *Richard III*, King John (with Sarah as Constance), Othello (with Sarah as Desdemona) – 'he wrapt', says Boaden, 'that great and ardent being in a mantle of mysterious solemnity' – Macbeth (replacing Smith in 1785 for one benefit night only), the Count in *The Count of Narbonne*, and a brilliant King Lear for his sister's benefit in January 1788. His new Lear was described by Boaden, who was in the theatre:

> I have seen him since in the character, but he never again achieved the excellence of that night. Subsequently he was too elaborately aged, and quenched with infirmity the insane fire of the injured father. The curse, as he then uttered it, harrowed up the soul: the gathering himself together, with the hands convulsively clasped, the encreasing fervour and rapidity, and the suffocating of the conclusive words, all evinced consummate skill and original invention. The countenance too was finely made up, and in grandeur approached the *most* awful impersonation of Michael Angelo.[3]

Like his sister, Kemble fancied himself in smart comedy, and attempted Sir Giles Overreach in Massinger's *A New Way to Pay Old Debts*, and the fashionable Lord Morden in Holcroft's *Seduction*. Like Sarah, he spent his summers on tour, collecting considerable sums of money, repeating his successes from town, but, according to Boaden, he was frequently underworked at Drury Lane – the reason being that what Boaden calls the 'Garrick School' had 'possession of management, leading characters, the press, and no slender portion of the public'. He had to play Bassanio, for example, to Sarah's Portia in 1786. However, Smith, Kemble's greatest stumbling-block when it came to casting the important parts, retired at the end of the 1787–8 season; Kemble played Macduff to Smith's Macbeth at the latter's farewell benefit in March.

Kemble's approach to his work was really that of the scholar-actor who had used his initial years at Drury Lane to become the intellectual master of what he was attempting to do while still growing in his capacity as a performer. Boaden's reference to this is of great interest, when he compares the artistry of brother and sister at this time:

> Their talents, although they bore a strong family resemblance, differed considerably as to their power, and, in some respects, character. The organ of the brother was weaker than his sister's; he was, besides, very far indeed from his meridian. His studies were ardent, and embraced every thing collateral to his art. No man applied more than Mr Kemble, at the same time that his habits were highly convivial. The mornings he devoted to business, the evenings, not

seldom, to his friends. He wrote out his parts accurately from the authentic copies; he possessed himself, by degrees, of every critical work upon the drama. He was intimate, according to their different habits, with Mr Steevens, Mr Malone, and Mr Reed, the editors and commentators of Shakspeare. On the vast ground of that poet, Mr Kemble, like them, made his stand; and it was fortunate that he did so. Fame was sure to be acquired by contributing any way to that of Shakspeare. The singleness of our object contributes to its attainment. He saw that much was yet to be done in the representations of his plays, and determined, when he should acquire the necessary power, to bend every nerve to make them perfect, beyond all previous example. To do this, he was first himself to study the antiquities of his own and other countries; to be acquainted with their architecture, their dress, their weapons, their manners; and he, by degrees, assembled about him the artists who could best carry his designs into effect. To be critically exact was the great ambition of his life.[4]

Boaden quotes from Sir Joshua Reynolds's discourses a passage on acting, claiming that what Reynolds observes comes close in spirit to what Kemble performed:

I must observe (says that judicious critic in his thirteenth discourse), that even the expression of violent passion, is not always the most excellent in proportion as it is the most natural: so great terror and such disagreeable sensations may be communicated to the audience, that the balance may be destroyed by which pleasure is preserved, and holds its predominancy in the mind; violent distortion of action, harsh screamings of the voice, however great the occasion, or however natural on such occasion, are, therefore, not admissible in the theatric art. Many of these allowed deviations from nature arise from the necessity which there is, that every thing should be raised and enlarged beyond its natural state; that the full effect may come home to the spectator, which otherwise would be lost in the comparatively extensive space of the theatre. Hence the deliberate and stately step, the studied grace of action, which seems to enlarge the dimensions of the actor, and alone to fill the stage. All this unnaturalness, though right and proper in its place, would appear affected and ridiculous in a private room; *quid enim deformius, quam scenam in vitam transferre?*

Such, I know, were the conceptions, which Mr Kemble entertained of his art; and on these principles labouring incessantly through life, he became, at length, the most scientific artist that perhaps ever graced the stage. But a great deal was to be done, to satisfy desires so extensive; he pleased others at a cheaper rate than would gratify himself; and he frequently expressed his dissatisfaction at an imperfect performance, by a very homely phrase – 'I acted to-night THIRTY SHILLINGS a week.'

Like Sarah, he never ceased to work on an established part throughout his career; Boaden comments on this:

> Mr Kemble . . . seemed to me always to consider the work as still to do: he never dismissed a part from his study, as having given to it *all* the consideration he was capable of. To the last of him, Hamlet and Macbeth had still, as he conceived, calls upon him for improvement. . . . Late in his career, I one morning found Mrs Kemble going over Zanga with him as carefully as if it had been a new part: he did not rely even upon his recollection, and in the preparation of his effects left nothing whatever to chance.[5]

Another aspect of the theatre to which Kemble was giving his attention was that of the art of scenic presentation. According to Boaden, he anticipated his later 'archeological' productions, with sets and costumes appropriate to the historical period of the play, by making a prolonged study of the subject:

> King John has revived the exact habiliments of the 13th century, and either as to materials or elegance, the dresses of the mimic scene might have been admitted at the ancient court. The old scenery exhibited architecture of no period, and excited little attention. The powers of De Loutherbourg's pencil were devoted to the decoration of some catching novelty of the time – a picturesque forest might aid the enchantments of Arthur and Emmeline, and an exact view of Tilbury Fort form a background to the sleeping centinels in the Critic; but nothing could be less accurate, or more dirty, than the usual pairs of low flats that were hurried together, to denote the locality of the finest dialogue that human genius ever composed. The error was too universal to admit of a speedy or radical corrective. The vast old stock could not be entirely condemned, and the treasury could seldom bear the expense of any very considerable novelties. The scale of dimension was also too small to admit of magnificent designs. The structure, for it really was one, that latter years saw erected for the play of De Monfort, would have been condemned as unnecessary, or pronounced impracticable by the artists of Garrick's theatre. But the great reform was to take place in those parts of representation, which nothing but propriety can raise above derision or disgust – the whole tribe of mobs, whether civil or military plebeians, and their pasteboard and leathern properties. Whatever credit might be taken by managers, and the

newspapers and playbills gave them much, for liberality in their expenditure, the fact is certain, that the expense which attended one of Mr Kemble's revivals would have defrayed the demands during a whole season of any former management. Such a change in theatrical arrangements he always desired, and through life steadily pursued; until at length he carried his design into complete effect, during his influence as a proprietor in Covent Garden Theatre. I have ventured this slight anticipation here, because it was at the period of which I am treating, that discerning persons saw Mr Kemble destined, at no distant time, to be the manager of Drury Lane Theatre. To this object the wishes of his sister, Mrs Siddons, no doubt powerfully contributed. He now turned his attention to various branches of scenic display, and read with infinite pains every thing that related to his art.[6]

Kemble had taken on a most difficult task in becoming Sheridan's deputy and stage manager. Tom King had suffered enough at the hands of the aggravating, charming, brilliant but utterly dishonest Sheridan. King, says Boaden, had returned to this post at Drury Lane in 1784 after a period of temporary retirement, though he was only in his fifties:

He accepted the management of the stage, disclaiming, however, very particularly, the having any power whatever as to the acceptance or rejection of the usual literary offerings to the theatre. This department was principally assumed by Mr Sheridan himself, who had neither leisure nor inclination to attend to it. Melancholy proofs of this appeared in piles of long forgotten tragedies and comedies, which he had promised to consider, and had never opened. Mr Kemble, whom I one day found sitting very patiently in this great man's library, pointed to this *funeral* pile, and added to his action the declaration of his belief, that in these morning attendances, he had read more of these productions than ever had been or would be read by the proprietor himself.

Sheridan's habit was to keep his visitors distributed variously, according to their rank or intimacy with him. Some, like ourselves, penetrated into the library; others tired the chairs in the parlours; and the tradesmen lost their time in the hall, the butler's room, and other scenical divisions of the premises. A door opening above stairs, moved all the hopes below: but when he came down his hair was drest for the day, and his countenance for the occasion; and so cordial were his manners, his glance so masterly, and his address so captivating, that the people, for the most part, seemed to forget what they actually wanted, and went away, as if they had come only to look at him.[7]

During the period immediately preceding Kemble's assumption of management, King had failed utterly to set up an enterprising season. Boaden says:

> Mr King evidently had too little power to enable him either to form a plan, or carry one into effect. He could get nobody in to attend to him, and property was certainly essential at every step. He was constantly remonstrating with Sheridan, but without the slightest effect.[8]

Sheridan refused, nevertheless, to delegate authority. King, worn out by his efforts, had taken latterly the line of least resistance, which was scarcely to the advantage of standards at Drury Lane.

This was the task Kemble accepted to fulfil in the summer of 1788. He had recently (on 8 December 1787) married Brereton's widow, the actress Priscilla Hopkins, whom he called 'Pop', a pleasant, talkative lady who had been forced to endure her former husband's confinement in the lunatic asylum at Hoxton, where he had died the previous February at the age of thirty-seven. The wedding-day seems to have been rather casually conducted; after the ceremony Kemble was asked where he and his bride (who was to perform that evening) were to dine. Kemble replied that 'he did not know; at home, he supposed'. Some friends, the Bannisters, who were present at the wedding, took pity on the bride and bridegroom and asked them to dinner. While the new Mrs Kemble acted that night with Mr Bannister, Kemble killed time playing with the Bannisters' children until it was time for him to fetch his wife from the theatre and take her to her new home in Caroline Street, Bedford Square. Priscilla Kemble needed to have patience and understanding to live with Kemble, who had as ready an eye for a woman as he had for a bottle of wine. But the marriage was to endure.

Sheridan and Kemble were both highly individual men. In 1788 Sheridan was thirty-seven, and therefore little older than Kemble, but at the early age of twenty-five he had, by characteristically enterprising means, acquired a share in Drury Lane on Garrick's retirement in 1776. The property was then valued at £70,000, of which Garrick held a half share, the other being possessed by Willoughby Lacy, an outsider in theatrical matters. Sheridan, already famous as a brilliant young playwright, set up £35,000 during the early months of 1776, £25,000 of which he obtained from his father-in-law and a Mr Ewart, while somehow managing to borrow the other £10,000 in order to set up this share in his own name. As his early biographer, Thomas Moore, says of him, with a frankness which is as commendable as it is entertaining:

> There was indeed, something mysterious and miraculous about all his acquisitions, whether in love, in learning, in wit, or in wealth. How or when his stock of knowledge was laid in, nobody knew; it was as much a matter of marvel to those who never saw him read, as the mode of existence of the chamelion has been to those who fancied it never eat. His advances in the heart of his mistress were, as we have seen, equally trackless and inaudible; – and his triumph was the first that even rivals knew of his love. In like manner, the productions of his wit took the world by surprise, – being perfected in secret, till ready for display, and then seeming to break from under the cloud of his indolence in full maturity of splendour. His financial resources had no less an air of magic about them; and the mode by which he conjured up, at this time, the money for his first purchase into the theatre, remains, as far as I can learn, still a mystery.[9]

So Sheridan became a sharer in the Drury Lane patent, and, in 1778, bought Lacey out at the cost of a further £45,000. No one seems to know where the money came from. As Moore puts it: 'That happy art – in which the people of this country are such adepts – of putting the future in pawn for the supply of the present, must have been the chief resource of Mr Sheridan in all these later purchases.'

Sheridan, therefore, was a pretty fly customer. He lived like a prince, though he seldom had more money than a pauper. His ready cash was always in transit from one enterprise to another, and the bailiffs were his familiars. Yet who could resist him? His grandfather had been the friend of Swift, while his father was to become the well-known manager of Smock Alley Theatre in Dublin. His mother was a novelist and playwright. From his youth he learned how to exercise charm; he idled his time at Harrow, but was loved by everyone, retaining the lifelong friendship of his schoolmaster, the learned Dr Parr, who recognized his latent gifts. As a young man living with his father and brother Charles in Bath (his mother had died in 1776 and his father, Thomas Sheridan, had moved to Bath in 1770), Sheridan fell in love with a young singer, Elizabeth Linley, a girl of sixteen much sought after by suitors. In 1777, while Thomas Sheridan was away in Dublin,

Sheridan snatched the beautiful Elizabeth from under the hands of one of her more importunate lovers, a Captain T. Mathews, by fetching her in a sedan-chair from her father's house in the Royal Crescent and dashing her off in a post-chaise to London, where Elizabeth was represented to a family friend, Mr Ewart the brandy merchant, as a rich heiress. Elizabeth thought she was being taken to a convent by a chivalrous protector; in fact she was induced by Richard to enter into a form of marriage in a village near Calais in March 1772. The celebrating priest was notorious for his conduct of such informal ceremonies. Sheridan was twenty and Elizabeth just eighteen. Meanwhile her father, enraged at her disappearance because she had concert engagements to fulfil, pursued her to France and brought her back from the retreat in which she had insisted Sheridan should leave her. She withheld from her father the fact that she was supposed to be married.

On his own return to England Sheridan had had to face the wrath of the frustrated Captain Mathews, who had been on the family doorstep ever since the elopement was known. A form of duel followed, Ewart acting as Sheridan's second; the outcome was that Mathews was forced to apologize for vilifying Sheridan's character. The disgrace proved more than Mathews could face, and Sheridan consented to a second meeting. Elizabeth Linley, her married state still a secret, was meanwhile singing at Oxford; Thomas Sheridan arrived from Dublin to look into his son's affairs, while Charles, Richard Brinsley's elder brother, was on the eve of leaving to take up an appointment in the British Embassy in Sweden. Meanwhile, the second duel degenerated into a brawl; the seconds intervened, and the principals retired, Sheridan this time wounded more seriously than Mathews. The news was kept from Elizabeth until her concert engagements were over and she had returned to Bath. The whole affair of the duel was reported in the press, and became the talk of the town, and in her anxiety Elizabeth revealed that she was in fact a married woman. Thomas Sheridan and Thomas Linley were appalled, and both determined to keep their young people apart. Sheridan sent his son to live with friends in Essex, while Elizabeth remained closely guarded by her father, and was eventually taken by him to Dublin. It was the firm intention of both parents to refuse to acknowledge that any form of marriage had taken place, while Richard himself apparently said little or nothing about it. Nevertheless, it would seem that he suffered deeply from jealousy because Elizabeth

was still undertaking concert engagements, even singing in oratorios
at Covent Garden in the spring of 1773. Sheridan slipped up from
Essex and, according to Moore, disguised as a hackney coachman,
drove her home from the theatre. It appears that the couple
quarrelled, and rumours were put about that Elizabeth was soon
to marry again. In April she did remarry, but the bridegroom was
once more Sheridan. Elizabeth's father, though not Sheridan's,
had finally consented to the match. Richard was now of age, and
could do what he liked.

Richard had no money except what his young wife brought
him; a previous, elderly suitor had settled some £3,000 on her.
In 1774 the young couple set up house in Orchard Street, Portman
Square. In spite of their need, Richard refused any longer to let
Elizabeth sing for money. He was determined to maintain his wife
as a gentleman should, and it was outright need which turned him
from an amateur man of letters into the author of *The Rivals*.
He thrust aside his natural indolence and wrote. *The Rivals* was
first produced with indifferent success at Covent Garden in
January 1775; a change of cast, however, brought a change of
fortune, and Sheridan was supposed to have earned some £700
from the piece. In February the play was performed with great
success in Bath. *St Patrick's Day* and *The Duenna* followed in
the same year, before Sheridan's purchase of his share of Drury
Lane. *A Trip to Scarborough* (a version of Vanbrugh's *The Relapse*)
and his masterpiece *The School for Scandal* followed more slowly,
but Sheridan was only twenty-six when he wrote the latter.
The School for Scandal was produced at Covent Garden on 8 May
1777 with Tom King as Sir Peter Teazle, Palmer as Joseph
Surface and Mrs Abington as Lady Teazle. Its success was
absolute. It played consistently throughout May to houses taking
between £195 and £272 a night. The King, of course, went to see it
on the tenth night. But Sheridan's main work as a playwright had
finished by the age of twenty-six. The only other considerable
piece he wrote was *The Critic*, performed in 1779.

Sheridan's interest by now was in the manipulation of money
to his own advantage and the forwarding of his ambitions in
politics. Had he lived in a modern capitalist society he would
have been in his element conducting shady deals, balancing the
losses of one company against the gains of another, and, above all,
in the skilful avoidance of taxes. But he was gambling against
time in making contracts he was in no position to fulfil. As charm-

ing as he was unscrupulous, he proved in the end more than a
match for the honesty of Kemble and the stupidity of William
Siddons.

Sheridan remains a complex man to understand. His fame rests
on plays which he only wrote when he was forced to make some
effort to earn money. Though he delighted in the success they
brought him, he never settled to become a dramatist, and, apart
from the money, he neglected any duties he assumed at the
theatre, such as the reading of playscripts. His heart lay in politics,
while the theatre was at once his cover, or front office – the centre
from which he could turn over a certain amount of money and
build up a permanent network of debt. His later biographer, Lewis
Gibbs, has estimated that while he gave no more than five years to
his career as a dramatist, he was to devote over thirty years to
politics. In spite of his tomb in the Poets' Corner of Westminster
Abbey, it would seem therefore that he might have preferred to
be remembered as a statesman. Nevertheless, he remained manager
of Drury Lane for thirty-three years – until, indeed, it was burned
down in 1809. To his friends he remained a boon companion, and
a brilliant political orator on behalf of the Whigs. He was twice
married, but he was not a faithful husband. His romantic youth
was sufficient to commend him to those women who were happy
to receive him as a lover. The other people who constantly sought
him out were the duns.

Kemble's accession to stage management had not come about
smoothly. Sheridan was just as unreliable when it came to keeping
appointments as he was in fulfilling his obligations to pay his debts.
It needed, says Boaden, a 'Troy siege to secure his attention'.
King had been left in the air, not knowing whether Sheridan
wanted to renew his contract with him or not; he finally took the
law into his own hands, announced his retirement, and on the
same day, before Sheridan could rouse himself to remonstrate
left London for the North of England, leaving the pressmen to
speculate as they liked on this sudden withdrawal from the theatre.
The trouble really lay in Sheridan's refusal to delegate authority
to his manager, while at the same time never being easily available
for consultation or firm in his contractual obligations. The
circumstances of King's retirement on the very eve of the new
season had forced the proprietors to be more precise in the terms
of the hasty appointment of their youthful manager. The usual
rumours circulated among the gossips of the town, and Kemble

thought it wise on 10 October 1788 to issue his own view of his appointment:

To the Public

I find myself arraigned, by an anonymous writer, as having undertaken the management of Drury Lane Theatre under *humiliating restrictions*. I do assure that writer, and the public, that no humiliation degrades my services to those who do me the honour to employ me; and that the power entrusted to me is perfectly satisfactory to my own feelings, and entirely adequate to the liberal encouragement of poets, of performers, and to the conduct of the whole business of the theatre.

The public approbation of my humble endeavours in the discharge of my duty will be the constant object of my ambition; and as far as diligence and assiduity are claims to merit, I trust I shall not be found deficient.

I am happy to add, that I find myself most fairly and ably supported, by the general zeal and exertions of a company of performers so capable of making the stage a source of pleasure and instruction.[10]

In any case, Sheridan was exceptionally preoccupied at this time with politics, since the King's health was in doubt and the question whether or not the Prince of Wales should become Regent exercising the minds of the political leaders. Sheridan was constantly on his feet in the House, and even more closely involved in the discussions taking place offstage. Drury Lane was in consequence left almost entirely to Kemble's discretion. He had a good company at his disposal; though both King and Smith, and Bensley later, were retired, Palmer was still acting, and so were such reliable and experienced players as Farren, Packer and Jack Bannister. On the women's side the position was equally satisfactory; in addition to Sarah herself as the principal attraction, there was the precise and ladylike Elizabeth Farren, for many years mistress of the odd-looking Earl of Derby until she became his Countess in 1797, and that ever delightful and witty comedienne, Dora Jordan, who had been reared and trained by Tate Wilkinson; she had what Charles Lamb called 'a steady, melting eye' as well as a beautiful figure. For twenty-six years she was the mistress of the Duke of Clarence, by whom she had five sons and five daughters, and who gladly shared with her the considerable professional income she earned. Among the supporting actresses at the theatre was the beautiful Mrs Crouch of whose appearance in *Macbeth* Boaden was to write:

The music of Matthew Locke in this tragedy has crowded the stage
with people to sing it; and in the crowd beauty, formerly and since,
forced its way into notice. The Witch of the lovely Crouch wore a
fancy hat, powdered hair, rough, point lace, and fine linen enough
to enchant the spectator. Perhaps in her vindication it may be
allowed, that in so enormous a rabble, one invariable squalidness of
attire would be merely disgusting. Among the mingling black, white,
red, and grey spirits some may be imagined fantastic enough to
assume the garb of beauty, as in all probability many must possess
the features. Let it be remembered that in the ancient traditions of
the fallen spirits, Azazel, having corrupted Naamah, and continuing
impenitent, still presides over the toilets of women.[11]

Smith's retirement left certain great parts in Shakespeare
(Macbeth, for example) open to Kemble, and in any case, his
policy was to develop more fully the spirit of 'ensemble' acting
among the company, so that its total strength could be deployed
to the best advantage rather than letting mere seniority decide
who should take possession of the star parts. Actors and actresses
who had been established at Drury Lane for many years knew
one another's performances intimately, and were well prepared to
respond effectively on the stage to one another's work. Kemble
wanted to strengthen this quality, while at the same time raising
the standard of production and presentation to fulfil his 'archeological' ambitions.

He worked hard during his first season. He transformed the
production of *Macbeth*, presenting it with fine scenery and costumes
and, as we have just seen, with singing as well as enchanting
witches and little elves – one of whom, a child called Edmund
Kean, misbehaved and was dismissed. He mounted *Henry VIII*
(November 1788) as a splendid pageant, with Sarah, of course, as
Katharine, and himself in the dual roles of Cromwell and Griffith
– until Burley's early retirement, when he took over Wolsey. For
himself he put on *Coriolanus* (February 1789), with Sarah a
striking Volumnia, playing her brother's mother, although she was
only thirty-four. *Romeo and Juliet* came in May, with brother and
sister playing the young lovers. As Boaden so nicely put it, she
'numbered twenty years more than the fond enthusiast of Verona'.
But this was by no means all that was new; there was *Mary
Queen of Scots* in March, a novelty by the Honorable John St.
John, brother of Lord Bolingbroke, which, for reasons which it is
easy to imagine, Kemble could not refuse from so noble a source.

He himself played Norfolk. Mrs Fawcett tried to get out of playing Queen Elizabeth, but finally consented because Sarah said she would appear as Queen Mary. This play can be forgotten, together with *Law of Lombardy*, adapted from *Ariosto* by Robert Jephson, in which Sarah played the Princess. Sarah was content to add Volumnia to her repertoire and leave it at that; but Kemble seemed insatiable in the demonstration of his talents, for so long dammed up at Drury Lane. He appeared as Hastings in *Jane Shore*, Zanga in *The Revenge*, Norval in *Douglas*, Sciolto in Rowe's *The Fair Penitent* (in which Sarah was Calista), and, turning to comedy (which was not his strongest suit unless the comedy were 'grave'), as Leon in *Rule a Wife*, and as Mirabel in *The Way of the World* (a part he took over from Smith) with Elizabeth Farren as Millament.

Sarah was to withdraw her services entirely from Drury Lane for the 1789–90 season, in effect going on strike, as we shall see, because of Sheridan's unwillingness or inability to pay her according to her contract. Although she returned to the stage in December 1790, she was to appear in no new parts before the closure of the theatre in the summer. The first phase of her brother's management, therefore – from the autumn of 1788 to the summer of 1791, when the theatre was pulled down so that a new, much larger structure should take its place – became a break-point in her career. It almost seemed as if she was ready to yield the stage to the comediennes, the tiny Eliza Farren and the ravishing Dora Jordan. Nevertheless, the partnership had started auspiciously, more especially with the new productions of *Henry VIII* and *Coriolanus*, and with Kemble taking over as Macbeth.

It must be remembered that parts such as these, which stayed in the permanent repertoire and became identified over the years with the players who performed them, in London and on tour, grew with renewed study and repetition. Neither Kemble nor his sister were casual with their work; they studied and re-studied before every performance, adding stature to both rendering and characterization. Sarah's Katharine and Volumnia of 1788 and 1789 would not have developed yet to the standard of her performances in the 1790s; they were, however, striking first appearances. The actor Charles Young recollects her as Volumnia around this earlier period:

I remember her coming down the stage in the triumphal entry of her son, Coriolanus, when her dumb-shew drew plaudits that shook the building. She came alone, marching and beating time to the music; rolling (if that be not too strong a term to describe her motion) from side to side, swelling with the triumph of her son. Such was the intoxication of joy which flashed from her eye, and lit up her whole face, that the effect was irresistible. She seemed to me to reap all the glory of that procession to herself. I could not take my eye from her. Coriolanus, banner, and pageant, all went for nothing to me, after she had walked to her place.[12]

In complete contrast, Campbell recalls the small touches of humanity she brought to the playing of Desdemona:

. . . in the scene of *Othello*, where she pleaded as Desdemona for Cassio, there was a fondness, most beautifully familiar, in Mrs Siddons's acting, which succeeding actresses have generally attempted to imitate.[13]

He remarks, too, on her 'power of softening tragedy by a condescension to what might almost be called playfulness'. Campbell also records a description of her as Katherine which he believes to have been written by the actor Daniel Terry after seeing her in Edinburgh; in the trial scene:

Wolsey opposes her request of delay until she may have the advice of her friends in Spain. Vexed to the uttermost by the artifices with which her ruin is prosecuted, and touched with indignation at the meanness and injustice of the proceedings, she interrupts *Campeius*, with the intention of accusing *Wolsey* of personal enmity towards her, and of refusing him for her judge, and calls, in a resistless tone of command, 'Lord Cardinal!' *Campeius*, who has been urging immediate trial, imagines it addressed to him, and comes forward as if to answer. Here Mrs Siddons exhibited one of those unequalled pieces of acting by which she assists the barrenness of the text, and fills up the meaning of the scene. Those who have seen it will never forget it: but to those who have not, we feel it impossible to describe the majestic self-correction of the petulance and vexation which, in her perturbed state of mind, she feels at the misapprehension of *Campeius*, and the intelligent expression of countenance and gracious dignity of gesture with which she intimates to him his mistake, and dismisses him again to his seat. And no language can possibly convey a picture of her immediate re-assumption of the fulness of majesty, glowing with scorn, contempt, anger, and the terrific pride of innocence, when she turns round to *Wolsey*, and exclaims, 'To you I speak!' Her form seems to expand, and her eye to burn with a fire beyond human. *Wolsey* obeys the summons, and requests to know her pleasure: she proceeds to make her charge and her refusal. And we cannot refrain from quoting the following passages, for the purpose of remarking that the mingled feelings of which they are composed, their natural gradations, their quick and violent transitions, are all unfolded and expressed with such matchless perfection of ease and truth, and in colours so far exceeding in force and brilliancy those of every other performer, that the learned and unlearned, the vulgar and the refined, feel alike the instantaneous conviction of their superiority, and the impossibility of adapting praise expressive of their own conceptions and adequate to her deserts.

Wolsey.
'Your pleasure, madam?'

Queen.
'Sir!
I am about to weep: but thinking that
We are a queen, or long have dream'd so, – certain
The daughter of a king, – my drops of tears
I'll turn to sparks of fire!'

There were none who did not feel the agonies of sympathy when they saw her efforts to suppress the grief to which her woman's nature was yielding, – who did not acknowledge, in her manner, the truth of her assertion of Royalty, and who did not experience a portion of that awe which *Wolsey* might be supposed to feel when her 'sparks of fire' darted through her 'drops of tears'.[14]

Sarah did not neglect her summer seasons. As we have seen, she had undertaken a short season in Scotland and northern England in 1788 before returning to work under her brother's management. Here she had taken some £900 in nine weeks. She also played in Norwich, and on 19 September Lord Buckinghamshire wrote to Sir Charles Hotham to say she had been well received there and 'her consequential Profit must have been more than £400'. During the same period Kemble himself had been playing Hamlet, Othello, Macbeth, and Richard for Tate Wilkinson in Leeds and Wakefield, though he was ill; like his sister, in the words of Wilkinson, 'he did not hate money'. In 1789 it was the same thing. In May Sarah was in the North again – 'that powerful theatric engine', as Tate Wilkinson calls her, 'the radiant Siddonian queen, that never-failing magnet'.[15] He could stand the hard bargaining she and William drove at his expense for the sake of the prestige it brought him, though her visits could lead to a drop in attendance afterwards. In York he took £453 in six nights, in Leeds £362.11.6d in five nights, and in Wakefield £495.17.6d in two nights. His profits in Wakefield were only £30.12.0d, but it was worth it. From Sarah's point of view it was worth it, too, though she sometimes found provincial audiences tiring. Tate Wilkinson writes:

> I heard Mrs Siddons say, that acting Isabella out of London, was double the fatigue; for there the applause on many of the striking passages, not only invigorated her whole system, but the space it occasioned assisted the breath and nerve, which when not relieved by the warmth of the auditors, chills and deadens the mind of the actor or actress, and sinks him or her into self; no matter how great the personage representing, or the fame of the representative.[16]

What Sarah could not bear were the interruptions with which the coarser wits in the audience would entertain their fellows, shouting ironic advice to the players during the more dramatic scenes. In addition to his own story of what happened at Leeds during *Macbeth*, Mathews recalled to Fitzgerald a further incident, probably during a performance of *Romeo and Juliet*:

> The elder Mathews was at that time engaged in the same company with her, and he described what she suffered from the barbarous frequenters of the Leeds galleries. When she was about to drink the poison, one called out, 'Soop it oop, lass!' . . . . No wonder, when the curtain came down, on the last night of her engagement at Leeds, that she said, 'Farewell, ye Brutes'.[17]

She also performed in Weymouth, where she was seen by Fanny Burney. Weymouth was in a festive mood because the King, recovered from his indisposition, was enjoying a holiday by the sea. Her own health was bad, and she really went to Weymouth with William for a cure. Fanny Burney met them briefly. On 3 August she was invited by the Royal Family to give them a performance of her Lady Townley in *The Provoked Husband*. The royal party, who had gone by sea to Lulworth Castle, could not get back owing to a contrary wind, and the loyal audience and loyal players had to wait. Eventually, the royal party arrived at ten at night. Servants rushed to fetch them their evening wigs, and the performance started. 'Mrs Siddons . . . was exquisite,' wrote Fanny Burney.

Sarah herself had observed signs of the King's mental disturbance at the beginning of his illness the previous year, as Campbell has recorded:

She was often at Buckingham House and at Windsor. But, when she was on a visit at the latter Palace, his Majesty one day handed her a sheet of paper, that was blank all but the signature of his name. She judged too highly both of her Sovereign and herself to believe that, in his right mind, he could shew such extraordinary conduct; and the event proved the justice of her conclusion. She immediately took the paper to the Queen.[18]

Following her appearance in Weymouth, Sarah went to Exeter, as a letter to Lady Harcourt dated 11 August 1789 shows: 'I am going to Exeter,' she wrote, 'where I shall be about five weeks, to act a few nights, and then I shall have done with tragedy for a long, long, time.' Earlier in the letter she describes her encounter with the Royal Family at Weymouth:

Dr Reynolds has prescribed so happily for me, that within this fortnight I am a new creature. It is impossible I suppose to give you any account of the Royal Family that you have not already heard. The King and Queen have done me the honour to be very gracious to me, and to little George. Her Majesty told me the other day he was a very fine little boy; and so civil. They saw him several times with his maid, for *I* did not take him on the Esplanade, when their Majesties were likely to be there, for fear his spirits should have grown boisterous, except when we went to bathe in the morning, and the Queen was never on the walk at those times. How it rejoices one's heart to see the King so well. I never saw him look so handsome in my life, and the Queen is absolutely fat.[19]

But no amount of natural desire to make money when the opportunity arose could hide the fact that Sarah's health was poor. Her appearances at Drury Lane were substantially cut back. She was thin, which no doubt assisted her in the 'breeches' part of Rosalind, where the standing joke always was how actresses with more delightfully prominent bosoms would fare once they were dressed up as a youth. But quite apart from her health, Sarah was very angry at the way she was being treated by Sheridan. Boaden claims that she also had 'some slight misunderstanding' with her brother, which Campbell denies absolutely on 'the best authority'; the whole blame, he says, rested on Sheridan's shoulders. He did not hand over the money due to her. Also, gossip or not, there is the strange story about Sheridan's misbehaviour which Samuel Rogers claims Sarah told him herself.

Mrs Siddons told me, that one night as she stepped into her carriage to return home from the theatre, Sheridan suddenly jumped in after her. 'Mr Sheridan,' she said, 'I trust that you will behave with all propriety: if you do not, I shall immediately let down the glass, and desire the servant to show you out.' Sheridan *did* behave with all propriety: 'but,' continued Mrs Siddons, 'as soon as we had reached my house in Marlborough Street, and the footman had opened the carriage-door, – 'only think! the provoking wretch bolted out in the greatest haste, as if anxious to escape unseen.'[20]

Since Sheridan's reputation with women was so bad, she had every right to be on her guard – though it is unlikely he would have molested her. However, gentlemen could be very uncertain where sex was concerned, especially with actresses. Who would have suspected that the great Kemble would so far have forgotten himself as to assault Maria Theresa de Camp, a Viennese dancer and one of the young ladies of the company, and be forced afterwards to make public apology in the press on 7 January 1795 in the most humiliating terms:

I, John Philip Kemble, of the Theatre Royal, Drury Lane, do adopt this method of publicly apologising to Miss de Camp, for the very improper and unjustifiable behaviour I was lately guilty of towards her, which I do further declare her conduct and character had in no instance authorized; but, on the contrary, I do know and believe both to be irreproachable.[21]

Miss de Camp later became his sister-in-law when she married Charles Kemble.

There were other reasons why Sarah broke temporarily with Drury Lane, with its strong company of actresses including Elizabeth Farren and Dora Jordan. Sheridan believed the town was tired of lugubrious tragedies and melodramas, and needed a diet of comedy. It is probable that he was at first quite pleased to be spared the expense of Sarah's salary, until he found that the public still clamoured for her and that it would be wise to come to terms and bring her back. She did not return, however, until December 1790, and then only when she had been assured that she would be paid correctly and punctually. The house was crowded to suffocation, and the *London Chronicle* of 8 December reported that the shouting and applause lasted for five minutes. The *Chronicle* reported on 22 March 1791, after she had performed in *Jane Shore*:

The langour of indisposition was visible in her countenance; but this langour gave a deeper interest to the illusion, by making it more perfect, for it was suited to the distress of the penitent, and never did we see her sufferings more chastely, more calmly, and more impressively delineated.[22]

Sarah was to appear only seven times during the remainder of the season, and she undertook no new parts in 1791. On her benefit night she gained £412 with *The Gamester*, and, harbouring her strength, she undertook no summer work in the provinces. Apart from these seven appearances in London, she was absent from the stage from the autumn of 1789 until January 1792. Then she was to appear at the company's temporary theatre, the Opera House, Haymarket, during the rebuilding of Drury Lane, which had been condemned as unsafe.[23]

Sarah, for the first time in her adult life, was enjoying an abundance of leisure as a result of her ample savings, and occasional munificent earnings. Sufficient letters of the period survive, supplemented by references in Mrs Piozzi's diary, to fill out the circumstances of her daily life. She certainly did not allow ill-health to prevent her from travelling about in the summer and staying with her friends. On 30 August 1789 she is writing to Sir Charles Hotham:

The truth is that I have been in so miserable a State of health and Spirits for a long time, as not to have written a line to anyone except my Physician, dear good Dr Reynolds . . . I have well grounded hope of being relieev'd [sic] from the tormenting complaint which has rendered the last twelve months burthensome to a degree that I cannot express: what torrents of tears has it drawn from my eyes! and prayers (I fear of impatience) from the bottom of my heart.[24]

According to Campbell, Sarah was in Bath in November and attended a play, *The Earl of Godwin*, written by Anne Yearsley, 'a poor woman who literally sold milk from door to door'. He adds that Sarah also visited Birmingham, where an eager shopkeeper sold her a stucco bust of herself without realizing who she was. He told her it was 'the likeness of the greatest and most beautiful actress in the world'. She thought its appearance appalling; she began studying statuary far more carefully, and took her own modelling in clay more seriously.

In the spring of the following year she began her prolonged stay at Streatham with Mrs Piozzi, who had lost her original antipathy to Sarah and, almost as if in reaction, became one of her closest friends. Indeed, Mrs Piozzi needed Sarah's friendship at this time.

Her love for her second husband was strong and lasting, but the antipathy this foreign musician had excited in her friends, and her own family, had hurt her so cruelly that she had thought it wise to leave the country for a while. From 1784 to 1787 she and her husband had lived abroad in great happiness. They had finally set up house in Streatham Park in 1790. In an entry dated 17 May Mrs Piozzi writes:

> Charming Siddons has spent some Weeks with me, I think mighty well of her Virtue, & am amazed at the Cultivated State in which I have found her Mind . . . that She loves *me* I am not so sure, but I love her exceedingly. The Physicians have mistaken her Case, & have under a silly notion of Scorbutic Humours – dosed that poor Dear with Mercurial Medcines, till they have torne the fine Vessells to pieces, & shattered all the nerves that her Profession had not ruined before – Sir Lucas Pepys will restore her however to Health as firm as mine which was still more ill used. Poor pretty Siddons! a warm Heart, & a Cold Husband are sad things to contend with, but She'll get thro'.[25]

This is one of the earlier hints that all was not well between Sarah and William. They called on the Piozzis – and were invited to stay for some weeks.

Mrs Piozzi, of course, had certain ulterior motives in inviting Sarah to stay with her:

> Kemble and his Sister both pretend to like my little Drama, but I dare say would see me hanged, rather than bring it out at the very slightest personal Hazard of ten Pence Loss, as well as they pretend to love me – My last set of Friends have however done me *one* Favour; they have cured me of suspecting kindness from any one. I am not cured of loving *others*, but shall never believe that any one loves *me*.[26]

Sarah seemed devoted to her new friend. While at Streatham she scribbled a personal postscript at the foot of one of Mrs Piozzi's letters to Sophia Weston:

> I fear my heart will fail me when I fail to receive the comfort and consolation of our dear Mrs Piozzi. There are many disposed to comfort me, but no one knows so rationally or effectually how to do it as that unwearied spirit of kindness.[27]

On 2 June, she wrote to another friend, Bedina Wynn: 'Doctors differ you know and it seems they are very much at odds about

poor me, for Sir Lucas Pepys says my Complaint is *Nerves* and
Nerves only.'

In June William returned to Gower Street. On 21 June, he
wrote to Sir Charles Hotham (revealing a certain discrepancy as
to when exactly the visit to Streatham had started):

Last Saturday three weeks we went merely to pay a morning visit to
Mr and Mrs Piozzi at Streatham Common. They were so good as to
wish our continuance there for some time to see what change of air
might do. It is a sweet quiet place, and Mrs Siddons gladly accepted
their offer and there she remains.

Mrs Piozzi persuaded her she should try some other medical
gentleman, as Dr Osborne seemed at a standstill and had a fair and
long tryal. Sir Lucas Peppys was fixed upon, and sent for, who
gave her great hopes, and prescribed for her. To be as brief as
possible, either from Sir Lucas, the air, or Mrs Piozzi's attention and
witty concorse, [*sic*] she is amazingly better, and sleeps the whole
night without waking – what she has not known for a year and a half
past. She has got her flesh again, and I think looks as well as ever
she did in her life. Sir Lucas says she may go to Calais and see her
children there, to bathe in the sea if she should go back again. I
understand he intends to recommend her Harrogate, but he advises
her to stay at Streatham as long as she can, so our departure is
unfixed.

I must inform you I have at last got a house, 'tis in what is called
an unfashionable street, but still 'tis more among our friends, and
though not so pretty as Gower Street, t'will be warmer (a thing Mrs
Siddons wished for) and have more room. It is in Great Marlborough
Street. The houses there are all in an old fashioned style, and there
are plenty of closets, which the ladies seem in general to be fond of.
I am just going to be very busy with painters, plaisterers and paper-
hangers, to get it ready against this winter, by which time the smell
will be pretty well gone.

Little other news is there stirring here. I have heard from Liverpool,
all well as to health, but electioneering likely to keep the play-houses
thin there and everywhere beside.

 'Tis at Mrs Siddons particular request I write this, who begs her
kindest regards to all at Dalton. She thinks she sees her Ladyship so
busy and so happy feeding her chicky biddys and Gallinis.[28]

The Siddons moved in 1790 to the less attractive surroundings
of Great Marlborough Street. The area had become fashionable
not so much for residence as for promenading; the *beau-monde*,
the bright ladies and gentlemen of fashion, had deserted the piazza

at Covent Garden and even the once-favourite walk under the trees of the Mall in preference for the wide thoroughfare near Great Marlborough Street. A fashionable friend, writing to Sir Charles Hotham, tells him how he was walking all alone in Covent Garden in his latest finery when an old basket-woman called out: 'Ho! Ho! here comes a farthing rushlight to stick in my window!' As for Mrs Piozzi, she found that 'the leaden goddess', as she had once called Sarah, had turned to gold, and Sarah herself, who had only recently told Lady Harcourt she could not possibly care for Mrs Piozzi, found that she loved her. These women of high talent and intelligence, both of whom had made their way in a difficult world and had their troubles, discovered each other, and seemed all the warmer for their previous coldness. Mrs Piozzi wrote of Sarah: 'The longer one knows that incomparable creature the more reasons spring up to esteem and love her.' The Hothams knew Mrs Piozzi well, and the actress Elizabeth Farren; they attended, though Sarah apparently did not, Mrs Piozzi's seventh wedding anniversary on 28 July – a fête of 'prodigious splendour and gaiety' – 'seventy people to dinner', wrote this tireless hostess.

The Siddons were almost certainly away from London at the time. Campbell records that she and William went during the summer to visit their daughters Sally and Maria, who were at boarding school in Calais, and that they subsequently toured the Netherlands, and visited Lisle. There is a reference to this visit in the reminiscences of Michael Kelly, the opera singer, who had a great admiration for Sarah. He writes, without giving a precise date, that he visited St Omer in 1790:

> At the hotel where we dined, the landlady told us that Madame la grande actrice Anglaise Siddons had just dined, and quelled the house. . . . She said, she 'thought her a fine woman, and thought she made it her study to appear like a French woman; but . . . she has yet much to learn before she arrives at the dignity and grace of one.' After this speech I could find nothing palatable in her house.[29]

A letter addressed to Lady Harcourt at Nuneham, dated merely 2 August and written from Sandgate, near Folkestone, describes this visit to the Continent; they were accompanied by friends, a Miss Wynn and her brother, a clergyman:

> I set out with Mr S., Miss Wynn, and her brother for Calais, and after a very rough passage of little more than two hours arrived at Calais, and found my dear girls quite well and improved in their

persons, and (I am told in the French) I was very much struck with
the difference of objects and customs, when I reflected how small a
space divides one nation from the other, like true ENGLISH. [*Sic.*] We
saw all we could, and I thought *of* my dear Lord Harcourt, though not
with him in their churches. I own (though I blame myself at the
same time for it), I was disgusted with all the pomp and magnificence
of them, when I saw the priests 'playing such fantastic tricks before
high heaven as (I think must) make the angels weep,' and the people
gabbling over their prayers, even in the *act of* GAPING, to have it over
as quick as might be. . . . We were nearly twenty hours on the sea
on our return, and arrived at Dover fatigued and sick to death.
Dr Wynn was obliged to make the best of his way to London on
account of a sermon he was engaged to preach, and took his charming
sister with him. *We* made haste here, and it is the most agreeable
sea-place, excepting those on the Devonshire coast, I ever saw.
Perhaps *agreeable* is a bad word, for the country is much more
sublime than beautiful. We have tremendous cliffs overhanging and
frowning on the foaming sea, which is very often so saucy and
tempestuous as to *deserve* frowning on; from whence, when the
weather is clear, we see the land of France, and the vessels cross from
the Downs to Calais. Sometimes, while you *stand* there, it is amazing
with what velocity they skim along. Here are little neat lodgings,
and good wholesome provisions. Perhaps they would not suit a
great *Countess*, as our friend Mr Mason has it; but a little great
actress is more easily accommodated. I'm afraid it will grow larger
though, and then adieu to the comforts of retirement. At present the
place cannot contain above twenty or thirty strangers I should think.
I have bathed four times, and believe I shall persevere, for Sir Lucas
Pepys says my disease is entirely nervous. I believe I am better, but
I get on so slowly.[30]

In 1791, while Sarah was making her limited appearances at
Drury Lane, William wrote on 6 April to Whalley expressing his
delight that last Monday was 'a golden letterday'; the takings had
reached £412.12s., 'sixty pounds more in the house than ever
known'. He then goes on to say that Sarah

. . . last night did the honours of her house to fifty people, till near
two in the morning, who all confessed they never saw her look
better, only that she's grown much thinner; but *that* Sir Lucas
Pepys holds as a favourable symptom. To-day, I think, she is better
still, and we are going to dine with the Chevalier St Michael, brother
of the King of Poland; you will be surprised to hear on what
account. He wishes to propose to her, as I understand, a journey to
Warsaw; his brother, the King, it seems, is fond of all that's English;

he was a long time at Oxford for his education, has heard of Mrs Siddons, and would give anything, could she be induced to visit his kingdom, that he might hear her read some English plays. God knows what it will come to; I think she ought to travel, and imagine it would be of service to her constitution. Whether that climate would suit or not, I know not, but it would be a very honourable circumstance to have such an offer from a crowned head, though it may require a great deal of consideration to adopt it. Italy and Switzerland I should delight in taking her to, and if, by a little stretch farther, one could pay the post-horses, would it not be pleasant. Do let me have your opinion. You are a friend, and nobody's judgment on such a business should we prefer to yours. . . .

Mr Piozzi, in his answer to me, said you were not well, nor Mrs Whalley. I hope nothing serious, and by this time you are both recovered. Mrs Jackson was with us last night, but it was in such a bustle I could hardly speak to her at all. I am going, in a few days, to put our cottage a little in order. I fancy that Mrs Siddons will be, while at Streatham, enjoying air and quiet. Your little Hercules, as you are pleased to call him, is a fine fellow still.[31]

This last referred to George, now aged five.

During the summer of 1791 Sarah's health was still bad, and, according to Campbell, she spent some part of the time at Nuneham Rectory, her country cottage as she called it, and at Guy's Cliffe with the Greatheeds. Her friend Lord Harcourt's estate was near by, which added to the attraction for Sarah, and the Whalleys occasionally came to stay in the area as well. While Sarah was at Nuneham, Mrs Piozzi paid her a visit; she wrote to Sophia Weston on 6 August that the cottage was:

a fairy Habitation, but [I] had not an Idea of finding as elegant a Thing as it is. England can boast no happier Situation; a Hill scattered over with fragrance makes the stand for our lovely little Cottage, while Isis rolls at his foot, and Oxford terminates our view. Ld. Harcourt's rich Wood covers a rising Ground that conceals the flat Country on the Left, and leaves no Spot unoccupied by cultivated, and may I say peculiar Beauty.

On 18 August she wrote again:

Dear, lovely, sweet Siddons is better, and at last tolerably reconciled to parting with me for the relief of those whose anguish is of the soul, while hers, I thank God, is confined wholly to the beautiful clay that fits it so neatly with its truly well suited enclosure.

In September, when passing through the village again, she wrote to Sophie Weston:

Dear charming Siddons is better; we stopt at her *village*, not at her *house*, returning, and heard that Sheridan and Kemble were with her; on *business*, no doubt, so we would not go in, but sent compliments.[32]

Later, writing in her private diary on 9 September, Mrs Piozzi gives a disenchanted picture of poor Sarah who, it appears, had had to endure a useless pregnancy once again:

Well! My Scheme was to reside with dear Mrs Siddons at Nuneham till they returned: but She miscarried, & to encrease her Illness came a Storm worthy of hotter Climates, which killed a Woman within our View, and fired ten Shocks of a neighbring Farmer's Corn under the very Windows. Our young Girls Cecilia and Miss Siddons fell into Fits, the Baby Boy George not 5 Years old was from home, gone o' merry-making with our Servants to some Village not far off – the Mother became a real Picture of Despair, supposing him killed by the Lightning: and I had to comfort & support them all: but my Task was too great, and gave me a Pain in my Bowels that might have had bad Consequences. Mean Time I had many petty Vexations: the Eating & Drinking at Mrs Siddons's was insupportably ill dress'd, dirty, & scanty: my little favourite Spaniel Phillis went proud; & as I had received a Charge from Mr Piozzi to let her have no Dog, She distressed me in that small House beyond all telling: my Maid was discontented with her Place of Residence, ill Lodged I believe She was sure enough, & worse fed: so the Plagues increased upon me, while the Pleasures faded away. At our first Coming I liked Nuneham vastly; the View from our Cottage Window was enchanting, Mrs Siddons sate spinning under a great Tree at the Door.[33]

Sarah, apparently, had been successful in her attempts, earlier in the year, to resolve the bitter quarrel which had arisen, largely over her remarriage, between Mrs Piozzi and her daughter Cecilia.

Sarah paid a visit to Guy's Cliffe late in August. On 9 September Mrs Piozzi wrote:

Mrs Siddons had a mind to go spend some Days at Guy's Cliffe, where Mr and Mrs Greathead had invited *her* not *me*, at which I felt offended.[34]

William wrote to Whalley from London:

So both our cottages are to be forsaken, and both for the same melancholy cause, ill health. A fresh arrangement is going to take place with Mrs Siddons . . . it was first necessary to consult Sir Lucas Pepys, who has so long attended her, and with so much care and attention, though with so little success. He has been here this morning, and says it is impossible that medicine can ever cure her, and that Lady Mordaunt's case was probably different; but he would have a consultation with Warren about her, and in a day or two let her know the result; but he begged she would, in the meantime, so settle her affairs as to leave herself at liberty to go to Harrogate. I imagine to that place we shall be obliged to go; if for any purpose I shall bless the suggestion. But alas! my hopes give way, and my faith in medicine is tottering; and yet everything must be tried, and shall, while we have a guinea at command.[35]

So Sarah spent Christmas in Harrogate. Two undated letters to another friend, a Miss Coates of Glasgow, with whom she sometimes stayed, appear to belong to this period. She writes in one: 'My spirits are absolutely worn out with fatigue, the springs of my poor machine have been overstrained, and I must have complete rest of body and mind to restore them to their natural tone again, so I fear you will find me very stupid.' In the other she says that she has come to Harrogate 'to try the effect of the water for a complaint, which tho' not dangerous has been an unspeakable torment to me'.[36]

Sarah eventually returned to the London stage with some diffidence. No doubt she felt it was time she earned some money to support the family. She was discouraged by further malicious attacks on her, apparently organized by her old enemy, Samuel Pratt. Anna Seward wrote to their mutual friend Sophie Weston in some alarm at Whalley's continued support of the man she now called the 'blasphemer':

It is past conjecture that P. is the source and master-spring of all the blasphemy against Siddonian excellence. Mr Siddons, as you know, traced to him the first malicious paragraphs that appeared against his wife; Mr W—— knows this, amongst other countless instances of his dark ingratitude – and yet it seems he corresponds with him. Alas! how does this weakness abase the dignity of Mr W's character![37]

A further reason for Sarah's diffidence was that while Drury

Lane was being rebuilt the company had to perform (until March 1794) in a much larger building than the old Drury Lane had been. This was the King's Theatre, Haymarket, the largest theatre in England, and primarily used for ballet and opera. Sarah feared that she would be unable to command her audiences to the same degree in this extensive auditorium. On the other hand, she knew that the days of working in small theatres were over. The new Drury Lane was being constructed on a huge scale; and during this same period, in 1792, Covent Garden itself was virtually rebuilt by the architect Henry Holland at a cost of £25,000.

Sarah set about remodelling her style of acting, using the circumstances forced upon her to prepare herself for the great theatre in which she would eventually have to perform. She played herself in gently after her return from Harrogate, appearing for the first time on 21 January 1792 in her most familiar play, *Isabella*, and giving in all only twenty-two performances during the remainder of the season, which ended on 15 June. Her only new parts were the very indifferent, lachrymose Queen Elizabeth in Cibber's version of Shakespeare's *Richard III* and Mrs Oakley in Colman's comedy, *The Jealous Wife*, in which she played opposite her brother.[38] Boaden comments on the enlargement of her style which she adopted when he refers to the

> . . . alteration in some degree of her style of action, which, moving in a greater space, certainly became more grand and imposing. . . . That the spectators in the front of the house lost much of her expression I know, though I seldom sat there; for the passage between the orchestra and the pit had a very comfortable seat for about thirty amateurs of the art, and, with a little activity and address, it was never very difficult to obtain a place there. And from this situation, in all her towering majesty of person, and in the maturity of her excellence, I received impressions which I could never consent to lose.[39]

Boaden is most revealing in describing her technique of deportment on this much larger stage area:

> In a small space the turns are quick and short. Where the area is considerable the step is wider, the figure more erect, and the whole progress more grand and powerful; the action is more from the shoulder, and we now first began to hear of the perfect form of Mrs Siddons's arm. Her walk has never been attempted by any other

actress, and in deliberate dignity was as much alone as the expression of her countenance. . . . Conspiring with the larger stage to produce some change in her style was her delight in statuary, which directed her attention to the antique, and made a remarkable impression upon her as to simplicity of attire and severity of attitude. The actress had formerly complied with fashion, and deemed the prevalent becoming; she now saw that tragedy was debased by the flutter of light materials, and that the head, and all its powerful action from the shoulder, should never be encumbered by the monstrous inventions of the hairdresser and the milliner.[40]

Having completed this partial season at the King's Theatre by May, Sarah appears to have gone north. By 1 June, we gather from Mrs Piozzi's diary, 'charming Siddons' was in Scotland, having left her daughter Sally (now aged seventeen) sick with asthma and in Mrs Piozzi's charge. Sarah's journey was probably linked with the movements of her brother Stephen, who in January 1792 had become manager of the new Theatre Royal in Edinburgh. He was unfortunately in the midst of legal trouble with John Jackson, the previous manager. Mrs Piozzi mentions Sarah again in a letter written in October from Guy's Cliffe to Sophie Weston, who during the year had become Mrs Pennington and had gone to live with her husband, William Pennington, in Clifton, a suburb of Bristol.[41] Sarah, she says, is still unwell, but Sally's health is worse:

> On the road hither however for we came softly, not to hurry poor Cecy, only 44 miles o' day, Sally Siddons was taken *illish*. I hop'd it was the Influenza, for cold she could not have catch'd, and I have kept her at all possible distance from my own girl ever since she threw up blood at Denbigh. Here however was she seized yesterday with *such* a paroxysm of Asthma, cough, *spasm*, *every* thing, as you nor I ever saw her attack'd by.[42]

In her diary, written about the same time, Mrs Piozzi is more frank about the nature of Sarah's illness:

> And so poor Mrs Siddon's Disorder that we have all been at such a stand about, turns upon close Examination to be neither more nor less than the P – given by her husband. What a World it is![43]

Sally, writing on 29 September to Sophie Pennington – who now preferred to be called by her other name, Penelope – claimed, 'my belov'd Mother is at length cur'd of her complaint, and quite an alter'd woman'. But Mrs Piozzi does not concur; writing to the same friend, she says, 'Poor Siddons pities my very soul to see her; an indignant melancholy sits on her fine face, and care corrodes her very vitals, I do think . . . she is all resentment.'

This was not the first time, as we have seen, that a rift in Sarah's relations with her husband had been suggested. Sarah's natural shyness and desire to be regarded as 'respectable' in the eyes of society – especially in view of her humble origins and the indifferent moral reputation actresses normally possessed – made her only too anxious to cover up any sign of domestic trouble under the mask of a conventional loyalty to her husband. Mrs Piozzi, on the other hand, having endured much personal trouble, had a nose for it in the affairs of others. Sarah, too truthful a person to be able to hide her problems from so close an observer, must have had her secret prized from her almost immediately after the establishment of her sudden, eager friendship with Mrs Piozzi, which seemed to satisfy some need for companionship and the sharing of confidences. But even before this there are hints in Mrs Piozzi of feminine resentment at the treatment she either knew or imagined Sarah was getting from her husband. As early as March 1789 she refers in her diary to the lack of 'immediate influence' of Sarah over her husband in spite of her beauty; and on 2 November the same year she wrote to Penelope Weston from Bath of 'his savage treatment of dear Siddons, whose present state of health demands tenderness'. In the spring of 1791 she entered in her diary:

I think Mrs Siddons tho' beautiful, and endowed with Talents not to support only, but to enrich her Family – is a woman by no means particularly beloved either by Parents, husband Brother or Son. They all like to get what they can out of her; but all the Affection flows from her to them, not from them to her. . . . I guess not the Reason, but five Thousand Women are better liked by their Families.[44]

This poor opinion, not only of William but of the whole Siddons-Kemble family, is probably an exaggeration of the truth, an example of feminine resentment against the whole race of men and their casual treatment of women. Whether William had passed on a venereal infection to Sarah or not, Mrs Piozzi burned with sympathy for her friend. At the turn of the year 1792–3, she is writing again to Sophie Pennington in an undated letter from Streatham:

I am sincerely afflicted for her suffering virtue, never did I see a purer mind, but it is now sullied by the thoughts that she has washed her hands in innocence in vain! How shall I do to endure the sight of her odious husband? I suppose he comes tomorrow.[45]

Influenza was, as usual, raging in London, and Sarah had her usual 'terrible cold'. Later, however, says Mrs Piozzi, she was 'in her business'.

Sarah made a number of appearances during the 1792-3 season, but only one new part was presented, Ariadne in Murphy's *The Rival Sisters*, which ran for six performances only. Part of the time the company performed at the Theatre Royal, Haymarket. When the season was finished it appears she went straight off to Guy's Cliffe. In April Mrs Piozzi tells Mrs Pennington she will be meeting 'charming Siddons' at Mr Greatheed's. In May she passes the opinion that Sally 'outlooks her sister'.

Sarah's own surviving letters resume in August 1793. She is back in her Rectory cottage at Nuneham in July, but, as she wrote to Mrs Piozzi on 5 August, is about to leave to take the waters at Cheltenham. 'What a blazing summer it has been and no terrifying Storms thank God! . . . I have sent a Head of George to London which I have made very like and have just finished one of Sally, they tell me this last is quite beautiful.' She ends her letter effusively: 'I *adore* you with all the faculties of my Mind and Love you with all the warmest affections of my Heart.' But she added an economical postscript: 'You Shoud write to me under Cover to Lord H. which Saves Postage remember this important point another time darling.'[46]

On 19 September Mrs Piozzi, writing to Mrs Pennington, reports that Sarah 'looks incomparably better, I'm told'. Then she refers to 'her setting off for Ireland in this stormy season, but it will answer to her husband and family, *she* has fame and fortune enough without running further hazards'.[47]

So another arduous provincial tour was started, this time in the depth of winter; Mrs Piozzi wrote to her friend in December that Sarah was 'doing delightfully in Ireland'. The tour spread into the New Year of 1794, because Sarah wrote to Mrs Pennington from Stephen's Green, Dublin, on 5 January:

I was very truly grieved my dear Friend to receive so uncomfortable a letter from you but I hope by this time the cloud has entirely disappeared and that dear Mr Piozzi is recovered from his terrible fit of the Gout.

I hope to be at home in about a Month, and I leave you to Judge whether it will be long before I haste to embrace you. I have reapd my lawrels plenteously and have considerably encreased the weight of my Purse pray tell my dear Sir Lucas so, but I am not yet well – we must not expect *all* the good things.[48]

On 23 January, Mrs Piozzi wrote: 'Mrs Siddons is come home, handsome, celebrated, enriched, adored. Every body worships that admirable creature except her own family – to *them* She is no Heroine – tho' contented to make herself Valet de Chambre,'[49] The tour must have represented a period of reconciliation with 'Mr Sid', if this were indeed necessary, for when she came back with him to London she was almost three months pregnant.

The new theatre was opened on 12 March 1794 with a concert of sacred music; the building was not quite finished, and there was no regular dramatic performance until 21 April, when *Macbeth* was played in a new production, Charles Kemble (aged eighteen and fresh from Douai) joining the cast in the part of Malcolm.[50] The theatre, naturally enough, was a reflection of John Philip Kemble's more grandiose conceptions. Whilst it was being built Kemble took Boaden into his confidence, and took him along to see the historical site which was being prepared for his productions:

Mr Kemble's active mind had full employment in the preparations for the stage itself. As the dimensions of the new theatre were calculated for an audience, the price of whose admission would amount, even at 6*s.* in the boxes, to more than £700, it was quite clear that for all grand occasions they would want scenery of greater height and width than had been exhibited at old Drury; and that in fact but little of the old stock could be used at all. On this occasion it gives me sincere pleasure to mention the very great acquisition Mr Kemble had met with in an old friend of mine, who really seemed expressly fashioned, as a scene-painter, to carry into effect the true and perfect decorations which he meditated for the plays of Shakspeare: the artist to whom I allude is Mr William Capon, who has the honour of being draughtsman to H.R.H. the Duke of York. Mr Capon, like his old acquaintance, the late John Carter, was cast in the mould of antiquity; and his passion was, and is, the ancient architecture of this country. With all the zeal of an antiquary, therefore, the painter worked as if he had been upon oath; and as all that he painted for the new theatre perished in the miserable conflagration of it a few years after, I indulge myself in some description of the scenery, which so much interested Mr Kemble. The artist had a private painting room, and Mr Kemble used to walk me out with him to inspect the progress of these works, which were to be records as well as decorations, and present with every other merit, that for which Kemble was born, – truth.

A chapel of the pointed architecture, which occupied the whole stage, for the performance of the Oratorios, with which the new theatre opened in 1794.

Six chamber wings, of the same order, for general use in our old English plays – very elaborately studied from actual remains.

A view of New Palace Yard, Westminster, as it was in 1793. – 41 feet wide, with corresponding wings.

The ancient palace of Westminster, as it was about 300 years back; from partial remains, and authentic sources of information – put together with the greatest diligence and accuracy – the point of view the S. W. corner of Old Palace Yard. About 42 feet wide and 34 feet to the top of the scene.

Two very large wings, containing portions of the old palace, which the artist made out from an ancient draught met with in looking over some records of the augmentation office in Westminster. It was but a pen and ink sketch originally, but though injured by time, exhibited what was true.

Six wings representing ancient English streets; combinations of genuine remains, selected on account of their picturesque beauty.

The Tower of London, restored to its earlier state for the play of King Richard III. . . . In our conversations, Mr Kemble now opened to me many of the great improvements that he meditated; and notwithstanding sundry difficulties, which would not always be charmed away, his ambition rose along with the splendid pile of Mr Holland; and the *grand national theatre* was the term that he not too partially appropriated to the edifice which Mr Burke thought an encroachment upon the architectural majesty of our temples. Mr Kemble now steadily pursued his object of forming a complete collection of the drama – the newspapers occasionally reported the large sums given by him for single plays. It became him, he thought, to possess every thing relative to his art, and his collection, at last, was greatly superior to that of his illustrious predecessor, Garrick. To give him ample room, he had enlarged the library of his house in Caroline Street, Bedford Square.[51]

When eventually the theatre was opened it was not found to be easy for the actors. All the intimacy of the old Drury Lane was gone. George Colman the Younger (who had a vested interest in maintaining small theatres since he had taken over management of the Little Theatre – the Theatre Royal – in the Haymarket from his father at the time the two big new theatres, Drury Lane and

Covent Garden, were being constructed, both under Holland's supervision) wrote:

> On 3 February 1794, their Majesties commanded the performances, and the crowd was so great at the pit entrance, that when the door was opened, a gentleman was thrown down the stairs, and the persons behind him being pushed forward, fell over him, and these again were trampled on by those impelled by the force of numbers who were still rushing on. The groans of the maimed and the dying were terrific, while those who were literally treading their fellow-creatures to death, had not the power to recede. Fifteen persons were killed, and nineteen others were severely injured! This melancholy accident was not made known to the King, until his return to the palace.[52]

As Colman points out, an actor can pitch his voice, but not his face. Both he and his father had memories of Garrick:

> Garrick, always tremblingly alive to his great ability, and judicious in nursing his fame, would not probably have risked his powers in theatres of the present magnitude, particularly in the sublime walk of Tragedy. His talents must have suffered a paralysis, a loss of half their vitality, when the rapid and astonishing transition of his eye and his features could not instantly, by their close fidelity to nature, electrify all who witnessed them.
>
> On the whole . . . it may be said that the principal London theatres are too large for all the purposes they should accomplish; too large for perfect convenience of vision, and for an easy modulation of speech; too large to 'hold the mirror up to nature'.

The art of acting, he felt, was being ousted by the glamour of spectacle.

Spectacle was the keynote of the reopening of Drury Lane. A huge iron fire-curtain was let down and struck with a hammer to demonstrate its resonance. The curtain then rose to reveal a lake of real water embellished with a cascade, while Elizabeth Farren spoke a Prologue defying the lethal fire to descend and destroy the new, fireproof theatre:

> The very ravages of fire we scout,
> For we have herewithal to put it out:
> In ample reservoirs our firm reliance,
> Whose streams set conflagrations at defiance.[53]

Needless to say, the new Drury Lane went the way of most theatres of the period, and was burnt down in 1809.

Even Sarah shared the general enthusiasm for the place which was to destroy the intimacy of her art. She wrote to Lady Harcourt on 11 April 1794:

> Our new theatre is the most beautiful that imagination can paint. We open it with *Macbeth*, on Easter Monday. I am told that the banquet is a thing to go and see of itself. The scenes and dresses all new, and as superb and characteristic as it is possible to make them. You can conceive what I feel at the prospect of playing there. I dare say I shall be so nervous as scarcely to be able to make myself heard in the first scene.[54]

Boaden claims that the theatre was 'the most chaste and beautiful structure that ever bore the name', but tended to attract an audience of sightseers. Sarah was later to realize what she had lost. She said to the actor Dowton: 'I am glad to see you at Drury Lane, but you are come to act in a wilderness of a place, and God knows, if I had not made my reputation in a small theatre, I never should have done it.'[55] But Boaden, who could scarcely be termed a mere sightseer, remained enthusiastic.

Mrs Piozzi, of course, anticipated that there might be trouble about Sarah's advanced state of pregnancy. She wrote in her diary:

> Mrs Siddons is going to act Lady Macbeth at the new Theatre Drury Lane next Easter Monday. She is big with child, and I fear will for that reason scarce be well received: for People have a notion She is covetous, and this unnecessary Exertion to gain Money will confirm it. And yet says Lord Deerhurst, She thinks I suppose to carry *all before her*. Lord Deerhurst is very comical.[56]

Sarah was indeed heavily pregnant. On 30 April she wrote to Mrs Piozzi to congratulate her on the success of her new book, and added, 'I am sure there must be *two* I am so frightfully large and heavy.'

She did not have twins. On 25 July 1794, about three weeks after her fortieth birthday, her seventh and last child, Cecilia, was born, a girl who soon became the favourite of all the family, and the only one of her daughters to survive her. She was named after Mrs Piozzi's daughter; on 27 August, Sarah wrote to her friend:

> I fancy that you will be rather glad to see my hand writing again, dull as my letters are. I will first thank you all very sincerely for the

s.s.—7*

concern you have so kindly felt for me, and your solicitude for my recovery which would be perfect coud I gain a little more strength, but such a lumping Lifey was neither brought forth, or can be now sustaind without humbing and bringing low its Mother. I had a very safe, tho a long, and *Laborious* time, and I bless God that I have brought you a perfect and healthful a Baby as ever Sun shone on. How I long for you to see the little dear fat lump. . . . Her Father doats on her and Maria does nothing but Dawdle about with her all day. . . . I know you will both be glad to hear that Mr Sheridan has been here to settle our business we expect him here again in a day or two to conclude upon the manner of discharging the account between us and I believe it will [be] by installments, heaven farther it to us evry way. . . . We shall soon go to Ramsgate – I hate all those places – but I believe one half of the world is born for the convenience of the other half – My husband likes it, and it is very natural that the Girls shoud. I shall never begin to live for myself I believe and perhaps I should not like it, were it in my power.[57]

With a further mouth to feed – and, possibly, as Mrs Piozzi believed at this time, driven out to work again by her husband, though this is most unlikely – Sarah prepared herself for another northern tour. She wrote to Whalley in an undated letter composed before setting off for Edinburgh to support her son Henry, now an actor, and her brother Stephen, who was still in difficulties with his management:

I intend if it please God, to be at home again for Passion week. I leave my sweet girl behind me, not daring to take her so far north this inclement weather, and could well wish that the interests of the best of sons and most amiable of men did not so imperiously call me out of this softer climate just now. . . . *Glad enough should I be never to appear again*; but while the interests of those so dear and near as those of son and brother are concerned, one must not let selfish considerations stand in the way of Christian duties and natural affection.[58]

This was to be the beginning of an arduous commitment to work in London and elsewhere from the autumn of 1794, following on her comparatively long period of semi-retirement and illness. Drury Lane was now virtually under Kemble's control until his later serious disagreements with Sheridan led to his temporary resignation from management in 1796. Sarah now found herself involved in a series of indifferent parts, mostly in more or less worthless plays; she appears to have undertaken these engagements for the sake of the money. Only one new part was in Shakespeare – the Queen in *Hamlet*. Each summer she toured the provinces, as well as making a visit comparatively early in 1795 to Scotland, immediately after her benefit performance in *Macbeth* on 25 April in London.

During the first season, 1794–5, poor Fanny Burney's play *Edwy and Elgiva* finally reached the stage on 21 March 1795; it did so in the most unfortunate circumstances, which led to Sarah having to die tragically amid laughter. Campbell describes what happened:

Miss Burney was peculiarly unfortunate in bringing bishops into her tragedy. At that time there was a liquor much in popular use, called Bishop: it was a sort of negus or punch, I believe, though the origin of its name I must leave more learned antiquaries to determine. But, be that as it may, when jolly fellows met at a tavern, the first order to the waiter was, *to bring in the Bishop*. Unacquainted with the language of taverns, Miss Burney made her King exclaim, in an early scene, '*Bring in the Bishop!*' and the summons filled the audience with as much hilarity as if they had drank of the exhilirating liquor. They continued in the best possible humour throughout the piece. The dying scene made them still more jocose, when a passing stranger proposed, in a tragic tone, to carry the expiring heroine to the other side of a hedge. This hedge, though supposed to be situated remotely from any dwelling, nevertheless, proved to be a very accommodating retreat; for, in a few minutes afterwards, the wounded lady was brought from behind it, on an elégant couch, and, after dying in the presence of her husband, was removed once more to the back of the hedge. The solemn accents of the Siddons herself were not a match for this ludicrous circumstance, and she was carried off amidst roars of mirth.[59]

Sarah wrote to Penelope Pennington on 25 March, referring in passing to a country cottage she was acquiring in Putney:

We shall not inhabit Putney yet, for I play twice a week and you know it will not do to divide our little establishment and otherwise I must go there after the play. – Oh there never was so wretched a thing as Mrs D-arblaye's [sic] Tragedy. . . . She was at the representation in Spite of all I coud say of the ill effects So much agitation as She must necessarily feel woud have upon an invalide for She has been extremely ill it Seems Since her lying in. In truth it needed no discernment to See how it would go, and I was grivd that a woman of so much merit must be so mortified. The Audience were quite Angelic and only laughed where it was *impossible* to avoid it. . . . She

went to my brother's the next day and nobly said, She had been
decievd by her friends, that She Saw it was a very bad thing, and
withdrew it immediately. . . . I hope you will not be later than the
15th for if you are I shall scarcely catch a glimpse of you before I go
to Scotland where my restless fate drives me this summer. . . . Pray
give all our loves and congratulations to Cecilia, her little namesake
is very *witty and pretty*.[60]

Sarah, accompanied by Harry, went to Scotland while the
weather was still bad. She wrote to Mrs Piozzi in mid-May that
there were four feet of snow in Edinburgh. Afterwards she wrote
to Miss Coates in Glasgow, with whom she had stayed with Harry
during the tour, about this son of hers who, against her advice,
had insisted on going on the stage. His presence was a comfort to
her, however, since he could replace her husband – whose foot
was giving him great pain – as an escort:

But my dear Harry having oddly and perversely enough taken into
his head . . . that it is my way to be late always, made me leave
Lancaster by eight o'clock the Sunday following. I got to Skipton
about five in the evening and was detained the next morning for
want of Horses. . . . I think when the crude materials of his composition are ripened by Time and observation, he will be a fine creature;
the more I conversed with him, the more I found instinctive fondness
heightened by his excellent understanding and very amiable qualities,
his mind is capable of every lively and great perception, and he only
wants to get rid of his unjustifiable portion of diffidence and to see
and hear good things, to make him a fine Actor. Do not fancy this a
blind partiality, for I look at those I love 'with all the malice of a
friend'.[61]

It was a restless year, as surviving diaries and correspondence
show. Mrs Piozzi wrote to Penelope Pennington from her home
in Streatham on 13 June: 'Charming Siddons is somewhere in
the North, setting up the individuals in her family, like Ninepins,
for Fortune to bowl at, and knock down again. *She* meantime
secures glorious immortality in both worlds.' Mrs Piozzi kept alive
her resentment at what she regarded as the exploitation of Sarah
by her family: 'Mrs Siddons remains,' she wrote in May 1795,
'indeed – but ever on the Wing – to serve some Brother, or save
some Sister, or satisfy cravings from her own hungry Family –
or something that calls her into Distant Regions – Scotland or
Ireland – one Week in the year (now She is got well) is all I can
obtain of *her* Company!'[62]

Sarah wrote to Whalley on 14 August:

I am but just returned out of the North. I have been travelling (for the first time by myself) near nine hundred miles this summer; have worked harder, I believe, than anybody ever did before; but I am very well, thank God! and have got a good deal of money. Mr Siddons is a victim to the rheumatism, and I am persuading him to go to Bath. . . . It is most likely that I must stay at home and mind my business, which will be unlucky for Sally and Maria, whom I should like to send with their father, if I knew any lady who would now and then *chaperone* them, in case of my being obliged to give up the pleasure of going with them. . . . We are now at our quiet little nutshell upon Putney Heath – a nice little snug, comfortable place it is. I wish we had ye both here.[63]

The cottage was to serve as a substitute for Nuneham Rectory during 1795 and 1796.

Sarah was in fact fortunate during the spring of 1796 to have managed to free herself from any connexion with the celebrated Shakespearian forgery – the play *Vortigern*, in which it was originally intended she would appear. She wrote to Mrs Piozzi in March 1796, and reveals that she had no time for this audacious bid for fame by the Irelands, which deceived so many scholars:

All sensible persons are convinced that *Vortigern* is a most audacious imposter. If he be not, I can only say that Shakespeare's writings are more unequal than those of any other man. I am studying for *Vortigern* and Almeyda, and only scrawl these few lines, for fear you should have been frightened at some story of my biting or barking.[64]

The forgery of *Vortigern* is a remarkable example of the gullibility of people in the literary world, as well as reflecting the almost pathological private obsessions of the forger, William Henry Ireland, and his father, Samuel Ireland, a topographical artist, etcher, and antique dealer.[65] Ever since Garrick's elaborate promotion of Shakespeare as the Immortal Bard at the Jubilee celebrations at Stratford in 1769, the dramatist was to become a national cult figure, handed on with reverence by the eighteenth century to the nineteenth, and by the nineteenth (with bowdlerization) to the twentieth – each generation of scholars, critics, actors, and devoted public remodelling him to suit their current tastes. The *entrepreneurs* soon entered the market, acquiring, manufacturing, or falsifying 'relics' for sale, as if Shakespeare had been some kind of saint with powers to heal. The unscrupulous exploitation of these antiquities, or Shakespeariana, had already created interesting market-values when Samuel Ireland and his son entered the stage.

Samuel Ireland realized that the Shakespeare document market was virtually a blank. If only some of his letters or manuscripts could be discovered, not only fame but fortune lay in the discoverers' hands. Aided by another scoundrel, John Jordan, a Stratford wheelwright, Samuel began to acquire 'relics' of Shakespeare. Both he and his eighteen-year-old son absorbed from Jordan all the necessary Shakespearian patter about the Bard's associations with Stratford, both true and fictitious. The only thing no one seemed able to supply were manuscripts, however fragmentary, from Shakespeare's plays or personal papers.

William Henry Ireland appears to have been illegitimate, born to Ireland's housekeeper and mistress, Mrs Freeman, a woman with both money and some education. William Henry's birth was shrouded in mystery, and his mother may well have been some other woman, though Mrs Freeman was held to be the mother of most of Ireland's children. A lonely child, to some extent despised and neglected by his father, William Henry's one idea during his adolescence was to impress his father and share in his cultural dealings. He was obsessed by Chaucer, filling his bedroom with 'relics' and medieval armour. He was also influenced by the astonishing career of Chatterton, who had died in 1770. So he began to try his hand at writing poetry in a kind of medieval style, with pseudo-medieval spelling.

It was in 1793 that William Henry had accompanied his father to Stratford. Here he learned of the absence of Shakespearian manuscripts, which Samuel found so frustrating. After they had returned to London, he began to experiment with forgery, using fragments cut from old vellum documents and special inks. From small beginnings, such as author's dedications in books, he progressed by the end of 1794 to present his first Shakespearian forgery, a property deed. This proved such a success with his father that in quick succession during January 1795 he produced a whole series of Shakespearian 'finds'. He was careful to use parchment scraps of the right period cut from documents in his employer's archives; since he was apprenticed to a lawyer who specialized in the conveyance of property, there was no shortage of parchment on which he could draw. He dried the ink of his inscriptions brown before the fire. He told his father the documents came from the collection of an aristocrat who refused to have his name revealed.

The forgeries of William Henry Ireland were to develop into one of the great hoaxes of literature. Both father and son were by now, in their quite different ways, in a state of compulsive excitement. They were 'possessed' by the possibilities of what lay before them. While Ireland senior put on a special exhibition of his new and most precious 'relics' in February 1795 at his place in Norfolk Street, his son hastened to create new and even greater ones, working away from home on his employer's premises. Among the exhibits was a ludicrous perversion of the second quarto of *King Lear*, and some 'leaves' from *Hamlet*, both manuscripts omitting Shakespeare's 'indecencies', and dressing what was left with bogus period spelling which became more eccentric than that of Chatterton. Boaden was among those who visited the exhibition, and he was at first as completely taken in as anyone. He wrote in his journal, *The Oracle*:

> By the obliging politeness of Mr Ireland, of Norfolk Street, the conductor of this paper is enabled to gratify, in a general way, the public curiosity. . . . There are various papers, the *domestica facta* of this great man's life, discovered. [The letter] 'to the lady he afterwards married! . . . [is] distinguished for the utmost delicacy of passion and poetical spirit. . . . The conviction produced upon our mind, is such as to make all scepticism ridiculous, and when we follow the sentiments of Dr Joseph Wharton, we have no fear of our critical orthodoxy.[66]

He was delighted to find that Shakespeare's mind was after all so pure; 'the *licentious* passages' as 'confirmed by the original! – they are not SHAKESPEARE'S, but the foisted impurities of buffoons.' Boswell himself went to Norfolk Street, where he excited the attention appropriate to his fame by kneeling and kissing the sacred relics. But the array of 'believers', including John Taylor and many well-known scholars such as Wharton, had from the first[67] to face the scorn of the 'unbelievers', led by the redoubtable, though rival, Shakespearian scholars, Steevens and Malone. But the believers were not to be put off, scholars or not. Meanwhile William Henry was excelling himself by writing an entirely original Shakespearian tragedy – *Vortigern*, adapted from Holinshed. It took him only two months to complete this, and he presented it to his father in hastily composed sections.

At the same time he protected his 'copyright' by forging a deed of gift of the plays to a fictitious ancestor, Masterre William Henrye Irelande. Then, to end the series of forgeries, since they had to end sometime, he produced an early Shakespearian Will, dated 1611, to challenge the genuine, later one, dated 25 March 1616, which had come to light in 1747. In this he gave Shakespeare a bastard son. While this work was being completed, Samuel Ireland was busy collecting subscriptions, at four guineas a time, for the publication of the documents, and at the same time pressing his son only too hard to introduce him to the unduly retiring aristocrat from whom the documents had come. Among the subscribers to the publication were Boswell, Burke, Pitt, Sheridan and Dora Jordan; neither Kemble's nor Sarah's name appears on the list. Sheridan – rather against his will because, on the whole, he did not much care for Shakespeare – signed a contract in September 1795 to produce *Vortigern* at Drury Lane. He felt that at least he owed it to himself and his theatre to be the first to present the great dramatist's newly-discovered work, for what it was worth, and he fully expected Kemble and Sarah, as dedicated Shakespearian players, to appear in it together.

Kemble, in fact, was violently opposed to *Vortigern* and did everything he could to postpone its production. Sheridan, too, procrastinated; he thought what he had read of the play to be most disappointing, and he did not live up to his word to give *Vortigern* a grand presentation with new scenery and the greatest *réclame* worthy of the occasion. Kemble and Sheridan were still pressing to get the completed script from Ireland before having any new scenery constructed. William Henry, however, though refused the patronage of Sheridan, Kemble, and Sarah, managed to secure more generous treatment from Drury Lane's second lady, Dora Jordan. She took him straight to her lover, the Duke of Clarence, who readily at her bidding joined the claque of believers in the authenticity of *Vortigern*, and put himself down for several copies of Samuel's publication. Thus encouraged, William Henry started to work on another Shakespearian play, *Henry II*. The papers were published on 24 December, but still *Vortigern* lacked a production date.

By the New Year, Boaden had lost his faith and moved over to the ranks of the unbelievers; he published a retraction of his initial support; he was, he said, victim of a 'wished impression' of the authenticity of the papers. By now it had become a race –

29. Drury Lane Theatre in 1804. From Thornbury,
Old and New London.

The Pit Entrance at Drury
Lane when Sarah Siddons is
playing Euphrasia; the play is
indicated on the poster. (*British
Museum*)

31. Edinburgh: Regent Bridge, Nelson's Monument, and the
Theatre (right), 1820.

32. King's Theatre, Haymarket, London. Drawing: William Capon, 1785.
(*Photograph from the Richard Southern Collection in the Theatre Collection,
Department of Drama, University of Bristol*)

33. King's Theatre, Haymarket, 1795. Performance of *The Three and the Deuce*, by Prince Hoare. (*Photograph by courtesy of the Theatre Collection, Department of Drama, University of Bristol*)

34. Contemporary print of the Pit Accident at the Theatre Royal, Haymarket, 3 February 1794.

35. Lawrence as a young man. Engraving from a drawing by the artist. (*Original in the British Museum*)

36.   Sarah Siddons. By Thomas Lawrence (1797?). Said to be in the part of
Mrs Haller, production 1798. (*National Portrait Gallery, London*)

37. Maria Siddons. A sketch in oils by Thomas Lawrence.

38. Maria Siddons. From an engraving after Thomas Lawrence.
(*British Museum*)

39. Sally Siddons. Lithograph after a drawing by Lawrence, 1800.

would *Vortigern* be produced at Drury Lane before the hoax was finally exposed? The production actually won by a very short head. The discussion for or against authenticity was still in balance when the play was presented on 2 April 1796; Malone's scathing 400-page *Inquiry into the Authenticity of Certain Miscellaneous Papers* appeared on 31 March. Sheridan by now did not care one way or the other, since he was certain the theatre would fill. He was right; the streets outside were crammed two hours before the start of the play at six-thirty.

Sarah's withdrawal from the cast was made tactfully but firmly:

> Mrs Siddons' compliments to Mr Ireland; she finds that *Vortigern* is intended to be performed next Saturday and begs to assure him that she is very sorry the weak state of her health after six weeks of indisposition renders her incapable of even going to the necessary rehearsals of the play, much less to act. Had she been fortunately well she would have done all in her power to justify Mr Ireland's polite sentiments on the subject when she had the honour of seeing him on Saturday.[68]

Kemble's hostility showed itself in a number of ways, most of all in his refusal to bill the play as written by Shakespeare. *Vortigern* was announced quite simply as 'a new play' without benefit of author. There were, however, 'new Scenes, Dresses and Decorations' and the presence in the cast of both Kemble himself and Dora Jordan. The Duke of Clarence was present, but not the Prince of Wales, who had granted an audience to Samuel Ireland the previous December. A musical entertainment was added, *My Grandmother*, with Miss de Camp in the cast; it dealt with the gullibility of an art collector. Samuel Ireland was there – in a box with Mrs Freeman, while William Henry remained behind the scenes with Dora Jordan.

The tension in the theatre ran high. The Prologue appealed to the audience to keep an open mind, and the first two acts survived fairly enough. Laughter only began during the third act, and Kemble had to appeal for silence. Ireland was by now sure that Kemble had maliciously miscast the play in order to encourage derision, and this was confirmed when a comedian, Mr Phillimore, having played a warrior who died in combat on the stage, lay in such a position that the drop curtain came down directly on top of him, and the audience could see him extricate himself. Gradually the production declined into a farce, at which even the actors seemed to connive. Kemble gave the *coup de grâce* to the evening by the way in which he spoke the line

'And when this solemn mockery is ended.'

When it was announced from the stage that the play was to be repeated, the house rose in uproar in spite of the presence of the Duke of Clarence, a 'wonderfully and ridiculously conspicuous' supporter of *Vortigern* as a Shakespearian discovery. The production was never repeated. Kemble, though his behaviour can scarcely be commended, never concealed the fact that he was determined the play should not succeed; he gave his own, much refurbished account of it, some years later. *The Annual Register* summed up the general verdict: the play, it said, was the work of 'a copyist who is more intent on imitating the language than the genius of Shakespeare'.

The melancholy end to the story is well known. William Henry's total profit for all his work, a gift from his father since he was still only a minor, was £90. Samuel persistently believed in the authenticity of both the papers and the play until his death. Perhaps the greatest tragedy for William Henry was his father's resolute refusal to accept any hint that he could have been the author of the Shakespeare papers; how could such an idiot have composed these wonderful writings? The very thought was, to William Henry's father, a further proof of his son's 'insolence and vanity'. William Henry left his father's house for good in June.

In 1796 came the first major break between Kemble and Sarah on the one hand, and Sheridan on the other. In May Sarah wrote to a friend whilst travelling in the North, where her earnings were at least paid to her in hard cash:

Here I am, sitting close in a little dark room, in a little wretched inn, in a little poking village called Newport Pagnell. I am on my way to Manchester, where I am to act for a fortnight; from whence I am to be whirled to Liverpool, there to do the same. From thence I skim away to York and Leeds: and then, when Drury Lane opens – who can tell? for it depends upon Mr Sheridan, who is uncertainty personified. *I have got no money from him yet;* and all my last benefit, a very great one, was swept into his treasury; nor have I seen a shilling of it. Mr Siddons has made an appointment to meet him today at Hammersley's. As I came away very early, I don't know the result of the conference; but, unless things are settled to Mr Siddons's satisfaction, he is determined to put the affair into his lawyer's hands.[69]

In an undated letter of about the same period, Sheridan wrote to John Grubb: 'Siddons is notifying her departure.'

Sheridan, however, knew how to blandish Kemble, who genuinely liked him in spite of the anxieties the partnership involved. An astonishing story is told by Boaden in his life of Kemble:

I was present one night in Suffolk Street, when he denounced his fixed, his unalterable determination. He expected Sheridan there after the house should be up, and aware of the great disarming powers of the orator, in a sort of inarticulate murmur, alarmed the party with the prospect of a scene; and as some very excellent claret was near him, he proceeded to fortify himself for the engagement. At length Sheridan arrived, took his place next to Mrs Crouch at the table, looked at Kemble with kindness, but the kindness was neither returned nor acknowledged. The great actor now looked unutterable things, and occasionally emitted a *humming* sound like that of a bee, and groaned in the spirit inwardly. Crouch whispered two words in Sheridan's ear, which let him know, I believe, the *exact* cause of the present moody appearance of his manager. A considerable time elapsed, and frequent repetitions of the sound before mentioned occurred; when at last, 'like a pillar of state', slowly up rose Kemble, and in these words addressed the astonished proprietor. 'I am an EAGLE, whose wings have been bound down by frosts and snows; but now I shake my pinions, and cleave into the general air, unto which I am born.' He then deliberately resumed his seat, and looked as if he had relieved himself from insupportable thraldom. Sheridan knew the complacency of man under the notion of a fine figure, and saw that his eagle was not absolutely irreclaimable; he rose, took a chair next to the great actor; in two minutes resumed his old ascendency. The tragedian soon softened into his usual forgiving temper; and I am ashamed to say how late it was when, cordial as brothers, I took one arm of Kemble, and Sheridan the other, and resolutions were formed 'that melted as breath into the passing wind'.[70]

In another undated letter, Sheridan, evidently annoyed with Kemble, nevertheless suggested they resolve their difficulties over four bottles of claret. Kemble's 'veneration for him was extreme', and, according to Boaden, though he took no interest in politics ('Newspapers he did not read'), he admired Sheridan's eloquence and thought he had something of the appearance of Shakespeare, as Kemble imagined him. Kemble was also, says Boaden, 'a child even in the forms of business', and strictly honest, so that only too often he found that materials would be

supplied to the theatre only if he personally guaranteed the payment for them. Players who had not received their salaries
naturally grew difficult, and would only appear if he personally
promised they would be paid. Finally, Kemble could stand it no
longer, and before the autumn season began in 1796 he resigned
as manager; he was succeeded by Richard Wroughton. The
theatre was deeply encumbered by debt, and Wroughton almost
immediately ran into trouble with both Elizabeth Farren and
Dora Jordan. Farington records on 30 November 1796:

> Miss Farren last night refused to appear in a new Play at Drury
> Lane which made much confusion in the House. The cause assigned
> was indisposition but that was not believed by the audience; and
> the fact Lysons [a friend of Farington; Keeper of the Tower
> of London] says is, that as she cannot obtain payment from the
> Theatre, she resolutely told them she wd not appear unless Her
> demands were paid. – Kemble keeps away for the same reason;
> so does Mrs Jordan, and Mrs Siddons will unless she is regularly
> paid. – Such is the unprincipled conduct of Sheridan.[71]

Although both Sarah and Kemble were still appearing at Drury
Lane, their money was hard to come by. On 9 November Campbell
quotes her as writing to a friend:

> I am, as you may observe, acting again: but how much difficulty
> to get my money! Sheridan is certainly the greatest phenomenon
> that Nature has produced for centuries. Our theatre is going on, to
> the astonishment of everybody. Very few of the actors are paid, and
> all are vowing to withdraw themselves: yet still we go on. Sheridan
> is certainly omnipotent.[72]

Boaden says that Sheridan always knew how to get round Sarah,
calling on her in his carriage and persuading her to go with him
in it to Drury Lane, pledging his honour that she would be paid
if only she would perform. In a letter to his wife written on 20
September 1796, he wrote 'I was obliged to go out of town to
meet Mrs Siddons and prevail on her to play on thursday [sic]'.
On the same day a notice had appeared in the *Morning Post*:
'Mrs Siddons has finally closed her engagement with the Proprietors of the Drury Lane Theatre.' Nevertheless, Sheridan got
round both her and Kemble yet again, and during the season
1796–7 she appeared in no less than eight new parts.

In one of these, *Tamerlane* by Rowe, she played Arpasia, a
character (says Campbell) in which 'she wrought herself up . . . to

a degree of agitation that was perilous almost to her life.' After witnessing her lover's strangulation,

> . . . it was Mrs Siddons's part to feign a swoon, but she swooned in earnest. Clutching her drapery with convulsive fingers, she fell back so that her head was heard striking the stage, and her limbs were exposed, which at once made it palpable to the spectator that her fall was neither studied nor voluntary. In a moment there was a rush from the pit and boxes to enquire for her on the stage. It was long before she recovered from the fainting fit.[73]

In another production of this period, Lillo's *Fatal Curiosity*, she became the cause of emotional disturbance in others. Crabbe Robinson as a young man in London was thrown into hysterics in the theatre. According to Campbell:

> When Mrs Siddons, as Agnes, was asked by Old Wilmot how they should support themselves, and when she produced the jewels of their unknown son, giving a remote hint at the idea of murdering him, she crouched and slid up to Wilmot, with an expression in her face that made the flesh of the spectator creep. Mr Robinson said that from that moment his respiration grew difficult, and in a few minutes he lost all command of himself. When the murder-scene approached he laughed aloud, and there was a general cry in the pit to turn him out. The process of his ejectment was even begun, and he had received some harsh treatment, when a humane woman interposed, who saw, and explained his real condition. He was in strong hysterics.[74]

In the season of 1797–8, during which Campbell claims Sarah appeared in over forty presentations, there was continual trouble with Sheridan, as a letter from William to Whalley, dated 15 and again 17 December 1797 reveals:

> . . . the worst of all situations is that of uncertainty. Such, I am sorry to say, is yours with respect to Mrs Siddons, who at this very time is withdrawn from the theatre again on account of the failure of 'Tercus', solemnly proposed before she began. They may patch it up again, and the next fortnight it shall be the same; in short, it is so disagreeable that I would to heaven she had done with them altogether.[75]

A remarkable letter, preserved at the Garrick Club in London, shows in some detail the nature of the negotiations which went on between Sheridan and William. It is dated 13 November 1799, but deals with the whole period of 1797–9; it is from William to Sheridan's treasurer at the theatre, Richard Peake:

My account and yours agree exactly as to the number of nights of last season and to the £970 received from you – but I wish before we start again to have all the accounts drawn upon a sheet of paper, or this filled up will do – signed by Mr Sheridan and you that we may fairly understand what they are –

My last account stood to you as follows –

In the beginning of the season 97–8 was owing to Mrs Siddons from the Proprietors of Drury Lane Theatre

Two Notes amounting to	1677. 15.	6
a third amounting to	410. 0.	0

In the course of the season 97–98 she performed 54 nights, which is	1080. 0.	0
Total		
	3167. 15.	6

In the season of 97–8 paid to her	1860. 0.	0
Due to her at the end of 97–98	1307. 15.	6
Interest upon the two notes of 1677.15.6		
from March 23 1797 to the same date 1799, somewhere about	167. 14.	0
Do. upon the third Note of £410 as from the end of April 1797 to same date 1799 somewhere about	41. 0.	0

Total before last season	1516. 9.	6
Last season deficiency of Salary	610. 0.	6
For Mrs Siddons benefit last Season	[Left blank]	

Total [Left blank]

Tickets £174.16.0
Mr Fosbrook sold 35.2. which I did not receive
Mrs Siddons sold 139.14.0

When the benefit money is added take 139.14.0 for tickets away and there remains the sum of [Left blank]

Now, *Sir*, as I think the opposite statement plain and correct I wish to have the Benefit filled up, and your signatures [illegible words; damaged paper], and for the future, Mr Peake, if I suffer you to go backward like a crab from the agreement of the thirty pounds per night even a single payment why –

Your very hum sert., Wm. Siddons

Sarah appeared in only two new parts during the season of 1797–8, Julia in Sheridan's *The Rivals*, a serious enough part for a comedy, and in the controversial character of Mrs Haller; this was in Kotzebue's play, *The Stranger*, translated and adapted initially from the German by Benjamin Thompson, but much revised by Sheridan, who made the adaptation his own. This play was all the rage in Germany, and Sheridan hoped to establish a similar success with it in London. The part of Mrs Haller was a relatively daring one for the period; it certainly shocked Boaden, who did not like it at all when he saw it for the first time in March 1798. Adelaide Haller is no less than a woman of sin. She is acting as housekeeper in the castle of the Count and Countess Wald-bourg, who discover that she is in fact as aristocratic as themselves, though she has deserted her husband and children under the influence of a man who has seduced her. Her husband arrives to claim her in the guise of a Stranger, living alone at the castle gates. Although at first she refuses to go back to him, preferring to remain in a permanent state of penitence, the sight of her children finally brings her to her senses. The play was remarkable for the absence of any conventional, moral retribution designed to fall upon the sinner's head. Mrs Haller is neither killed nor does she kill herself. It came as something of a shock to the sentimental audiences in London, almost like Ibsen's *A Doll's House* which shocked conventional audiences a century later.

The play was a sensation, and was performed twenty-six times in the season. Campbell gives some idea of the restraint and subtlety with which Sarah played the part:

Mrs Siddons's performance of the part of *Mrs Haller* was the most delicate and judicious that can be imagined. She shewed what the poet clearly intended us to feel, namely, that the reconcilement was not a conclusion anticipated as a matter of reason or principle by either party, but a burst of nature, overwhelming all abstracted feelings of pride and considerations of stern propriety. She therefore sustained the part with tearless but touching self-command till the end of the very last scene, denoting that she had neither hope nor wish, beyond a promise from her husband that he would not hate her. All other actresses of the part let fall their tears too soon; and, in the shower of their grief, dimmed to us that only redeeming light in which we can view *Mrs Haller*. Though a penitent woman, she is conscious that she has no claim to more than her husband's dry-eyed forgiveness, and is therefore aware that she has no right, in their trying interview, to affect him with voluntary demonstrations of her sensibility. Mrs Siddons accordingly conducted herself with a reserve and calmness that threw pride into humility; and thus, by contrast, made the effect of her agitation, in the last scene, undescribable.[76]

In spite of the moral strictures of certain critics (one of whom forecast that the time would come 'when not a child in England will have its head patted by its legitimate father'), curiosity brought in large numbers to see it, and Sarah was to appear in the part no less than twenty-six times during the season. She played it, says Boaden, with 'subdued power'; but, as Sally was to write, it affected her deeply, 'My Mother cries so much at it that She is always ill when she comes home.' There can be little doubt that her own unhappy relations with Sid did not help her. And there were soon to be other, deeper reasons to disturb her emotions.

Another man was deeply impressed by her, and painted her (possibly in the character of Mrs Haller, though we cannot be certain of this) in 1797. This was Thomas Lawrence, now at the height of his fame as a fashionable portrait painter. He was in love, now with one, now with the other, of Sarah's two daughters, and it would seem almost certain that he was in love with Sarah herself. His was a strange, collective love affair with all the women in the Siddons family. Sarah's own relations with Lawrence were to become the greatest drama in her life offstage.

6

Lawrence

===========⌘===========

IN 1787, AT THE age of eighteen, Lawrence had begun his career in London, full of confidence that he would soon establish himself as a great portrait painter. More than a dozen years had passed since the days when, as a boy, he had pursued Sarah with the passionate admiration a youth of his nature might feel for a mature and beautiful young woman.

Lawrence's career in London had developed rapidly and brilliantly. He gained the immediate help of Sir Joshua Reynolds, who thought well of his work and, seeing that his talent was indeed for portraiture, realized that all he needed, apart from the full development of his technical mastery, was the right kind of introduction into society which would enable him to obtain commissions. Lawrence lived briefly in Leicester Fields (later Leicester Square), near to Sir Joshua Reynolds's own house, and his round of introductions soon increased when the fashionable world adopted this handsome, accomplished, reserved and polite young man, who wrote them appreciative letters couched in the correctly formal terms of the eighteenth century. Friends in Bath sent him on to friends in London, and since everybody in London Society tended to know everyone else, it was not difficult for Lawrence to advance. He had all the social graces; he danced, fenced and boxed well; he was outstanding at billiards; he was a good shot. And, the ladies noted, he was a good amateur actor; after all, he had once seriously thought of becoming a professional player. He was soon in demand at the London dinner-tables; according to one observer, 'his chestnut locks flowing on his shoulders gave him a romantic appearance'. He wore his hair in this fashion until 1789. The artist William Hoare thought that he had an ideal head to model for Christ.

It would seem to have been Miss Delany, who had originally introduced Fanny Burney to the Royal Family, who first showed Lawrence's work to the Court. Within a year of his arrival his name was widely known; his new studios in Jermyn Street became crowded, and his visitors included John Philip Kemble. He was talked of in both Court circles – that of the King, and that of the Prince of Wales – before he was twenty. He was the 'talk of the town'. He exhibited in the Royal Academy from 1787, and was for a while a student at the Academy School. By 1788, he was exhibiting oils as well as crayon drawings. The only blight on his life, though he does not appear to have regarded it as such, was the presence of his father in London, doing his best in the most absurd fashion to 'puff' his son's work when it needed no puffing, and certainly not of the kind in which Lawrence senior indulged.

In September 1789, six months before he came of age, he received his first Royal command. In 1790 he moved to Old Bond Street; his earnings were now large, though his expenses were always larger, and he allowed his father £300 a year. Lawrence was doomed always to be overworked in the hopeless effort to cancel his debts, and he wisely placed his affairs in the hands of the financier John Julius Angerstein and his friend Joseph Farington, R.A., the celebrated diarist. Even with their help, Lawrence's debts grew, and were a constant source of embarrassment to him. Among his many subjects exhibited between 1790 and 1798, in addition to his Royal portraits, was one of Elizabeth Farren – the 'picture of the year' in 1790, when Sir Joshua himself said on seeing it: 'In you, sir, the world will expect to see accomplished what I have failed to achieve' – and others of Miss Moulton Barrett ('Pinkie', the future mother of Elizabeth Barrett Browning), William Cowper and the portraits of Sarah herself. In February 1892, after Reynolds's death, he was appointed Painter in Ordinary to His Majesty. He had become an Associate of the Royal Academy the year before, and was elected an R.A. in 1794, when he was twenty-six. The same year he moved to an expensive house in Piccadilly, facing on to Green Park. His debts increased.

In his social and private life he showed a marked interest in women without, it would seem, going to the final length of proposing either a liaison or marriage. A flirtatious letter from Ann Theresa Fleming of Bath lends a little substance to the rumour he felt forced to deny in 1792 that he was paying his addresses to a Miss Anne Foldsone. He excelled as the painter of beautiful women, achieving a sensitivity of expression which revealed response and understanding of the emotionalism beneath the surface charm and elegance of the vivacious women who sat for him; they felt that he painted their 'souls'. This exceptional, sensitive response to women made him subject to violent attachments which he did not carry further than passionate declarations, and his love affairs developed into obsessions which preyed on his nerves and rendered him 'desolate' for love. From the point of view of the girls who became the object of such nervous passions it was either exhilarating or distressing according to whether they had progressed beyond the stage of enjoying adolescent 'crushes' on romantic-looking men or had more realistic desires to engage a man in the kind of relationship which might lead on to marriage. Lawrence, indeed, was developing into a spiritual philanderer whose need for believing himself to be violently in love was greater than his need actually to fulfil it by becoming a husband and father. It is notable that one of his sisters was also subject to obsessive passions for unobtainable men, and that, though his sisters indeed married, neither Lawrence nor his two brothers, Andrew and William, ever did.[1]

By the time Lawrence had reintroduced himself into the Siddons household during the 1790s, when he was still only in his mid-twenties, he came as the most brilliant young painter of the age, an R.A. at twenty-six, a darling of the Court, athletic but highly cultured and sensitive, overworked but also romantically well set up, a handsome socialite given to gallantry and polite philandering, but also known to be in debt. His flattering responsiveness to young women had already been noted by the King himself, who 'quizzed' him for flirting with Miss Papendieck, wife of his German musician, while little Princess Amelia rushed to his Majesty in tears of jealousy because he had only given her one drawing while her sisters had received two. Georgiana, the beautiful Duchess of Devonshire, was among the fine ladies who had taken a fancy to him; she had adopted him during his boyhood in Bath, and often entertained him when he came to London. Indeed, Lavinia Forster, who knew him when he was young, wrote of him later: 'His manners at that time appeared to me so frivolous, that I neither sought, nor supposed I obtained, his notice.' However, portrait painting of the kind he executed at such speed became an ethereal form of love-making, and when Miss Farren protested to him – 'teased' as she was by her friends about the portrait of herself for which she considered her lover, Lord Derby, to have been overcharged – the letter seems written in terms almost like an attempt to make things up after a lovers' tiff:

> Mr Lawrence, you will think me the most troublesome of all human beings, but indeed it is not my own fault; they tease me to death about the picture and insist upon my writing to you. One says it is so thin in the figure, that you might blow it away – another that it looks broke off in the middle: in short, you must make it a little *fatter*, at all events, diminish the *bend* you are so attached to, even if it makes the picture look ill, for the owner of it is quite distressed about it at present. I am shocked to tease you, and dare say you wish me and the portrait in the fire.

One can well imagine the intimate, flirtatious discussions which went on around the canvas between the intense, responsive young painter and his beautiful, highly self-conscious subjects, ever curious to find out what he could 'see' in them.[2]

Sarah was forty-two when Lawrence, aged twenty-eight, painted the full-face portrait of her which was exhibited in the Royal Academy in 1797, and is now in the National Portrait Gallery. It appeared in the catalogue of the period as 'Portrait of a Lady'.[3] There seems little need for John Williams (who wrote acid comments and criticisms about art under the name of Anthony Pasquin) to have written so scathingly of this picture:

> It is no more like her than Hebe is similar to Bellona. We have here youth, flexibility of features, and an attempt at the formation of beauty, to denote a lady who is proverbially so stern on her countenance that it approaches to savageness, – so determined in the outline of her visage, that it requires the delusion of the scene to render it soft and agreeable, and who is so far from being young, that her climacteric will be no more.

In the same exhibition, Lawrence had a portrait of Kemble, catalogued as 'Portrait of a Gentleman'.

According to Lawrence's recent biographer, Goldring, he had already fallen in love with Sally Siddons by 1796, and wanted to marry her. A letter to him from William Godwin, dated 20 February, shows that the philosopher was highly sympathetic to the state Lawrence was in, perhaps all the more so because he was himself involved at the time with the unhappy Mary Wollstonecraft, whom he was finally to marry the following year, which was also the year of her death in giving birth to Shelley's future wife. Godwin wrote:

> I have felt considerable anxiety about you. I could plainly perceive, when I breakfasted with you a few weeks ago, something extraordinary passing in your mind. It showed itself principally in a sort of listlessness, which might almost at first sight have suggested the idea of paralytic affection, but might easily be supposed to be disconsolateness and dissatisfaction, arising from some cause, not of a physical, but an intellectual nature. I longed I confess to probe you, but dared not.
>
> And now you hint to me that your uneasiness is sacred, and that no one must intrude upon it. I am sorry for it. My sympathies, active and reactive, should have been much at your service. . . . Nothing is more inimical to the restoration of cheerfulness and activity than this obstinate silence. Let me add, that it seems a peculiar refinement of pride, of which I should not have suspected you, to resolve to be uneasy and that the world shall know nothing of the matter.[4]

Whatever Lawrence was able, or unable to express, he set about painting the most extraordinary genre picture, completely alien to his normal work – *Satan Summoning up his Legions*. This was exhibited at the Royal Academy in 1797. Lawrence's pugilist friend, 'Gentleman Jackson', posed for the vast, nude figure of Satan; the face is that of Kemble, while a writhing demon in a pit at Satan's feet has the profile of Sarah, though Lawrence was later to obscure the face with clouds. According to Mrs Piozzi, Sarah's face belonged to a *rising* angel, not a *falling* one. However one may care to interpret the presence of the faces of his friends in this obsessive work, the fact remains that they are there, and were recognized when the picture was exhibited with Lawrence's other portraits of Kemble and Sarah.[5]

By 1797, the tensions of Lawrence's relations with the whole Siddons family had reached fever-point. Sally was a young lady already established in society. She had returned to London with Maria from her finishing school in Calais when the international situation did not look reassuring. From 1793 both sisters were living at home with their parents, and we have Mrs Piozzi's judgement in that year that Sally was 'finely dressed' and 'prettier than Maria'. In 1796 Sally was twenty-one and Maria seventeen;

both were gay, enjoying their mother's position and money and, unlike her, loving the balls and parties which did their delicate health little good. Sally, as we have seen from Mrs Piozzi's alarming accounts, was subject to spasmodic attacks of asthma, while Maria, like so many women of the period, suffered from a weakness of the lungs.

Owing to their mother's preoccupation with the theatre, and frequent absence from home, and their father's declining health, which was eventually to force him to retire to live in Bath, it seems the two girls were in a somewhat freer position than most young women of their age, who had to live with their parents constantly watching over them. By 1797 Lawrence was frequently drawing their portraits, as he was their mother's, and this might well have led to periods of privacy in his studio. There were frequent parties at Great Marlborough Street, with the sisters escorted by their Uncle Charles (who was, within months, the same age as Sally) and attended in particular by the gay young men who did not find it at all difficult to fall in love with Sally – Lawrence openly and effusively, and, entirely secretly, Charles Moore, younger brother of General Sir John Moore who was fated to die at Corunna. Sally described Charles in her observant way as a 'merry creature. . . . I think I never saw anyone laugh so heartily in my life; it is impossible not to join him, even tho' one is ignorant of the cause of his mirth'. Charles, who was handsome, was reading for the Bar. Other girls in this circle of friends were Sarah Bird, who became in 1797 a partner with one of Lawrence's sisters in founding a school, and Amelia Locke, daughter of William Locke, who lived at Norbury Park and was one of Lawrence's wealthy patrons.

The divergent character of the two sisters will become apparent from what they said and what they did in the difficult situation in which Lawrence placed them during 1798. Sally might in many respects have made a good wife for Lawrence, had she been stronger in health and he brought to the point of accepting one woman in his life with whom he could live in a state of intimacy. She was an intelligent girl and, like Lawrence, she loved music and even composed songs. There seems no doubt that Sarah knew of the attachment, but opposed any open acknowledgement of it in the form of an official engagement, partly because of Lawrence's financial troubles and partly because of the acute worry she always felt about Sally's health.[6] With William by now

little better than her dependent, it would have been her responsibility to maintain Sally and Sally's family should Lawrence ever
become bankrupt. She knew all about men who could not keep
their wives and families. Lawrence's affairs were in a very bad way,
and on 17 October 1797 he had to write to John Graham, the Bow
Street magistrate, to plead for a postponement of execution by
the Sheriff against his possessions. However much Sarah knew,
or did not know, about this, the fact remains that she opposed a
formal engagement in 1797, but not the love affair itself. Lawrence
came to the house, therefore, as a friend of the family and as the
more or less acknowledged beau of Sally. Sarah, apparently,
wanted the relationship to be kept secret from both her husband
and her brother. She therefore carried the burden of this knowledge, if burden it was, herself; after all, she was very fond of
Lawrence, whose open admiration of her was expressed in the
beautiful drawings he made of her at this time. The affection of
this young man no doubt meant much to her, perhaps more than
she would have been prepared to acknowledge even to herself,
now that she was, emotionally at least, estranged from her
husband.

Maria, meanwhile, was developing fast. By 1797 she was
eighteen, and she was a very different girl from Sally. She was
spoilt, shallow and selfish; she set no store by her sister's moral
scruples in her effort to attract men, and it would seem she gave
way only too easily to passion and that she was by nature jealous.
In the autumn Sally fell ill again, and Maria took advantage of
her sister's enforced separation from Lawrence to alienate his
affections. She was successful. He fell madly in love with her; she
had more obvious sexual attraction than Sally, who was always
restrained and self-controlled.

The story of Lawrence's relationship with the women in the
Siddons household has been preserved in the letters written in
1798[7] – Lawrence, Sally and Maria Siddons and Sarah all wrote to
Penelope Pennington at Clifton in Bristol, who, as it happened,
had to bear a great part of the strain which the brief, passionate
relationship between Lawrence and Maria brought on, followed
by his even more passionate return to Sally, to whom he had been
virtually engaged in the first place. Mrs Pennington, who was
quite out of her emotional depth in dealing with Lawrence, kept
the letters, apparently, in case she was ever called upon to account
for her part in the strange and disturbing story. Other letters,

written earlier in the year by the girls to their friend Sarah Bird, have also been preserved, and give some introduction to the story.

The initial change in Lawrence's affections, his rejection of Sally and passion for Maria, appears to have taken place late in 1797, and certain private meetings with Maria may well have taken place in Greek Street, possibly with Sarah Bird as an intermediary. There are hints of this in an undated letter from Maria to her friend written at this time:

> I came home so late that I went to my room directly, and would not ring for Candles that they might fancy I had been in a *great while*. I *felt* how to dress myself, absolutely, and came down about the middle of dinner, and my Father ask'd me where I had been! I told a *story*, and there was an end of it.[8]

She was sending Lawrence notes, evidently against her mother's wishes but almost certainly with her knowledge: 'Tell *Mr Tom* he shall hear from me to-morrow morning,' she writes to Lawrence's sister, 'because my mother don't like to bear a letter.' Sarah Bird also brought letters back from Lawrence, because Maria in another letter is 'vex'd and impatient that . . . no note makes its appearance from Greek Street'.

Early in 1798 a final consent was given to Lawrence's engagement to Maria, with the Siddons agreeing to pay Lawrence's current debts by way of a marriage settlement. This unwilling consent was given because Maria's own health was failing, and it would appear she made it clear to her parents that their opposition to her engagement was the cause of her decline. Sally herself wrote to Miss Bird, now in Warwickshire, on 5 January; more than a little can be read between the lines. Sally began by referring to the doctor's report on her sister:

> He says she is in a *very* doubtful state, and has given us too plainly to understand that a Consumption may be the consequence. I cannot however see her so very much recover'd without great hopes that her youth, and the unremitting attention that is paid her, may conquer this complaint. Do not for Heaven's sake breathe a syllable of this which may reach Mr Lawrence's ears, for I suppose, if he could imagine her so seriously ill, he would be almost distracted, now especially, when every desire of his heart is, without opposition, so near being accomplished. For now, dear Miss Bird, I must tell you a piece of good news, which will I know surprise and please you; my Father at length consents to the marriage, and Mr Lawrence has been receiv'd by him in the most cordial manner as his future son-in-law.

Maria determin'd to speak to my Father when she was much worse than she is now; she did, and he, mov'd by the state in which she was, and considering, no doubt, that the union must take place with or without his consent, thought it most wise to agree to what was inevitable. Some letters pass'd between him and Mr L., and now all is going on smoothly, and he regularly makes us a visit every evening. Should not this happy event have more effect than all the medicines? At least I cannot but think it will add greatly to their efficacy. But what will our friend do without some difficulties to overcome?[9]

Later in this, and in subsequent letters, she pokes fun at Sally Bird because she will not reveal which of the two Charleses she likes the better – Charles Kemble or Charles Moore: 'You are a sly thing,' she says, and obviously wants to become the intermediary for the chosen Charles's messages.

In February it is Maria who takes up this coy, allusive correspondence, in which love affairs form the serious undercurrent to the flow of gossip: Maria scarcely hides her resentment at Sally Bird's freedom of movement, while she hopes to excite her jealousy by references to Charles Moore's possible feelings for Amelia Locke:

> I am anxious to go out of the house for air, but I must not till April. I agree with you that nothing can be so delightful as the *unremitting* attention of those we love. . . . I am here all day, and very seldom see anybody so kind. . . . There [are] more real delights at home than I thought there were, the love of a mother and sister never fails. . . .I shall see Mr Charles Moore here on Monday, and I shall talk to him about you; I am sure he cannot have ceas'd *mourning for you*! I dare-say you have put even Miss Amelia Locke out of his mind.[10]

Then, still in February, came Lawrence's second precipitate switch of affection. It seems, as before, to have been brought on by the prolonged sickness of the girl with whom he was supposed to be in love. Maria's hypnotic hold on him was broken by her confinement to her room; the romantic assignations were over, and Lawrence, we must presume, came to his senses and realized that Sally, after all, was his true love. However, according to Sarah's niece, Fanny Kemble, daughter of Sarah's brother Charles, Lawrence became hysterical with anxiety when he realized the situation he was in. Instead of trying to resolve the matter as quietly and tactfully as he could, he appears to have undergone a torment of conscience in his desperate desire to be accepted once more by Sally, who had appeared so placid and kind when he had deserted her a few months before, and released by the possessive Maria, of whom he was possibly by now afraid, or at least fearful of the effect his change of affections might have on her health. Fanny Kemble recalls that Lawrence became

> . . . deeply dejected, moody, restless, and evidently extremely and unaccountably wretched. Violent scenes of the most painful emotion, of which the cause was inexplicable and incomprehensible, took place between himself and Mrs Siddons, to whom he finally, in a paroxysm of self-abandoned misery, confessed that he had mistaken his feelings . . . and ended by imploring permission to transfer his affections from one to the other sister.[11]

Sally, not Sarah, is the first to give her own, restrained, account of the new situation in a letter dated 5 March 1798 to Sarah Bird, excluding her own place in it, but giving an almost clinical account of Maria's reactions, an account which reveals her own feelings about her sister's duplicity in stealing her lover from her. She began by apologizing for not writing for some while:

> A great, great change has taken place in our house; when you write to Maria avoid, if possible, mentioning Mr Lawrence, at least for the present; all that affair is *at an end*. Are you astonish'd? Had you been present for some weeks past you would not be so much surpris'd. Maria bears her disappointment as I would have her, in short, like a person *whose heart could never have been deeply engag'd*. Mr Lawrence has found that he was mistaken in her character, his behaviour has been evidently alter'd towards her, as I told you, for weeks; his letters too, she said, were chang'd – in short, we see him no more. I long to be with you that I might tell you *all* and *everything*, for I am sure you are much interested in this affair, but I cannot write half I would say. It is now near a fortnight since this complete breaking off, and Maria is in good spirits, talks and thinks of dress, and company, and beauty, as usual. Is this not fortunate? Had she *lov'd him*, I think this event would almost have broken her heart; I rejoice that she did not.[12]

She also adds that her mother, who had not been able to work for a while, is better, but 'a good deal fatigued after the Play on Saturday night'.

The next letter is Maria's, also addressed to Sarah Bird and written a little over a week later, on 14 March. Maria seems to take some literary pleasure in presenting her sorrow to her friend:

I yet think I shall not live a long while, it is perhaps merely nervous [sic], but I sometimes feel as if I should not, and I see nothing very shocking in the idea. . . . You know I suppose the cause of too much of this misery, therefore I shall be spar'd the hateful task of mentioning it. Yet from the love I have for you I cannot bear that you should think I have been in the wrong, ah no, indeed, he himself, if it is possible any feeling can remain in him, will acknowledge how little he deserv'd the sacrifices I was willing to make for him. . . . I know you will be sorry to hear how ill I have been, and how nervous I still continue, though I am again mending.[13]

She says that she is to stay in Clifton during the summer, actually with Penelope Pennington, while her mother, accompanied by Sally, is on tour in England and Scotland. She likes the idea of Clifton – 'you may enjoy the beauties of nature there whenever you like, and yet be very gay in the evening, for the balls are generally crowded'. Sally, a fortnight later, followed up her letter with another in which she says: 'It is very certain they were not suited to each other, but had he lov'd her, he would not have found these deficiencies in her character which now he has discover'd.' She also adds, about Charles Moore, who was still secretly in love with her, 'I see him appear with pleasure, I think he is very agreeable company, and I see him depart without regret. Don't you think this is a comfortable way of going on? Oh, if I had always done so, I should have been happier than I am.' Mrs Piozzi visited the house in Great Marlborough Street late in April, and sensed the tension in the household. She wrote to Penelope Pennington of Sarah: '*She* is not cold to her old friend Heaven knows, yet there *is an iciness in the house* that I cannot describe. One reason may be that as everybody takes sides now, and many go there that are not on *your side and mine*, it must be as it is.'[14]

Sally, writing on 16 April, hastens to reassure Sarah Bird about the continued coolness of her relations with Charles Moore. Then she adds:

I feel certain that you, like me, *have been* unhappy; but let me hope that the recollection only remains with you, and that however similar our cases *may have been*, you are not, like me, surrounded with doubts, fears, and perplexities, from which I see not how to extricate myself – oblig'd to appear chearful, while everything about me at times distresses or is totally forgotten by me. Oh, you cannot guess my situation, but you pity me, I am sure . . . have either of you heard from Mr Lawrence? I once took it into my head you corresponded . . . this time last year – good heavens! – what changes have I seen since that time. Do tell me if it does not to you appear almost impossible for that violent passion, of which you were so close a witness, to be entirely vanish'd? And yet so it must be, or would the treasure, almost in his possession, have been resign'd? Ten weeks ago, who could have foreseen this?[15]

Sally's inquiries concerning the whereabouts of Lawrence appear to have been meant to deceive Sarah Bird. Two letters survive among Lawrence's papers; they were sent to him by Sally in April. They make it clear that, though they were not meeting, they were exchanging letters, and that she welcomed and returned his love. She starts in her teasing way by writing of their relationship in the third person:

Our friend in Dorset Street (Mrs Semple) is a good and kind friend, and you may, if you please, tell her all; and that will not, I imagine, be more than she suspects, for I believe I thank'd her a little too warmly when she put your letter in my hand. He is such a creature (says she), there is really no denying him anything. Ah! Mrs Semple, thought I, and do *you* feel his strange, resistless power? No wonder, then, that Sally is thus led on, step by step, to feel and to confess that she is again upon the point of surrendering that heart which (plaguing thing that it is!) was lost for a great while some time ago, and now is teasing and tormenting her to let it go where it is sure of being well receiv'd. And, besides, it is jealous of *another heart*, which it declares it sees plainly enough I do 'to every heart prefer'; and so I have a good mind to bid it begone, and rid myself of its importunity, especially as it has the generosity to assure me that, delighted as it shall be with its new abode, *it will obey my call* and, should its rival prove inconstant, will immediately return to Sally. Yet I think I should consult some friend before I make so dangerous a change. What do you think of it? I know you will tell me of *friends averse*, of *circumstances embarrassed*, of the *time that must elapse in secrecy and anxiety*, and, above all, of the *inconstancy of man*. My good friend, I have thought of all this twenty and twenty times. Your last is indeed a serious (forgive me if I differ from you and say I think it is the only) objection, for constancy and perseverance may surely overcome the others. The time that must pass before we could avow our sentiments may be employ'd by him (you know who I mean) to extricate himself from all pecuniary difficulties, for *do not suspect me of being so mad as to add to the embarrassments of him I love by giving him a wife to support. Indeed, you wrong me if you do. The more I love him the stronger will be this resolution.* But tell me, you who are his friend and mine – and tell me, I charge you, the truth, for I know you can – will his exertions, if he perseveres, enable him at last to marry one who will have nothing but a heart to offer? I know that this must be the work of perhaps years. I do not start at the idea, for *I know myself*; but will he be constant for *years*? I do not mean that we are to pass all this time situated as we are at present. I wait but for the time when Maria shall be evidently engaged by some other object to declare to her my intentions, and then there will be no more of this cruel restraint and we may overcome the objections of those whose objections are of importance. And now, having finished my letter to *your friend*, I will begin one to you. You cannot be in earnest when you talk of being soon again in Marlborough Street; *you know it is impossible*. Neither you, nor Maria, nor I could bear it. Do you think that tho' she does not love you, she would feel no unpleasant sensations to see those attentions paid to another which once were hers? Could you bear to pay them, could I endure receiving them? Oh no! banish this idea. Your *absence* indeed affects Maria but little – so little that I am convinced she never lov'd – but your *presence*, you must feel, would take us all in the most distressing situation imaginable. I was told that you pass'd thro' our street yesterday; I did not see you. If chance should ever bring you this way at nine o'clock in the morning and if it should occur to you to look towards our house, you might see a friend of yours at one of the parlour windows, where she is generally writing or reading at that hour, and where she now is, the clock just striking nine. . . . It seems like mockery when you talk to me of being *my pupil*. No, no; I have too much pleasure in the hopes of becoming yours to make any such agreement. I know that, should the prospect I now have before my eyes ever be realised, you will be much employ'd. So much the better. The more I see of men that have nothing to do, the more I wish that my husband may be oblig'd to do something. This temporary separation will, in my eyes, have many advantages. I can find employment for a morning as well as you. It is my choice to be alone in the morning; no one in an evening has greater delight in society. Need I tell you there is *one* (*if he is but constant*) whose company I would prefer to all the world? I inquire after you whenever I have an opportunity, and I am rejoic'd to hear that you paint diligently, and that the 'Coriolanus' is likely to leave all behind it at the exhibition, as 'Satan' did last year. I recall my words. Yes, I will suffer a rival: I permit you to be almost as much devoted to your divine Art as to Sally. . . . Adieu! In the present circumstance your plan of secrecy is an excellent one. Nobody need know what passes; from me they certainly will not. I will try to make myself easy, since my conduct is no secret to her whose approbation is as dear to me as my life; but I shall have much to endure.

I foresee it. I am not one of those who can set at nought the opinions of my friends. But you should be the better pleas'd that I am not, for is it not a sacrifice I make you? Oh, then, judge me not by others; think not that when you have won my heart you may abandon me and I shall soon recover. I tell you now, before you proceed any further, that *if I love you again* I shall love more than ever, and in that case *disappointment* would be *death*.[16]

It would appear from this letter that Sarah knew something, at least, of the contact between Lawrence and her daughter. On 24 April Sally wrote to Lawrence again, after they had met briefly, either by contrivance or by accident:

And did I indeed see you, speak to you, last night? Good heavens! was it not rather a dream? No, no, it was reality. How short, how cruelly short, did the time appear! It seem'd to me that I had a thousand thousand things to say to you, and yet, I think, I said nothing. But was it necessary to *say*? Oh! could you not read in my eyes the ecstacy of my heart? I could scarcely imagine it was reality; and yet 'such sober certainty of waking bliss I never felt (*but once*) before'.

You will not be surprised at my writing to you; you will guess that the cause which oblig'd me to resign this pleasure is *in part* remov'd. I will tell you more on Thursday. Yes, I will *tell* you; for if it is fine I mean to walk before breakfast, as I have done every fine morning lately. I shall be in Poland Street before nine. You have a key of Soho Square: shall we walk there? Oh time, time, fly quickly till Thursday morning! But alas! as hours last night appeared but moments, so will moments now be long, *long hours*.

I looked for you all over the pit last night, and had almost despair'd of seeing you; but I found you out before you saw me. You were on both sides up one pair of stairs; then in the stage-box, where I believe Mr Lysons pointed me out. Sunday and Monday – happy days! They have repaid me for a month of anxiety. I can hardly hope that I shall be so happy as to see you, as I intend, on Thursday. If I should, Thursday will acquire another charm for me. *One o'clock* – how often, how impatiently do I look at my watch from breakfast till that hour! And when it comes – tell me, tell me – do you think of Sally? I sit where you have sat; I stand where you have stood; I look round on those Shakespeare prints, I try to recollect your observations on them. And which do I look on longest, most intently? *Orlando – dear Orlando*! And then I write. Would you know what? You shall *read*.

I can no longer continue my Journal as I us'd; I dare not write my thoughts now; but, since I am forbid to express the feelings of my heart in my own words, I transcribe those lines, wherever I find them, which best accord with my own sentiments and situation. *This* is what you shall read. Have you taken your ring to Cowen's? But do not learn the puzzle of him; let me only teach it. Do you know its name? Have they told you it is a True Lover's Knot? I bought it for you. I have worn it, kissed it, and waited anxiously for an opportunity to give it you. Last night, beyond my hopes, it presented itself. You have it, keep it, love it, nor ever part with it till *you return me my letters.*

You like my locket. Your hair and my mother's are in it – think if I prize it! I wear it always. Have I not told you that the first song I set to music was that complaint of Thomson's to the Nightingale? I compos'd it at Harrow Weald. You then liv'd in my heart, in my head, in every idea; every moment your image was present. *You did not love me then*. But now! Oh, mortification, grief, agony are all forgot!!![17]

Maria, presumably, knew nothing of this. She was still an invalid, though allowed to drive out in the park. In a letter of 6 May to Sarah Bird, she expresses her resentment at being called 'conquest-making', and puts down some pious resolutions in self-defence:

I am a little angry with you for some part of your letter, where you wish I may resume my favourite employment of *conquest-making*. You are deceiv'd, I assure you, I have an *abomination* of it. Some people may do it innocently enough, but *I* particularly feel how wrong it is, and I hope I shall always shun it. I am very serious, you think, but I always am when I am suppos'd, even in joke, to be a *conquest-maker*. . . . I had much rather be lov'd, I assure you, than admir'd, tho' I am so *fond of this admiration*. Well, when you knew me there was more justice in this accusation than there is now, I hope.[18]

Maria, perhaps, had learned something of a lesson from Lawrence's desertion of her. She then says of Sarah in *The Stranger*:

You were not in Town, I believe, when *The Stranger* came out; I long to see it much, and you, I daresay, have heard enough of it to wish to see it too. My Mother crys so much at it that she is always ill when she comes home.

The family moved to Clifton early in June. Sally wrote to Sarah Bird on 13 June from Princes Buildings in Clifton which overlooked the Avon Gorge. Maria, though she survived the journey well, could not yet go to a ball which Sally says she attended. She sent Sarah Charles Moore's *love* – 'What do you think of it, my dear girl? I did not know that *Gentlemen* sent their *loves* thus to Ladies without any meaning.' She adds about Sarah's summer tour, which was to begin in July:

> My Father and Mother will stay here a month, I fancy. If Maria is pretty well, and in good spirits, I shall accompany my Mother, who wants a companion sadly in her Summer excursions. If however dear Maria should be low, or unwilling to part with me, I will not leave her. She will be with a very kind and old friend of ours, who lives constantly at Clifton, so we are certain that she would have every tender attention paid her.[19]

The kind friend is, of course, Penelope Pennington, of whom in a further letter of 1 July Sally complains that 'her incessant talk is rather fatiguing'. Her praises of natural beauty were too much for Sally: 'It seems to me quite impossible she can feel the sensations she finds such fine language to explain. When I am most affected I am most silent.' She looks forward to another ball:

> I am fond of the mere exercise of dancing, and my partner must be odious indeed if I am not pleas'd to dance; if he is agreeable, the pleasure is double. I wish it may be my lot to meet with such a one on Tuesday, though I trouble myself but little about that, since, if I dance, I am *satisfied*.[20]

For a month Sally was to live at Cheltenham, while her mother appeared for seasons of a week or so there and in the neighbouring towns, such as Gloucester, Worcester and Hereford. William was with them. It was from Worcester that Sarah wrote to Penelope Pennington on 26 July about Maria:

> Your goodness to my dear girl is what I expected, but I am not able to express my gratitude for it. I know she went to the Ball, I hope it did her no harm. This weather has prevented her riding too; tell me about her pulse, her perspirations, her cough, everything! and tell me too that your mind is at ease about your brother. I am playing every night to very full houses, but how the people can sit to see such representations is quite wonderful, for anything so bad I never yet beheld, and I have seen strange things. The fat cakes, however, are quite as good as formerly, only that I find one suffices my appetite now, and formerly, I verily believe, I could have eaten half-a-dozen. I hope to get a frank for this scrawl, which I can tell you has not been written without stealing the time from other affairs. I have a maid who is not us'd to my exhibitions, and of course, playing every night,

it is as much as I can do to prepare all day for my appearance in the evening. God bless you and yours, and your dear charge![21]

Maria was able to go for rides, but if she went to a ball, she was not allowed to dance. Sally, however, went to a ball in Cheltenham and 'danc'd all that was to be danc'd' since, she says, she was 'an indefatigable' whom 'three hours will not satisfy'.

After a week in Cheltenham, Sarah played a short season in Hereford. Her gratitude to those tending her daughter was becoming more desperate; it is evident she hated her enforced parting from Maria, whom Penelope Pennington came to realize during the summer had only a short while to live:

... how shall I ever sufficiently repay your goodness to my sweet girl, or express the comfort I feel in having such tenderness to repose my aching heart upon? ... I thank you, my dearest, kindest friend, for your promise of faithful and frequent accounts of my precious child. We leave this place for Cheltenham, where we shall stay a week. Thank Heaven I shall play only *three* times there – and then to Birmingham for another week; in the course of this time I hope to God to hear something comfortable from you! But do not, dearest soul, do not, I beseech you, flatter me, for inured as I am to disappointment, it is still to me the *most painful of feelings*.[22]

By the time Sarah had reached Cheltenham early in August, Sally herself had fallen ill. When Sarah wrote to Penelope on 9 August it is clear she was beginning to realize the truth about Maria, but that she also fears that Sally herself would prove too much the invalid to make Lawrence a suitable wife; her own ill-health, apparently, was one at least of the causes of her estrangement from her husband:

Mine is the habitation of sickness and of sorrow. My dear and kind friend, be assur'd I rely implicitly on your truth to me and tenderness to my sweet Maria. I do not flatter myself that she will be long continued to me. . . . How vainly did I flatter myself that this other dear creature had acquired the strength of constitution to throw off this cruel disorder! Instead of that, it returns with increasing velocity and violence. What a sad prospect is this for her in marriage? for I am now convinc'd it is constitutional, and will pursue her thro' life. Will a husband's tenderness keep pace with and compensate for the loss of a mother's, her unremitting cares and soothings? . . . Dr Johnson says the man must be almost a prodigy of virtue who is not soon tir'd of an ailing wife; and sad experience has taught even *me*, who might have hop'd to have assured that attention which *common gratitude* for a life of labour in the service of my family shou'd have offered, that illness, often repeated, or long continued, soon tires a man. To say the truth, a sick wife *must* be a *great misfortune*.[23]

It appears that Maria did not at first reveal to Penelope Pennington her past feelings for Lawrence. However, when Penelope to pass the time read her a novel, *The Memories of Miss Sidney Biddulph*, by Mrs Sheridan (the mother of the dramatist), the truth came out. In this story the hero, Orlando, is portrayed as in love with both the daughters of his benefactress. Maria broke down and naturally enough told the whole story entirely from her point of view, at the same time declaring that her greatest anxiety now was that Lawrence would succeed in inducing her sister, Sally, to be his wife. Everything Penelope might argue in favour of leaving Sally free to make her own decisions or mistakes, was met by Maria's unalterable determination to oppose any relationship which might grow up between her sister and Lawrence. Maria was adamant.

In view of Sally's letters to Lawrence, Sarah's letter to Penelope, written from Birmingham but undated, is of great interest. Was Sally beginning to change her mind, once she was free from the direct influence of Lawrence's hypnotic presence?

Sally is well again. . . . I *have* done *all*, my dear friend, that it is possible to do; for before your last and most excellent letter I had suggested to her my doubts, my fears. The GOOD SENSE and TENDERNESS it was evident had *needed no prompter*, and, while she ingenuously confessed her predilection, she was as well aware of Mr L.'s blameable conduct as any one could be, and declar'd that (Maria *totally out of the question*) she felt the weight of many other objections that seem'd to preclude the possibility of the dreaded event. 'Parental *authority*' therefore, were I inclin'd to exert it, you see is needless. But in this *most* IMPORTANT *object of their lives* it has always been my system that they must *decide* for themselves. I will *advise*, I may *entreat*. Had Maria listen'd to my advice she had been spar'd the mortification she has felt, for *my* heart *never approv'd* her union with Mr L., but restraint in these cases, we, who know the perversity of human nature, are well aware will only excite a *greater* desire, and *stimulate* to the attainment of our wishes. Had their intercourse been longer prohibited I doubt not the marriage wou'd have taken place, and poor dear Maria (even in health), after the first raptures of possession had subsided, would have found herself in a situation, to a girl of her turn of mind, EXTREMELY PAINFUL; for *with* that decided way of thinking, she always honestly confess'd herself incapable of

any exertion either of mind or body. So that there is an end of *that*.
. . . What relates to Mr L. and Sally in this hasty scrawl you may
perhaps think it right to communicate to Maria.[24]

Sarah was now moving about the country fulfilling a variety of
engagements. From Brighton on 1 August she wrote to Penelope,
describing a meeting she had with the Prince and his strange
mistress, Lady Jersey:

> In my poor Maria I expect no material change; but Sally, she, I
> hope, is better, and augur'd truly, that her fit would be short – yes,
> she, I hope, is well again? My poor Husband is quite lame, absolutely
> walking on crutches. Something is the matter with his knee, but
> whether Rheumatism, or Gout, or what it is, heaven knows; and the
> terrible, yet not irrational dread of becoming a cripple makes him
> very melancholy – Alas! alas!
> This place is crowded with people that I know nothing of; so much
> the better, for I am ill dispos'd to gaiety. I have played twice to fine
> Houses, and the Prince frequents the Theatre with great attention
> and decorum. He had issued his sublime commands (which, it seems,
> nothing but death or deadly sickness will excuse one from obeying)
> to have me asked to supper with him, which I, disliking the whole
> thing, had declin'd; but when I came to talk it over with Mr Sid.,
> he thought it best that I shou'd recant my refusal; and so I went to
> sup at Mr Concannon's, where, as I had fear'd, I met Lady Jersey.
> However, the evening went off much more easily and agreeably
> than I had imagin'd, and as it is not likely to happen often, perhaps
> it was better to avoid giving the offence which I am assur'd I shou'd
> have incurr'd by a refusal. Lady Jersey is really wonderful in her
> appearance. Her hair was about an inch long all over her head, and
> she had ty'd round her head one single row of white beads: this I
> thought was ill judg'd. She certainly wou'd look handsome if she
> wou'd not affect at forty-eight to be eighteen.[25]

The Prince was now living almost entirely in Brighton, where he
had built his oriental Pavilion as a palace by the sea. His connexion with Lady Jersey, a lady-in-waiting to the Princess, and
married to a Master of the Horse, was the latest scandal.

Sally meanwhile had been sent back to help look after her
sister. Sarah wrote a letter to Penelope which Sally herself brought;
it reveals that Lawrence had come to Birmingham in pursuit of
his love:

> I felt some days since what a comfort it wou'd be to you as well as
> us that one of us shou'd come to your relief, and this day have

determin'd to deprive myself of the companionship of my darling Sally, who sets out in a Post-chaise with a good soul who has undertaken to be her Guardian. By this means, too, we shall avoid the distress of meeting with Mr L., who is come here, I understand, upon a visit to his sister. This charming girl has determined, and this day I told him so, to put an end to his expectations.[26]

The charming girl was, of course, Sally, bearer of the letter. She was later to reveal that while she was in Birmingham she had written a letter to Lawrence 'in which I most positively assur'd him there must be a total end to all intercourse between us'.

Sarah was afraid Lawrence would follow Sally to Clifton, and wrote a second letter of warning to Penelope:

I know not if Sally has told you that this Mr L. was at Birmingham when she left me. He has left this place without letting a soul know whither he is gone. His hopes with regard to Sally, I, with her own concurrence, told him were entirely at an end, representing at the same time the situation of her sister. I suppose he is almost mad with remorse, and think it is likely he may be at this moment at Clifton. I pray God his phrenzy may not impell him to some *desperate action*! What he can propose by going thither I know not, but it is fit they should both be on their guard. Mr S. knows nothing of *all this*, the situation of dear Sally, when one recurs to her original partiality for this wretched madman, placing *her* in so delicate a situation, we thought it best to keep the matter entirely conceal'd, as it was *impossible* that anything *cou'd* come of it, if *ever*, NEVER, she was RESOLV'D, till her sister shou'd be perfectly restor'd. I hope it will always be a secret to Mr S., as it could answer no end but to enrage *him* and make us *all* still more unhappy. Miss Lawrence tells me that her brother is expected at his Hotel to-day. I wish to God he may come, for the uncertainty of *what is become* of him is dreadful to us all. . . . If he *shou'd* be at Clifton and be impell'd to make an eclat of this business, he will *ruin himself for ever*, and make us the talk of the whole world – it is dreadful to think of, and the effect on my *poor Maria*! Oh God! His mind is tortured, I suppose, with the idea of hasting her end. I REALLY, my dear friend, do not think so, and if one knew where he was, to endeavour to take this poison from it, he *might* be persuaded to be quiet. Dr Pearson premis'd from the *very beginning* all that has or is likely to happen to her. But the agonies of this *poor wretch*, if he thinks otherwise, *must* be INSUPPORTABLE.[27]

Sarah's continual concern and sympathy for Lawrence is evident, in spite of her desire to protect her daughters from him.

Lawrence did in fact follow Sally to Clifton, staying at an hotel under an assumed name. He then began to importune Penelope Pennington, who scarcely knew how to deal with the hysterical man. He seemed by now oblivious of the effect of his actions on Maria's health; his most urgent need was to keep the love of her sister who, it seemed to him, had been persuaded by Sarah to refuse to have anything further to do with him. His aim, in Sarah's absence, was to persuade Penelope to become his friend and ally, and act as an intermediary between himself and Sally:

MADAM, – If you are generous and delicate (and talents should be connected with these qualities), not only the step I take will be excus'd, but you will render me the service I solicit, and keep it an inviolable secret. If you are not, or let suspicion of the person who requests it weigh against the impulse of your nature – it indeed matters not much, I shall only have heap'd on myself an aggravation of misery that at present is all but madness!

My name is Lawrence, and you then, I believe, know that I stand in the most afflicting situation possible! A man charg'd (I trust untruly in their lasting effect) with having inflicted pangs on one lovely Creature which, in their bitterest extent, he himself now suffers from her sister!

I love – exist but for Miss Siddons, and am decisively rejected by her.

If I have touch'd her heart – would I knew I had – her present conduct is the more noble, correct, and pure as every thought and action of her sweet character! If founded on the consideration I hope it is, I will not, dare not rail, hardly murmur at the decision which exalts the Object of my Love.

Be assur'd, Madam, the Paper I have enclos'd has in it nothing contrary to this sentiment, and it is therefore I have confidence in requesting that you will, at a fit but speedy moment, *give it into her own Hand.*

I know, Madam, that secresy should always be justified by Reason; and the reasons for it in the present case are very obvious. Miss Maria's situation is, I know, a very dangerous one. *If it is* REALLY *render'd more so by feelings I may have excited, the least mention of me would be hazardous in the extreme.*[28]

His greatest anxiety now appears to have been that Maria was influencing her sister against him; he is fearful –

. . . when the querulousness of Sickness becomes the Complaint of Injur'd Virtue; when Hints are Commands, and implied Wishes (however irrational or fancifully construed) binding as the most sacred duties; – should that moment soon arrive – God! God! avert it! – how dangerous will it be to that trembling Hope which, half-broken as it is, my heart still cherishes as its sole spring of Life![29]

So Lawrence wrote in the course of this lengthy letter to Penelope. He begs her to understand why he has made such an abnormal approach to her, a stranger: 'I have done it,' he writes, 'and perhaps *all of my future happiness is at stake, and in your Power.*'

What transpired (and we do not have Penelope's reply) can only be surmised. But against (one can be sure) the wishes of Sarah, this rather foolish, over-romantic but well-meaning woman gave way to Lawrence's impetuous demands. It would seem from Lawrence's second letter to her that she must have told Sally, and that Sally's response must have struck Lawrence as favourable. He wrote immediately to Penelope:

My blessings on you both! A thousand times! But do not say that I come to add to your distress and affliction! God knows I meant not that. Yet, too true, my coming must do it. How strange it is today that I am comparatively happy. What can have made me so? O! I thought she was dead!! But your window somewhat convinces me that it is not so. The Almighty be praised for the hours, the minutes, he spares us! Sally, dear angel, shall I indeed see you!!! Dearest, dearest friend, adieu!
I will be compos'd. You shall see I can.[30]

Having won the first round, Lawrence met Sally again, and then, turning away from Clifton, the centre of all his hopes, he rushed off to Birmingham to do battle again with Sarah, whom he appears to have terrified by his conduct – though she never ceased to feel for him, however much she cries out against his 'madness'. The great actress who could strike terror into her audience, and command their willing tears, was herself the victim of an actor, as 'possessed' as she. Lawrence burst into her presence, shouting and pleading; afterwards Sarah, still tied down by the hard work of a provincial tour, poured out her anxieties in an undated letter to Penelope in Clifton:

I shudder to think on the effect this wretched madman's frenzy has had on you. *I* know the effect too well, for he well knows he has TERRIFIED me into my *toleration* of his love for Sally by the horrible desperation of his conduct; and if his own words are to be believed, I have more than once shut upon him the Gate of SELF-DESTRUCTION by compromising (thou' without that self-possessing wisdom) as you have now done. Yes, that dear Sally is indeed an Angel, and, my dear Friend, she lov'd him; I think then on the tremendous situation I was placed in, and let my tenderness for his feelings be the excuse for my weak indulgence. *You* now *know* the whole, and *she* has *seen* and *known* enough of *him* to make her *wary.* You will advise, you will warn this best beloved of her Mother's heart – you, to whom it has been given to calm the sea when it roars wildest, for to that dreadful image have you well compared this unhappy man, on whom an EVIL FATE *seems to attend, and wreaks its vengeance on all the most* UNFORTUNATE SOULS WITH WHOM HE IS CONCERN'D. That so many excellencies shou'd be thus alloy'd by ungovernable Passion is lamentable indeed. A duteous Son, a tender Brother, a kind and zealous friend: all these he is. I have *seen* him, and I bless God and you that you have reason'd him out of some extravagance that might have been dreadful in its present or future effects upon my POOR GIRLS or on himself. He appeared to be extremely repentant, and I was impell'd not only by policy but commiseration to treat him with more lenity than I thought I cou'd have done. I gave him my sincere forgiveness and calm advice, but told him positively that he had NOTHING MORE to hope from ME except my good wishes for his success and happiness. Oh, may I never have the painful part to play again! . . . I have receiv'd my belov'd Sally's comfortable letter. Oh, tell her how proud her *Mother is of such a child.* Mr L. set off for London last night after pacing about here for three hours in agonies that brought me almost to fainting three or four times. He went off calmly, however, and with resolutions to be all that cou'd be wish'd. I hope for his own sake he will, for *we* I trust have seen the end of our sufferings from him. How I long for the 24th, yet dread to see the alter'd face of my sweet Maria.

Wednesday.

You will receive a letter of mine to Mr L. from Miss Lee. I was wild with my fears, and thought she might know something of him. Send it to me if you please, for it will save you the trouble of again requesting him to burn the letters. I was so shaken by his wild transports yesterday, that, on rising to ring for some hartshorn and water, I should have fallen upon the floor if he had not fortunately caught me at the instant, and was totally incapacitated to play last night.[31]

Sarah sent Penelope another letter two days later, in which her affection for Lawrence is again apparent:

Dearest, wisest, best of creatures. Oh! *imagine* all that I *wou'd* say to you, for it is impossible for me to express it. Yet do not let your affection for *me* induce you to be too resentful of this poor wretch's conduct, for indeed I *do* believe the violence of his grief for all the sufferings he had been the cause of, was the then powerful feeling which he cou'd *not* command: and when one adds to this that he has so *completely* thrown away his *own happiness*, let us temper our indignation with pity, even for his weakness and folly. We must also take into account that the agitated state of *my* nerves acted perhaps *more powerfully* on me than there was just cause for. You tell me that you are to be 'very good friends'. Perhaps you are to write to him; your wisdom needs no warning from *me* not to let his arguments (and he can wield them with some force) induce you to depart in a *single instance* from the present arrangements, and, as I *gave* him my FORGIVENESS, do not let his mind be *again* IRRITATED by bringing his parting visit to me to his recollection. No, let us keep him quiet by all means that are *consistent* with our *own safety*; do not name it to him, for God's sake! lest he shou'd be flying off in ANOTHER *whirlwind*! We have already had too many proofs of the weakness of his Character, we have felt by sad experience how little he is master of himself, and no wonder that the sight of her on whom he has heap'd so many and bitter sorrows should have operated powerfully on a mind thus irritable, and stung almost to madness on the retrospect of *them* and his OWN FOLLY. Let it compensate *you* and DEAR Sally that his visit, in the end, quieted my agonis'd spirit so completely that I rested well, and have been a *new creature* ever since. It was *necessary* that he shou'd see me, and I really believe that he came resolv'd to be *compos'd*, but he is the *creature* of *impulse*, and I verily believe the REMORSE he felt was too powerful to be mastered by HIM. I believe I told you that he went away *compos'd*, grateful for my forgiveness (tho' that comfort was allay'd by my *solemn assurances* that he had nothing *more* to hope for from *me*), and determin'd steadily to pursue a course of conduct which shou'd regain his credit. I hope to God he *will*, for his *own* sake, but I fear his natural propensities have been so strengthen'd by the habits of indulgence that there is little to be expected in point of improvement from a man who at the age of THIRTY appears to have so little control over himself.[32]

After expressing her fears for Maria in a line or two, she reverted again to Lawrence and Sally:

P.S. – Let not my belov'd Sally fear *my* persevering *firmness*, dearest of creatures! Does she not know it was the dread of making HER *unhappy*, which, ever since that terrible visit that followed Miss Linwood's Exhibition, has forced me into toleration: when, without the least consideration for poor Maria, I was even on my knees to prevent his rushing into her presence. Yes, I will own that tho' I cou'd not

wonder at the effect my adorable Sally's perfections had wrought
upon him who was in the daily contemplation of her perfections, I
believe no time, no change, could wear away the unfavourable
impression of his selfish, unfeeling conduct at that tremendous
moment. He said it was madness, and the fear of losing them both,
for, next to Sally, he adored Maria. And will this insanity be ever
cured? – there's the terrifying doubt. But I have long had some
reason (for she is truth itself), from her own mouth, to see her mind,
recover'd from the surprise at these sad events, and from the terror
he had thrown her into, had meditated the ill consequences of this
attachment, and the instability of the character of Mr L. These late
efforts of her extraordinary wisdom and unparallel'd sweetness have
shown me her *whole heart*, and I shall now pursue the *straightforward
path* without the fear of *wounding* HER *peace*. . . . I am afraid there is
but too much reason to believe the affairs of this unhappy man are
very much derang'd. He told me some time ago, when he was *as*
mad about Maria as he is now about Sally, that, if she rejected him,
he would fly, to compose his Spirit, to the mountains of Switzerland.
Maria reign'd sole arbitress of his fate for *two years*, or more. The
other day he told me, if he lost *Sally*, SWITZERLAND was still his
resource. Oh! that caprice and passion shou'd thus obscure the
many excellencies and lofty genius of this man![33]

Then she adds again, as if unable to let the letter leave her hands
without writing more and more to relieve her feelings:

I am afraid there is but too much reason to believe the affairs of this
unhappy man are very much derang'd. . . . Oh! that caprice and
passion shou'd thus obscure the many excellencies and lofty genius
of this man!

What is lacking is any evidence to account for the change in
Sally, who only four months earlier had written letters of the most
dedicated love to Lawrence. Did she put up any resistance to
Sarah's pressures on her to give up her lover? Did she realize the
effect her rejection of him would have on a man of Lawrence's
uncontrollable sensibilities, sending him into paroxysms of
frustrated passion? According to her mother, there seems to be
little sign of suffering on her side, only of 'reasonableness' in the
face of Lawrence's self-torture; as Sarah put it, Sally had
become 'wary', and had written her a 'comfortable' letter from
Clifton which makes her 'proud . . . of such a child'. She had
indeed 'meditated the ill consequences of this attachment'. There
is a further hint of her attitude in a passage from Lawrence's

next, very (for him) reasonable, letter to Penelope, written from London:

> In the course of our conversation you told me that you were conjur'd to say nothing that could be hurtful to my feelings, at least as little as possible. Now don't be offended with me! but did she insist on your telling me that 'I was mistaken *in my system* – that she was not a girl to be won by rant and violence?' To say truth I did not sit down coolly to consider the most POLITIC mode of securing her affections. She was gone, and I flew after her, because I could neither know peace nor rest till I had seen her, or at least had such an explanation from her as satisfied me that I ow'd the loss of her Society to Necessity, and not to Choice.
>
> I have not much of the Cameleon about me: the color of my actions will be that of my mind, changing, I am told, too often, but always belonging to the real Creature and not taken from Surrounding Objects. Even the woman that I love I must love in my own way, and, at the moment when I most dread her displeasure, will not hesitate to tax her with Indelicacy and Injustice, if she accuses me of endeavouring to influence her affections by dishonourable means. No! if I win the prize it must be by the genuine emotions of my Heart: One that feels Passion perhaps in too wild excess, but would disdain the proudest (ah! *this*) Conquest, if only Hypocrisy could atcheive it. I hop'd I had been *known*.[34]

Lawrence's letter is a long and subtle one. He recognized that Penelope was, unlike Sally, a 'romantic', and that, for all her 'dread' of him, she was perhaps unconsciously enjoying her close involvement in the passionate love affair. Behind everything written, said and done it is necessary to remember that they all realized by now that Maria was dying and should be sheltered from any further distress which the sight of Lawrence might cause her. Lawrence, however, knew by now how to appeal to Penelope's soft nature; he recalled their secret meetings in Clifton:

> Was ever love-lorn Shepherdess under the Hawthorn so interesting as Mrs Pennington under that scrubbed Oak, with not one atom of Romance about her, AS SHE SAYS, and only the victim of it in others; – but Romance – where is it to be found if not in you? You are the very Creature of it.[35]

Having, as he hoped, prevailed over Penelope's weakness, he returns to the main attack, giving some account of his second meeting with Sarah:

Surely there are some Beings sent into our sphere for the sole purpose of showing us 'they are not of this World'. That Dear Woman has suffer'd more from this wayward Child, whose Tears are now attesting his repentance, than all the agonising feelings her Genius has excited. Yet she is willing to forgive and almost to forget them, could Memory be commanded – my most inveterate Foe. . . . On you, my dear kind Enemy, I throw the labour; and *I beseech you enter upon it with all the energy of your Character; with your very Heart and Soul! Think that you are working out the happiness of two Beings destin'd (yes, with all my frailties), destined for each other by Love and Mind, by every feeling and perception of Heart and Intellect.* . . . It is a new Soil her bounty has now to work upon, and its fruit shall be happiness and peace. . . . May the end of these exhausting agitations bring tranquillity to all, but only *can* it do so by *Sally's being mine.*[36]

Lawrence's appeals were again successful. But even Penelope realized that she was involving herself in something which might well get her into serious trouble. So, with time on her hands, she began to keep copies of the more important letters she sent to Lawrence so that Sarah, in particular, could see what she wrote to this fascinating but disturbing man. Lawrence's letters were also forwarded to Sarah, and a few have in consequence become lost. Penelope's letter in reply to Lawrence was, as can be expected, as long as his, and as carefully worded, and it reveals not only that Lawrence had threatened suicide, but that Sally had finally decided to postpone any further consideration of Lawrence's suit during her sister's lifetime:

Yes, I perceive you are a great Magician, and I will frankly confess you have found me out. . . . I could not see the violent agitations which shook your Frame, without becoming once again the Creature of Impulse, and obeying the dictates of the moment, which were to console you at any rate. . . .

And now you have gained so much ground, compleat your victory. . . . Love this dear Girl (Sally), but love her with a sacred and reasonable devotion: with that love which shall consecrate her true interest in your heart superior to all selfish considerations. . . . I saw so much 'method in your madness' in the first ten minutes I passed with you, that I am convinced you *can be* all this. . . . Be it so, and then you shall live in my memory also with the few whom I wear in my 'Heart of Hearts'. One way only lies open to this salutary end, by governing your passions, and by preferring the peace and tran-quillity of those so deservedly dear to you, to the gratification of those impetuous propensities, which I call selfish, but to which, doubtless, you give some finer and more agreeable name. . . .

You are very saucy, and give me a most ridiculous picture of myself, and of the inconsistencies I was guilty of in our late conferences. Surprise and agitation left me very little Mistress of my own powers, and I am conscious I was much more influenced by Sensation than by Reason in my mode of arguing. It was difficult to compose a Medicine suited to your case . . .; but whatever I said in the name of dear Sally, I must gravely assure you, was simple fact. I did not exceed my commission . . . pray permit me to ask, what less can a man of sense and principle expect from a creature of rectitude and intelligence like S.S., than that if he were weak enough to shock her with the horrible idea of *Suicide*, she should assume energy enough of Character to give him the reproof he merited, by shewing him she despised the threat? . . . True Love does not seek to scare or wound the peace it values by such hideous Phantoms; – as a momentary flash of delirium she regards it, which she well knew the better man would rise up and master. . . . What end can such rash and violent expressions answer, but to fright gentle Love from a pure and guileless Mind, and to fix a sort of Horror there? Therefore, believe me, a Woman is not to be accused of '*Injustice*', who presumes to shew her Lover an honest resentment and contempt of such conduct. This dear Girl's Mind is as firm as her Heart is tender and affectionate. The present critical and uncommon state of circumstances in which she is placed calls forth all her energies. . . . She declares her soul is so full of the present mournful claims upon her, that she will not trust herself with a thought of the *future*, nor will she promise anything but to esteem you as you may deserve, and always to retain a sincere interest in your Honour and Prosperity. . . .

We talk often of you – sometimes with a kindness which would be flattering – often in a style that you would not at all approve; because we lament that so many good Gifts as you possess, should be rendered in a great measure abortive by the eccentricities that shade your character; and instead of the excelling Thing you *might* be, leave you the mere Slave of Passion. . . .

You have much to do, and to *undo*, my friend, before you can be deserving of this excellent Creature, should fortune and circumstances ever favor you so far as to put the prize within your reach.

Think only, for the present, of subjecting and governing your mind.[37]

Lawrence followed up his advantage (and, no doubt, his acute disappointment at Sally's present rejection of him) by sending Penelope a drawing of Maria with a covering letter dated 1

September. On 4 September Penelope sent a reply to a letter from Lawrence which is now lost, but which evidently was not to her taste; this letter, too, reveals Sally's character as cold, and even, as Penelope puts it herself, somewhat 'masculine':

> You have favoured me with a Letter compounded of ingenuity, wit, and sarcasm. . . . I am inclined to think a great part of what lies before me is rather written *at* dear Sally than *to* me; and it is only honest to tell you, that she has the firmness to resist taking any part in this correspondence, and will neither peruse, nor hear read, your Letters, nor my Replys. This is a very masculine trait of character, for which, I dare say, she will appear highly reprehensible in your eyes.[38]

She goes on to blame Lawrence for having suspected, as he did while in his desperate mood, that Sally might have another, more favoured, suitor. Sally, she tells Lawrence, was ill again and confined to her room, 'her sweet faculties . . . locked up by the power of that dangerous medicine, which alone releases her from the effects of the dreadful constitutional complaint, for which there appears to be no efficient remedy'. This was laudanum, which sometimes left her barely conscious. As for Maria, she grew weaker – even Penelope admits to her possession of 'that degree of self-love which is interwoven into most of our characters, and which was certainly a prominent feature in this sweet creature's'. She had said that she 'wished Mr Lawrence no ill, and freely forgave him the uneasiness he had caused her'. Penelope adds that Sarah is expected on 24 September in Clifton: 'I long for, yet dread, the hour of her arrival; it will, however, somewhat relieve me from a degree of care and anxiety that I find at times almost too much for me.' She concludes by thanking him for the drawing which 'has the stamp of a great Artist, and, what I prize more, a striking resemblance of features'. Rather surprisingly, she invites him to stay with her and Mr Pennington at Clifton 'in happier times' to come.

A further complication appears to be that Lawrence, in some desperate moment, had shown, or said that he would show, certain of Sally's letters (possibly the very ones preserved among his papers) to an unnamed third person, a friend of Sarah's in London. He had said as much to Penelope, and this immediately roused her against him. She added a severe postscript to her letter, implying that any such inconsiderate action would be more than sufficient to justify Sally refusing to enter into any further correspondence with him. Lawrence was, naturally enough, deeply troubled .o learn of Sally's illness, and he makes a revealing admission in his next letter, written 7 September, to Penelope; he admits that he had on one occasion stolen into her bedroom and seen her under the influence of laudanum:

> Never have I lov'd her more, never with so pure an ardour, as in the last moment of sickness I was witness of (the period she must remember), when, in spite of the intreaties of her dear Mother and Maria, I stole into her room, and found her unconscious of the step of friend or relation; her faculties ic'd over by that cursed poison, and those sweet eyes unable to interpret the glance that, at that instant, not apathy itself could have mistaken.[39]

The following day Lawrence wrote denying that he had ever shown Sally's letters to anyone – the suggestion that he had, or might do so being 'a retort just dull enough to be mistaken for truth'. Penelope wrote again on 11 September to say that she, however, had shown all *their* letters to Sally, and that this had done nothing to alter Sally's resolve, though Penelope adds, for her part: 'I feel for you most sincerely, and I wish you happy with all my soul – but I *fear* more than I hope for you.'

At last, on 25 September, we find a letter from Sally, written to Sarah Bird, whom Sarah had met; apparently, she had been told as much of the situation between Sally and Lawrence as Sarah thought fit to pass on. Sally, therefore, after a melancholy reference to Maria, describes how much she owes to her mother – 'not only the tenderest of parents, but the sweetest and most indulgent of friends, to whom my whole heart is open, and from whose sympathy and consolation I have found comfort and happiness in moments of severe affliction'. Then she feels free to speak of Lawrence with a coldness, a power of analytical observation, which is astonishing after her letters written only the previous April:

> Heaven grant that restless being may be quiet, at least with respect to us. That he can ever be happy is, I fear, impossible. His strong genius and disposition impel him to seek for and to conquer difficulties; the object of his desires, once obtain'd, *becomes indifferent*, some new idea fills his imagination, more danger must be encounter'd to fulfil his wishes, and thus, I greatly fear, a life will be pass'd, which might have been spent, *oh, how differently!* with more steadiness and consistency of character, joined to talents and fascination

which no mortal ever was so highly gifted with!! Thank heaven, dear Maria's mind is perfectly tranquil concerning him, she thinks not of him, or if she does, it is only to hope that I will never have anything to do with this, *our common enemy*, as she calls him.[40]

It is clear that Maria, as much if not more than Sarah, had turned Sally against her lover.

During the final days of Maria's life, Penelope kept Lawrence informed of the health of both the sisters – Lawrence in his replies being particularly flattering to his confidante – 'Do you expect my gratitude to be so disinterested as that I should love you equally when you send me bad, as when you are the herald of good news? You know my nature, and the human mind too well, and that at this moment I am only not *worshipping* your image.' And he adds in this letter of 29 September: 'Be not apprehensive about my composure', and inquires after the 'Immortal', who is, of course, Sarah. On 2 October he is furious that the newspapers in London were already reporting Maria's death: 'Those unfeeling Blockheads . . . have been torturing us with the death at full length. Would to God there were a penalty that might teach them humanity!' He is concerned that the reports should reach Sarah's eyes. Sally, he is relieved to learn, 'has walk'd out. Dear Creature!' In a letter of 2 October which crossed with his, Penelope admits 'that both Mrs S and myself have spoken to *her* of *you*; and that I request you to be satisfied with the assurance, that SHE awards you what is generally understood as CHRISTIAN forgiveness, and to entreat you will enquire no further.'

Perhaps because Penelope could no longer bear it, Maria (whom she describes to Lawrence as having 'not one trace of even prettiness remaining – all ghastly expression, and sad discolouration!!') was taken away in a sedan-chair to a lodging-house across the square; she was receiving doses of laudanum which, says Sally in a letter to Sarah Bird, 'keep her in a continual stupor'. Sarah and Sally sat by her bedside, Sally reading because the sound of her voice soothed her sister's brain. Lawrence was meanwhile receiving what scraps of news he could from John Philip Kemble and from Mr and Mrs Twiss, who were in London, as well as from his daily correspondence with Penelope, who appears to have become as regular in her letter-writing as he. 'Dear, dear Mrs Siddons,' writes Lawrence to his 'ever-valued friend' on 3 October, 'she must be worn to nothing. I am almost thinking of writing to her.' And again on 4 October: 'If you can, a thousand grateful remembrances to my beloved Mrs Siddons for the effort she made for me. An humble sign or two for my Mistress!' And in his next: 'Call it madness, or what you please, but were my wishes gratified not a groan or look, not (of all the most fearful) the ghastly smile, should be hid from me. I would know *everything*.' And he adds, referring to his suggestion of writing direct to Sarah, which Penelope had thought ill-advised: 'I won't write yet, since you fear it; but there's no fear of Mr S. getting it *if I enclose it to you*.' Penelope is now 'his dearest friend – God, God, bless you!'

Maria died on 7 October. She was still only nineteen. The following day Penelope set down, as Lawrence had begged her to do, every detail of the death-bed scene, during which, from Lawrence's point of view, the worst that he suspected did indeed happen – which was why, no doubt, Penelope opened her letter so emotionally: 'Dear, afflicted, and unfortunate Being, who attack, agitate, interest, and *distract* all that are intimately connected with you.' Then she described what had happened the night before, beginning: 'If ever creature was operated on by the immediate power and Spirit of God, it was Maria Siddons, in the last forty-eight hours of her life:' She then continued:

In her *dying* accents, her last solemn injunction WAS given and repeated some hours afterwards in the presence of Mrs Siddons. She call'd her Sister – said how dear, how sweet, how *good* she was – that one only care for her welfare pressed on her mind. 'Promise me, my Sally, *never* to be the wife of Mr Lawrence. I *cannot* BEAR to *think* of *your* being so.' Sally evaded the promise; not but that a thousand recent circumstances had made up her mind to the sacrifice, but that she did not like the positive tye. She would have evaded the subject also, and said, 'dear Maria, think of nothing that agitates you at this time'. She INSISTED that it did not agitate her, but that it was necessary to her repose to pursue the subject. Sally still evaded the promise, but said: 'Oh! it is *impossible*,' meaning that she cou'd *answer* for *herself*, but which Maria understood and construed into an impossibility of the event *ever* taking place, and replied: 'I am content, my dear Sister – I am satisfied.' The moment she saw her Mother, she told her that her mind was perfectly made up, and talked with her in a most wonderful manner on her approaching change. She was extremely sollicitous to know *when* it might be supposed to take place, and was anxiously inquisitive about time, but check'd herself, and said 'perhaps that was not right'.

She desired to have Prayers read, and followed her angelic mother, who read them, and who appear'd like a blessed spirit ministering about her, with the utmost clearness, accuracy, and fervor. She then turn'd the conversation to *you*, and said: '*That man* told you, Mother, he had destroy'd my Letters. *I* have no opinion of his honor, and I entreat you to demand them;' nor would be easy till she had given the strongest assurances that she wou'd use every means in her power to procure them from you, or a confirmation that they were destroy'd. Strong and delicate were the reasons she alledged for this request. She then said, Sally *had promised her* NEVER to think of an union with Mr Lawrence, and appeal'd to her Sister to confirm it, who, quite overcome, reply'd: 'I did *not* promise, dear, dying Angel; but I WILL, and DO, if you require it.' 'Thank you, Sally; my dear Mother – Mrs Pennington – *bear witness*. Sally, give me your hand – you promise never to be his wife; Mother – Mrs Pennington – lay your hands on hers' (we did so). – 'You understand? bear witness.' We bowed, and were speechless. 'Sally, sacred, sacred be this promise' – stretching out her hand, and pointing her forefinger – 'REMEMBER ME, and God bless you!'

And what, after this, my friend, can you say to SALLY Siddons? She has entreated me to give you this detail – to say that the impression IS sacred, IS indelible – that it cancels all former bonds and engagements – that she entreats you to submit, and not to prophane this awful season by a murmur.

If you can sanctify passion into friendship, still you may be dear to their hearts, and, at some future time, but even that far distant, enjoy their society. If you *cannot* do this, never approach, or, if you can help it, think of them more. I think Sally will not lightly or easily, if ever, make another election; but *yours* she NEVER *can*, never WILL be. She is wonderfully well, and wonderfully supported; feeling all that she can, and all that she ought. Mrs Siddons is fortitude and tenderness united and personified.[41]

Her descriptions of Maria's manner of facing her imminent death, even allowing for the pious licence thought necessary at that period, make her out to be little less than a saint, in spite of her exacting this fearful oath. Penelope describes Maria's appearance when she was at last dead:

When I look'd at her *cold remains* a few hours before she was shut for ever from our sight, conceive my astonishment on beholding the *exact resemblance* of HER MOTHER, GROWN OLD! even to seventy years!! A strong character, an expression of divinely solemn, and grave composure, but not one trace of *youth* remaining.[42]

In a further letter, written a few days after the funeral, which took place on 10 October in Clifton, she wrote to Lawrence: 'It is but poor consolation to offer you my constant friendship and tender sympathy; but if you will accept the gift, and can bind it with soothing efficacy to your heart, it is sincerely yours.' But her account of Maria's end launched a storm upon her which she could certainly never have foreseen. On 13 October, in a state of distraction bordering upon madness, Lawrence sent her what came to be called his 'diabolical' letter:

> It is only my Hand that shakes, not my Mind.
> I have play'd deeply for her, and you think she will still escape me.
> I'll tell you a Secret. *It is possible she may. Mark the End.*
> You have all play'd your parts admirably!!!
> If the scene you have so accurately describ'd is mention'd by you to *one Human Being*, I will pursue your name with execration.[43]

Penelope, whose feeling for Lawrence had clearly amounted almost to love, was deeply, bitterly hurt. She wrote back on 15 October what was to be her last letter to him:

> I THANK you, – you have made a *Grateful* return for a long and painful task, imposed on me by YOURSELF, which I have endured patiently, and discharged with integrity, and the truest, tenderest sympathy.
> From all uneasiness from that source you very kindly relieve me.
> The mind that is uncorrected under such circumstances, and which feels only for itself, deserves not a thought.
> I deign not to reply to your unmanly *threat*.
> Any further letters from your hand will be return'd unopen'd.[44]

Sarah herself was on her way back to London; she was probably staying overnight with the Whalleys in Bath when she wrote from there to Penelope, after having received from her the latest news of Lawrence; prior, that is, to Penelope's receipt of the diabolical letter:

> Write to your correspondent immediately, and remember by the same post to send me the transcript of your letter ... 'Spare not him', but have compassion on his *reputation*, or the blest work of reformation your counsels are likely to effect may be frustrate, and he may think it labour lost to aim at it. . . .
> Direct your letters to Sally Briggs, lest it should fall into improper hands. . . .

e. Thomas Lawrence's so-called diabolical letter to Penelope Pennington.
(*By permission of the Syndics of the Cambridge University Library*)

Query whether you shou'd promise him that Sally will make no other election? This hint is merely for your caution – you know with such a character one must speak by the card – and I would shield you from further trouble on this unhappy subject.[45]

The 'improper hands' were, of course, those of William Siddons, who was travelling with her. The proper hands, those of Sarah Briggs, probably belonged to her maid.

As soon as she reached London, Sarah wrote again to Penelope:

I take the first opportunity of telling you that we arrived safe at home; but poor Sally's malady was not to be diverted. Her breath grew more and more oppress'd from the time I wrote to you from Bath; all day yesterday she was extremely ill indeed. I hope, however, the violence of the fit is past! Today she breathes more freely. . . . Of our wretched friend I hear only that he is miserable. May your wise and sweet counsels operate to soothe and purify his mind![46]

Sarah had written to her friend, Mrs FitzHugh, her own account of Maria's last moments, using the elevated terms of the period:

Although my mind is not yet sufficiently tranquillized to talk much, yet the conviction of your undeviating affection impels me to quiet your anxiety so far, as to tell you that I am tolerably well. This sad event I have been long prepared for, and bow with humble resignation to the decree of that merciful God who has taken to himself the dear angel I must ever tenderly lament. I dare not trust myself further. Oh that you were here, that I might talk to you of her death-bed, – in dignity of mind, and pious resignation, far surpassing the imaginations of Rousseau and Richardson, in their Eloise and Clarissa Harlowe; for hers was, I believe, from the immediate inspiration of the Divinity.[47]

It was on 15 October that Penelope wrote to Sarah about Lawrence's 'diabolical' letter:

I have this morning received a letter from that *wretched man* not likely to calm my slumbers I pray God preserve *your* peace, my dearest Friend, from the attacks that I fear it will be assailed by from that quarter. . . . This letter has the stamp of a DARK and DESPERATE character, to which I do not *chuse* to fix the *proper* name. . . . It is critical to *advise* under such circumstances, but I am much inclined to think *I* should at all hazards put the affair at once into the hands of Mr Siddons, and trust to his candour and good sense. I should also consult with Mr Kemble. It is necessary, in my opinion, that

Sally shou'd be placed under the protection of those who are naturally inclined and able to afford it her. While *he* thinks he has ONLY the timidity of WOMEN to operate on, and to oppose him, there is no saying *what* he may not *attempt. . . . What a wretch!* My nerves and my nature shudder at this man. What will you do to save yourself, and above all, dear, dear Sally, from him? Let me have his *diabolical* letter at a future day. God only knows what occasion I may have for it. I send you a copy of my reply. . . . I cou'd wish dear Sally's mind kept quiet; yet surely she *ought* to know of this *outrage*, which I shou'd imagine must cast him from *her* heart for *ever*. Much am I mistaken if there is not more wounded *Interest* than *Love* at the bottom of all this. *It is desperate*, because his FORTUNES *are so*.[48]

Sally, who had recovered from her relapse, took up the correspondence with Penelope:

I seriously believe he is, at times, *quite mad*; there is no other possibility of accounting for his conduct. Poor, wretched creature! let him inflict still farther torments on those who love and are interested for him, *he will still be the most tormented*.

Do not fear upon my account, dearest friend! where can there be any danger, since I am myself more unwilling to put myself in his power than any of my relations can be? AM I NOT BOUND BY A PROMISE, THE MOST SOLEMN, THE MOST SACRED, – is not that sufficient to preserve me, even should my own treacherous heart dictate a thought in his favour! *But that it does not*, even when I thought of him as unhappy but resign'd I did not regret my promise given. But now, his shocking violence. . . . *It may be love, but such love as I never wish to inspire; I fly with* HORROR *from such a passion!* . . . We cannot, you know, quite conquer all our *feelings*, but virtue and reason may regulate our *conduct*, and, with the help of heaven, I fear not for myself in that respect; whatever I may *feel* I will *act* AS I HAVE PROMISED.[49]

The situation after the death of Maria was painful and impossible. Sarah had known Lawrence almost from his childhood. She had, most evidently, a deep affection for him. If it was short of actual love, it was still far more than she had for any other man. But now she was torn between fear of the deep trouble he could bring upon her family if he maintained his ungovernable passion for Sally, and a real desire to have him as a constant companion in her private circle, if not in her family. He disturbed her inner emotions more than any other man was ever to do, and her anguish at what she felt was his unreasonable, unbalanced behaviour was the greater because she did not want to harm him in defending her beloved Sally from his attentions. Only when we realize how moved she was beyond reason by strong and contrary emotions can we account for the weakness and vacillation of her judgement at this time. Normally, any conventional mother in her position would have told her husband about Lawrence's intolerable behaviour and left him to deal with the matter. But Sarah took every care to secure Lawrence from William's disapprobation, once Lawrence had told her it was Sally, not Maria, whom he loved. The only action she appears to have taken was to warn Sally that Lawrence would be a very unsuitable husband for a girl in weak health. William, obtuse and self-centred, and worried about his health, was (according to Mrs Piozzi) by no means indifferent to his daughters, whom he seems to have loved far more than he loved his wife. Sarah did not want him to visit his petty wrath on Lawrence's head, and so drive him for ever from her intimate circle. We do not know how much she herself had come to depend upon Lawrence's affection; her name was to be linked with his on more than one occasion in the future, in spite of the difference in their years. Perhaps her anger with him was even a little motivated by jealousy. In her letters to Penelope, who, as we have seen, had until the end come to relish her part in the drama and proved as susceptible to Lawrence's fascination as Sarah or any other woman who knew him intimately, she felt she must play the part of the good mother, protecting her daughter against the violent attention of a distracted lover. But neither she nor Penelope attempted to hide their extraordinary partiality for Lawrence. Penelope's last letter to Lawrence is that of a woman who had been deeply hurt by a man of whom she had allowed herself to become too fond. As for Lawrence himself, he does not say a single word against Sarah, even though he knew very well that she was doing everything to oppose a possible marriage with Sally. It had been Maria he had really feared, and he was right. She had not been the kind of girl, once she had stirred a man to love, to accept outright rejection unavenged. Lawrence's instinct for women, that of a sensitive rather than a blindly virile man, made him realize where his enemy lay – the girl could exploit the conventional pieties of the deathbed to exact a ritualized oath from her sister in order to deprive him of the woman she knew by now he truly loved.

The question of whom he really did love remains open. It was

probably Sarah herself, fourteen years older than he. Though she
was as starved of private affection as she was overwhelmed by
public admiration, she was too correct, too puritanical ever to
entertain the idea of taking him as a lover. But he could link
himself to her through marriage with one of her daughters. His
initial love for Sally, who though intelligent was placid and cold
by nature, had been supplanted by that for Maria, whose youthful
and far more sensual beauty had at first, no doubt, taken his
senses by storm – until, within a few months, he found her
possessiveness, and perhaps her sensuality, oppressive and
ultimately repellant. Sally, beautiful, intellectual and sociable,
seemed then like some bright angel to this man who, though he
worshipped women, may never have gone to bed with one. No
wonder, therefore, he was driven to sudden distraction when he
felt that Maria, his evil angel, had deprived him of the one woman
he thought might bring both beauty and companionship into his
life.

Sarah's next letter to Penelope, written on 17 October, only a
week after Maria's funeral, is unusually revealing. There are signs
too in her manner of writing, normally so clear and controlled,
that she is deeply uncertain of herself:

> Of the infatuated creature, whose diabolical letter you have astonish'd
> me with this morning, I hear from Mr and Mrs Twiss, that after
> every species of frantic behaviour (which you yourself have borne
> so sweetly, and for the agitating effects of which you have met *so fit
> a return* – of course, if you have opened his letters, he has been
> upon his knees to you, BODY AND SOUL, for his unmanly outrage),
> for several days together, that he is now PERFECTLY COMPOSED, and
> determined, by a course of proper conduct, to deserve the blessing
> he hopes for. *I* wish him every good *but that*, for I am more and
> more convinc'd they would both be wretched. Dear Sally loves you
> with all her heart. I thought it right to show her that shocking letter.
> 'If this is love, defend me from it!' were her words. She is shock'd at
> his behaviour to you. I wou'd follow your advice implicitly, but that
> Mrs Kemble, with a thousand good qualities, is so fond of talking
> over other people's concerns, and that so indiscriminately, that it is
> no exaggeration to say this affair would be known in every Milliner's
> shop in Town, had she the least intimation of it. The confidence
> between Mr S. and my Brother is unbounded, and I fear, were I to
> acquaint my Husband of it, there is no doubt of the forenam'd
> consequences. Mr S. too, is, unhappily, so cold and repelling, that
> instead of tender sympathy I shou'd expect harsh words, 'unkind

reproof, and looks that stab with coldness'. Yet all this I wou'd and will *boldly encounter* the very moment that I see occasion.[50]

Lawrence, meanwhile, was trying to make his peace with Penelope. Though she did not send his letters back, as she had threatened, it would seem that she never replied to them. There is no more correspondence from him preserved, and we only learn of the aftermath from the letters which passed between Sally, Sarah and Penelope. Lawrence's 'diabolical' letter continued to prey on Penelope's mind:

> Me he has agitated so dreadfully, that I know not when I shall recover it. My spirits were weak before, and two SUCH nights have succeeded to the receipt of his *savage* letter as I shall not soon get the better of. Nothing but scenes of gloom and images of *horror* floating on my fancy, and ever present to my sight![51]

Hers was a susceptible imagination which would have responded to such Gothic novels of the macabre as *The Castle of Otranto* and *The Monk*. Sarah's letter of 21 October, however, continues to reveal her (and Sally's) indulgent feelings for Lawrence:

> If our Tormentor will but cease his persecutions, we shall not only be content, but happy; for my dear, sweet Sally still assures me that it is impossible *she* should be otherwise while I am with her. And while she acknowledges (what we all feel) the powerful fascinations of this creature, she is as well aware as any of us that to be his wife would be to be *completely wretched*. . . . Though she contended the other day that what *we* have seen of him *lately* has not been the *character* of the man, because it is so unlike all that we have seen of him *heretofore ourselves*, and all that we have ever *heard* of him. . . . I sometimes fear this calm precedes a storm – yet let me be thankful for this short respite! . . . *Tell me, tell me how you are.* I am to play next Saturday. I have chosen Isabel, in 'Measure for Measure', because it is a character that affords as little as possible to open wounds which are too apt to bleed afresh.[52]

A few days later, in an undated letter, she is writing about Lawrence again:

> All is still quiet. I am astonished at it, and so is Sally. He goes to the Play, and in all respects appears quite easy. . . . Sally seems still quite determin'd; but when I talk'd of the importance of their *first meeting anywhere*, she told me it was impossible for her to treat him with coldness or neglect: poor thing! I feel the difficulty, yet anything short of it will, I fear, encourage him to hope that he may one

day attain his end. She is not likely to meet him anywhere in private, except at Mrs Semple's, where she assures me she will not go without me, and has promis'd that if he shou'd be at the Theatre, etc., she will seem not to see him. . . . Her Father or myself will always, I hope, be able to accompany her on such occasions, and, by these precautions, I hope he will be tir'd of the pursuit. I wish, and so does Sally, that we had her letters out of his hands, for he may think, perhaps, their being suffer'd to remain with him is a sort of tacit encouragement; yet, on the other hand, we sometimes think it best not to awaken the sleeping embers of those passions that may again *upon a breath,* break forth to torment us. I perceive he has interested Mrs Twiss very much, though she is convinc'd of the imprudence of Sally's listening to him . . . as to Maria's injunction (to my great surprise), she seems to say an *extorted* promise goes for nothing. This, I fear, is his opinion too. Sally does *not* think *so,* yet thinks her sister shou'd not have exacted such a promise, and that she was actuated as much by resentment for *him,* as care and tenderness for *her* in it. . . . Poor Sally has had another severe attack; she has been in bed ever since Tuesday; today she is better, and I hope will be well enough to come downstairs. Oh! my dearest Friend, shou'd she think of marrying a man more steady in his attachments than this versatile creature?[53]

Penelope, in her reply of 5 November, reads easily enough between the lines, and refers to 'those waverings which you relate to me, which, in conversation on the subject, betray the power this man still has over her heart'. She goes on to argue that 'dear Sally, though in love' gave a voluntary, not extorted, promise to Maria, which is 'as binding as any human engagement CAN be'; Mr and Mrs Twiss, as we have seen, had been arguing otherwise, which shows that some members of the family, at least, had been expressing their views on the subject, and Penelope warns Sarah that the gossips are at work: '. . . sorry am I to say, the subject has spread much more widely than we any of us expected. Everybody's eyes will be on you and dear Sally, and your conduct respecting this connexion closely watch'd and commented upon.'

Two days later, on 7 November, Sally herself wrote to Penelope about 'Mr Lawrence's unfortunate attachment', speaking as if she were in the position of a penitent:

I do not shut my eyes to conviction; *I see him as he is.* Yet, oh pardon me, if I sometimes cast over him that brilliant veil of enchantment which conceal'd his errors from our fascinated eyes – I do indeed. I cannot help viewing him sometimes as *he was,* or rather, such as he appear'd to be; and I then think that the world does not contain another creature who could so answer my idea of perfection. *But that creature was ideal!* such as my heart imagin'd it, IT NEVER EXISTED, – hard, hard task, to return to the reality! But I am now, perhaps, leading you to believe, that while I can indulge in such retrospections, while I think thus of the past, I cannot consider the present and the future *as I ought.* You see I do not conceal even *these thoughts* from you: I let you read the weakness that yet remains in my heart. But do not doubt the firmness of my mind or of my conduct, – do not so wrong me! I do not think I shall ever so love again as I have lov'd that man, but this is most certain, I LOVE HIM NO LONGER. The creature *I would have liv'd and died for,* EXISTS NO MORE, or, as I have before said, *never did exist.* Time and circumstances have discover'd to me a character which nothing could tempt me to unite myself to.[54]

Sally also reveals that Lawrence, having lost Penelope as an intermediary, had attempted unsuccessfully to replace her with Patty Wilkinson, Tate Wilkinson's daughter, who had recently come to London to join the Siddons household and act as a 'companion' for Sarah. He had also been forbidden to discuss the matter further with Sally's aunt, Mrs Twiss. Everything, in fact, was being done to enable the whole unfortunate affair to be forgotten. 'My Mother tells me she means to be very gay this Winter,' says Sally to Penelope.

But it is obvious that Sally was neither ready nor able to forget Lawrence. On 18 November, she writes to Sarah Bird about her feeling for him:

If indeed he loves me, I pity his present situation from my soul. But I feel certain that I shall soon share the fate of those who have gone before me, and that he, poor creature, will get out of this distress only to plunge himself into a new one. Well, let us only be out of the scrape, and that will be some comfort. I do assure you I should, on my own account, rejoice to hear that he had given up all thoughts of me, and was in love with Miss anybody else.[55]

This is possibly a reference to Amelia Locke, in whom Lawrence had expressed some interest. But did Sally mean this? Lawrence himself had certainly not given up his hopes of Sally, as Sarah evidently knew. In her next letter to Penelope, Sarah writes on 19 November:

Last Sunday we saw the unhappy disturber of our peace at church, whose self-love was naturally wounded by our total inattention to his presence. He went to Mrs Twiss's, and was betrayed into his usual excesses of passion. He persuades himself that Sally still loves him, and is only operated upon by some powerful influence to *appear indifferent* to him. He terrified Mrs Twiss so completely, that both she and Mr Twiss have told him that they shall EITHER of them quit the room at the very first mention of the subject. – Mr Siddons, my dear Friend, is now inform'd of all; for since I was mistaken in supposing, from this interval of peace, that he, Mr L., might in time be induc'd to desist from the pursuit of this vain shadow, I determined, last Monday morning, to hazard everything uncomfortable to myself from Mr S.'s disapprobation, rather than leave my darling unprotected by the strong fence of a Father's care and caution. . . . There is a corner yet left in my heart that feels for this unhappy creature, and still yearns towards him, when I think of the hours we have all spent together under this roof, – the happiness I proposed to myself in spending the last hours of my life in the bosom of that domestic peace, which my fond imagination had pictured in his virtues and rare endowments, as the husband of my child.[56]

This was perhaps the most revealing expression of Sarah's devotion to Lawrence that she was ever to write, or which is now known to us.

It is not clear what action William took. He probably took none at all, for Lawrence still vainly persisted in his suit. Sally writes to Sarah Bird on 23 November:

I am sorry to tell you that Mr L. will not yet believe I can keep the determination I made at Birmingham, but time will, I trust, reconcile him to what at present he looks on as a loss. I grieve most sincerely for all he has, or may suffer. . . . He has never address'd himself to my Mother or me since our return to Town, but he has so persecuted Mr and Mrs Twiss by his violence, that I fancy he has excluded himself from their house. . . . Good heavens! my dear girl, when we look back to this time last winter, when we think of those clandestine meetings, those various scenes of love and terror that we were witnesses to, is it not wonderful to reflect on the events which have happen'd in one short year? . . . In little more than two years, during every month, circumstances have happen'd which would almost make a history; – indeed if *ours* were known from first to last, what a *romance* it would appear.[57]

Sarah unburdened herself still further to Penelope about her unhappiness with her husband:

You desir'd me to tell you how Mr S. received the information which I told you had been communicated; with that coldness and reserve which has kept him so long ignorant of it, and that want of an agreeing mind (*my* misfortune, though not *his fault*), that has always check'd my tongue and chilled my heart in every occurrence of importance *thro' our lives*. No, it is not his *fault*, it is his *nature*. Nay, he wou'd never have hinted to Sally anything of the matter, if I had not earnestly represented to him how strange such a reserve must appear to her; whereupon he testified his total disapprobation, nay, abhorrence, of any further intercourse with Mr L.[58]

The rest of the letter is full of Lawrence, more especially concerning a drawing of Sally which he wants to copy before returning the original to Great Marlborough Street. The persistence of her anxious curiosity as to what might happen next is very revealing:

All this while, *God be praised!* my dear child is well, and I really think is as far easy about him, as the uncertainty of his designs (which must excite a sort of restless curiosity) will allow. What will be the end of it? I suppose, if they shou'd chance to meet, we shall have another explosion; and all my fear is, that she shou'd be surprised, or frighten'd, or soften'd into some *expression* that may encourage him to *hope*, which I am *sure she does not* MEAN.[59]

Lawrence in fact had written a joint letter to Sarah and Sally about the portrait, and then another to Sally, to which she replied, according to Sarah, 'in so decisive a manner . . . to extinguish in a short time all hope'.

During the hard months of winter the health of the family suffered; only Sarah remained well, in spite of 'the piercing cold of that stage'. But the differences with Sheridan over the non-payment of her fees recurred – 'I wonder if Mr Sheridan has any notion that she is really at last determined to have no more to do with him,' writes Sally to Penelope on 19 January 1799. As for Lawrence, she adds, 'all I can tell you is that *I am just as* firmly determin'd as when I first determin'd, and that he is, I fear, still guilty of loving me too well. Why will he not give us one more proof of his inconstancy? But we must have patience, it cannot fail to happen soon.' Later in the month she saw him in Covent Garden theatre, and 'was very much distress'd to be oblig'd to pass close to him'.

Sarah left London with the family for Bath, where she was due to fulfil an engagement postponed on account of Maria's death. Sally managed to get there, but a severe attack of asthma followed,

which angered her because she was missing the local balls at which
she so much enjoyed the dancing. Writing on 8 February to
Sarah Bird, she says: 'The people are all as mad about my Mother
as if they had never seen her.' Sarah, however, began to be
tormented by her recurrent erysipelas, which affected her lips,
and for which she could get no relief until she returned to London
in March. Sally's letters of the period, once she had recovered, are
full of references to the rumour, apparently obtained from the
newspapers, that Lawrence was shortly to marry 'a young Lady
of distinguish'd talents, and extensive possessions' who lived in
Clapham, and 'paints extremely well, I know'. But on 23 March,
she writes to Sarah Bird:

> I have heard no more of Mr L. since my return to town, but am told
> that he denies any *particular attraction* being the cause of his frequent
> visits to Clapham. . . . If he was indeed going to be married, I think
> he could not deny my request, which was *that he should return me
> all my letters.* Tell me whenever you hear of him, for, separated as
> we are for ever, I must, while I have sense or feeling left, be more
> interested in the fate of that being than I ever was, or perhaps ever
> shall be, in the fate of any other.[60]

Sally's illness recurred in April; she tried a new cure, 'Dr
Barton's fix'd air, or vital air' which 'almost kill'd me; so I have
done with experiments, and will return to Laudanum'. Meanwhile, Sarah had been induced to return to Drury Lane, and was
appearing in Whalley's tragedy which – according to Sally, at
any rate, writing to Penelope on 29 April – though not considered
a 'standing' play, was pretty well received. 'My Mother really
acts most divinely in it, and looks as beautiful as possible.' By
May, apparently, Lawrence was being talked about in connexion
with a Miss Jennings; Sally, writing about this to Sarah Bird on
3 June, claims that this new lady friend lacks

> . . . that expression of an intelligent mind, without which all beauty
> is, in my eyes, defective. . . . You know I have resign'd all thoughts
> of Love, or Jealousy, but if I had not, I do not think Miss Jennings
> would make me jealous. I have once or twice seen Mr L. by chance,
> and I thought I should have dropp'd the Sunday before last, in
> Kensington Gardens, when I passed him so close that I might have
> touch'd him! Whenever I meet his eyes with that glance that pierces
> thro' and thro' one, it is like an electric stroke to me, and it is well
> I had hold of Dorothy's arm. I pass'd his door too, the other day,
> and my heart sank within me when I pass'd the windows of that

Parlour where we have pass'd so many pleasant hours! Ah, my dear friend, these are sad recollections, and such vain regrets will follow, that I always strive, and now must, to banish them from my mind.[61]

It is evident Sally was still in love.

Sarah's appearances in London continued until well into the summer, when the theatre grew as hot as it had previously been cold in mid-winter. Writing on 11 June to Penelope, Sarah complains that 'playing every night a laborious part this hot weather, induces a langour, both of body and mind'. A walk in Kensington Gardens brings back sad memories of Maria:

> Mr S. forced me out to walk in Kensington Gardens. – I was there *once before*, about this time last year, and my sweet Maria's fading image (for she was there too) haunted me at every step. . . . I shall go there no more, I think. . . . I fancy our friend Whalley will not be much richer for his play, for *nobody is paid*. *I* can get no money. I rely on my Husband's good judgment, and am resolv'd not to dispute with him any more on the subject of going on with Mr Sheridan, which, he says, is the only chance I have of getting a shilling of my money.[62]

Lawrence was still on her mind, and she writes strangely about him, almost as if she wanted to prevent a possible marriage from her own rather than Sally's point of view:

> Our poor dear Sally has had a sad winter of it. . . . And so you think Mr L.'s mind is sober'd, and there's an end of the affair. I wou'd I cou'd persuade myself that it is so! And yet my fears are surely groundless, for he has been perfectly quiet now for some months. And, good God! a man *must* be out of his senses to build his happiness on the possession of a poor creature who brings such an affliction for her *portion*.[63]

As soon as the London season was over at the beginning of July, Sarah went north to play in Edinburgh where her brother Stephen was still in management, following this with a tour of the English provincial towns. Sally went with her, and liked Edinburgh as much as her mother did. Before she left London, Sarah went so far as to write to Lawrence asking him to return both her letters and Sally's. Sally, in her next letter to Sarah Bird written from Edinburgh on 15 July, tells her of Lawrence's reply, in which he said that he would return the letters 'when he is married . . . but that that event he believ'd to be at a great distance'. She begs for any news of him her friend can send, and ends by admitting that 'from you I wish not to conceal the interest I must ever feel in all that concerns him'. The following November, Sarah, in a letter to Penelope, was to make a shrewd comment on Sally's attitude to Lawrence: 'Poor Soul, she thought (I suppose naturally enough for her), that his adoration was to last for ever, even against Hope, and I think is rather piqued to find that "these violent transports have violent ends".'

The summer tour went on until September. William was negotiating as hard as he was able with Sheridan concerning terms for Sarah's return to London. Matters were not finally settled to William's satisfaction until November; Sarah agreed to appear once again at Drury Lane in *Pizarro*, on which Sheridan set great store because he knew it would fill the theatre, provided Sarah was in it. Late in November they were back in London. On her return to Drury Lane, Sarah proved as popular as ever, but William seems to have been duped once again by Sheridan – 'Not a farthing of money has my Father yet touch'd,' writes Sally to Penelope on 24 November, 'but *he* seems satisfied with his agreement, and that is enough for me.' As for Lawrence, she repeats again and again that she considers herself 'completely cur'd of that *disease*, A TENDER PASSION'. In another letter of this period she says that her Mother has 'frequently said she never believ'd Mr L. lov'd me' – though Sally cannot make out how this could have been the case, since she has only herself, and no fortune, to offer a man.

Sarah's own relations with Lawrence were apparently resumed in 1800; some contact seems to have been made through Sarah Bird herself, who came to stay at Greek Street in February with Lawrence's sisters. Sarah had resumed sufficiently formal relations with Lawrence to write on 7 February to Sarah Bird: 'Will you be so good as to ask Mr L. where I can get some very fine Carmine? I find it the best Rouge, cover'd with a little hair-powder; but I can get none at all equal to some he gave me about two years ago.' Shortly after this, Lawrence was permitted to come and visit her. Sally then wrote to Sarah Bird:

I am glad my Mother has seen Mr Lawrence, I mean, talk'd with him, as I think the composure of his manner the most likely method to convince her of his sincerity. I have not entertain'd the smallest doubt of it, but I am perhaps better able to judge in this case, as *I know from myself* what a change may take place in one's feelings in the course of some months. . . . Remember me to *all* the Greek Street party.[64]

Just before Sarah Bird left Greek Street, Sally wrote to her again:

It seems to me I had many things to ask of, and to say to you, that I have neglected, but perhaps these things are best *unsaid, unheard.* . . . In your departure I think I lose *two* instead of one. You will not be sorry that I blend your idea with one for whom you know I have so true a regard, so lively an interest. . . . It should be my constant prayer to be *always kept at this same distance from that being, whose fascination I have not the power to escape, should I be drawn within the circle of his magic.* Time and absence have work'd wonders in me, let me then not seek to counteract their salutary effects. My heart is so restor'd, that, can I but keep clear of that one rock, it will, I think, split on no other. . . . Do not forget to say something kind and friendly for me to Mr Lawrence.[65]

In a moving letter, not published before, Sarah expresses on 25 November 1799 her deep gratitude to Penelope Pennington and to Mrs Piozzi, who was apparently on a visit to Bath and therefore only a few miles from Penelope in Bristol:

I am very sorry for both your sakes that you will not meet our dear Mrs Piozzi at Bath, but *She* has the satisfaction of being mistress of her time and within a *Dozen miles of you* woud to God I were so too! She will come to you, and what do I not expect she will not operate on you, to whose tender attentions, sweet and wise consolations, I verily believe I owe that *I* am still in the land of the living – Oh tell her tell her I can *never* forget her goodness and that I love her to the bottom of my heart – Was ever Woman Blessd with *two such Friends?* No never; But yours dear Soul was the greater tryal and by so much the deeper is my sense of gratitude – I shall hope soon to recieve [sic] this promisd Letter but do not I conjure you fitigue yourself – You must imagine I shall be anxious to hear day by day the progress of your recovery but only just in *three words* from time to time. Say '*I am better*'

May God almighty bless and speedily restore you prays Your ever affte and faithful S. Siddons.

Remember me kindly to Mr P. and Mrs W. Our darling Sally is quite well and in riotous spirits. May God preserve her body and *Mind* Mr L. is not in Town.

These dangerous flirtings with passionate memories supposed to be suppressed for ever apparently led to nothing but some private excitement for Sally. On account of William's health, the summer of 1800 was spent away from town, two months at Broadstairs and two at Brighton. The northern provincial tours were cancelled, though Sarah earned some much-needed money in the south. On their return to London, Sally saw Lawrence in the theatre, 'looking,' she thought, 'very pale and ill'; but whatever she might construe from this, Miss Lee of Bath, who saw Lawrence frequently, told her that in December 'he was quite well, quite gay, and she believ'd, just at present, heart-whole'. But Miss Lee went on to imply that Betty Tickell, a society beauty whom Sally detested, was engaging Lawrence's attention. Sally's interest in Lawrence became, if anything, more active. First she writes on Christmas Eve, 1800, to Sarah Bird:

> You may have heard (and it is true) of Mr L. being in Mrs Kemble's Box, and with my Mother. I fancy she often sees him at the Theatre, but you have indeed been misinformed by those who told you he was ever of *our party*. All I ever see of him is now and then at the Theatre, when he just appears for a minute, as if *purposely* to make me a formal bow, and then he generally goes away, to some other part of the house, I suppose. . . . He is frequently at my Uncle's house, and I believe scarcely ever misses a night when my Mother performs, when he generally pays her a visit in her dressing room. This I hear not from my mother, for unless I force her to it, she never mentions him.[66]

Then on 23 January 1801, Sally writes far more frankly to Sarah Bird, whose house in Rugby, Lawrence had been visiting:

> I confess the last time I saw him, I made him as distant a Curtsy as he made me a Bow. I know my Mother sees him often, and I know she cannot cease to look on him with the partiality she always did, and always I believe will feel for him, yet she never mentions him to me, never tells me he has spoken of me, or desires to be remembered to me – perhaps indeed he never *does* think or speak of me – but can I ever forget the days that are past? . . . However *right* I may think it that we are separated, I would not have him *forget me*!
> I know that his is an inconstant heart, that he has lov'd many, yet I think there were circumstances attending my attachment to him and his to me, which (though love be gone) should ensure me for ever a portion of his recollection and his tenderness. As for *my heart, it is a single and a constant one*, it never gave itself *but once* away, and I believe it *incapable* of change.[67]

s.s.—9*

Sally no longer felt able to sing at parties, and there is even a hint of estrangement from her mother, probably on account of Lawrence:

> I sing but little now, to what I once did, and indeed I think *all* my energy is weaken'd since I have ceas'd to give delight to the three beings who were dearest to me on earth; one is gone for ever, the second *is as dead to me*, and the third no longer takes the same delight in me she once did.[68]

There followed next an attempt by Sally to exchange 'speechless messages' with Lawrence in the theatre, but she was deeply hurt when he appeared not to take notice of her repeated attempts to attract his attention; she writes to Sarah Bird on 13 February:

> Separated for ever as we are, I would still live in his memory as a friend he esteems and regrets, and to think that he can quite forget me, and after not seeing me for so long a time behave to me as he did last night, gives me great uneasiness. Be diligent to send me an answer. I know you sometimes write to him, ask him *from me* what I have done, for I would rather think him angry than suppose he wish'd to make me understand I was more forward than he dsired I should be to acknowledge him. . . . I have never ceased to express the interest I take in him, in his fortunes, in his sentiments, and I had flatter'd myself that tho every former hope was *by both of us resign'd*, I should not in passing from his heart, be mixed with the many who had gone before and were forgotten.[69]

A tense situation immediately followed. Lawrence wrote direct to Sally about some imagined grievance, which hurt her bitterly. She could not restrain herself from complaining of this to Sarah, and a feminine tangle developed between her and her mother (who thought Sally had broken her undertakings about Lawrence), and Sarah Bird, who Sarah rather unfairly thought had been interfering. The fracas eventually died, but it did not prevent the gradual development of the close friendship of Sarah and Lawrence. He was never to have any further relationship with Sally, who appears to have resented her mother's continued affection for the man she herself still loved. Sally passed out of Lawrence's life, and the long, painful correspondence came to an end. Within little more than a year, Sally was to be dead.

Lawrence's distraught experiences of love have to be understood in the light of what little is known of his subsequent relationships with women, and, above all, with Sarah herself. It must be realized that his conduct was comparatively innocent for the period in which he lived and for the society in which he moved. The Prince Regent, who was married in 1795 against his will to Caroline of Brunswick, had a voracious appetite for women and set the pace for the English upper classes. The profligate living and sexual indulgence of both his brothers and sisters was no less than his own. He separated from his wife after the birth of their daughter Charlotte the year following their marriage. London Society was resolved into gossiping cliques, reflected at their best in Farington's diaries and at their worst in, say, those of Greville, who was to write somewhat later. No one at once so prominent and so unattached as Lawrence could escape calumny. Gossip ebbed and flowed about his relationships; his official biographer, D. E. Williams, wrote of him soon after his death: '. . . in affairs of love, Sir Thomas had need of the fortitude of St Anthony, for he was often tempted, and was more sinned against than sinning.' One woman, who knew him well, claimed he was 'oftener wooed than wooing', but another woman wrote:

> . . . it cannot be too strongly stated, that his manners were likely to mislead without his intending it. He could not write a common answer to a dinner invitation without its assuming the tone of a billet-doux: the very commonest conversation was held in that soft low whisper, and with that tone of deference and interest, which are so unusual, and so calculated to please. I am myself persuaded, that he never intentionally gave pain. He was not a male coquette; he had no *plan* of conquest.

Susceptible women, therefore, in an age of widespread sexual licence, were often misled by his manner and frustrated by the evident pleasure Lawrence took in their company without inviting himself to their beds. Apart from Sally and Maria, he appears to have sought to marry only one other woman – one of the two Miss Uptons, which of them even is not known. According to Williams, 'He fell *éperdument amoureux* of the Honourable Miss Upton, sister of Lord Templeton', but she rejected him, apparently, on the grounds of inequality of birth, having played with his affections for two years.[70] Since he painted both girls, exhibiting their portraits in 1801, we can only assume this second unhappy love affair occurred at some time after Sally's death in 1803, but before the development of what Williams calls the 'intellectual attachment' of his later years to Mrs Isabella Anne Wolff. This, a friend told Williams, 'innocent as it was, absorbed all his feeling and his time, and left no room for other attachments'.

Lawrence first met Mrs Wolff about 1803 when she was a little over thirty, but the friendship between them only reached intimacy many years afterwards when, in her early forties, she had separated from her husband. Lawrence's beautiful portrait of her, so full of evident affection, was exhibited in the Royal Academy in 1815, the year he was knighted by the Prince Regent.

But this final relationship came in quieter days, when Lawrence was himself over forty. In 1801 his relations were at least relatively intimate with the Princess of Wales, then aged thirty-six, whom he painted in 1804 and whom he was in the habit of visiting at her residence in Blackheath. The Princess's conduct, after her virtual separation from her husband, was considered officially to have 'more levity than was acceptable' and in 1806 a commission was set up – though not by the Prince – to carry out what was called a Delicate Investigation into her behaviour and morals. Since Lawrence was currently rumoured to be one of the men involved, he had to swear an affidavit in September 1806 that he had never been alone with Her Royal Highness 'with door locked, bolted or fastened' against unwanted intrusion.

The only other rumour which had to be openly contested concerned an alleged sexual relationship with Sarah herself. On 27 November 1804, a Captain Thomas called on Farington and 'spoke of the reports of Mrs Siddons being gone off with a young man, an artist, who had courted two of Her daughters in succession, both of whom had died, and now had adressed [sic] the mother. – I surprised him by strongly reprobating all that related to His going off with Mrs Siddons, and told him it was a foul calumny.' Again on 30 November Farington reports: 'Lord Thomond called on me – He spoke of the public report of Lawrence and Mrs Siddons having formed a connexion, and concluded it to be true, as He had heard a Divorce was to be sued for. – I told his Lordship that the whole was a most unfounded calumny.' Then again on 1 December Farington writes:

In this morning paper the following advertisement appeared. It proves to what length the reporters of the wicked calumnies against Mrs Siddons and Lawrence have carried their endeavours to asperse their characters and impute to them their having formed an illicit connexion. The object undoubtedly has been double, viz: to drive Her from the Stage and from Society, – and to injure him in his profession. Mr Siddons, Her husband, being lately returned from Bath has then publickly come forward to conteract the infamous attempt. –

> Having been informed on my recent arrival in town, that the most wicked and injurious slanders have been circulated of late respecting Mrs Siddons, I do hereby offer a Reward of One Thousand Pounds, for the first discovery and conviction of any Person who had been, or shall be concerned, directly or indirectly, in the circulation thereof. Wm. Siddons. Upper Terrace, Hampstead. Nov. 30 1804.

Lysons told me that he and Morris had drawn up the advertisement which *appeared this morning*, and had shewed it to Kemble who at first hesitated, about the publication of it. – The calumny is shocking. Mrs Siddons has been a long time confined by a sort of rheumatick complaint.[71]

The advertisement foiled this attempt to destroy the reputations of both Sarah and Lawrence, and in spite of these designs, and the great tensions in their past relationship, they were to remain friends for as long as they lived. But, as we shall see, Lawrence was to die before Sarah, his heart engaged once more by the girl who most reminded him of her, her niece Fanny Kemble.

7

The Dangerous Years

⸺⟩⟨⸺

SARAH'S BEAUTY was a lasting one, maturing in her later
middle age in spite of the periods of ill-health from which
she suffered. As an actress she was to remain fairly consistently
on the stage until her final season in 1812, and she never stood
higher in public esteem than during these later years. Young
writers of distinction, such as Hazlitt, Byron, Crabb Robinson,
and Haydon were to put on paper some of the best, most illuminating descriptions of her. But in her private life, she was lonely,
unhappy, and for a brief while, as we shall see, vulnerable and
indiscreet in her behaviour.

She was, then, at the peak of her success at the turn of the
century, sustaining her talent almost entirely on established work.
Only in that semi-notorious play, Kotzebue's *The Stranger*, had
she taken the opportunity to create an entirely new kind of
character, a daring portrayal, in its way, and an entirely contemporary part. After this, her only great opportunity to create a
new part in London was in *The Winter's Tale*, in which she
appeared as Hermione in 1801.[1] The remainder of her new roles
were of negligible value.

But she was used to success, and the theatre brought her more
labour than happiness. This was the period when her domestic
troubles were at their height. It was the period when she had to
face the death in 1802 of her father, to whom she was deeply
attached. She had a grain or two of comfort when her son Henry,
an utterly undistinguished actor, played Hamlet at Covent Garden
in 1801. She wrote to Elizabeth Inchbald:

258

It is so long since I have felt anything like joy, that it appears like a dream to me, and I believe I shall not be able quite to convince myself that this is real till I am present 'to attend the triumph and partake the gale'. I am all anxiety and impatience to hear the effect of Hamlet; it is a tremendous undertaking for so young a creature, and where so perfect a model has been so long contemplated. I was frightened when I yesterday received information of it. Oh, I hope to God he will get well through it.[2]

She saw her son act, but she was away in Ireland when he got married in Bath in 1802.

The success of Sarah as Mrs Haller meant that the cultish fashion for Kotzebue was on in London; Sheridan was in no financial position to resist it, even if he had wanted to do so. But he became himself a part of it. In 1799 he adapted an English translation of Kotzebue's *Rolla's Tod*, a tragedy set in the period of the Spanish conquest of Peru. Sheridan gave the play the title *Pizarro*. Sarah played Elvira, the mistress of Pizarro, in effect a camp-follower whom, says Campbell loyally, she raised into respectability. In spite of its fustian, *Pizarro* was an immense success, and Sheridan managed to give it a contemporary political twist by introducing words he had used in his orations, particularly from his speech on the trial of Warren Hastings. Sheridan, apparently, was in a state of nervous perturbation about this piece, in which Charles Kemble, as well as John Philip, appeared, together with Dora Jordan, who was, apparently, very bad in a wholly unsuitable part. But the play was demanded repeatedly; it ran for thirty-five nights by the end of the season. So once again, in 1799, another play by Kotzebue was put on, *Adelaide of Wulfingen*. This however failed, like the other new plays in which Sarah was to appear, *Aurelia and Miranda* (based on Lewis's 'Gothic' novel, *The Monk*), the unhappy Dr Whalley's *The Castle of Montval*, Joanna Baillie's *De Montfort* (29 April 1800), for which, says Boaden, Kemble had 'a very unusual pile of scenery' created in 'seven planes in succession' representing a church of the fourteenth century – 'positively a building', Sotheby's *Julian and Agnes* and William Godwin's *Antonio*.

The labours of committing lines to memory and of rehearsal were arduous enough for Sarah, without the additional nervous strain of appearing in plays which failed with the public. There was also the continuous uncertainty of receiving proper payment from Sheridan's barren treasury, so the labour of the provincial tours went on to keep her own finances even. On 14 July 1801 she wrote to her friend Mrs FitzHugh from Preston:

> In about a fortnight I expect to commence my journey to Bath. Mr Siddons is there; for he finds no relief from his rheumatism elsewhere. His accounts of himself are less favourable than those of any one who writes to me about him; but I hope and trust that I shall find him better than he himself thinks; for I know, by sad experience, with what difficulty a mind, weakened by long and uninterrupted suffering, admits hope, much less assurance. I shall be here till next Saturday, and after that time at Lancaster, till Tuesday, the 28th; thence I shall go immediately to Bath, where I shall have about a month's quiet, and then begin to play at Bristol for a few nights. '*Such resting finds the sole of unblest feet!*' *When* we shall come to London is uncertain, for nothing is settled by Mr Sheridan, and I think it not impossible that *my* winter may be spent in Dublin; for I must go on *making*, to secure the few comforts that I have been able to attain for myself and my family. It is providential for us all that I can do so much. But I hope it is not wrong to say, that I am tired, and should be glad to be at rest indeed. I hope yet to see the day when I can be quiet. My mouth is not yet well, though somewhat less exquisitely painful. I have become a frightful object with it for some time, and, I believe, this complaint has robbed me of those poor remains of beauty once admired, at least, which, in your partial eyes, I once possessed.[3]

The end of the previous year, Sarah had endured a painful operation, as Mrs Piozzi records in a letter to Penelope Pennington: 'she is now thin as a lath, and light as air, but safe, as everybody thinks. Her behaviour – angelic creature – was in this tryal, as in all her tryals, exemplary; firm but unostentatious.' Later, as we have seen, she suffered from erysipelas, which attacked her lips with burning pain. She was never to be entirely cured of this. In July 1801, Mrs Piozzi wrote:

> Poor dear pretty Siddons! What has she been doing to her mouth? Picking it, my master says, as I do my fingers, which, he threatens me, are one day to resemble poor Mr Pennington's toes. But in earnest and true sadness, what can be the matter with her lips? Lips that never were equalled in enunciation of tenderness or sublimity! Lips that spoke so kindly *to* me and *of* me! Dear soul! what can ail her? She dreamed once that all her teeth came out upon the stage I remember; I told her she would go on acting till age had bereft her of them; but God forbid that she should lose them *now*. Her husband will mend at Bath. . . . Sally's death will be no *loss* to

40. Edmund Kean as Sir Giles Overreach. Attributed to George Clint.
(*Victoria and Albert Museum, Crown Copyright*)

41. Covent Garden Theatre, 1804.

42. Exterior Covent Garden Theatre, from Bow Street, 1809. Ackermann.

43. Covent Garden Theatre, after rebuilding, 1810. (*Photograph from the Richard Southern Collection, the Theatre Collection, Department of Drama, University of Bristol*)

44. Riot Act being Read during the O.P. Riots at Covent Garden Theatre in 1809.

45. Mrs Piozzi. By George Dance. (*National Portrait Gallery, London*)

46a. (Below left) John Philip Kemble. Sketch for a portrait by Thomas Lawrence. (*National Portrait Gallery, London*)

47. Silhouette of Sarah Siddons.

48. (Right) Sir Thomas Lawrence, President of the Royal Academy. Self-Portrait. (*National Portrait Gallery, London*)

46b. (Left) Sarah Siddons. By John Flaxman. A hitherto unpublished drawing in a series by Flaxman. (*By courtesy of Miss Yvonne ffrench*)

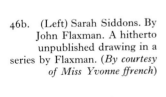

49. Make-up Table designed by Sheraton for Sarah Siddons.
(*British Theatre Museum*)

50. Sarah Siddons's cottage at Westbourne Green.
(*By courtesy of Miss Yvonne ffrench*)

51.   Covent Garden Theatre, 1815.

52.   Covent Garden Theatre: Saloon to the Private Boxes, 1810.
Ackermann.

53. Fanny Kemble. Lithograph after the drawing by Thomas Lawrence.
(*Lawrence Collection, British Museum*)

her dear mother, altho' a very poignant affliction without doubt; and Cecilia will be her delight I dare say: but Sally and her Father both will yet last many years I am confident. Shall we have a Bath Winter all together and be comfortable? Or will they pay her, and lure her back to Drury Lane? You must get her mouth in good order, that she may look like my *little* miniature of the *greatest and only unrivalled* female this century last expired has pretended to produce. When her lips close, what good will our ears do open? . . . Comfort the charming creature all you can tho', and get her into her accustomed beauty.[4]

Sickness and worry wore Sarah down, and her creative work suffered. At times she became ponderous, both on and off the stage, and stories circulated about her as a tragedy queen who could not free herself from her decasyllables once she was off the stage. Her friends were worried about her, and in a burst of feminine confidence, Mrs Piozzi wrote at this time to Mr and Mrs Chappelow, who were only acquaintances of Sarah:

She commissioned me to tell you . . . that *nothing* does her any good . . . or produces any but a momentary Relief . . . that anxiety of mind increases it almost to Distraction but that she has martyr'd herself with unavailing Remedies, and will *try no more*. Since Maria's Death it has returned upon her Terribly, and she is as lean as yourself; but very beautiful, and light and grace in her Figure. . . .
. . . We passed yesterday evening together, and she was half asleep all the while with Laudanum taken externally and internally for this horrid Torment – poor Soul!
So now *swear* to me you *will not tell*; but say Mrs Siddons is here and acting divinely, which is the strictest Truth: and that she looks better than ever, which is the strictest Truth likewise: Confession of Illness is to her a Ruin. . . . Say not that anything ails her for Heaven's sake.[5]

Kemble had resumed the management of Drury Lane at a fee of £50.14s a week for the 1800-01 season with some tacit understanding that he might gain a share in the property, and so emulate Garrick. He told Boaden that the theatre 'fairly treated, was a profitable concern'. Yet the only way for Drury Lane to get fair financial treatment was to take it out of Sheridan's hands. But it was useless; Sheridan, however much one liked him, proved impossible to work with, and negotiations to take over a share in the property collapsed on legal grounds; the risk was too great. There was criticism when at the close of the 1801–02 season the

Kemble family, John Philip and Sarah, removed themselves from the sinking ship which for so long they had prevented from foundering by their presence.[6] So they went over to the rival house, Covent Garden, where they were to work together for the remainder of their joint careers. This was the only move open to them in the capital, which was still dominated by the two principal patent theatres. Here Kemble's old friend, Elizabeth Inchbald, was to help him negotiate the purchase of shares which by 1803 were to make him part-owner of the Covent Garden Theatre. The theatre was managed by Thomas Harris with notable efficiency and a keen eye to profit.

Both John Philip and Sarah withdrew entirely from the London stage for the period of a year. Kemble went with his wife on a Continental tour, staying for a considerable while in Spain, where he studied Spanish. He was abroad when his father died. Sarah, accompanied only by Patty Wilkinson, undertook a prolonged tour of Ireland to make money; she was to be absent from home for a year, from May 1802 until May 1803. The family were to spend the summer in Bath, including her beloved Sally and her little daughter Cecilia (aged now eight); she entrusted them to the care of William, while at the same time begging Mrs Piozzi to watch over them as well:

> Farewell, my beloved friend! a long, long farewell! Oh, such a day as this has been! to leave all that is dear to me. I have been surrounded by my family, and my eyes have dwelt with a foreboding tenderness, too painful, on the venerable face of my dear father, that tells me I shall look on it no more. I commit my children to your friendly protection, with a full and perfect reliance on the goodness you have always manifested towards Your ever faithful and affectionate S. Siddons.[7]

During the period she was away her father was to die – as her sensitive emotional state prompted her to forecast.[8] Only Patty Wilkinson remained to give Sarah the loving care she so much needed. They left London together in May 1802 for Holyhead, passing through Stratford, where some horrible representative of the new Shakespeare reliques industry tried to pass off a child with a cloven tongue as a descendant of the poet. Patty kept a diary of their journey, which Campbell quotes:

> 'On the 25th of May,' she says, 'a beautiful day, we entered Wales, and got to Conway before sunset. Mrs Siddons walked about the

romantic castle for more than an hour. There were harpers below
the building. She sat at one of the windows of the ruins, looking
out upon the lovely scenery, – the river glowing in the balmy sun-
shine, – the vessels gliding up and down, – and the glorious Welsh
mountains, till she seemed absorbed in a luxuriant reverie. We
returned to our inn, and during supper a harper was admitted,
according to custom, to entertain the strangers. He was the most
venerable looking man I ever saw. Mrs Siddons said that he gave
her mind the image of a Druid. In that romantic time and place
Mrs Siddons honoured the humblest poet of her acquaintance by
remembering him; and let the reader blame or pardon my egotism,
as he may think fit, I cannot help transcribing what the Diarist
adds, – "Mrs Siddons said, I wish that Campbell were here."

'We left Conway,' Miss Wilkinson continues, 'next morning, and
ere long crossed Penman Mawr, where, like other travellers, we
alighted from our carriages to look from a bridge that commands
the fullest view of the sublime landscape, with all its rocks and water.
A lady within hearing of us was in such ecstacies, that she exclaimed,
"This awful scenery makes me feel as if I were only a worm, or a
grain of dust, on the face of the earth." Mrs Siddons turned round,
and said, "I feel very differently." '9

The season in Dublin began in June and lasted until August,
when Sarah left for another season of some weeks in Cork,
followed by a month in Belfast. Letters from William urged her
to keep at it; money was short owing to heavy expenditure on
their house in Great Marlborough Street, and preparations for
fitting out George for service in India. Sarah decided to stay the
winter in Ireland, where her continued success at least ensured a
good income.

But there appear to have been other considerations which
attracted her to Ireland. It was during this period that Sarah
indulged herself in what many regarded as the greatest indiscretion
of her life. Every circumstance must be taken into consideration
if a full and compassionate understanding of what happened is
to be reached. The more obvious facts appear simple and undisputed. While in Dublin she befriended a young actress,
Catherine Galindo, and her husband, a fencing instructor.
Catherine Galindo was a member of the company in Dublin.
Her stage name was Kitty Gough, and she was a friend of some
long standing of Patty Wilkinson. By her own account, she came
of a good family whose fortune was lost through the irrespons-
ibility and extravagance of her father. She had become an actress

in order to gain a living for herself and give assistance to her
father; finally, after appearing in English and Scottish theatres
with some success, she had secured a long-term engagement in
Dublin. She had met her future husband, whom she always calls
Mr Galindo, in Bath. She says she won the lasting disapproval of
her family by marrying him; she experienced 'a strong and perhaps
fatal attachment' to him. When she first met Sarah she was the
mother of one child, a little boy called Johnny, to whom Sarah
stood as godmother. Later, after Sarah had left Ireland, she gave
birth to a daughter.

Since both Boaden and Campbell, Sarah's contemporary
biographers, make no mention whatsoever of the Galindo affair,
we are left with Catherine Galindo herself, the most biased of
witnesses, as the only exponent of what happened. In 1809 she
published her notorious open 'Letter to Mrs Siddons' in which
she attacked her for alienating her husband's affections seven years
previously. This letter is, in effect, a prolonged indictment of
Sarah's wantonness and duplicity, as well as her cruelty to a
young wife whom she professed to love and to one of whose
children she had stood as godmother. In all this she appears to
have been aided and abetted by Patty Wilkinson, who was supposed to be Catherine's friend. Mrs Galindo published for good
measure twenty of Sarah's private letters to her and her husband,
and charged the public five shillings for her eighty-page booklet.[10]

Later biographers who mention the affair rush to their subject's
defence, which is quite natural. To Fitzgerald, a Victorian, the
matter is obviously most distasteful, but he has to admit that
Sarah formed an 'extraordinary intimacy' with this disreputable
'adventurer', and that she was 'a little impulsive and rather
indiscriminate in her friendships'. For Mrs Parsons, the open
letter 'proved nothing beyond the irresponsible and violent nature
of the writer'.[11] For Naomi Royde-Smith the whole affair was 'the
indulgence of a little vanity' by Sarah, showing her to be 'femin-
inely silly', a passing phase for which she was forced to pay a
bitter price by the 'pushing and venomous wife' of a 'handsome
and plausible young man'. It was her 'autumnal season of foolish-
ness'. Yvonne ffrench surely comes far nearer the truth in calling
the relationship a 'violent friendship', though she qualifies this by
adding that it was also 'thoroughly silly'.

But Sarah had never before been foolish, let alone silly. It was
not in her shy, emotional nature to be so. Throughout her life she

had felt she needed all the protective covering she could assume. She was still only forty-seven, a period when a woman can still be richly endowed with sexual needs. Every contemporary account of her emphasizes how beautiful she was, in spite of her sporadic ill-health, though the descriptions are always qualified by emphasizing her dignity, her aloofness, her grandeur of manner, the masks with which she protected her emotional nature, as in the *persona* of the 'tragedy queen' which she borrowed from the stage. So long as she was youthful and kept enough of her husband's affection at least to secure an occasional increase in her family, she could keep herself content. But after the birth of Cecilia eight years before, we have to assume she had no further relations with poor 'Sid', whose prolonged humiliation as a result of his wife's fame drove him finally into hypochondria, taking refuge in his love for Sally. No doubt he had had at one time or another some unassuming mistress, discreetly housed in Chelsea, and knowledge or suspicion of this could hardly have inspired Sarah to maintain her original love for him. Her letters to Mrs Piozzi during the Lawrence affair prove that all real warmth and affection between them had gone. More and more she was driven to expend her lively emotions on her children, especially on Maria, Sally and the youthful Cecilia, and on her few more intimate friends. Above all else, she spent herself on the stage, where some of her sexual energy could be drained away in the performance of such emotional parts as Isabella or Mrs Haller. She would return from the theatre worn out by her physical and emotional exertions, still weeping the real tears of her projected emotion. As her sons left her to discover their own lives and find their own women, she was driven increasingly into the emotional vortex of Lawrence, who, if the truth were known, was possibly the one deep, if partially unconscious, love of her life. Lawrence, the cerebral lover, had given her a notional love uncomplicated by demands on her bed. Seeing she was already married and much older than he, she had hoped to knit him to her through marriage to one or other of her daughters; she had not allowed for the complications in Lawrence's own nature, and had suffered with him the tortures of his indecision and his self-lacerating exhibitionism. Only Sally had managed to emerge relatively unscathed from this encounter; her protective mask was well in place. But Sarah's had proved wholly inadequate in the face of her own and Lawrence's suffering during the months before Maria's death, and the period afterwards when she felt forced, against her evident affection for Lawrence, to induce Sally to reject him.[12]

In a letter to Whalley written as early as 13 January 1801, Sarah had said in despair: 'I wish I could tell you something comfortable of poor Mr Siddons, but I see no material change; and as for poor Sally, I now feel so convinced that her complaint is part of her constitution, that I have done hoping.'[13]

Now Sally was slowly wasting away. There was no one left but Cecilia, the little prodigy, wise, they all said, beyond her years, but, like her elder sister, not strong. As early as 1799, Mrs Piozzi was writing:

> I think She is not happy in her Children tho'. The eldest Son will be a strolling Player, the Second has bad Eyes – almost to blindness. The pretty Daughter died; and Sally seems almost entirely ruined by an Asthma which they call Constitutional, and scarce try to remove. The little Baby my *God* Child, called Cecilia, is sick and spoild, and fretful and fragile, – her Mother has put her to Miss Lee for Education, but they are fearful that she will *not* live.[14]

More than a year later, in November 1800, she paid Sarah a quick visit, and notes that she 'is lean and nerve-shaken, but lovely as ever, and was preparing to shine in Elvira the evening of our visit. Her husband walked in with his two sticks and chatted cheerfully; her eldest daughter appeared to *me* in high health and spirits, and Miss Lee, who was there, made a good report of the youngest'. Cecilia, aged six, was at Sophia Lee's school for young children at Belvedere House. Only a few months before, on 4 June, Mrs Piozzi had written to Penelope Pennington:

> I reckon her as having only *one* daughter to portion out; Sally will never marry, I suppose, if half of what I have *heard* of her ill health be true. . . . Siddons will repeat over to two or three generations the lamenting strains I heard him recite in 1788, and his Daughter will think herself young when everybody else sees her grown old, because she has a father to nurse.[15]

Sarah's desire to love was being slowly starved; Lawrence, much as she must have wanted the company of a man of creative capacity equal to her own, was still all but estranged at this time.[16] Her own peak achievements on the stage were, she knew, passing. She was to create nothing new at Covent Garden. She was facing, or was soon to face, her menopause. She was worn out by too much emotion and the strain of earning her family's living while suffering from frequent debilitation through ill-health.

It was not, therefore, either a foolish or a silly woman who went to Ireland with Patty Wilkinson, who was by now virtually her adopted daughter. It was a woman with a great, if unspoken, need for affection and support far beyond what poor Patty, a helpful, willing, substitute daughter, would be capable of supplying. What she needed could probably only be given her by a man. In her uncertainty Sarah had proved to be afraid of the gathering strength of her emotionalism; she had channelled it all into her performances on the stage to such a powerful degree that even the most sophisticated audiences were shaken by her and returned again and again for more. But what of her own inner needs? She had carefully stood by her own chosen image of quiet domesticity, even of piety, while other decent and fashionable actresses whom she knew so well had openly enjoyed the affectionate patronage of their lovers – the feminine Elizabeth Farren, now at last married to the Earl of Derby after a lengthy liaison, and the charming and lovely Dora Jordan, acknowledged mistress of the Duke of Clarence and mother to several of his children. Sarah had no lover, though not for lack of sexual attraction, but this could have strange side-effects. In 1804 a twenty-three-year-old Irish law student at Lincoln's Inn fell violently in love with her and so pestered her with letters he had to appear before the magistrates and be bound over to keep the peace. According to Farington, the 'mad Irishman' fancied Sarah was in love with him. As Mrs Piozzi describes in her diary entry of 17 June:

> Dear lovely Siddons has had an Adventure of a curious Nature – a Lover so mad with Passion for a Woman more than twice his Age, that she has been forced to swear the Peace against him – Comical enough! and that odious Husband of hers never coming forward to protect her: but thinking of his own Health, drinking Bath Waters, etc., etc. How everybody does hate that perverse Fellow! and how he does hate his beautiful and enchanting Wife.[17]

Mrs Piozzi's hostile reference to William is interesting. She was somewhat erratic in her attitude to him. On 20 May the following year she was writing: 'Mrs Siddons and *her* Husband not living at *all* together. Mercy on us!', while in the following October she is beginning to warm to him, perhaps because he evidently liked her (since he had no access to her diary and correspondence about him), and wrote her amusing, domestic letters. On 25 October she writes:

> Mr Siddons has been a very agreable and comfortable Companion to us; I know not why his Wife turned him out so in his Old Age Poor Fellow! or whether he turned *himself* out; but the World is beginning I see to blame *her* and pity *him*; they had better have gone on together.[18]

William was probably a nicer man when he was away from Sarah. He liked the small things of life, and loved cats. It is doubtful, as we shall see, if William and Sarah ever formally separated. It is far more likely that they drew almost entirely apart during this period of emotional stress in Sarah's life.

In Ireland, therefore, Sarah suddenly found herself confronted by a young married man who made no secret of his adoration for her. If Patty was a substitute for Maria and Sally, Galindo was to become the substitute for Lawrence. He is a somewhat shadowy character; we do not even know his first name, though his initial was P. It would seem that in her response to him Sarah let her emotions run away with her and behaved 'badly', at least to Catherine Galindo, who surely had considerable cause for the furious jealousy which eventually drove her to take a vicious and calculated vengeance on the woman she considered had destroyed her marriage, which was probably none too secure in the first place. To the Galindos Sarah was obviously a person whose friendship was overwhelmingly flattering and likely to make their fortune. For Sarah, these young friends of Patty's helped to fill the void of her unhappiness until the young man's infatuation broke down the weakened barriers of her resistance, and she gave him her affection in return. There are only too many precedents for such anomalous attachments between women in their forties or fifties who, lacking any firm emotional anchor in their lives, respond unwisely to the exuberance of a man much younger than themselves. As often as not, the young men involved in such relationships are unscrupulous and out to exploit both the affections and the fortunes of their victims.

Catherine Galindo certainly tells her offensive story in such a manner as to justify herself for resorting to its publication, but there seems little reason to doubt that the main outline is true. Sarah is introduced to Catherine and her husband by Patty, and she takes a fancy to them. Catherine, in her initial efforts to impress the great actress who could be so helpful to her in forwarding her career, suggests that her husband should take Sarah for rides in Dublin in a little curricle, or open carriage, which the young couple own. It is during these rides alone together that Galindo falls in love with his beautiful companion, whose loneliness and emotional needs he is no doubt quick to sense. Galindo is represented as a fencing instructor, rather than an actor.[19] As Sarah responds to his warmth a plan is evolved by means of which they could work together; she will revive her old production of *Hamlet*, in which she appeared as the Prince, and so give him the opportunity of teaching her (at the age of forty-seven) to fence. The costume design which she wore for this production of *Hamlet* survives.

Galindo appears to have neglected his wife and run after Sarah, carrying her on summer and autumn journeys to Cork and Limerick in his little open carriage, while Patty and Catherine travelled by post-chaise. Catherine Galindo's story continues:

> When you came to Limerick and Cork, Mr G. spent his whole time with you, generally driving you out of a morning, and, whether engaged at the theatre or not, spending all his hours with you. I saw and felt myself so entirely neglected that I will own, I became very unhappy, and often expressed my dissatisfaction to Mr G. I was also much distressed at the expenses we were every day incurring without a hope of renumeration; for, as I scarcely ever performed, I had no chance of any benefit of mine succeeding, having no claim as formerly upon the public.[20]

For a while her work parted her from her husband, who stayed with Sarah and Patty in Dublin. He even went for a while to England 'upon a scheme which he and Miss W. had planned together, entirely against my wishes'. She saw Sarah's decision to prolong her stay in Ireland for the full winter as a blow to her hopes of winning back her husband's affections:

> As if your passion for Mr G. had overcome all considerations for propriety, you never suffered him to be from your side, he spent all the day and half the night with you, scarcely ever returning home sooner than one, two, and sometimes three in the morning. Provoked beyond all patience at such conduct, I remonstrated in the warmest manner to Mr G. and, though in milder terms, to Miss W. and even to yourself. I told both you and her that though I believed Mr G. to be in very good company, yet that I could not be content at his

entirely abandoning his home; you seemed vexed at what I said, but notwithstanding pursued the same conduct.

One circumstance I must not omit: you were very ill for about a week, the nature of your illness I am to this day ignorant of.[21]

She even claims she was turned from Sarah's door by Patty during the period of Sarah's illness, while her husband was always encouraged to come. Whether or not Catherine Galindo is exaggerating or twisting the facts, the broader nature of Sarah's relationship with Galindo must be true. According to his aggrieved wife, an engagement at Covent Garden was engineered for her against her wishes so that Galindo could be with Sarah when she finally returned to London. An engagement for Mrs Galindo was indeed negotiated between Sarah and Harris behind Kemble's back when he was abroad. Kemble was furious when he returned and found out about it, for he had worked with Catherine in Dublin and thought nothing of her as an actress. He went storming round to his friend and confidante, Elizabeth Inchbald, making a strange request of her, his oldest friend, which upset her, as she reveals in a letter quoted by Fitzgerald:

> When Kemble returned from Spain, in 1803, he came to me like a madman; said Mrs Siddons had been imposed upon by persons whom it was a disgrace to her to *know*, and he begged me to explain it so to her. He requested Harris to withdraw his promise of his engaging Mrs G., at Mrs Siddons's request. Yet such was his tenderness to his sister's sensibility, that he would not undeceive her himself. Mr Kemble blamed me, and I blamed him for his reserve, and we have never been so cordial since, nor have I ever admired Mrs Siddons so much since; for though I can pity a dupe, I must also despise one. Even to be familiar with such people was a lack of virtue, though not of chastity.[22]

Kemble, as it happened, came to Dublin himself and, says Catherine Galindo, was publicly rude to her, and in the end her engagement at Covent Garden was abandoned. Nevertheless, the Galindos came to London because, it would seem, of Galindo's relationship with Sarah.

Once there, Catherine Galindo claims she was forced to support herself and her family out of her savings. Nevertheless, her relations with her husband were such that another child was born to her at this time in London. Catherine Galindo writes of this period:

You were shortly after this taken ill of a complaint which confined you to your bed, when you were somewhat recovered, you went to live at Hampstead; there Mr G. was your constant visitor, and as he could sleep upon a sopha in your parlour, he always stayed at night. I visited you occasionally twice or thrice; from some circumstances I was asked to stay at night; but though I did not then observe it, not supposing it proceeded from any cause, my *little* boy was always asked to accompany and sleep with me, Mr G. being as *usual* on the *sopha*. Upon your recovery, you took your present residence near Paddington, which, for what reason I know not, was kept a profound secret from me. One day before you went to reside there, Mr G. took me to see it, we met you on the road, you seemed extremely offended with Mr G. for having done so. I did not see you again for near a month, when I went by invitation for the first time to Westbourn. Having heard you were thinking of performing, from Mr G. I said I was happy to find you thought yourself well enough to venture doing so; from what cause I am still ignorant, you flew into so violent a rage no words can describe, and in your passion, which astonished me, you used these words, 'I suppose Mr G. you keep nothing a secret that concerns me from Mrs G.' As I could not comprehend what so much good passion was wasted for, and disgusted with your conduct, I left the room, secretly resolving to visit you in future but as seldom as possible. . . . When you returned home, things fell into their former course; Mr G. continually dining with you, and always staying at nights. I never seeing you but at a morning visit, and that seldom.[23]

The association between Sarah and Galindo appears to have lasted about four years, that is from 1802 to around 1806 or 1807. It finally broke up, as these associations inevitably must, and in this case over money. Sarah unwisely, and without William's knowledge, lent her friend £1,000 to assist him set up a theatrical venture with William Macready in Manchester. Interest was supposed to be paid on this, but the venture failed and in the end Sarah had to write off the debt along with the relationship in 1807.

Catherine describes two further extraordinary meetings with Sarah. The first was in Birmingham, where she unaccountably found herself sharing the same lodging with Sarah, who was on tour:

. . . you met me with more warmth and seeming kindness, than I had for a long time seen in your manner . . . I was affected even to tears, my mind was in a dreadful state, as I shall explain hereafter. In a few days we parted, when you took your leave of me, I told you I was very unhappy, and that you were the object of my un-easiness, but that when next you saw me, let it cost me even my life, all should be explained; you seemed shocked and surprized at my words; taking my hand in the most *affectionate* manner, you said, 'if you ever should believe me any other than your sincere friend, you will wrong me much.'[24]

The second meeting took place in London in 1807:

I was so agitated on seeing you I could scarcely speak; you said you were going to *church*; I told you I should not detain you, as I had only come to fulfil the promise I had made when last we parted, and in a few words to tell you, I was no longer your dupe, as I was now perfectly informed as to the nature of your attachment to Mr G. for these many years. You changed from red to extreme paleness, and with trembling lips and great hesitation of speech, after some time you said, 'you cannot believe what you say, and on what do you found your accusation?' I answered, 'that is of no consequence, you know what I say to be *true*.' I then walked out of your house, not chusing to prolong the conversation; you and Miss W. followed me, and endeavoured to say something like persuading me I wronged you; to which I answered, 'you know, Madam, I would not lightly accuse one whom I have so long believed my friend, indeed the opinion I once had of you was beyond any other created being. How could you then have the barbarity, the cruelty to betray in every thing that concerned my peace, one who thought so highly of, and who trusted you so unboundedly?' you answered me in these most extraordinary words: 'why then did you think so highly of me, did you believe me superior to the weaknesses of humanity?' upon which I replied, 'I have indeed been punished for thinking too well of you.' At that moment I left you, seeing Mr G. coming towards me, who had followed me from home. You may suppose he was much displeased at this visit to you, but at that moment I was too much afflicted to attend to what he said. I left town in a few hours after.[25]

In one's desire to condemn Catherine Galindo for her infamous publication, one must not overlook her genuine grievance. There are faults and occasional inconsistencies in her narrative, and it is shameful that at one point she should publicly hint at her know-ledge of the venereal complaint Sarah is said to have caught from William, so revealing that Sarah had at some time early in their acquaintance felt a need to unburden herself about intimate matters at home. The euphoria of a new and untried intimacy of the kind she formed with the Galindos might well have led her to refer to this deep-felt resentment against her husband. But Catherine's observations on the initial relationship with Galindo himself are not without interest:

> . . . though I was not blinded on the subject, I never believed it more than a ridiculous passion, chiefly arising from liking to have the attention of a man, who, being young enough to be your son, flattered your vanity by his apparent attachment to you. Never could I suppose it could go beyond a weakness of that description. I have known such folly even in the most worthy natures. Your character and principles, which I believed of the purest kind, your supposed extreme *piety*, together with your *age*, and other *causes*, which I shall be silent on, preserved me from feeling any sensations like jealousy, which I might have felt had any other but yourself been in question.[26]

Later the nature of the relationship changed, according to Mrs Galindo:

> From my coming to England, I remarked a kind of mystery in your conduct towards Mr G., that I could not develope the source of, particularly continual quarrels, the subject of which I could never guess at: for though those disagreements were no secret to me, the cause always was. Your conduct on these occasions was repeatedly this, you had a quarrel with Mr G.; when a few days were past, Miss W. was despatched to me, requesting my company alone, and to complain of Mr G.'s rudeness to you and to her: if I went, I was obliged to listen to a long detail on the subject, which I endeavoured to excuse as well as I could, not knowing how he had *offended*, then perhaps the very next day, a letter was written by Miss W. to say all should be forgiven if I would come and bring Mr G. with me: this had been so often repeated, it became at last quite ridiculous, and I used frequently to say to Mr G. what indeed was but the truth, 'Mrs Siddons or Miss W. scarcely ever call on me, but when they have quarrelled with you.' These and many other circumstances which I could not account for, such as long private conversations, letters received from you which I never knew the contents of, not directed to our residence, but to a coffee-house at a distance from it, which by an accident I became possessed of. Those letters written from the residence of your friend Mrs ——, and from Bath when you went to visit Mr Siddons, were written in a FALSE ALPHABET, one of which I saw Mr G. writing an answer to; upon my asking him what it was, he appeared confused, but said, 'it is a puzzle Mrs Siddons has given me to decipher for her'. My suspicions once awakened, I followed the clue, as I before said, which at last

exposed the whole of such a character as must shock all good minds to contemplate; what you really are is known but to a few, but they do exist.[27]

Running through the whole of Catherine Galindo's narrative are the morbidities of acute jealousy, almost amounting to mania. Everyone appears to be plotting against her – her husband, Patty, Kemble, as well as Sarah herself. The desire of all is to be rid of her so that Sarah may indulge in an unlawful relationship. All she can actually prove, however, is that Sarah and Galindo spent a very great deal of time together, though when the relationship was at its height she did not scruple to have relations with her husband, with the result that yet a third child was born to her in London. That she was both wicked and foolish to publish her accusations in the manner she did, goes without saying; all she could hope to gain from this were the profits resulting from a wide sale. The risk she took was that Sarah would prosecute her.

But in addition to Catherine Galindo's narrative there are Sarah's intimate letters, the first ever to be published; they provide us with a gloss on the whole affair and do little in fact to harm Sarah's reputation, however much light they throw on new aspects of her nature. However unwisely she may have revealed her unhappiness to the Galindos in conversation, Catherine Galindo had no letters to include which reveal Sarah as the kind of monster she is made to appear in the narrative.

It is in Sarah's letters that we discover something of Galindo's character, and not in his wife's story. Perhaps what appealed to her initially was his gaiety – 'gaiety', she wrote to him after she had returned to London,

is your natural turn, and I have too great a regard for you not to be very sensibly affected, when I see or know you otherways. I have been very low myself all this day, and have often wished for the friend who knew so well how to keep me 'up up up'. – About this time last summer, we used to be practising the noble science of *defence*, it served the purpose of the moment well, very well indeed.[28]

In another letter, written this time to Catherine from Cheltenham, she writes: 'This has been a sad dull day, and I have wished myself in —— Street, very often indeed, in the course of it. Mr G.'s *oddity* would have done me a great deal of good, and I wanted to be made to stare, to wonder and to laugh, to rouse me from my lethargy . . .'[29] On the other hand, he was touchy and perhaps rather lazy; he told her he did not like writing letters, and when she lightly reproved him ('you know you began your last letter very ungallantly, by telling me you were a very bad correspondent; and in short intimating that you found it rather troublesome to write letters'),[30] but adding that she, too, was an indifferent correspondent, he apparently took offence, so that she had to write and explain herself more fully:

> I am very sorry to find that any thing I have written has made you uneasy, for I assure you on my honour, I should not have been the least offended if you really *had* been tired of writing. I have often heard you say you *could not write letters*, and I can easily imagine it must be a great restraint upon you; for my own part I confess there is nothing I dislike so much, and were it not that I fear my friends would accuse me of neglect or unkindness, I should never write a line to any one: to say the truth I have a dread of having my letters thrown about, to be picked up by servants, or other *officious persons*; with this fear before my eyes, no wonder my correspondence is not very voluminous, – there is an insatiable curiosity both in my own family, and in those whom one would imagine could have no earthly concern about me, to find out what I write and to *whom* I write, that robs me of all the pleasure I could receive from opening my own heart or reading that of my friend. – You will therefore allow the reasonableness of my dislike to writing letters or even of receiving any, but those of the *commonest* sort, and you can imagine that such an intercourse can but ill supply those sallies of good humour and pecularities of cordiality, which might be misinterpreted by those who were not acquainted with the *characters of the writers*.
>
> And now I hope I have explained myself, and that you will believe me *unalterably your sincere friend.* If there be, as I have sometimes thought, some yet unknown causes, that in a more particular manner unite separated friends at particular times, I should imagine those causes must have operated powerfully for the last ten days, with respect to me and my distant friends, for certain it is, that though I have been very ill, and rise from my bed *only to quiet your mind at this moment*, yet I have thought more of the dear farm (that is to be) than of my own illness.[31]

This strange letter, like others in the book, hints at so much more in their relationship than it says, for the very reason she gives, that she fears to be too revealing. Indiscretion, though, is surely at work in the following letter written to Galindo on 18 October 1803:

. . . I have been in such an agitated state of mind from domestic sorrows and cares that *I could* not write; the present cloud is dispersed, but how soon it may gather again I fear to think: at all events this I am resolved upon, the *next* storm SHALL BE THE LAST: I beg that you will divulge this only to Mrs G.; be kind and gentle to her, if you value my regard and esteem? Oh! I have suffered too much from a husband's unkindness, not to detest the man who treats a creature ill that depends on her husband for all her comforts; give my love to her and tell her she owes me a letter. I love and think of you both, and those sweet days that are fled for ever, – with the sincerest interest. I shall send you another watch chain soon, in the mean time assure yourself of my *unchanging regard*; I have time only to add that I hope you do not swear, and that you keep your beautiful hands very clean.[32]

Was it a failing in Galindo that he did not wash as often as he should, in what was, after all, an age of increasing personal cleanliness, among the upper classes at least? But, in its main content, how painful the publication of this letter must have proved to Sarah, appearing as it did so shortly after her husband's death.

More serious, perhaps, are the references which make Galindo appear to be both violent and hysterical. Sarah writes to Catherine:

I have a most sincere and affectionate regard for him, and I wish for your sake as well as his own, he would endeavour to correct that avidity of imagination, that at one time hurries him into what he mistakes for happiness, but which is indeed no other than intoxication; a sort of drunkenness of the mind, and the next moment plunges him into despondency. Indeed, indeed, I wish you would tell him it is my most earnest request that he would, and that by making this exertion, and in the effects it will produce on your *mutual comforts*, I shall be richly overpaid for all I have done; if *he* thinks himself unfortunate, let him look on *me* and be silent.[33]

How exactly this description would seem to fit Lawrence. The passage comes in the midst of one of the noblest and most moving letters she ever wrote, and shines like a jewel in an Ethiop's ear in the venomous context of Catherine Galindo's book. It was written after the prolonged struggle she had with Harris to secure the longed-for engagement at Covent Garden which was to bring the Galindos to London. Although writing formally to Mrs Galindo, it is to the husband that she is really addressing herself. After explaining the difficulties she has had with her new manager, she goes on:

This letter is to serve as an answer to Mr G.'s, and I most sincerely hope I may never receive such another: for alas! the pressure of my own affliction has not yet hardened me into an insensibility to the sorrows and mishaps of my friends, my friends too should *know* this; but I say no more, I most sincerely wish his spirits may be again restored; he tells me, I have taken too much trouble about this engagement, and that 'happiness is purchased at too dear a price'. I will own, in answer to the first assertion, that it *has* cost me much and various and very bitter contention; but I have gained the victory at last, and it depends on the moderation of the wishes and expectations of us all, whether the conflict is ended peaceably and honourably. I pray God it may, for to live in a state of contention with a brother I so tenderly love, and a husband with whom I am to spend what remains of life, would be more than my subdued spirit and almost broken heart would be able to endure.

In answer to the second, I can only say that the testimony of the wisdom of all ages, from the foundation of the world to this day is childishness and folly, if happiness be anything more than a *name*, and I am assured our own experience will not enable us to refute the opinion. No, no, it is the inhabitant of a better world, content, the offspring of moderation, is all we ought to aspire to *here*, and moderation will be our best and surest guide to that happiness to which she will most assuredly conduct us.[34]

There follows the passage in which she begs Galindo, through his wife, to practise such moderation. Then she goes on to discuss her own tragedy:

Two lovely creatures gone, and another is just arrived from school with all the dazzling, frightful sort of beauty that irradiated the countenance of Maria, and makes me shudder when I look at her. I feel myself like poor Niobe grasping to her bosom the last and younger of her children; and like her look every moment for the vengeful arrow of destruction. Alas! my dear friend, can it be wondered at that I long for the land where they are gone to prepare their mother's place. *What have I here?* Yet *here*, even here, I could be content to linger still in peace and calmness: content is all I wish: but I must again enter into the bustle of the world. For the *fame* and *fortune* have given me all I wish, yet while my presence and my exertions here may be useful to others, I do not think myself at liberty to give myself up to my own selfish gratifications.[35]

Only some kind of tenderness can surely prompt such a letter as this, sent on 14 December 1803, to Mrs Galindo, but plainly written through her to the man with whom she was perhaps somewhat absurdly in love:

> Do you remember this day twelvemonth, for I have had it so strong in my memory, that I have lived in N—— Street every moment of this day. Well, I trust we shall see some of those happy hours again; in the mean time do tell me something of your little Sarah, and what Mr G. is doing, for though I received a letter from him yesterday, he tells me nothing, only that he is as much my *slave as ever*.[36]

Mrs Galindo adds an ironic note in reference to the day she is invited to remember:

> I have no recollection of this day, but as my sensations were only that of calm friendship, I did not feel those *very tender* impressions which so strongly marked particular days to this lady; and perhaps those days she found so very pleasant were not always so to me; to sit and see Mr G. adoring her, was sometimes rather disgusting to me.[37]

No amount of bitter jealousy excuses the despicable way in which Catherine Galindo interprets Sarah's failure to return home in time to say goodbye to Sally on her deathbed; this is how Mrs Galindo describes the sequence of events:

> The week before you left town you received letters informing you that Miss Siddons your daughter was very ill; you were then reading Paradise Lost at the Lying-in-Hospital rooms, and had engaged to give the last night's receipt to the charity. The day before it was to take place, Miss W. received a letter saying Miss S. was past all hopes of recovery, and urging you to return home; she asked my advice how she should act, and we both agreed that as it was but one day's delay it would be best to defer the sad news until after the charity night was over. On your return home that night we gave you those letters to read; you seemed much affected by them, but never can I describe my astonishment when, instead of instantly resolving to return home, you said that you thought your honour obliged you to fulfil your engagement at Cork. You set out the next day for thence accompanied by Mr G.; all who knew the circumstances were disgusted at such conduct, and it was so much the subject of reprobation, that you know it was openly censured in the newspapers; letters came every day, (which I sent you) pressing your return home. By this time you had performed a few nights to very indifferent houses, and getting some way out of the engagement,

you at last resolved to leave Ireland. The event was, your *daughter's death before you could reach home.*[38]

As far as one can ascertain, what happened was as follows, as Campbell reconstructed it. On 2 February Sally had written to say she was well and happy; George had spent a fortnight with his mother in Ireland during mid-February before leaving for India; a letter from home gave no hint of Sally's approaching illness. On 10 March William wrote to Patty, not Sarah, saying Sally was very ill, but that it was better Sarah should not be told. (Those hostile to William like to imply he could not bear the thought of money being unnecessarily forfeited.) Patty, however, thought that she should reveal the news, but nothing could be done to secure them a passage to England, since gales were confining all boats to harbour. As the winds died, a further letter arrived from William to say that Sally was sufficiently recovered, and that Sarah could undertake her engagement in Cork. She therefore went to Cork with Patty and Galindo, and performed there on 21 March. On the same day she wrote to Mrs FitzHugh:

How shall I sufficiently thank you for all your kindness to me? You know my heart, and I may spare my words; for, God knows, my mind is in so distracted a state, that I can hardly write or speak rationally. Oh! why did not Mr Siddons tell me when she was first taken so ill? I should then have got clear of this engagement, and what a world of wretchedness and anxiety would have been spared to me! And yet, good God! how should I have crossed the sea? For a fortnight past it has been so dangerous, that nothing but wherries have ventured to the Holy Head; but, yet, I think I should have put myself into one of them, if I could have known that my poor dear girl was so ill. Oh! tell me all about her. I am almost broken-hearted, though the last accounts tell me that she has been mending for several days. Has she wished for me? but I know, I feel, that she has. The dear creature used to think it weakness in me, when I told her of the possibility of what might be endured from illness, when that tremendous element divides one from one's family. Would to God I were at her bedside! It would be for me then to suffer with resignation what I cannot now support with any fortitude. If anything could relieve the misery I feel, it would be that my dear and inestimable Sir Lucas Pepys had her under his care. Pray tell him this, and ask him to write me a word of comfort. Will you believe that I must play to-night, and can you imagine any wretchedness like it in this terrible state of mind? For a moment I comfort myself by reflecting on the strength of the dear creature's constitution, which has so often rallied, to the astonishment of us all, under similar serious attacks. Then again, when I think of the frail tenure of human existence, my heart fails, and sinks into dejection. God bless you! The suspense that distance keeps me in you may imagine, but it cannot be described.[39]

The storms returned, and letters from home were delayed a week while she stayed on at Cork, uncertain what to do for the best. The manager of the Cork Theatre acted humanely and released her from the remainder of her contract, at great loss to them both. Sarah and her companions returned to Dublin, where the seas were still high and, in consequence, no news from home was possible. Mrs FitzHugh had sent a letter to Cork, where she believed Sarah still to be. On 2 April Sarah wrote from Dublin in so great an agony that she did her friend a grave injustice:

I am perfectly astonished, my dear friend, that I have not heard from you, after begging it so earnestly. Good God! what can be the reason that intelligence must be extorted, as it were, in circumstances like mine. One would think common benevolence, setting affection quite aside, might have induced some of you to alleviate, as much as possible, such distress as you know I must feel. The last letter from Mr Siddons stated that she was better. Another letter, from Mr Montgomery, at Oxford, says that George gave him the same account. Why, why am I to hear this only from a person at that distance from her, and so ill informed as the writer must be of the state of her health? Why should not you or Mr Siddons have told me this? I cannot account for your silence at all, for you know how to feel. I hope to sail to-night, and to reach London the third day: God knows when that will be. Oh God! what a home to return to, after all I have been doing! and what a prospect to the end of my days.[40]

At last Sarah managed to secure a passage to Holyhead; here, while she waited for the post-chaise to Shrewsbury, she wrote to the Galindos:

For some hours we had scarce a breath of wind, and the vessel seemed to leave your coast as unwillingly as your poor friend. About six o'clock this morning, the snowy tops of the mountains appeared, they chilled my heart, for I felt they were emblematic of the cold and dreary prospect before me. Mr —— has been very obliging, he has just left us, but it is probable we may meet again up on the road. I thought you would be glad to know we were safely landed. I will hope, my beloved friends, for a renewal of the days we have known, and in the mean time endeavour to amuse and chear my melancholy, with the recollection of *past joys*, though they be 'sweet and mournful to the soul.'

God bless you all, and do not forget

your faithful, affectionate
S. SIDDONS.[41]

She reached Shrewsbury only to find a melancholy letter from William awaiting her; it had been written only an hour or so before Sally's death. As she was reading the letter, further news came by word of mouth that Sally was dead. Patty recorded in her diary that Sarah 'sank into speechless despondency' and took at once to her bed, 'cold and torpid as a stone'. When she had recovered sufficiently to travel, she began her journey home (according to Campbell, who received his details from Patty Wilkinson), by way of Oxford. Here her brother Charles came to meet her, and took her to see their widowed mother. By 16 April she was back in London, and from there she wrote an agonized letter to the Galindos in Ireland, using the love she bore them as a salve for the grief she felt for Sally:

> What can I say to you? And why should I write to you, since the dark cloud that hangs over my destiny will not, cannot, be dispersed, *and every ray of sunshine departed from it at the time I left you, never to return?* If I am to write or to speak to those I love, I must speak and write from genuine feeling, and why distress you with my over- whelming sorrows? God knows the portion of each individual is sufficient for himself to bear. I make the attempt to tell you many things that press upon my aching memory, but I feel myself unequal to it. I hope a little time will restore my tranquillity, at present my head is so confused, it is not without difficulty I have said thus much; though I should write volumes, I could never describe what I have lost in you, my beloved friends, and the sweet angel that is gone for ever. Good God, what a deprivation in a few days! Adieu! Adieu![42]

Then, in another short, undated letter, she added:

> Pray ask Mr G. to send me those sweet lines To Hope: that which he gave me is almost effaced by my tears, and let it be written in the *same hand*.[43]

The reference was to a sonnet which Galindo must have copied out for her. It was out of her need for affection that she sought to bring the Galindos from Ireland, and so forfeited to some degree the professional regard of her brother, as well as of Harris and such friends as Elizabeth Inchbald, who knew a little of what was going on. She wrote in an undated letter that a contract for Catherine Galindo might be possible for the 1804–05 season a considerable time ahead. Then she continued:

> If I do vow a friendship, you know I will perform it to the last article, write to me immediately, for I will not let the matter cool if I can avoid it. We talk of you every day, and think of you every moment. Surely, surely, we shall meet again, and though the manner of our intercourse be *different* yet our *affections* will be unaltered except that *deprivation* will teach us to estimate even more *highly* what we were near losing for ever. Do not let sweet little Johnny or his father forget her who loves them very affectionately.[44]

She admits that she is 'confused and stupified with anxious agitation and perpetual crying. I am still unwell, very unwell . . .' Then she refers to the prospect of them all living together on a farm near London, a project she appears to have discussed with them often, or with Galindo when she was alone with him.

Worn out with grief, she retired in May with Patty and little Cecilia to a farm near Cheltenham to recover herself. From there she wrote on 15 May to the Galindos of a way of life she loved:

> Our little cottage is some distance from the town and perfectly retired, surrounded by fields, and hills, and groves. The air of this place is peculiarly salubrious; I live out of doors as much as possible, sometimes reading under the haystack in the farmyard, sometimes rambling in the fields, and sometimes musing in the orchard; all which I do without spectators: no observers near to say I am mad, foolish, or melancholy; thus I keep the 'noiseless tenour of my way', and you will be glad to hear this mode of life so well suited to my taste. Rising at six and going to bed at ten has brought me to my comfortable sleep once more; the bitterness and anguish of selfish grief begins to subside. . . .[45]

In July she left Cheltenham for a tour of the Wye Valley with John Kemble and Charles Moore, Sally's silent lover, a young man she held in high regard. Then, after a visit to her close friend, Mrs FitzHugh, at Bannisters, near Southampton, she returned to work in London at Covent Garden.

Covent Garden Theatre had been refitted for the grand opening, and sixteen private boxes had been added to those taken by the aristocracy at a rent of £300 a year. Kemble, as usual, opened with *Hamlet*, on 24 September 1803, and Sarah, as usual, with *Isabella*, three nights later. Between September and May she made sixty appearances, those parts most often repeated being Elvira, Lady Macbeth, Desdemona, and Belvidera.

In 1804, while they were still together, Sarah and William had removed themselves to a cottage in Hampstead, where Sarah underwent the agonising new electrical treatment for rheumatism, which nevertheless brought her some temporary relief. A letter written by Elizabeth Inchbald describes this:

> Mrs Siddons is restored as by a miracle. She had a nervous affection from her hip to her toe, which made that side totally useless, yet in torturing pain that kept her sleepless for months. All medical art, such as embrocations, etc., failed. She heard of a new-invented machine that performed surprising cures by electricity. Her physicians all told her such an operation would make her disorder still worse. Her surgeon, Sir James Earle, said, No; but he assured her it would do her no good. On his word, fearing no harm, she tried it, and was almost instantly cured. But the agony she suffered in the trial she describes as if burning lead was running through her veins where the sparks touched; and Mr Siddons says her shrieks were such that he really expected the mob would break open the door, and think he was killing her.
>
> By-the-bye, what wicked accusations have been laid against this woman! Poor John Bull loves to set up, but then he loves equally to pull down.[46]

The wicked accusations to which Elizabeth Inchbald refers were doubtless the rumours about her relations with Lawrence, with whom she was now in touch once again. According to Farington, he was engaged during March in painting 'a whole length of Mrs Siddons', mostly by candlelight, and in an entry in his diary dated 2 March, Farington adds, 'Lane told me that Mrs Siddons sat to Lawrence for a *whole length last night by Lamplight*, till 2 o'clock this morning.[47] We cannot know to what extent this renewed contact brought her any real solace, nor what they talked of so far into the night. All Farington can add, on 7 May, is that his friend Taylor had received a letter from Sarah 'of a despairing kind. She expressed how incapable she was of feeling happy, but acknowledged she was sensible of kindness.' This renewed intimacy was the cause of the slanders against Sarah and Lawrence during the summer which led William the following December to make a public offer of £1,000 in order to discover their originator. No one responded, and the matter was gradually forgotten.

During the autumn of 1804 came the final domestic parting from William, who retired to Bath; he was crippled by lumbago, and could not walk without the help of sticks. The house in Great Marlborough Street was given up, and Sarah and Patty lived for a while in lodgings in Prince's Street, Hanover Square. During the winter of 1804–05 Sarah appeared only twice at Covent Garden, though she acted in Edinburgh and in Ireland during the summer of 1805. In Belfast Edmund Kean, then an eighteen-year-old stroller, played opposite her. The 1804–05 season was the one in which the celebrated child actor known as Master Betty stole the London audiences.[48] Sarah wisely withdrew until the furore had died down; she went to see him act, and said as she sat in her box, 'He is a very clever, pretty boy, but nothing more.' She preferred to spend the winter preparing her little country house at Westbourne, near Paddington, paying visits and dining with her friends, who included Mrs Damer of Strawberry Hill, where on more than one occasion she met the Prince Regent socially; he admired her, and, according to Campbell, 'she was never at Brighton, when the Prince was there, without being a guest at the Pavilion'. She wrote to Mrs Piozzi on 29 September 1804 in a letter otherwise full of London gossip:

> My little Cis is a great source of anxiety to me, she has that cruel tendency in her Constitution that has already cost me so many sighs and groans and tears – these will never cease to flow, and grief has done more than time to destroy those eyes, which showed no symptom of decay to *common observers*, but which fail me very much indeed when I stand in need of them.

She makes in this letter an unusually acid reference to Master Betty:

> As for *the Baby with a Woman's name* . . . the young Roscius as he is called, I hear a great deal, and *remember* nothing.[49]

Campbell calls the parting of Sarah and William one of 'convenience', dictated as much by their health as their mutual disagreement. Nevertheless, William came to stay at Westbourne while Sarah went to stay at Bath, the climate of which, though good for William, had proved to be bad for her. His warmer relations with Mrs Piozzi led to his being asked to keep an eye on her property in Bath, and he writes to the Piozzis detailed letters about servants, sub-letting, and the like, adding, for good measure,

a patriotic verse or two he has composed. On 12 October 1805
he wrote:

> There was a letter from Mrs Siddons upon my Table when I
> arriv'd telling me she was well – and pressing me to come up directly
> to see her little Box – which she continues to think is very pretty –
> I have wrote her word – I had rather she first woud come to Bath –
> as I had rather pay my visit to London after Christmas. She performed
> on Wednesday evening in Isabella – the Newspapers of yesterday
> were all very liberal in their praise – but all agree as to the 'en bon
> point' since her last engagement.[50]

All of which sounds friendly enough.

Since everything Sarah did encouraged rumour, Boaden, who,
like Campbell, knew her well, acknowledges their mutual disagreement – which Campbell was later to deny, largely on the
strength of the testimony of Patty, who was virtually an adopted
daughter and who liked William as much as he liked her. While
smoothing things over in his good-natured way, Boaden, however,
regards the separation as a real one:

> I know that he used to consider himself on some occasion neglected,
> and that he was deemed of slight importance compared with the
> object of universal attention, his own wife. . . . This unhappily
> produced in a most honourable and high-spirited man some in-
> equalities of temper, which occasionally seemed harsh to a woman
> conscious of the most unremitting diligence in her exertions, and
> often endangering her health to secure, along with fame to herself,
> the present and future comforts of her family. . . . But he retained
> at all times the sincerest regard for his incomparable lady.[51]

Campbell prints a letter sent by Sarah on 16 December 1804 to
her husband:

> My dear Sid – I am really sorry that my little flash of merriment
> should have been taken so seriously, for I am sure, however we may
> differ in trifles, *we can never cease to love each other*. You wish me
> to say what I expect to have done – I can expect nothing more than
> you yourself have designed me in your will. Be (as you ought to be)
> the master of all while God permits, but, in case of your death, only
> let me be put out of the power of any person living. This is all that
> I desire; and I think that you cannot but be convinced that it is
> reasonable and proper. Your ever affectionate and faithful S.S.[52]

The previous June a settlement had been reached over money.
The all-knowledgeable Farington records on 20 June 1804:

'Lysons told me that Mr and Mrs Siddons have acquired £40,000 and that Mr Siddons has lately settled upon Her £20,000, which He will also leave and all the rest *at Her disposal*. Her £20,000 brings in £1,000 a year.' Lysons was to act as a trustee along with Kemble.[53]

In his final years, 'Sid' never lost touch with Sarah. In the summer of 1806 he went to stay with her for six weeks at Westbourne Farm; he wrote to the Piozzis on 7 July:

Tis a very pretty Birds nest Mrs Siddons has made here. . . . I think Mrs Siddons is in better health – and looks handsomer in the Face than for some years past – so much does she enjoy 'this Shepherds life' – yet in three weeks we shall be in a different scene, namely the Sea side – you must know we have two as pretty Grand daughters at least we think so – as any England boasts . . . they have just had the Measles – and Sea Bathing is recommended – to strengthen them again. Tis for their sakes that Grandpa and Grandma make this excursion – we have fix'd on Broadstairs for the purpose as so much more retir'd than Brighton, Margate or Ramsgate. We leave this on the 24th – and shall stay six weeks.[54]

With William no longer acting for her, it would seem that Sarah hoped to make Galindo her manager. Correspondence, as we have seen, had passed back and forth between her and the Galindos during the summer of 1803; she is almost playful in an undated letter of the period written to Galindo as she contemplates living with him and his family in 'the dear farm (that is to be)'. She thinks of visiting Ireland again and going to Cork, and then adds:

I will put on my green turban as soon as I am out of mourning; certain old garments and shoes are become dear to me, because they remind me of some little compliment or joke in those days that are gone, like the memory of past joys, pleasant and mournful to the soul of your friend. – Present me to your fireside and *adieu*![55]

She begs him to write her gay and entertaining letters, and sends him little gifts such as silk handkerchiefs. From Bannister Lodge in July she writes: 'Oh, how I wish you were comfortably set down on this side of the water. I long for that time.' In August she writes to congratulate Mrs Galindo on the birth of her daughter, to whom she was to become a godmother. In November she says that, 'We talk of you all incessantly, indeed *that* is the only solace of my dejected mind. Alas! alas! how happy we all were together this time last year.' The little farm is much on her mind – 'Patty and I have been making a little arrangement for next summer'. In February 1804, Galindo left Dublin to join Sarah, but Catherine Galindo did not follow him for seven months. During this time she claims that Sarah only wrote to her once.

The last letters Catherine Galindo publishes are those which belong to the distressing period when Sarah's relationship with Galindo was foundering. After the unhappy interview between Sarah and Catherine at Birmingham, she wrote to her from Manchester, where she had seen him:

> Mr G. has just been here. . . . I need only tell you that he was as violent as usual, and wondered what he had done to offend me. . . . I asked him if he had ever heard me utter a word respecting you, that was not dictated by esteem and cordial good will, and how he could imagine that if I had an idea that his acquaintance with me would give *you one* moment's uneasiness, that I should not in *that moment* have broken it off. . . . I always thought you were desirous of keeping it up, as being sure of his at least being in society that could not be disreputable. I tell you this, WHICH IS ALL THAT PASSED BETWEEN US IN THIS INTERVIEW. . . . He was talking so much all the time, that I believe, he hardly heard me, when I assured him I was sorry to see him carried away by the violence of his temper. . . . He went away in a rage, or perhaps I might have talked him into a little reason.[56]

Finally, it would appear, her quarrels with Galindo – mainly, of course, about the loan she had made him – grew so violent she refused any longer to see him, and by the close of 1808 she would not open any letter he sent her. However, when Catherine Galindo published her 'open letter', Sarah decided it would be best to ignore it. She wrote to her nephew, Horace Twiss:

> Patty tells me, you have been urging the Prosecution of these people which surpris'd me a good deal now in the first place. It is the opinion, I do assure you upon my honor, of *all my friends*, that it would be lowering myself, to enter the lists with persons, the indecency of whose characters is become so notorious, and in the next place, what would be the result of a Prosecution Damages or Imprisonment I suppose, and in failure of the first, what should I gain by inflicting the second? . . . They have already cost me too much money, and what's more important, too much tranquility, to renew a subject so Shoking. . . . It would be HUMILIATING, HARRASSING, AND EXPENSIVE. . . . There is no species of suffering that I woud [not] prefer to

encountering the horrible indecency of that wretched woman, whom everyone supposes to be quite mad, too.[57]

Meanwhile, Sarah's professional engagements had kept her well occupied. With the first furore over Master Betty subsided, she appeared thirty-nine times at Covent Garden during the 1805–06 season, her most frequently repeated performances being Queen Katherine, Lady Macbeth, and Elvira, while in 1806–07 she appeared as Volumnia fifteen times in a season of thirty-four performances. On 15 July 1807 she wrote from Liverpool to a friend, probably Mrs Piozzi:

The houses are tolerably good. I can't expect to be followed like the great genius, Master Betty, you know; but I hope to put about £1,000 into my pocket this summer. 'Tis better to work hard for a short time, and have done with it. If I can add three hundred a year to my present income, I shall be perfectly well provided for.[58]

Acting at this time affected her deeply. In November 1805 she wrote to a friend:

I never played more to my own satisfaction than last night in Belvidera: if I may so say, it was hardly acting, it seemed to me, and I believe to the audience, almost reality; and I can assure you that in one of my scenes with my brother John, who was the Jaffier of the night . . . the real tears 'coursed one another down my innocent nose' so abundantly that my handkerchief was wet with them when I got off the stage. . . . I never was more applauded in Belvidera certainly; though, of course, as a piece of mere acting, it is not at all equal to my 'Lady']Macbeth].[59]

On 11 March 1808, William died at the age of sixty-seven. Sarah had been performing only intermittently at Covent Garden the previous autumn, and had been free to visit him for six weeks in Bath from late in December to February for what was to be their last time together. She was appearing in Edinburgh at the time of his death, and had been forced to interrupt her season there to observe a period of mourning. In March she wrote to Lady Harcourt from Westbourne Farm: 'May I die as poor Mr Siddons died and prayed to die, without a sigh, without a groan; and may those to whom I am dear remember *me* when *I* am gone as *I* now remember *him*, forgetting and forgiving all my errors, and recollecting only my quietness of spirit and singleness of heart.'[60] She wrote to Mrs Piozzi also, on 29 March, using almost exactly the same words, but adding at the close: 'My head is still so dull . . . that I cannot see what I write. Adieu, dear soul, do not cease to love your friend.'

'Sid', poor worthy man, was gone. But at least he left Sarah a gracious tribute in verses written after his visit to Westbourne Farm.[61] They show his own last touch of feeling for her:

> Would you I'd Westbourne Farm describe,
>   I'll do it then, and free from gall,
> For sure it would be sin to gibe
>   A thing so pretty and so small. . . .
>
> But when the pleasure-ground is seen,
>   Then what a burst comes on the view!
> Its level walk, its shaven green,
>   For which a razor's stroke would do. . . .
>
> The mansion, cottage, house, or but,
>   Call't what you will, has room within
> To lodge the King of Lilliput,
>   But not his Court, nor yet his Queen. . . .
>
> Perhaps you'll cry, on hearing this,
>   What! every thing so very small?
> No: she that made it what it is,
>   Has greatness which makes up for all.

8

'Grateful Memory'

———————⚬〰⚬———————

URING THE SMALL hours of 20 September 1808, there
occurred that disaster at the Covent Garden playhouse
which is only too common in the history of the eighteenth-
and early nineteenth-century theatre. The play that night had
been *Pizarro*, and Campbell tells the story:

> About four o'clock on the morning of the 20th of September this
> noble building, which was erected in the year 1733, and enlarged,
> with considerable alterations, in 1792, was seen suddenly to be on
> fire: the flames continued to rage so fiercely, that in three hours the
> whole interior of the theatre, with the scenery, wardrobe, musical
> and dramatic libraries, &c., became a heap of smoking ruins. The
> loss of property of all descriptions, including that of the organ,
> bequeathed to the house by Handel, and of the unpublished MS.
> music of first-rate composers, was estimated at 150,000*l*.
>
> But the damage done to property by that dreadful event was light
> in comparison with the horrors which it occasioned by human deaths
> and sufferings. A number of firemen were crushed under the falling-
> in of the burning roof, and several unfortunate individuals, having
> approached the conflagration too nearly, were scalded to death by
> the steam of the water that arose from it. I shudder in calculating
> the number of victims – they must have amounted to thirty! Many
> of them were dug out of the ruins in such a state that they could not
> be identified.[1]

He adds: 'It was generally attributed to the wadding of a gun,
that was discharged in the performance of *Pizarro*, having lodged
unperceived in some crevice of the scenery.'

This was one of the worst fires of the period; many neighbour-

ing houses and other properties were burnt out, and at one time
it was feared that the flames would reach Drury Lane as well.
Many firemen were numbered among the dead. The theatre and
its contents were insured for only £50,000, and Boaden hurried
round to offer what comfort he could to Kemble. He gives an
extraordinary account of the actor in a state of shock in his house
in Great Russell Street:

> He was standing before the glass, totally absorbed, and yet at
> intervals endeavouring to shave himself.
>
> Mrs Kemble was sitting in tears upon a sopha, and on seeing me
> exclaimed, 'O Mr Boaden, we are totally ruined, and have the
> world to begin again!'
>
> His brother Charles, wrapt up just as he came from the fire, was
> sitting *attentive*, upon the end of the sopha; – and a gentleman,
> much attached to Mr Harris, who in and about the theatre was
> familiarly styled *old Dives*, with his back to the wall, and leaning
> upon his cane, sat frowning in a corner. It was not a situation that
> called for speech; our salutations were like those at a funeral. I took
> a chair, and sat observing the manner and the look of Kemble.
> Nothing could be more natural than for Mrs Kemble to feel and
> think of their *personal* loss in this dreadful calamity. Her husband,
> I am convinced, while I saw him, never thought of *himself* at all.
> His mind was rather raised than dejected, and his imagination
> distended with the pictured detail of all the treasures, that had
> perished in the conflagration. At length he broke out in exclamation,
> which I have preserved as characteristic of his turn of mind.
>
> 'Yes, it has perished, that magnificent theatre, which for all the
> purposes of exhibition or comfort was the first in Europe. It is gone,
> with all its treasures of every description, and some which can never
> be replaced. That LIBRARY, which contained all those immortal
> productions of our countrymen, prepared for the purposes of repre-
> sentation! That vast collection of MUSIC, composed by the greatest
> geniuses in that science, – by Handel, Arne, and others; – most of it
> manuscript, in the original score! That WARDROBE, stored with the
> costumes of all ages and nations, accumulated by unwearied research,
> and at incredible expense! SCENERY, the triumph of the art, un-
> rivalled for its accuracy, and so exquisitely finished, that it might be
> the ornament of your drawing-rooms, were they only large enough
> to contain it! Of all this vast treasure nothing now remains, but the
> ARMS of ENGLAND over the entrance of the theatre – and the ROMAN
> EAGLE standing *solitary* in the market place!'[2]

Sarah wrote to her Scottish friend, James Ballantyne about the
losses she and her brothers had sustained:

The losses to the proprietors are incalculable, irreparable, and, of all the precious and curious dresses, and lace, and jewels, which I have been collecting for these thirty years, not one article has escaped. The most grievous of these, *my* losses, is a piece of lace which had been a toilette of the poor Queen of France. It was upwards of four yards long, and more than a yard wide. It never cou'd have been bought for a thousand pounds, but that's the least regret. It was *so* interesting! But, oh! let me not suffer myself in the ingratitude of *repining* while there are so many reasons for thankful acknowledgment. My brothers, God be praised, did not hear of the fire till every personal exertion woud have been utterly useless. It is as true, as it is strange and awful, that everything appeared to be in perfect security at *two* o'clock, and that at *six* (the time my poor brother saw it) the whole structure was as compleatly swept from the face of the earth as if such a thing had never existed. Thank God that it *was* so, since, had it been otherwise, he woud probably have perished in exertions to preserve something from the horrible wreck of his property. . . . Lord Guilford and Lord Mountjoy have nobly offer'd to raise him any sum of money, and a thousand instances of generous feeling have already afford [sic] that evince the goodness of human nature, and its sense of his worth.[3]

Her brother, cries Sarah, 'bears it like an angel. . . . Oh! he is a glorious creature; did I not always *tell* you so!' And indeed, they had one great cause for thankfulness, the marvellous way in which those with the wealth to do so rallied to their help. Most generous of all was the Duke of Northumberland, who gave Kemble the loan of £10,000 on his simple bond and, on 30 December 1808, the day the foundation stone of the new theatre was laid by the Prince of Wales, destroyed the bond and donated the money to the building fund.

Sarah wrote more intimately to Mrs Piozzi of her losses:

I lost every stage ornament so many years collecting and at so great an expense of time and money – all my Jewels, all my lace, and in short nothing nothing left. The Duke of Northumberland has given my brother Ten Thousand pounds! and the manner of bestowing this noble gift was as great as anything I have ever heard or read of. . . . But poor fellow, he is I fear in a wretched state of health yet he looked the other night in Macbeth, as beautiful as ever –

And of the point lace which had once belonged to the Queen of France:

I us'd to wear it *only* in the Trial Scene of Hermione in the Winter's Tale, it covered me all over from head to foot. I suppose my losses

coud not be repaird for Twelve hundred pounds. But God be praisd
– that the fire did not break out while the people were in the House!!![4]

The Covent Garden company, meanwhile, presented a full
season at the King's Theatre (the Opera House) and at the
Haymarket, Sarah, appearing forty times – with Lady Macbeth,
Queen Katherine and Mrs Beverley far outstripping all her other
parts. She appeared as Lady Macbeth on fifteen occasions. A
letter of contract, signed by Thomas Harris on 16 May on behalf
of Covent Garden, outlines the terms on which it was proposed to
engage Sarah during the 1809–10 season; it was understood this
was to be her final season (though this was, of course, to be extended later), that she was to perform not less than thirty-five
times (sixteen nights before Christmas, and nineteen afterwards),
that the last appearance was to be a clear benefit in her favour,
that she was to receive 50 guineas for each normal appearance,
and that she was to play 'her whole range of characters according
to her List sent in'.[5]

The new theatre rose on the site of the old in an incredibly
short time. The building was in fact ready for the reopening two
days before the anniversary of the fire, a tribute to the architect,
Robert Smirke, and his builders. The theatre was reopened on
18 September with a performance of *Macbeth*, and this became
the first occasion for one of the most extraordinary as well as
notorious events in English theatrical history – the O.P. riots, as
they were called. These were, in effect, organized and prolonged
public demonstrations against the raising of admission prices;
the demonstrators were noisy, interrupting the actors, and they
frequently became violent. The protests lasted throughout the
season. A press account of the opening night, in which Sarah was
involved, is quoted by Campbell:

> The interior of the house was brilliantly lighted up, and served most
> impressively to display the beauteous order of the edifice, raised, by
> the creative power of the architect, from a late dismal chaos. The
> groups of admiring spectators, as they entered, burst into the warmest
> expressions of applause; and, for some time, no sentiment obtruded
> but that of self-complacency, and the satisfaction arising from novel
> enjoyment. Before six, the house was overflowingly full, and yet at
> least three times the number of those admitted, remained in the
> entrances and lobbies, making vain endeavours to obtain farther
> entrance.
> Mr Kemble made his appearance in the costume of *Macbeth*, and

NEW THEATRE ROYAL, COVENT GARDEN,

This present MONDAY, April 30, 1810, will be acted *Shakspeare's* Tragedy of

MACBETH.

The NEW SCENES painted by Mr. PHILLIPS, Mr. WHITMORE, Mr HOLLOGAN, and by Mr. CAPON.
The Dresses by Mr FLOWER & Miss EGAN. *The Machinery and the Decorations by Mr Saul & Mr Bradwell*
The *Overture* and *Symphonies* between the Acts *by Mr WARE—The Vocal Musick by Matthew Lock.*

Duncan, King of Scotland, by Mr. CHAPMAN,
Malcolm by Mr. CLAREMONT, Donalbain by Mr. MENAGE,
Macbeth by Mr. KEMBLE, Macduff by Mr. C. KEMBLE,
Banquo by Mr. MURRAY, Fleance by M. BRISTOW,
Lenox by Mr. CRESWELL, Rosse by Mr. BRUNTON,
Siward Mr ATKINS, Seyton Mr JEFFERIES, Physician Mr DAVENPORT
Lady Macbeth by Mrs. SIDDONS,
Gentlewoman by Mrs HUMPHRIES,
Hecat' by Mr BELLAMY, Witches, Mess. BLANCHARD, FARLEY, SIMMONS
The Choral Witches by
Mess. I. Bellamy, Bishop, Bond, Burden, Denman, Dixon, Everard, Fairclough, Lee, Linton, Norris, Odwell
Sawyer, Street, Taylor, Terry, Tett. Treby, Williams—Mesdames Bolton, Bristow, Coates, Emery,
Fawcett, Findlay, Hagemann, Hardy, Iliff, Leserve, Liston, Logan, Martyr, Price, Watts.
To which will be added a musical Farce, called

"WE FLY BY NIGHT;" or, Long Stories.

General Bastion by Mr. MUNDEN, Count de Grenouille by Mr. FARLEY,
Captain Winlove by Mr. BRUNTON, Mr. Skiptown by Mr. CLAREMONT,
Stubby by Mr. SIMMONS, Humphrey by Mr BLANCHARD,
Ferret by Mr. FAWCETT, Gaby Grim by Mr. LISTON,
Lady Lynx by Mrs. DAVENPORT, Countess de Grenouille by Miss LESERVE,
Emma by Miss BOLTON, Mrs Stubby by Mrs LISTON, Barmaid Miss Cox.

Printed by E. Macleish, 2, Bow-street. Vivant Rex & Regina.

Tomorrow will be revived the Comedy of ALL IN THE WRONG.
Sir John and Lady Restless by Mr. YOUNG and Mrs C. KEMBLE,
Beverly and Belinda by Mr. C. KEMBLE and Mrs H. JOHNSTON
To which will be added, The BLIND BOY.
On Wednesday, *for the Benefit of the FUND for the Relief of aged and infirm Actors, and the*
Widows and Children of Actors deceased, will be performed the Tragedy of
DOUGLAS.
Norval, Mr C. KEMBLE, Glenalvon, Mr. COOKE, The Stranger, Mr. KEMBLE,
Lady Randolph, Mrs. SIDDONS,
(Who has most kindly offered her services on the occasion.)
And the Committee who conduct the Institution, have the pleasure to announce, that
Mr. BRAHAM and Madam CATALANI
have both, in the handsomest manner, volunteered their assistance, and will sing
Some of their most popular Songs.
To which will be added the musical Farce of LOCK and KEY.
On Thursday, the Tragedy of The GAMESTER.
Beverley, Mr. YOUNG, Stukely, Mr. COOKE, Lewson, Mr. C. KEMBLE,
Mrs Beverley by Mrs SIDDONS,
To which will be added the Burletta of TOM THUMB the GREAT.
On Friday the Comick Opera of The CASTLE of ANDALUSIA.
(The Characters as before.)
To which will be added, The CHILD of NATURE.
On Saturday will be revived, *with new Scenes, Dresses & Decorations*, Shakspeare's Historical Play of
KING HENRY the EIGHTH.
King Henry, Mr. COOKE, Cardinal Wolsey, Mr. KEMBLE,
Queen Katharine by Mrs SIDDONS.
To which will be added the musical Farce of The WATERMAN.
Mr. Bundle, Mr. BLANCHARD, The Waterman, Mr. INCLEDON, Robin, Mr LISTON
Mrs Bundle, Mrs DAVENPORT, Wilhelmina, Miss BOLTON.
On Monday, *Shakspeare's* Tragedy of HAMLET, PRINCE of DENMARK.
Hamlet by Mr. KEMBLE.
The Publick are respectfully informed that a NEW MUSICAL AFTER-PIECE is in rehearsal,
and will very soon be produced.
Shakspeare's Historical Play of KING JOHN, is in preparation, *with new Scenes, Dresses, &c.*

f. Playbill: Sarah Siddons and John Philip Kemble in *Macbeth* at
Covent Garden, 1810.

amidst vollies of hissing, hooting, groans, and catcalls. He made an
address, but it was impossible to hear it. His attitudes were imploring,
but in vain. . . . The play proceeded in pantomime; not a word
was heard, save now and then the deeply modulated tones of the
bewitching Siddons. On her entrance she seemed disturbed by the
clamour, but in the progressive stages of her action she went through
her part with wonderful composure. Kemble appeared greatly
agitated, yet in no instance did his trouble interrupt him in carrying
on *'the cunning of the scene'*. Perhaps a finer dumb shew was never
witnessed.[6]

The Riot Act had to be read from the stage by magistrates from
Bow Street. From the theatrical point of view, the season was
disastrous, and Sarah virtually retired from Covent Garden. The
following March and April she was in Edinburgh. She was not
prepared to exhibit her art when in the pit, ready to launch their
tirades upon her, sat the O.P. rioters described by Boaden:
'contemplate,' he writes,

the efficient O.P. rioter, dressing for exhibition in the theatre. He
had to pass, though unsearched, at the doors, and to squeeze himself
through an iron or wooden hatch, of our usual width, encumbered
as he might be with his watchman's rattle, or dustman's bell, or
post-boy's horn, or French-horn, or trombone, with a white night-
cap in his pocket – his placards of a dozen feet in length wound
about his body, and his bludgeon for close action with the enemy.
He had to practise his O.P. dance, and rave himself as hoarse as a
night coachman in winter – he, at the hazard of his limbs, had to
make the central *rush* from the back of the pit down to the orchestra,
which trembled at every nerve of catgut it contained. And, in
addition to all this, he became skilled in the most seemingly desperate
sham-fights, ending with roars of laughter, or real combats, to
maintain his position in the field.[7]

Sarah wrote more precisely to her daughter-in-law, Harriott
Siddons:

the papers give as I understand a tolerably accurate account of this
barbarous outrage to decency and reason, which is a National
disgrace: where it will end heaven knows and is now generally
thought, I believe that it *will not* end without the interference of
Government, and if they have any recollection of the Riots of the
year 80, it is wonderful they have let it go thus far; I think it very
likely that I shall not appear any more this season, for nothing shall
induce me to place myself again in so painful and degrading a
situation, Oh glad am I that you and my dear Harry are out of it all![8]

She wrote in disgust at what was going on in the theatre to her friend Mrs FitzHugh on 2 December 1808:

> Surely nothing ever equalled the domineering of the mob in these days. It is to me inconceivable how the public at large submits to be thus dictated to, against their better judgment, by a handful of imperious and intoxicated men. In the meantime, what can the poor proprietors do, but yield to overwhelming necessity?
>
> Could I once feel that my poor brother's anxiety about the Theatre was at an end, I should be, marvellous to say, as well as I ever was in my life. But only conceive what a state he must have been in, however good a face he might put upon the business, for upwards of three months; and think what his poor wife and I must have suffered, when, for weeks together, such were the outrages committed on his house and otherwise, that I trembled for even his personal safety: she, poor soul, living with ladders at her windows, in order to make her escape through the garden, in case of an attack. Mrs Kemble tells me his nerves are much shaken. What a time it has been with us all, beginning with fire, and continued with fury![9]

Though she was not to retire officially until 1812, withdrawal from the stage was in her mind as early as 1810. With William gone, she was now mistress of her own fortune. According to Mrs Piozzi, there was a rumour in 1808 that she might marry Lord Erskine, but it was no more than a rumour. She was only fifty-four at the time of William's death, a beautiful and highly eligible widow. But she was never to remarry. She had grown somewhat stout, and she realized she could no longer represent the fine tragic figure of the past. Nevertheless she played fifty-seven times at Covent Garden during the 1811–12 season. Like Garrick before her, she dreaded leaving the stage. For Garrick, it may be remembered, retirement had seemed like the parting of his soul and body.

Lawrence, hypersensitive to her beauty and reputation, still went to the theatre to see her, but in September 1811 he told Farington that he thought she ought to retire. According to Farington, he 'saw her as Lady Constance in *King John*. Her voice failed in one passage; when he asked Kemble about this, Kemble replied, 'she had not the power to express the passage properly, Her voice failed for want of strength'. Nevertheless, Lawrence wrote to Farington on 20 December that *Coriolanus* was 'the best got-up Play that has been acted', and added: 'The Town is fashionably and I had almost said rationally mad after it.

I have seen it but once. It will give you the best specimen of Kemble, and a fine one of Mrs Siddons.'[10]

She did, in fact, complete her final season during 1811–12, though she was to appear from time to time for several years to come. Summoning her strength, she appeared in every part she had made famous by her interpretations, and on the final night of the season, on 22 June 1812, it was as Lady Macbeth that she chose to retire from the London stage.[11] Farington wrote a fine account of the event:

When Mrs Siddons walked off the stage in the last scene, where she appears as walking in her sleep, there was a long continued burst of applause, which caused Kemble etc to conclude that it was the wish of the Spectators that the Play should there stop. The Curtain was dropped and much noise was continued. One of the Performers came forward to request to know whether it was the pleasure of the audience that the Play shd stop or go on.

A tumult again ensued, which being considered as a sign that the Play shd stop, some time elapsed till at length the Curtain was drawn up and Mrs Siddons appeared sitting at a table in Her own character. She was dressed in White Sattin and had on a long veil. She arose but it was some time before she could speak the clapping and other sounds of approbation rendering it impossible for Her to be heard. She curtsied and bowed, and at last there was silence. At 10 o'clock precisely she began to speak Her farewell address which took up Eight minutes during which time there was profound silence. Having finished, the loudest claps followed, and she withdrew bowing and led off by an attendant who advanced for that purpose. . . . Her appearance was that of a person distressed and sunk in spirits, but I did not perceive that she shed tears. J. Kemble came on afterwards to ask whether the Play shd go on? – He wiped His eyes, and appeared to have been weeping. – The Play was not allowed to go on. – . . . The heat of the House was very great.[12]

Suddenly, it was all over. There was nothing left but Westbourne Farm, and a quiet life with relatives and friends. How could such a life ever be enough to satisfy the woman who for over thirty years had turned night after night to the theatre to fulfil her deep emotional needs, which had been so starved and frustrated outside it? In a letter to Mrs Piozzi, written ten days before her final performance, Sarah forecast what her retirement from the stage would mean to her; she writes with suppressed emotion:

I am free to confess it will to me be awful and affecting – to know
one is doing the most indifferent thing for *the last* time induces a
more than common seriousness, and in this case I own 'the healthful
hue of resolution is sicklied o'er with the pale cast of thought'. I
feel as if my foot were now on the first round of the Ladder which
reaches to another world. Give me your prayers my dear friend to
help me on my way thither and believe me ever and ever Your
faithful and affectionate S. Siddons.[13]

In 1812 she had taken lodgings for a few months in Pall Mall,
where Campbell remembers her, during this period of her final
season, receiving guests on such a scale that the street was lined
with carriages suggesting a royal levée was in progress. Apart
from this, she lived at Westbourne Farm from 1805 to 1817, when
she leased a house, number 27 at the top of Upper Baker Street,
on the right-hand side facing towards Regent's Park, the site now
occupied by a part of Baker Street Station. She had built here, as
she had at Westbourne Farm, a studio for her modelling. The house
at Regent's Park was nearer to town for the parties her daughter,
Cecilia, who in 1817 was twenty-three, was anxious to attend, but
even so Mrs Piozzi regarded 'the top house in Baker St' as 'out
of town'. But it had a handsome drawing-room on the first floor
with tall sash windows and an open view over the Prince Regent's
new park; Nash cut back Cornwall Terrace to leave Sarah's
prospect unobstructed. Underneath this fine salon was the
dining-room, and Sarah, now in her sixties, gave parties and
entertained to the limits of her fairly substantial means. She did
not want to vegetate. She would regale her guests – who included
Mrs Piozzi, Lawrence, Lady Harcourt, Sidney Smith, Maria
Edgeworth, Joanna Baillie, Mrs Anna Jameson, Mrs Damer, as
well as the circle of her other friends, such as the Whalleys and
the Kemble family – with her readings from Shakespeare.

For a while things seem to have been gay enough. Attended by
Patty and Cecilia, who was not to marry until 1833, after her
mother's death, Sarah did her best to live without her art, re-
calling it only by these nostalgic readings and recitals, and the
rare, very rare, reappearances she made in the theatre itself,
usually in support of benefit performances for members of the
family.[14] And, of course, she dined out and visited her friends
inside and outside London. In 1813 she took Cecilia and Patty
to Paris on a two-month visit during a brief period of peace
between England and France. She went to the Louvre, accom-

panied by Campbell. Neither she nor Campbell had seen the Apollo Belvedere before except in plaster casts. Campbell writes:

> The Louvre was at that time in possession of its fullest wealth. In the statuary hall of that place I had the honour of giving Mrs Siddons my arm the first time she walked through it, and the first time in both our lives that we saw the Apollo Belvedere. . . . She was evidently much struck, and remained a long time before the statue; but, like a true admirer, was not loquacious. . . . When we walked round to other sculptures, I observed that almost every eye in the hall was fixed upon her; yet I could perceive that she was not known, as I overheard the spectators say, 'Who is she? – Is she not an Englishwoman?' At this time she was in her fifty-ninth year, and yet her looks were so noble, that she made you proud of English beauty, even in the presence of Grecian sculpture.[15]

After seeing the Apollo and eating a seventeen-franc dinner, she was seen asleep at the Opera, but 'splendidly dressed'. Later she went to Lausanne to visit her brother and his wife. On John Philip's retirement from the stage in 1817 at the age of sixty, they had settled permanently on the Continent for the benefit of his health.

But, like other retired actresses, she could not easily be kept out of the theatre once she was thoroughly rested. In 1813 there was an organized attempt to induce her to return to the stage. Signature-books were placed at Hookham's and Ebers's in Old Bond Street and at the London Coffee House on Ludgate Hill to collect the names of influential people whose persuasion might make her change her mind. One of these books, stamped 'Recall of Mrs Siddons to the Stage' survives with 518 signatures of distinguished people. Sarah wisely resisted this 'recall', coming so soon after her official retirement. A second attempt to bring her back to the London stage for a single season was made in July 1815 by Lord Byron, acting as a member of the Drury Lane Committee, but again she refused.[16] Byron had seen her in London in December 1811; he had subsequently made her acquaintance. He held her to be the 'beau idéal of acting'; 'nothing ever was, or can be, like her' and, compared with actors even of the stature of Kean and Kemble, 'worth them all put together'. Apparently even Kemble recognized this, and told Lawrence 'that he never played with Mrs Siddons without feeling her superiority'. But her close friends and relations were very much against the various

reappearances which she did consent to undertake, because the
insufficiency of her performances blurred the bright memory of
what she had once been. However, when she appeared on 7 June
1815 at Covent Garden as Lady Macbeth, she was said by
Farington's friend, Sir George Beaumont, never to have 'performed better. Her acting was most powerful, and the House
felt it unanimously'. At the same time she acted Queen Katherine
for Charles Kemble's benefit – 'most excellent', commented Sir
George, though Thomson, another of Farington's friends, said
'age is visible in the falling-in of the lower part of the face'.
Hazlitt, one of the most enthusiastic of her panegyrists, who saw
her Lady Macbeth a year later, on 7 June 1817 during John
Philip Kemble's farewell performances, was severe with her,
though he manages with some grace to add a tribute to his reproof:

> It is nearly twenty years since we first saw her in this character; and
> certainly the impression which we have still left on our minds from
> that first exhibition is stronger than the one we received the other
> evening. The sublimity of Mrs Siddons's acting is such, that the
> first impulse which it gives to the mind can never wear out, and we
> doubt whether this original and paramount impression is not
> weakened, rather than strengthened, by subsequent repetition. We
> do not read the tragedy of the Robbers twice; if we have seen Mrs
> Siddons in Lady Macbeth only once, it is enough. The impression
> is stamped there for ever, and any after-experiments and critical
> inquiries only serve to fritter away and tamper with the sacredness
> of the early recollection. We see into the details of the character, its
> minute excellences or defects; but the great masses, the gigantic
> proportions, are in some degree lost upon us by custom and familiarity.
> It is the first blow that staggers us; by gaining time we recover our
> self-possession. Mrs Siddons's Lady Macbeth is little less appalling
> in its effects than the apparition of a preternatural being; but if we
> were accustomed to see a preternatural being constantly, our astonish-
> ment would by degrees diminish.
>
> We do not know whether it is owing to the cause here stated, or
> to a falling-off in Mrs Siddons's acting, but we certainly thought her
> performance the other night inferior to what it used to be. She
> speaks too slow, and her manner has not that decided, sweeping
> majesty which used to characterise her as the Muse of Tragedy
> herself. Something of apparent indecision is perhaps attributable to
> the circumstance of her only acting at present on particular occasions.
> An actress who appears only once a-year cannot play so well as if
> she was in the habit of acting once a-week. We, therefore, wish
> Mrs Siddons would either return to the stage, or retire from it

altogether. By her present uncertain wavering between public and private life, she may diminish her reputation, while she can add nothing to it.[17]

Hazlitt's great passage on her, when she was at the height of her power, must not be omitted. No one wrote more illuminatingly of her:

> We can conceive of nothing grander. It was something above nature. It seemed almost as if a being of a superior order had dropped from a higher sphere to awe the world with the majesty of her appearance. Power was seated on her brow, passion emanated from her breast as from a shrine; she was tragedy personified. In coming on in the sleeping-scene, her eyes were open, but their sense was shut. She was like a person bewildered and unconscious of what she did. Her lips moved involuntarily – all her gestures were involuntary and mechanical. She glided on and off the stage like an apparition. To have seen her in that character was an event in every one's life, not to be forgotten.[18]

Other stars were pressing to take possession of the stage, above all Edmund Kean, whose passionate, but undisciplined powers were in violent contrast to the cold sublimities of Kemble. Comparing Kean's achievements with those of Sarah, Hazlitt wrote:

> . . . we do not think there has been in our remembrance any tragic performer (with the exception of Mrs Siddons) equal to Mr Kean. Nor, except in voice and person, and the conscious ease and dignity naturally resulting from those advantages, do we know that even Mrs Siddons was greater. In truth of nature and force of passion, in discrimination and originality, we see no inferiority to any one on the part of Mr Kean; but there is an insignificance of figure, and a hoarseness of voice, that necessarily *vulgarize*, or diminish our idea of the characters he plays: and perhaps to this may be added, a want of a certain correspondent elevation and magnitude of thought, of which Mrs Siddons's noble form seemed to be only the natural mould and receptacle. Her nature seemed always above the circumstances with which she had to struggle: her soul to be greater than the passion labouring in her breast. Grandeur was the cradle in which her genius was rocked: for her *to be*, was to be sublime! She did the greatest things with child-like ease: her powers seemed never tasked to the utmost, and always as if she had inexhaustible resources still in reserve. The least word she uttered seemed to float to the end of the stage: the least motion of her hand seemed to command

awe and obedience. Mr Kean is all effort, all violence, all extreme passion: he is possessed with a fury, a demon that leaves him no repose, no time for thought, or room for imagination.[19]

Sarah, as we have seen, had stood on the same stage as Kean in 1794, when he was only a child.

Crabb Robinson is another writer whose absolute devotion to Sarah made him regret these reappearances. After seeing her performance as Queen Katherine on 31 May 1816, he wrote:

An immense crowd was assembled at the door to hear these more last words and I was rejoiced at the opportunity of once again hearing and seeing an actress who has delighted me beyond all comparison more than any man or woman on the stage. I was gratified by the performance but it was not an unmixed pleasure – Mrs Siddons is not what she was – It was with pain that I perceived the effect of the [sic] time in the most accomplished of persons – There was more audible to the ear than visible to the eye – There was occasionally an indistinctness in her enunciation and she laboured her delivery most anxiously as if she feared her power of expression was gone – In person she has become more thin – and I thought her step was not quite so majestic as it used to be but her face retains its expression and her judgment and the exquisite propriety of her performance were as they always were admirable.[20]

He returned to see her on 8 June as Lady Macbeth:

We were not at the Pit door of Covent Garden till a little after 4 O'clock – We had to endure a very sad squeezing and when the rush at the door took place Mrs Suchet and I were thrown out of line and went to the right hand door – However with great difficulty we got in and obtained a tolerably central situation about the tenth row of the Pit. –

However we were amply rewarded – Mr and Mrs Suchet both appeared to feel the astonishing powers of the actress and Mrs Siddons exertions were more successful than on Friday – Her voice was apparently as strong as ever but I fear the first impressions ought to be relied on – Yet I thought her step was not quite so majestic as it used to be – In the first scene in which she holds the letter from Macbeth, she was peculiarly excellent – her transitions of passion were admirable – In the banquet scene she was less admirable, but in the night scene she again raised herself to a level with all my recollections of her youthful powers. Though indeed my knowledge of Mrs Siddons does not reach back to her youth – it extends only twenty years.[21]

me very kindly to dear Mrs. Piozzi. God bless and support
you my very dear friend! I am unalterably

Your affte
S. Siddons

I lost in the fire a Toilette of the poor Queen of France
a peice of beautifull Bocent lace an ell wide and two
yards long which having belong'd to so interesting a person
of course I regret more than all the other things – It
cou'd not have cost at first, less than a thousand pounds
I had to wear it only in the Trial scene of Hermione in the
Winters Tale, it cover'd me all over from head to foot –
I suppose my losses cou'd not be repaird for Twelve hundred
pounds. but God be praisd – that the fire did not break
out while the people were in the House !!!

g. Sarah Siddons's Autograph.
(*Letter in the possession of the Folger Shakespeare Library, Washington, D.C.*)

In Newcastle, in 1812, she had appeared with William Charles Macready. An apprentice actor aged only nineteen, he had to play Beverley in *The Gamester*, and therefore appear as the husband of Sarah at the age of fifty-eight. He admired in her, above all things, 'the unity of design, the just relation of all parts to the whole, that made us forget the actress in the character she assumed'. He records the advice she gave him: 'Remember what I say, study, study, study, and do not marry till you are thirty. Beware of that. Keep your mind on your art, do not remit your study and you are sure to succeed.'

Sarah made her final appearance on the stage on 9 June 1819 for the benefit of Charles Kemble and his wife. But she was to continue to give the private readings at her house in the years that followed. Haydon has an amusing passage in his diary about Lawrence, who was present at a reading of *Macbeth* which Sarah gave on 10 March 1821, with an interval for tea and toast after Act III:

> While we were all eating toast and tingling cups and saucers, she began again. It was like the effect of a mass bell at Madrid. All noise ceased; we slunk to our seats like boors, two or three of the most distinguished men of the day, with the very toast in their mouths, afraid to bite.
>
> It was curious to see Lawrence in the predicament, to hear him bite by degrees and then stop for fear of making too much crackle, his eyes full of water from the constraint; and at the same time to hear Mrs Siddons's: 'Eye of newt and toe of frog', and then to see Lawrence give a sly bite, and then look awed, and pretend to be listening.[22]

Two glimpses of Sarah show both her humour and the awe in which she was held by those who tended to see her as a Tragedy Queen, retired. The first is by her little niece, Frances Kemble, daughter of Charles, who was brought as a child into the presence of this awful aunt after she had been naughty:

> Melpomene took me upon her lap, and, bending upon me her 'controlling frown', discovered to me of my evil ways, in those accents which curdled the blood of the poor shopman, of whom she demanded if the printed calico she purchased of him 'would wash'. The tragic tones pausing, in the midst of the impressed and impressive silence of the assembled family, I tinkled forth, 'What beautiful eyes you have!' all my small faculties having been absorbed in the steadfast upward gaze I fixed on these magnificent orbs.

Mrs Siddons set me down with a smothered laugh, and I trotted off, apparently uninjured by my great-aunt's solemn suasion.[23]

The other amusing glimpse is given by Haydon, when he records her visit to the private view of his huge canvas, *Christ's Entry into Jerusalem*, in 1820:

Everybody seemed afraid, when in walked, with all the dignity of her majestic presence, Mrs Siddons, like a Ceres or a Juno. The whole room remained dead silent, and allowed her to think. After a few minutes Sir George Beaumont, who was extremely anxious, said in a very delicate manner: 'How do you like the Christ?' Everybody listened for her reply. After a moment, in a deep, loud, tragic tone she said: 'It is completely successful.' I was then presented with all the ceremonies of a levee, and she invited me to her house in an awful tone, and expressed her high admiration of the way in which I had so variously modified the same expression. 'The paleness of your Christ,' she said, 'gives it a supernatural look.'[24]

Washington Irving was among her admirers, and said when he first saw her in 1805, 'I hardly breathe while she is on the stage. She works up my feelings till I am like a mere child. And yet this woman is old, and has lost all elegance of figure.' She was far older when he first met her, after the publication of his *Sketch Book* in 1820. She was introduced to him at a party. He says that she looked at him 'for a moment, and then, in her clear and deep-toned voice, she slowly enunciated: "You've made me weep." ' Two years later, in 1922, after the publication of *Bracebridge Hall*, he was re-presented to her. 'You've made me weep again,' she said. He took both remarks as a great compliment.[25] She kept her rather private sense of humour mostly to herself.

Her humour becomes rather ironic in her letter of 12 July 1819 to Mrs FitzHugh on the occasion of the Prince Regent's fancy dress ball:

Well, my dear friend, though I am not of rank and condition to be myself at the Prince's ball, my fine clothes, at any rate, will have that honour. Lady B. has borrowed my Lady Macbeth's finest banquet dress, and I wish her ladyship joy in wearing it, for I found the weight of it almost too much for endurance for half an hour. How will she be able to carry it for such a length of time? But young and old, it seems, are expected to appear, upon that 'high solemnity', in splendid and fanciful apparel, and many of these beauties will appear in my stage finery.

Lady C. at first intended to present herself (as she said very drolly) as a vestal virgin, but has now decided upon the dress of a fair Circassian. I should like to see this gorgeous assembly, and I have some thoughts of walking in in the last dress of Lady Macbeth, and swear I came there in my sleep.[26]

In 1815 Sarah lost her son Henry, who died of tuberculosis in Edinburgh at the age of forty. The shock of this was very great, as two letters written from Westbourne Farm to her friend Mrs FitzHugh reveal; the first is undated:

This third shock has indeed sadly shaken me, and, although in the very depths of affliction, I agree with you that consolation may be found, yet the voice of nature will for a time overpower that of reason; and I cannot but remember 'that such things were, and were most dear to me'. I am tolerably well, but have no voice. This is entirely nervousness, and fine weather will bring it back to me. . . . The little that was left of my poor sight is almost washed away by tears, so that I fear I write scarce legibly. God's will be done![27]

The second is dated 7 April 1815:

I don't know why, unless that I am older and feebler, or that I am now without a profession, which forced me out of myself in my former afflictions, but the loss of my poor dear Harry seems to have laid a heavier hand upon my mind than any I have sustained. I drive out to recover my voice and my spirits, and am better while abroad; but I come home and lose them both in an hour.[28]

One of the most sustained of her reappearances was a ten-night engagement in Edinburgh to raise money for her daughter-in-law and the children, to all of whom she was devoted. She wrote to her friend Ballantyne in Scotland on 22 October 1815:

I hope my visit to Edinburgh will be beneficial to my dear son's family. At least it will evince the greatest proof of respect for that public on whom they depend, which it is in my power to give. I have some doubts whether the motives which induce me to return to the public after so long an absence will shield me from the darts of malignity, and when I think of what I have undertaken I own myself doubtful and weak with respect to the performance of the task I am called on to make, but I will not suffer myself to think of it any longer. . . . I fear I shall never be able to present myself in Mrs Beverley, who should be not only handsome but young also . . . I look forward with the greatest satisfaction the moment of seeing you again, in the meantime do not exalt me too much.[29]

Gradually, during the 1820s, she began to find herself losing through death her closer friends and relatives. Mrs Piozzi died in 1821, and John Philip Kemble in 1823. The sharp, unfeeling eyes of her niece Fanny Kemble watched her decline:

> The vapid vacuity of the last years of my aunt Siddons' life had made a powerful impression upon me, – her apparent deadness and indifference to everything, which I attributed (unjustly, perhaps) less to her advanced age and impaired powers than to what I supposed the withering and drying influence of the overstimulating atmosphere of emotion, excitement, and admiration in which she passed her life; certain it is that such was my dread of the effect of my profession upon me, that I added an earnest petition to my daily prayers that I might be defended from the evil influence I feared it might exercise upon me.[30]

If Lawrence may be regarded as the one man to whom Sarah gave her deepest affections – as he, it might seem, experienced for her the strongest feeling of which he was capable – then this might explain the curious aftermath of their strange relationship. The few notes passing between them in later life which have been preserved are written in the most formal terms, as if after so much public scandal they dare no longer write a single line which could be misinterpreted. She was obviously touched when she heard he had declared in his presidential address to the students of the Royal Academy in 1824 that 'the Picture by Sir Joshua Reynolds of Mrs Siddons as the Tragic Muse, is the finest female portrait in the world'. She wrote him an odd and, for her, a complicated little letter from Bognor on 23 December:

> Situated as I am, with respect to the glorious Picture so finely eulogised, and with its illustrious Panegyrist, what can I say, where should I find words for the various and thronging ideas that fill my mind? It will be enough, however, to say (and I will not doubt it will be true to say) that could we change persons, I would not exchange the Gratification you have experienced in bestowing this *sublime* tribute of praise, for all the fame it must accumulate on the Memory of the Tragick Muse.[31]

What was this lady, now seventy, but living with her powerful memories, 'the various and thronging ideas' which filled her mind, trying to hide behind the maze of these two confused, confusing sentences? What can they mean but that such 'sublime' praise from him, whom she calls 'illustrious', is worth more to her than

the whole accumulated memory of her fame? But her feelings
choked her words, and they fell about her in embarrassed pieces,
fragments of emotion which she left him to decipher, as she knew
he would. Too much had passed between them for it to be
otherwise.

Other and later letters filter the warmth of their affection, so
that it is confined within conventional expression which nevertheless grows clumsy with hidden feeling. In 29 June 1826 Lawrence
wrote her a hasty, worried note asking what he should do about
Boaden's request for an engraving of one of his portraits of her
for his biography – he wants, Lawrence says, to secure the right
one because he is 'anxious that no representation of you should
be given to the World that had not *something* of you'. He signs
himself – 'With a thousand respects and a fixed, the very highest,
Esteem, that has never known diminution, Ever, Dear Mrs
Siddons, Oblig'd and Devoted Lawrence'. How could she, who
felt the same as he, fail to understand him? Another letter survives which Sarah wrote to Lawrence two years later, on 12 June
1828, to ask his help on behalf of a mutual friend seeking an
appointment. She ends, quite simply, 'I have no more to say but –
Farewell! and God bless you! Sarah Siddons'.[32]

In June 1828, Sarah was seventy-three and Lawrence fifty-nine.
The following year he lost the closest friend of his later years,
Mrs Wolff, with whom he had formed what was almost certainly
a wholly platonic relationship. With her death came his own
rapid decline in health; he survived her by little more than a year,
working until the end. But a final, romantic overflow of emotion
long since suppressed, though never forgotten, attended the last
months of his life in his relationship with Fanny Kemble. Fanny,
Sarah's niece, was a girl of only nineteen at the time; she was the
daughter of Charles Kemble and his wife, the Viennese dancer
Maria Theresa de Camp. Like her mother, she was an actress.

Half a century later, when she was herself almost seventy,
Fanny was to write an intimate account of what happened between
her and Lawrence during those final months of his life. Fanny
had been educated in France, where she says she kept a copy of
Byron hidden under her schoolgirl pillow. Her book reveals her
as an active, sharp, perceptive, intelligent, vain and somewhat
aggressive woman.[33] As a beautiful girl these characteristics,
though present, were overlooked in the face of her youth and
talent. She was a friend of her cousin Cecilia Siddons. Covent

Garden, of which her father was at this time manager, was in great financial difficulties, and it was her début in 1829 which saved the situation for him.

Since Lawrence was a great friend of Charles Kemble and his wife, he knew Fanny well, and by the time she began to flower as a young woman she claims he fell in love with her. Her account, however coloured in her own favour, is still remarkable:

When in town, Lawrence never omitted one of my performances, always occupying the stage box, and invariably sending me the next morning a letter, full of the most detailed and delicate criticism, showing a minute attention to every inflection of my voice, every gesture, every attitude, which, combined with expressions of enthusiastic admiration, with which this discriminating and careful review of my performance invariably terminated, was as strong a dose of the finest flattery as could well have been offered to a girl of my age, on the very first step of her artistic career. I used to read over the last of these remarkable criticisms, invariably, before going to the theatre, in order to profit by every suggestion of alteration or hint of improvement they contained; and I was in the act of reperusing the last I ever received from him, when my father came in and said, 'Lawrence is dead'.

I had been sitting to him for some time previously for a pencil sketch, which he gave my mother; it was his last work, and certainly the most beautiful of his drawings. He had appointed a day for beginning a full-length, life-size portrait of me as Juliet, and we had seen him only a week before his death, and, in the interval, received a note from him, merely saying he was rather indisposed. His death, which was quite unexpected, created a very great public sensation, and there was something sufficiently mysterious about its circumstances to give rise to a report that he had committed suicide.

The shock of this event was terrible to me, although I have sometimes since thought it was fortunate for me rather than otherwise. Sir Thomas Lawrence's enthusiastically expressed admiration for me, his constant kindness, his sympathy in my success, and the warm interest he took in everything that concerned me, might only have inspired me with a grateful sense of his condescension and goodness. But I was a very romantic girl, with a most excitable imagination, and such was to me the melancholy charm of Lawrence's countenance, the elegant distinction of his person, and exquisite refined gentleness of his voice and manner, that a very dangerous fascination was added to my sense of gratitude for all his personal kindness to me, and my admiration for his genius; and I think it not at all unlikely that, had our intercourse continued, and had I sat to him for the projected portrait of Juliet, in spite of the forty years' difference in our ages, and my knowledge of his disastrous relations with my cousins, I should have become in love with him myself, and been the fourth member of our family whose life he would have disturbed and embittered. His sentimentality was of a peculiarly mischievous order, as it not only induced women to fall in love with him, but enabled him to persuade himself that he was in love with them, and apparently with more than one at a time. . . . At the end of my next sitting, when my mother and myself had risen to take leave of him, he said, 'No, don't go yet, – stay a moment, – I want to show you something – if I can;' and he moved restlessly about, taking up and putting down his chalks and pencils, and standing, and sitting down again, as if unable to make up his mind to do what he wished. At length he went abruptly to an easel, and, removing from it a canvas with a few slight sketches on it, he discovered behind it the profile portrait of a lady in a white dress folded simply across her bosom, and showing her beautiful neck and shoulders. Her head was dressed with a sort of sibylline turban, and she supported it upon a most lovely hand and arm, her elbow resting on a large book, towards which she bent, and on the pages of which her eyes were fixed, the exquisite eyelid and lashes hiding the eyes. 'Oh, how beautiful! oh, who is it!' exclaimed I. 'A – a lady,' stammered Lawrence, turning white and red, 'towards whom – for whom – I entertained the profoundest regard.' Thereupon he fled out of the room. 'It is the portrait of Mrs W——,' said my mother; 'she is now dead; she was an exceedingly beautiful and accomplished woman, the authoress of the words and music of the song Sir Thomas Lawrence asked you to learn for him.'

The great painter's devotion to this lovely person had been matter of notoriety in the London world.[34]

Later she adds:

Mrs Siddons, dining with us one day, asked my mother how the sketch Lawrence was making of me was getting on. After my mother's reply, my aunt remained silent for some time, and then, laying her hand on my father's arm, said, 'Charles, when I die, I wish to be carried to my grave by you and Lawrence'.

Lawrence was to hear of this, Fanny tells us:

He asked eagerly of her health, her looks, her words, and my mother telling him of her speech about him, he threw down his pencil, clasped his hands, and, with his eyes full of tears and face convulsed, exclaimed, 'Good God! did she say that?'[35]

What did Lawrence see in this pert, hard girl but some irresistible recollection of the tortured emotions of the past? On her birthday, he sent her a finely framed proof-plate of the engraving of the Tragic Muse, which he inscribed: 'This portrait by England's greatest painter, of the noblest subject of his pencil, is presented to her neice and worthy successor, by her most faithful and humble friend and servant, Lawrence.' Then, whatever his feelings for Fanny, he found an excuse to call the picture back, claiming it needed reframing, but in reality because he wanted to remove the words 'worthy successor'. He felt he was being disloyal to Sarah. Looking at the picture again as it stood in his room, he said to his servant, 'Cover it up. I cannot bear to look at it.'

It would seem Fanny combined something for him of Sally and Maria, as well as a reminder of Sarah herself in her youth when he had first seen her at Bath.[36] When he showed his drawing of Fanny to her mother, she said, without thinking she might cause him any pain, that the portrait reminded her of Maria. Lawrence's voice became suddenly choked, and he said: 'Oh, she is very like her! She is very like them all!' He wrote to John Angerstein that Fanny had 'eyes and hair like Mrs Siddons in her finest time', and a voice 'at once sweet and powerful', and that she was 'blest with a clear "Kemble understanding" '.[37] He deserted his work and hastened to the theatre to see her:

> I have for many years given up the theatre (not going above once or twice in the year), but this fine genius has drawn me often to it, and each time to witness improvement and new beauties. . . . Her manner in private is characterised by ease and that modest gravity which, I believe, must belong to high tragic genius and which, in Mrs Siddons, was strictly natural to her, though, from being peculiar in the general gaiety of society, it was often thought assumed.[38]

Following each performance, he took further time to send her detailed letters of helpful criticism.[39] On 4 January 1830, only three days before his death, he wrote of her to a friend, Mrs Hayman:

> I have the shackles of 'sixty' upon me, and therefore these Love-chains would turn into skeletons of Roses, did anyone attempt to throw them round me. But tho' I seldom see her, I have almost a Father's interest in her, and a Father's resentment towards those who will not see the promise of almost all that Genius can do, because they have seen the unequall'd power, the glorious countenance and Figure of Mrs Siddons.[40]

Lawrence died on 7 January 1830. Fanny Kemble, on hearing the news, had the heart to realize what his death would mean to Sarah. Much can be forgiven her in later life for the letter she sent round immediately to her cousin Cecilia:

My dearest Cecy, . . . in case your Mother should not yet have heard of it, you had better prepare her for the news of Sir Thomas Lawrence's death – if she has not yet been apprised of it you may save her in some degree the shock which I fear the intelligence must give her. With love from all, ever affectionately yours, Fanny Kemble.[41]

Sarah survived Lawrence only seventeen months. She passed this final period quietly with Cecilia, who stayed with her mother until the end. There was nothing left in life for her, now so many of her friends had died. When she was on the stage, she had longed for the peacefulness of retirement. She had had in all nearly twenty years of it, and it had brought her little of the compensation for which she had once longed. She sighed to be back on the stage, to recover once more the nervous strength to sustain a performance in the grand tradition, the strength of her youth and middle years. The private recitals she gave until late in life gradually declined into ghostly attempts to recall the splendour of those past nights at Drury Lane and Covent Garden.

She died at the age of seventy-six on 8 June 1831 at her house by Regent's Park, 'peaceably, and without suffering, and in full consciousness', wrote Fanny later the same day. Five thousand people, it was said, gathered to mourn her at Paddington Church on 15 June – among them the combined companies of the Theatre Royal of Drury Lane and Covent Garden; the mourners from the profession Sarah had so greatly illuminated filled eleven coaches. But there remained another mourner. A veiled girl came out of the crush and knelt weeping beside the coffin. No one ever discovered who she was.[42]

On the evening following Sarah's death, Fanny Kemble played Lady Macbeth, Sarah's greatest part, at Covent Garden. But the mantle of Sarah's distinction was not for her shoulders, nor for those of any other actress. Sarah had been unique in her performance, as the greatest artists must be.

Notes

=========c◯AA◯)=========

Principal Biographical Sources. The principal biographies of Mrs Siddons are: *Memoirs of Mrs Siddons* by James Boaden, published in 1827, an infectiously enthusiastic and often highly observant book, marred by Boaden's extremely garrulous style and tangential interests; *Life of Mrs Siddons* (1834) by Thomas Campbell, the poet and writer chosen by Sarah Siddons herself to write her life, but who found his task a chore and lightened it (which makes him most valuable) by quoting extensively from important documents and letters and from the autobiographical memorandum with which Mrs Siddons provided him, but which Campbell edited to some extent for publication; *The Kembles* (1871) by Percy Fitzgerald, a most useful and sympathetic survey of the Kemble family as a whole, and quoting more widely than Campbell from correspondence; *The Incomparable Siddons* (1909) by Mrs Clement Parsons, a well-researched but somewhat untidy study by a devoted admirer of the actress, a book full of new details on which all future biographers must draw; and *Mrs Siddons, Tragic Actress* (1936; revised 1954) by Yvonne ffrench, the most thorough recent study and by far the most perceptive of the complexities of Mrs Siddons's character.

The original manuscript of Mrs Siddons's autobiographical notes written for Campbell is preserved in the Harvard Theatre Collection. It was published in 1942 as *The Reminiscences of Sarah Kemble Siddons*, edited by William Van Lennep. I am grateful to the Curator of the Harvard Theatre Collection, Miss Helen D. Willard, for permission to quote from this text, rather than from Campbell's revisions as published in his biography. Considerable numbers of Sarah Siddons's letters survive; single items change hands now and then in the antiquarian market; the larger collections may be found in the University Library, Cambridge, the John Rylands Library, Manchester, the Harvard Theatre Collection, and the Folger Shakespeare Library.

NOTES: I. PORTRAIT OF A YOUNG ACTRESS

1. Southerne, *Isabella*. Act IV, Scene 2.
2. Roger Kemble (1721–1802) came of a Catholic family associated

with Herefordshire. Several of his ancestors had been priests, including Father John Kemble, who died a martyr's death after being wrongly accused of involvement in Titus Oates's plot. See Parsons, *The Incomparable Siddons*, p. 3 *et seq*; ffrench, *Mrs Siddons, Tragic Actress*, p. 4 (revised edition, 1954). I am grateful to Mr J. F. W. Sherwood, City Librarian and Curator of Hereford City Library and Museums, for drawing my attention to papers held in the Library: (i) L.C.Deed 9300, a Bill dated 2 May 1741, of Roger Kemble, barber, to 'Madam Monington' with a receipt signed by his son, Roger (the actor); (ii) L.C.Deed 707, being the lease of a house in Capuch Lane to Richard Bethel; the house is mentioned as having been in the possession of Roger Kemble, barber.

3. John Ward (1704–73) had acted as a small child with Thomas Betterton (who died in 1710), and Peg Woffington had once been a member of the company of which he was manager in Dublin. Needless to say, he did not approve of her morals. See ffrench, *op. cit.* (1954), p. 4.

4. The Act of 1713 was 'for reducing the laws relating to rogues, vagabonds, sturdy beggars and vagrants, into one act of Parliament; and for the more effectual punishing (of) such . . ., and sending them whither they ought to be sent'; 'Common players of Interludes' were held under the act to be 'rogues and vagabonds'. The Act of 1737 gave for the first time statutory recognition of the Lord Chamberlain in his relation to the theatre; in the Act it was decreed that anyone acting 'for hire, gain or reward' in any place where he has no settlement, or 'without licence from the Lord Chamberlain of His Majesty's Household for the time being, shall be deemed a rogue and vagabond'; a further section of the Act decreed that no new plays or additions to old ones could be acted until a copy of the play, or additions to old plays, had been approved by the Lord Chamberlain.

5. See *Memoirs of the late Thomas Holcroft* (1816), Vol. I, p. 183 *et seq*.

6. The Shoulder of Mutton in Brecon has undergone some changes since 1755, including a completely new façade. See the comparative pictures given in Parsons, *op. cit.*, opposite p. 2. It has now the name 'Siddons' prominently displayed, and was once known as the Siddons Wine Vaults.

7. The sharing system was normal for companies working in the provincial theatres of England in the earlier part of the eighteenth century. All profits were shared equally among the members of the company, whether senior or junior, except that the manager had four extra shares because he provided the scenery and certain costumes. The system, liable to abuse by unscrupulous managers,

lapsed in mid-century. Actors depended on their benefit nights, occurring once or twice a season, for their main income. See Chapter 2, note 14. For Roger Kemble's income for 1757, see Percy Fitzgerald, *The Kembles*, II, p. 68.

8. Holcroft, *op. cit.*, I, p. 221.
9. See *Thraliana, the diary of Mrs Hester Lynch Thrale* (later Mrs Piozzi), pp. 842–3.
10. Campbell, *Life of Mrs Siddons*, Vol. I, pp. 35–6, for both quotations.
11. The handbill is reproduced by Fitzgerald, *op. cit.*, I, pp. 21–2. Fitzgerald also gives a traditional story that Sarah's first appearance 'took place in a barn at the back of the old Bell Inn, at Stourbridge, Worcestershire, when some officers quartered in the neighbourhood gave their services. It was said that she burst into fits of laughter at the most tragic moment, and inflamed to fury the military tragedian who was playing with her.' (I, p. 20.)
12. The letter is reproduced in T. C. Thomas's *Sarah Siddons*, pp. 11–12.
13. Samuel Rogers, *Recollections*, p. 135.
14. James Boaden, in *Memoirs of Mrs Siddons* (1896 edition), p. 13, is enthusiastic enough to put the dawn of the love affair as early as her fifteenth year; Campbell, more sedate and official, says 'about seventeen' (*op. cit.*, I, p. 41).
15. Campbell, *op. cit.*, I, p. 47 *et seq.*
16. Campbell, *op. cit.*, I, p. 51. According to the Ward, Lock guide to Warwick, Sarah attracted the attention of Lady Mary Greatheed when Roger Kemble's company performed at Warwick. Lady Mary Greatheed was the widow of Samuel Greatheed, M.P. for Coventry. She was born Lady Mary Bertie, daughter of the second Duke of Ancaster. Bertie Greatheed, Lady Mary's son, was eleven at the time of Sarah's residence at Guy's Cliffe. Guy's Cliffe, which Sarah was to come to know so well as the guest of Bertie in his adult life, was unfortunately burnt out in the twentieth century.
17. Campbell very rightly expresses his doubts that this early meeting with Garrick ever took place. See Campbell, *op. cit.*, p. 65.
18. The city in which Sarah was first announced as Mrs Siddons on the playbills is given as Worcester by Mrs Parsons (*op. cit.*, p. 17); Fitzgerald gives it as Wolverhampton, which Yvonne ffrench follows.
19. Fitzgerald, I, p. 35.
20. Sarah Siddons, *Reminiscences*, pp. 2–4.
21. Tom King (1730–1804) was a well-established actor in Garrick's company, playing such comedy parts as Peter Teazle, Puff and Sir Anthony Absolute in Sheridan's plays. Hazlitt was to write of him: 'His acting left a taste on the palate sharp and sweet like a quince.

With an old, hard, rough, withered face like a sour apple, puckered up into a thousand wrinkles ... he was the real amorous, wheedling or hasty, choleric, peremptory old gentleman.' He was to squander his considerable fortune in gambling and unfortunate ventures into management at Bristol and at the Sadler's Wells Theatre.

22. Fitzgerald, *op. cit.*, I, pp. 32–3.
23. *The Letters of David Garrick* (1963), Letter 926, p. 1021.
24. British Museum, ADD. MSS., No. 25,383.
25. *The Letters of David Garrick* (1963), Letter 932, p. 1026.
26. British Museum, ADD. MSS., No. 25,383.
27. British Museum, ADD. MSS., No. 25,383.
28. *The Letters of David Garrick* (1963), Letter 944, p. 1038.
29. Ditto, Letter 947, p. 1040.
30. Ditto, Letter 956, p. 1047.
31. British Museum, ADD. MSS., No. 25,383.
32. See Mrs Parsons, *op. cit.*, p. 22, and note to Letter 932 in *The Letters of David Garrick* (1963), p. 1028.
33. John Taylor, *Records of my Life*, I, p. 350.
34. Sarah Siddons, *op. cit.*, pp. 4–6.
35. British Museum, ADD. MSS., No. 25,383.
36. Sarah Siddons, *op. cit.*, pp. 6–7.

NOTES: 2. BATH

1. Tate Wilkinson (1739–1803), who came of good family, was established as a small-part actor by Garrick, and became the friend of Peg Woffington, although he had offended her initially by imitating her in public. Imitation of other actors and actresses was, apparently, his most notable talent on the stage. His greatest success as an actor was in Dublin, not London. His fame, however, rests on his distinguished career as a provincial manager.

2. Royal patents were given in the provinces as follows: Bath and Norwich, 1768; York and Hull, 1769; Liverpool, 1771; Manchester 1775; Bristol, 1778; Newcastle, 1788. Places of royal residence (Brighton, Windsor, and Richmond in Surrey) received licences direct from the Lord Chamberlain. In 1788 an Act was passed making acting in the provinces legal through the local justices, who were empowered to licence players for a period of up to sixty days. Many theatres had been built earlier in the century, for example, in Bath in 1705, in Bristol in 1729, in York in 1734, and in Ipswich in 1736. See also Chapter 1, note 4. Theatres were normally built by public subscription, the subscribers becoming the proprietors, and holding silver tickets which admitted them to all performances. The company manager then leased the building from the proprietors.

3. Tate Wilkinson, *The Wandering Patentee*, I, pp. 104–5.

4. Tate Wilkinson, *The Wandering Patentee*, I, p. 101.

5. Tate Wilkinson, *Memoirs*, III, p. 146 *et seq.*

6. *Ibid.*, p. 148 *et seq.*

7. *Ibid.*, p. 156.

8. *Ibid.*, p. 160 *et seq.*

9. *Ibid.*, p. 163 *et seq.*

10. Tate Wilkinson, *The Wandering Patentee*, I, p. 144.

11. Tate Wilkinson, *Memoirs*, III, p. 148.

12. *Op. cit.*, p. 69 *et seq.*

13. Tate Wilkinson, *The Wandering Patentee*, I, pp. 117–18.

14. The benefit system, which lasted until the nineteenth century, brought the popular player, both in London and the provinces, his main opportunity to make money. If his benefit night were 'clear', the actor drew the total takings, clear of any deduction for the theatre's expenses. A 'shared' benefit meant splitting the night's profits with another player. If star performers consented to act for a fellow-player's benefit, they frequently charged a fee for appearing, mostly below their normal one. Their presence might greatly increase the takings, and the deduction of the star's reduced fee from the takings might still result in a substantial increase in a lesser known player's benefit.

15. Tate Wilkinson, *Memoirs*, III, pp. 172–3.

16. Tate Wilkinson, *The Wandering Patentee*, I, pp. 252–6.

17. Fitzgerald, *op. cit.*, II, pp. 74–5.

18. According to the actor John Edwin, Mrs Siddons took snuff on advice as helpful against blindness, to which her family, apparently, was prone. See Pasquin, *The Eccentricities of John Edwin*, Vol. II, p. 157.

19. Boaden, *Memoirs of Mrs Inchbald*, I, p. 71.

20. *Idem.*, I, pp. 83–4.

21. *Idem.*, I, pp. 91–2. P.S.=prompter's side of the stage, O.P.= opposite the prompter.

22. According to Mrs Parsons, *op. cit.*, p. 36: 'Palmer's prompter, Floor, who saw Mrs Siddons act in Liverpool, was in part . . . instrumental in effecting her Bath engagement.'

23. For the building of the theatres in Bath, see Walter Ison, *The Georgian Buildings of Bath*, London, Faber and Faber, 1948.

24. Sarah Siddons, *op. cit.*, pp. 7–8.

25. Among the parts other than from Shakespeare which she played, were Lady Townly, Mrs Candour, Mrs Lovemore, Belvidera, the Countess of Salisbury, Euphrasia, Emmeline, Elvina, Millwood, Sigismunda, Lady Randolph, Jane Shore, and many others.

26. Boaden, *Memoirs of Mrs Siddons*, pp. 168–9.

27. According to Mrs Parsons, *op. cit.*, p. 38*n*, only two baptisms for the Siddons family are listed in the records of Bath Abbey: Maria, on 24 February 1779, and Frances Emilia, on 26 April 1781. There is no record of the baptism of the daughter born to Mrs Siddons while she was still at Bath, Eliza Ann. (See note 38 below.)

28. According to Mrs Parsons, *op. cit.*, p. 45, the Siddons lived for a while in lodgings at 'Mr Tilling's on Horse Street Parade', identified later with Southgate Street.

29. Frances Burney (1752–1840) was the daughter of Dr Burney, historian of music. She had been brought up in a cultured environment, and Dr Johnson included her among his women friends. When she became prominent through her novels, she was appointed Second Keeper of the Robes to Queen Charlotte (1786). In 1793 she married General d'Arblay, a French refugee in England. From 1802–12 she was interned in France by Napoleon. Her fame rests as much on her published diaries and letters as on her novels.

30. Fitzgerald, *op. cit.*, I, pp. 88–9.

31. This account of Lawrence's career is based on Douglas Goldring's book, *Regency Portrait Painter: the Life of Sir Thomas Lawrence*.

32. John Timbs, in his *Anecdote Biography*, publishes some verses attributed to Lawrence, but written sixteen years after his initial meeting with Sarah in Bath. The painter recollects how eagerly in his boyhood he ran to the theatre:

'Tis, let me see, full sixteen years,
And wondrous short the time appears,
   Since, with enquiry warm,
With beauty's novel power amazed,
I follow'd, midst the crowd, and gazed
   On Siddons' beauteous form.

Up Bath's fatiguing streets I ran,
Just half pretending to be man,
   And fearful to intrude;
Busied I looked on some employ,
Or limp'd to see some other boy,
   Lest she should think me rude.

The sun was bright, and on her face,
As proud to show the stranger grace,
   Shone with its purest rays;
And through the folds that veil'd her form,
Motion displayed its happiest charm,
   To catch the admiring gaze.

The smiling lustre of her eyes,
That triumph'd in our wild surprise,
  Well I remember still:
They spoke of joy to yield delight,
And plainly said, 'If I'm the sight,
  Good people, take your fill.'

33. Sarah Siddons, *op. cit.*, p. 8.
34. *Idem.*, pp. 8–9.
35. I am grateful to Dr Levi Fox, Director of the Shakespeare Birthday Trust, for informing me that the Trust preserves four pages in Mrs Siddons's autograph containing the part of Nell in *The Devil to Pay*, said to date from the occasion on which she played the part for her husband's benefit at Bath in May, 1782. William's benefit, with Mrs Siddons playing, would add to the family income.
36. Quoted by Yvonne ffrench, *op. cit.* (1936), p. 63.
37. See Campbell, *op. cit.*, I, p. 90.
38. This is the daughter whose relatively unrecorded existence caused Mrs Parsons so much concern. See Mrs Parsons, *op. cit.*, pp. 290–1. Yvonne ffrench, however, was shown by Mr Rupert Siddons a family Bible presented to Mrs Siddons by Cambridge University in 1819, on the flyleaf of which she recorded the births, marriages and deaths of her family. Among the entries is the following: 'Eliza Ann, Bath, 2 June 1782. Died April 16, 1788. Was buried at Marylebone Church at 5 in the evening.'

Additional Note:

Sarah Siddons in Bath. I am grateful to Mrs Mary Gibson and to Mrs Brackenbury of Bath for unearthing the following references in the Bath press to Sarah Siddons's appearances in that city:

DATE	JOURNAL	PLAY	PARTS
1779	*Bath Journal*	Romeo and Juliet	S.S. as Juliet.

(The performance had taken place on 4 March. On 8 March a letter appeared signed A.B.: 'I think I never beheld a Juliet till Mrs Siddons showed me one at that time, and yet for these 30 years past I scarce ever miss'd this favourite play, both in London and elsewhere.')

DATE	JOURNAL	PLAY	PARTS
3 May	*Bath Journal*	The Law of Lombardy	S.S. as the Princess.
8 May	*Bath Chronicle*	The Grecian Daughter	S.S. as the Daughter for her benefit.

27 May	*Journal*	The Funeral, of Grief a-la-Mode	S.S. as Lady Blumpton.
23 June	*Journal*	Siege of Sinope	S.S. as Thamyris; W.S. as High Priest.
30 Oct.	*Journal*	Jane Shore	S.S. as Jane Shore.

1780

8 Feb.	*Chronicle*	Braganza	S.S. as Duchess of B.
10 Feb.	*Chronicle*	Measure for Measure	S.S. as Isabella.
12 Feb.	*Chronicle*	Edward and Eleanora	S.S. as Eleanora; W.S. as Apasin. S.S. also recites Monody by Sheridan.
15 Feb.	*Chronicle*	The Conscious Lovers	S.S. as Indiana.
17 Feb.	*Chronicle*	The Countess of Salisbury	S.S. as Lady Salisbury.
19 Feb.	*Chronicle*	The Careless Husband	S.S. as Lady Easy.
28 Feb.	*Journal*		

(A paragraph in the *Theatrical News* reads: 'Our admirable Mrs Siddons acquires fresh laurels from every character she plays ... whether she aims her powers at our tender or mirthful feelings she appears alike the absolute mistress of them.')

28 Feb.	*Journal*	Edward and Eleanor	S.S. as Princess, for her benefit.
4 March	*Chronicle*		

(A fanciful letter, signed Melpomene, complains that 'your incomparable Mrs Siddons' is unfaithful to Melpomene – 'Nay, I am piqued to think that . . . in the part of Lady Townly, Indiana, the Fine Lady of Lethe, etc. etc. that the Saucy Goddess (Thalia) is thus favoured.' The letter ends with a demand that she should appear again as Isabella in *The Fatal Marriage*.)

7 March	*Journal*	Cymbeline	S.S. as Imogen.
9 March	*Chronicle*	Tancred and Sigismunda	S.S. as Sigismunda.
13 May	*Chronicle*	The Countess of Salisbury and The Clandestine Marriage	S.S. as Countess and Miss Sterling.
3 June	*Chronicle*	Douglas	S.S. as Lady Randolph; W.S., an Officer.
3 July	*Chronicle*	The Grecian Daughter (at the Theatre Royal, Bristol)	S.S. as Grecian Daughter; W.S. as Arcas.

1781
18 Jan.　　*Chronicle*
　　　　('Mrs Siddons is, "take her for all in all" what perhaps . . .
　　　　"we shall never see the like again".')

10 Feb.	*Chronicle*	The School for Wives	S.S as Mrs Belville; W.S. as Leech.
22 Feb.	*Chronicle*	The Funeral	S.S. as Lady Brumpton.
— March	*Chronicle*	She Stoops to Conquer	S.S. as Miss Hardcastle.
24 June	*Journal*	The Fair Penitent	S.S. as Calista.
27 Oct.	*Journal*	The Rivals	S.S. as Julia.
20 Nov.	*Journal*	The School for Wives	S.S. as Mrs Belville; W.S. as Leech.

1782

29 Jan.	*Journal*	The Fair Circassian	S.S. as Almedia.
19 Feb.	*Journal*	Venice Preserved	S.S. as Belvidera; W.S. as the Duke.
21 Feb.	*Journal*	The Inconstant	S.S. as Bizarre.
23 Feb.	*Journal*	Tancred and Sigismunda	S.S. as Sigismunda.
26 Feb.	*Journal*	The Jealous Wife	S.S. as Mrs Oakley.
28 Feb.	*Journal*	A Chapter of Accidents	S.S. as Cecilla, for benefit of Mr and Miss Siddons.
5 March	*Journal*	The Gamester	S.S. as Mrs Beverley.
7 March	*Journal*	Much Ado about Nothing	S.S. as Beatrice; W.S. as Don John.
2 April	*Journal*	The Countess of Narbonne	S.S. as the Countess.
7 May	*Journal*	Jane Shore	S.S. as Jane Shore.
18 May	*Journal*	The Mourning Bride	S.S. as Zara.
21 May	*Journal*	The Distressed Mother	S.S. as Mother.
25 May	*Journal*	The Rivals	S.S. as Julia.
29 May	*Journal*	King John	S.S. as Constance.

Sarah Siddons in Bristol. I am grateful to Miss Kathleen Barker for
the following press references to Mrs Siddons's appearances in
Bristol:

Felix Farley's Bristol Journal	14.10.1780	Chapter of Accidents
Bristol Gazette	23.11.1780	Elfrida
Felix Farley's Bristol Journal	23. 6.1781 &	
	30. 6.1781	Hamlet

Felix Farley's Bristol Journal	27.10.1781	Countess of Salisbury
Felix Farley's Bristol Journal ⎱	20. 4.1782 ⎱	King John
Sarah Farley's Bristol Journal ⎰	20. 4.1872 ⎰	
Sarah Farley's Bristol Journal	27. 4.1782	Count of Narbonne
Felix Farley's Bristol Journal	6. 7.1782	'The Three Reasons'
		&c.

In the papers of 10 February 1782 Mrs Siddons is advertised as too 'indisposed' to play on Monday, 12 February. We now know that she was at this time already five months pregnant with her child Eliza Ann. (See Note 38 above.) Miss Barker also contributes the following interesting note:

The remarks of 'Mrs Summers' who is said to have played confidantes to Mrs Siddons at Bath, on the influence of William Siddons's 'production' of his wife's acting, have been much quoted. Genest refers to this lady as 'Mrs' because apparently in later life she took this courtesy title, but she should properly be referred to as 'Miss', not just because she was unmarried, but because at the time of Mrs Siddons's engagement there was also a Mrs Summers as well as a Miss Summers (her daughter) in the company. And it is definitely to *Miss* Summers that the ascription of the confidante parts belongs (not very many of those! – she was really only a Columbine and small-part actress but she did on occasion play, e.g. Anna to Mrs Siddons's Lady Randolph). Mrs Summers properly so called was the Company's Second Old Woman.

The following appeared in the *Bath Journal* for 5 April 1779, Miss Barker points out:

The following Lines were written by a Young Lady on seeing our justly admired Actress, Mrs. SIDDONS, at the Theatre Royal in Bristol. As she has become the greatest, and most deserving favorite that ever appeared on our Stage, the insertion of them in your next will yield as much satisfaction to your readers, as it will oblige.

W.M.

OH! thou, whose soul, with perfect feelings fraught,
Can'st add new beauties to the Poet's thought,
Whose voice harmonious, melts to grief's soft pain,
And bid'st its sacred anguish round thee rain;
From the warm'd heart, its greatful tribute share,
That gives thee sigh for sigh, and tear for tear.

In thee, no cold, dull passion mars the line;
The fiction ceases – real sorrows shine;

From eyes expressive starts th'unbidden tear,
The soft effusions of the soul sincere;
And the fair face to the fine heart allied;
Speaks all the griefs – the joys which their reside.
When SIDDONS grieves, lo! pity wakes in all,
From every eye the pearly, sad drops fall,
Soft as the Breeze that swells thro' opening flowers
And wakes the groves, each bosom feels her powers;
With her we weep along the sorrowing page;
Or rise with her in all the fire of rage;
Each heart excites; and melts to grief or love,
And one fine transport varying bosoms move.

   The Stoic Wretch who Nature's feeling scorns,
Dear Gifts! that blest humanity adorns,
Who ne'er to sorrow gave a pitying tear,
Nor from his bosom heav'd a sigh sincere,
Owns, weeping owns, the Power that gave us birth,
A greater blessing ne'er consign'd to Earth
Than the soul's feelings, which by gracious Heaven
To soothe, and pity others woes were given.
     HOT-WELLS.

Through the courtesy of Peter Pagan, Director of the Municipal Libraries in Bath, I was able to inspect the five manuscript notebooks in their possession which formerly belonged to Mrs Siddons. The contents include appreciations of her acting, poems, sermons in extract, recipes written by various hands, including hers. One volume is headed 'Mrs Siddons receipt Book August 16 1808 written by Mrs FitzHugh'. Mrs FitzHugh, wife of the Member of Parliament for Tiverton in Devon, was one of the actress's closest friends, and often entertained her at her house near Southampton.

   Among the verses in tribute to Mrs Siddons are these by Lord Palmerston:

The varying charms that on thy Accents dwell
And bind attention like a magic spell
Thy looks still faithful to thy feeling heart
Thy taste refin'd that shames laborious art
Thy graceful Action whose unstudied ease
Still pleases most when least intent to please.

The following tribute by Thomas Erskine is copied up:

Mrs Siddons is a strong instance of the power of looking up to Nature, and following her genuine impressions. Her acting is so truly natural, that tho' she is the greatest favourite of the Public that has appear'd upon the stage since the death of Garrick she receives less visible Applause *during her performances* than very inferior Actors daily receive.

Persons of exquisite taste and sensibility are so overpower'd with real feeling and distress, that admiration which is the Palm of Art is swallow'd up in genuine emotions of Nature, and the Actress is applauded only by tears which she cannot see and by sighs which she cannot hear. . . .

The book also contains prayers for use morning and evening written in Mrs Siddons's own hand. The third volume is full of recipes, some of which are interesting. For example:

To keep eggs for months, use 'unslacked lime'.

For the disordered Stomach – 40 Grains of Sal-Polechrust, 20 grains of Rhubard in a glass of peppermint water.

For cough mixture – Oil of Sweet Almonds, 2 Oz; Syrup of Balsam, 2 Oz; Sal Volatile, 35 drops; Barley Water, 4 Oz; take a teaspoonful occasionally, shaking the bottle.

For Cholera – 'take three tablespoonsful of pure brandy: if you can possibly bear Calomel, 4 grains on a piece of Bread, or Bread and Butter; and an hour after a dose of Castor Oil or 15 grains of Rhubard with 15 grains of Sal Polychrust, taking it in warm water with a teaspoonful of Sal Volatile; if the spasms continue 15 drops of Laudanum in a little Brandy and water to be repeated every quarter of an hour till the pain be subsided.'

In another volume there is a recipe for the bite of a mad dog:

One pennyWeight of Native Cimabar, ditto of factitious Cimabar, fifteen grains of Musk . . . all ground and taken in a cupfull of Arrack, Brandy or Rum as soon as possible after the bite. And another dose thirty days after. But if any symptoms of Madness appear two of the doses must be taken in an hour and a half at farthest, and a third dose the next morning.

NOTES: 3. DRURY LANE REGAINED

1. Fitzgerald, *op. cit.*, I, pp. 93–9.
2. Campbell, *op. cit.*, I, p. 156, quotes the *Morning Post* for 10 October 1782 as follows: 'Mrs Siddons, of Drury Lane theatre, has a lovely little boy, about eight years old. Yesterday, in the rehearsal of *The Fatal Marriage*, the boy, observing his mother in the agonies of the dying scene, took the fiction for reality, and burst into a flood of tears, a circumstance which struck the feelings of the company in a singular manner.'

3. Sarah Siddons, *op. cit.*, pp. 9–10.
4. *Idem.*, pp. 10–11.
5. *Idem.*, pp. 11–12.
6. Fitzgerald, *op. cit.*, I, p. 111. Pratt, a friend later to become an enemy, wrote an Epilogue which Sarah in her agitation failed to speak. See Note 14 below.
7. Boaden, *Memoirs of Mrs Siddons*, p. 195.
8. Fitzgerald, *op. cit.*, I, pp. 122–3.
9. Anna Seward (1747–1809), another of Dr Johnson's women friends, was privileged to have her poetry published posthumously by Sir Walter Scott in 1810. Six volumes of her letters appeared the following year.
10. Whalley, *Journals and Correspondence*, I, p. 389.
11. *The Swan of Lichfield*, pp. 68–70, for both quotations.
12. See *Selected Letters of Horace Walpole*, Everyman Library, pp. 104–05. For the other two letters quoted, see *Walpole Letters*, edited in sixteen volumes by Paget Toynbee, XII, pp. 381 and 386.
13. Sarah Siddons, *op. cit.*, p. 12.
14. Fitzgerald, *op. cit.*, I, p. 115. Samuel Jackson Pratt, who wrote under the name of Courtney Melmoth, had in 1769 written a curious begging letter to Dr Johnson (see Rylands Library Bulletin XVI, p. 46) and in 1779 had been a suitor to Sophia Weston (Penelope Pennington), and later to Frances Kemble. In 1781 his tragedy *The Fair Circassian* was sustained for nineteen performances by Elizabeth Farren and her supporters; his comedy *The School for Vanity* had failed. Pratt was the author of the lines inscribed on Garrick's tomb in Westminster Abbey.
15. For both quotations, see Boaden, *Memoirs of Mrs Siddons* p, 217.
16. Sarah Siddons, *op. cit.*, pp. 12–13, 21–2.
17. The term 'Blue-Stockings' for women intellectuals with literary tastes, originated in the mid-eighteenth century with parties organized by such hostesses as Mrs Vesey and Mrs Montagu to promote literary discussions in place of the inevitable card-playing among women of fashion. They came to be called blue stockings not because they wore them, but because their male guests came wearing everyday, blue-worsted stockings instead of the black silk which was *de rigueur* for polite evenings. Hence the gatherings became known as Blue-Stocking Clubs, and the ladies concerned, Blue-Stockings.
18. *Diary and Letters of Madame d'Arblay*, II, p. 141.
19. *Idem.*, II, p. 141.
20. Sarah Siddons, *op. cit.*, pp. 15–16.
21. Fitzgerald, *op. cit.*, I, pp. 164–5.
22. Boaden, *Memoirs of Mrs Siddons*, pp. 170–2.
23. Campbell, *op. cit.*, I, pp. 191–2.

24. Boaden in his *Memoirs of Mrs Siddons* gives one of the very rare references to the grooves to be found in contemporary theatrical literature. See p. 403: 'the scoring line where the flats meet each other, the grooves in which they move. . . .'

25. Tate Wilkinson, *Wandering Patentee*, III, pp. 138–42.

26. For more of Palmer's extraordinary character, see Boaden, *Memoirs of John Philip Kemble*, I, p. 365. He was, says Boaden, 'idle and yet energetic, specious and fallacious, a creature of the moment, adopting hurry and pathos as the means of carrying his point; combined with a personal address for which I know no other name but that of *proud humility*'. Another member of the company was James Aickin, who, says Campbell, was best as an honest steward or affectionate parent.

27. See Boaden, *Memoirs of Mrs Siddons*, p. 244: 'She is believed to have carried away £1,100 from Dublin, about £700 from Cork, and on touching her native shores £160 at Liverpool.'

28. Fitzgerald, *op. cit.*, I, pp. 136–7, 139.

29. See Esther K. Sheldon, *Thomas Sheridan of Smock Alley*.

30. Fitzgerald, *op. cit.*, I, pp. 144–5.

31. Campbell, *op. cit.*, I, p. 18n.

32. There are many stories which refute the charge of meanness against Mrs Siddons. For example, see her discussion of a gift for Mrs Pennington, Fitzgerald, *op. cit.*, II, p. 35.

33. Boswell, *Life of Johnson*, Everyman edition, II, pp. 484–5.

34. Sarah Siddons, *op. cit.*, pp. 13–15.

35. Boswell, *op. cit.*, II, p. 484. Genest, in *Some Account of the English Stage*, VI, p. 251, reports Johnson's opinion of Mrs Siddons: 'Sir, she is a prodigious fine woman.'

36. It should be remembered that the King was also a great supporter of Covent Garden; he particularly admired the acting of Henderson.

37. Sarah Siddons, *op. cit.*, pp. 17–18, 19–20.

38. *Idem.*, pp. 20–1.

39. Connell, *Portrait of a Whig Peer*, p. 154.

40. Sarah Siddons, *op. cit.*, p. 25.

41. Campbell, *op. cit.*, I, pp. 259–60.

42. On her return to Edinburgh in July 1785, over £2,000 went into the box-office. The highest takings were for *Isabella* – £139. *Macbeth* took £125. At the end of July she made her first appearance in Glasgow. The takings in 1784 enabled Sarah to clear £967.7.7. See Dibden, *The Annals of the Edinburgh Stage*, p. 186 *et seq.* See also Fanny Kemble's *Record of a Girlhood*, II, p. 128:

> Of the proverbial frigidity of the Edinburgh public I had been forewarned, and of its probably disheartening effect upon myself. Mrs Henry Siddons had often told me of the intolerable sense of

depression with which it affected Mrs Siddons, who, she said, after some of her grandest outbursts of passion, to which not a single expression of applause or sympathy had responded, exhausted and breathless with the effort she had made, would pant out in despair, under her breath, 'Stupid people, stupid people!'. Stupid, however, they undoubtedly were not, though, as undoubtedly, their want of excitability and demonstrativeness diminished their own pleasure by communicating itself to the great actress and partially paralysing her powers. That this habitual reserve sometimes gave way to very violent exhibitions of enthusiasm, the more fervent from its general repression, there is no doubt; and I think it was in Edinburgh that my friend, Mr Harness, told me the whole of the sleep-walking scene in *Macbeth* had once been so vehemently encored that my aunt was literally obliged to go over it a second time, before the piece was allowed to proceed.

43. Dibden, *op. cit.*, pp. 189–90.
44. Whalley, *op. cit.*, I, p. 436.
45. *Idem.*, pp. 436–7. For Pratt, see Note 14 above.
46. Sarah Siddons, *op. cit.*, pp. 27–8.
47. *Idem.*, pp. 26–7.
48. Connell, *op. cit.*, pp. 358 and 360.
49. Stirling, *The Hothams*, II, p. 221.
50. Campbell, *op. cit.*, I, pp. 269–72.
51. Sarah Siddons, *op. cit.*, pp. 28–9.
52. Boaden, *Memoirs of Mrs Siddons*, pp. 291–2.
53. *Idem.*, p. 293.
54. *Idem.*, p. 295.
55. Sarah Siddons, *op. cit.*, pp. 29–31.
56. Campbell, *op. cit.*, I, p. 279.
57. Boaden, *Memoirs of Mrs Siddons*, pp. 296–7.
58. Stirling, *op. cit.*, II, p. 221.
59. *Idem.*, pp. 223–4.
60. Sarah was undoubtedly in reaction against the common reputation of actresses as the courtesans of royalty and men of fashion. The popular Anne Bellamy of Covent Garden, for instance, behaved like a courtesan, and lived in high style until her premature death in 1788; her *Memoirs*, called an *Apology*, appeared in 1785 in six volumes and caused some sensation through their frankness. Other well-known actresses of the eighteenth century who lived hard and freely were Peg Woffington, Fanny Barton (Mrs Abington), who began life as a prostitute and Harriet Wilson (who also published some revealing memoirs). The memoirs of Mary Robinson (published in the Beaux and Belles series by the Grolier Society) show

something of the moral dangers to which young actresses were exposed. See Ivan Bloch, *Sexual Life in England*, Chap. IX. Bloch emphasizes how firmly in reaction against this kind of loose tradition in behaviour Sarah Siddons was set.

61. Brit. Mus. ADD. MSS. 35,350. Lord Hardwicke was to lend Mrs Siddons a life of Pericles; the MSS in the British Museum include a letter of thanks from her to Lord Hardwicke, in which she says:

> I think the memoirs of Pericles laid the strongest hold on me, this may perhaps be accounted for by my presumption, having felt myself in some measure in his situation having been the favourite of the Mob one year and the *next degraded* by them – it remains only that I *may* like him be reinstated when Malice is cool'd and Candour takes its turn. (11 March 1785.)

62. Mrs Parsons, *op. cit.*, p. 106.
63. Fitzgerald, *op. cit.*, I, 215–16.
64. *Idem.*, p. 220.

NOTES: 4. 'CHARMING SIDDONS'

1. Campbell, *op. cit.*, II, p. 11 *et seq.* See below pp. 356–7.
2. She did not, of course, escape attack from certain critics for her Lady Macbeth. George Steevens, in particular, published a satirical review, which included the following paragraph:

> The soul of Mrs Siddons . . . (Mrs Siddons, whose dinners and suppers are proverbially numerous) expanded on this occasion. She spoke her joy on beholding so many guests, with an earnestness, little short of rapture, bordering on enthusiasm. Her address appeared so like reality that all the Thanes about her seized the wooden fowls, etc. in hopes, alas! to find every dish as warm and genuine as her invitation to feed on it.

See Boaden, *Memoirs of John Philip Kemble*, I, p. 245.
3. Her attempts at comedy included *The Way to Keep Him* in 1785, *As You Like It* also in 1785, *All in the Wrong* in 1787, and *The Taming of the Shrew* in 1788.
4. I am grateful to Gerald Burden for drawing my attention to this unpublished letter which passed through Sotheby's salerooms in 1958.
5. Whalley, *op. cit.*, I, p. 443.
6. Whalley, *op. cit.*, II, p. 19.
7. Campbell, *op. cit.*, II, pp. 3–4.
8. Yvonne ffrench, who saw the original which is in private ownership, gives this example. See *Mrs Siddons, Tragic Actress* (1954), p. 67.

9. Boaden, *Memoirs of Mrs Siddons*; for the quotations which follow, see pp. 186–7, 192, 209, 308, 314–15.
10. See *Diary and Letters of Madame d'Arblay*, II, p. 343.
11. *Idem.*, III, p. 401.
12. *Thraliana*, II, p. 715.
13. *The Swan of Lichfield*, pp. 91–2.
14. Genest, *op. cit.*, VI, p. 251.
15. *Thraliana*, II, p. 725.
16. *Idem.*, p. 748.
17. *Piozziana*, pp. 85–6.
18. Boaden, *Memoirs of Mrs Siddons*, pp. 179–80. Mme de Staël comments on the noble person and profound feeling of Sarah Siddons which captivates Corinne, who finds the English style of acting more immediately moving, and far less formal than acting in France; she even finds the style of dramatic writing nearer to real life. Sarah Siddons never loses her dignity even when prostrate on the ground. Corinne is especially impressed by her performance as Isabella.
19. Mathews, *Memoirs*, II, pp. 165–7.
20. Tate Wilkinson, *Wandering Patentee*, II, p. 261.
21. Campbell, *op. cit.*, I, pp. 205–06.
22. As for sculptural monuments, there was eventually, but only after a struggle waged by Macready, the memorial installed in Westminster Abbey in 1849. This was a large statue by Thomas Campbell, the sculptor. A miniature sculpture by L. Chavalliaud stands in Paddington Green. Mrs Siddons executed a bust of herself, which is in the Dyce Collection at the Victoria and Albert Museum
23. Taylor, *Records of my Life*, 11, pp. 84–6.
24. Fitzgerald, *op. cit.*, I, pp. 216–17.
25. *Idem.*, pp. 256–7.
26. See Chapter 2, note 38. The letter to Mrs Soame is in the Harvard Theatre Collection. See also *Thraliana*, II, p. 714. Bedina Wynn added a MS. note to the letter: 'Mrs Siddons in this letter alludes to the recent Death of her youngest daughter Eliz. Ann Siddons, aged Six Years.' For the quotations following in the text, see Parsons, *op. cit.*, pp. 290–1. See also Chap. 2, note 38, and p. 360.
27. Whalley, *op. cit.*, II, p. 20.
28. Fitzgerald, op. cit., II, p. 286.
29. Sarah Siddons, *op. cit.*, pp. 22–3.
30. Whalley, *op. cit.*, I, p. 445. According to William, writing on 18 September to Sir Charles Hotham, they 'did her the honour to hear her read the part of Hamlet' while they were at Nuneham. See *The Hothams*, II, p. 225.
31. *Diary and Letters of Madame d'Arblay*, III, pp. 305–7.
32. Fitzgerald, *op. cit.*, II, pp. 292–4.

33. *Idem.*, II, pp. 289–90.
34. *Idem.*, p. 257.
35. *Idem.*, I, p. 218.
36. Whalley, *op. cit.*, I, pp. 478–9.
37. Whalley, *op. cit.*, I, p. 453.
38. *Idem.*, II, p. 17.
39. For further information about George Steevens's notorious prejudice against Mrs Siddons, see Boaden, *Memoirs of John Philip Kemble*, I, pp. 184 *et seq.*
40. Whalley, *op. cit.*, I, p. 478.
41. Boaden, *J. P. Kemble*, I, pp. 284–5.
42. Fitzgerald, *op. cit.*, I, p. 219.
43. Whalley, *op. cit.*, I, p. 453.
44. Fitzgerald, *op. cit.*, I, p. 258.
45. *Thraliana*, II, p. 681.
46. Whalley, *op. cit.*, II, p. 22.
47. *Thraliana*, II, p. 692.
48. See above, Chap. 3, note 14.
49. Fitzgerald, *op. cit.*, I, pp. 216 and 221–4. Letters 13, 15 March 1785.
50. *The Hothams*, II, pp. 232–3.
51. Whalley, *op. cit.*, I, p. 479.
52. *The Hothams*, II, p. 240.

Additional Note:

I am grateful to Miss Norah C. Gillow of the City of York Art Gallery for pointing out to me the existence of a summary of the life of Sarah Siddons in *The Yorkshire Magazine* of July 1786, p. 198 *et seq.* This must be the earliest known biographical study of the actress of any length.

NOTES: 5. THE KEMBLE PARTNERSHIP

1. Taylor, *Records of my Life*, I, p. 131 *et seq.*
2. Boaden, *Kemble*, I, pp. 91–2. See also for descriptions of Kemble's work, Odell, *Shakespeare – from Betterton to Irving*, and Bartholomeusz, *Macbeth and the Players*.
3. Boaden, *Kemble*, I, pp. 378–9.
4. *Idem*, I, p. 157.
5. *Idem.*, pp. 178–9.
6. *Idem.*, I, pp. 280–1.
7. *Idem.*, I, pp. 203–4.
8. *Idem.*, I, pp. 372–3.
9. Thomas Moore, *Memoirs . . . of Richard Brinsley Sheridan*, I, pp. 192–3.

10. Boaden, *Kemble*, I, pp. 407–8.
11. *Idem*, I., pp. 418–19.
12. Campbell, *op. cit.*, II, p. 157.
13. Campbell, *op. cit.*, II, p. 160.
14. Campbell, *op. cit.*, II, pp. 142–3.
15. While in the north, Sarah Siddons visited the Reverend William Mason, the eccentric old parson-dramatist, who had at first resented her because she seemed to have displaced his idol, Mrs Pritchard. For her account of this meeting in Sheffield, see Fitzgerald, *op. cit.*, II, 295–7.
16. Wilkinson, *The Wandering Patentee*, III, p. 102.
17. Fitzgerald, *op. cit.*, I, p. 269. See above p. 135.
18. Campbell, *op. cit.*, p. 129.
19. Fitzgerald, *op. cit.*, II, p. 295.
20. *Recollections of the Table-Talk of Samuel Rogers*, p. 134.
21. Fitzgerald, *op. cit.*, I, p. 316.
22. Campbell, *op. cit.*, II, p. 168.
23. For the theatres in the Haymarket, and their various names, see Mander and Mitchenson, *The Theatres of London*, p. 95 *et seq*. During the period with which we are concerned, the theatre on the site now occupied by the Theatre Royal, Haymarket, was first The Little Theatre (1720); it became the Theatre Royal in 1776; it was then replaced by a second theatre in 1821, slightly resited, and with the present Corinthian portico by John Nash. The theatre first on the site of the present Her Majesty's Theatre was the Queen's Theatre (1705), which was renamed the King's Theatre in 1714; this was followed by a second theatre in 1791, which was also known as the King's Theatre. This second theatre was renamed Her Majesty's in 1837. The present theatre, the fourth to be built on the site, was built in 1897.

    The King's Theatre was also known as the Opera House owing to the associations of the building with the performance of opera and ballet; during the period the Drury Lane company occupied the building, 1791–4, they brought their patent for the performance of plays with them.
24. *The Hothams*, II, p. 246.
25. *Thraliana*, II, p. 769.
26. *Thraliana*, II, p. 771.
27. Piozzi-Pennington, *Intimate Letters*, pp. 27–8.
28. *The Hothams*, II, pp. 250–1. Sir Lucas Pepys, a celebrated doctor, 1742–1830. After Jenner's discovery he was an active supporter of the National Vaccine Institution.
29. *Reminiscences of Michael Kelly*, I, p. 213.
30. Fitzgerald, *op. cit.*, II, p. 297 *et seq*.
31. Whalley, *op. cit.*, II, p. 50.

32. *Intimate Letters*, pp. 32, 39, 47.
33. *Thraliana*, II, p. 814.
34. *Idem.*, II, p. 816.
35. Whalley, *op. cit.*, II, p. 60.
36. Enthoven Collection, Victoria and Albert Museum, Siddons file.
37. ffrench, *op. cit.* (1936), quotes this, p. 175.
38. During this season, Kemble fought a duel with James Aickin, a member of the company who felt himself unfairly treated by Kemble as manager, and had said so in public. Another event of the period was the death of Sheridan's wife, the former Miss Linley, in June 1793.
39. Boaden, *Mrs Siddons*, p. 400.
40. *Idem.*, pp. 402–3.
41. Penelope Sophia Weston came from Bath and Ludlow, and was related to the Whalleys. William Pennington, an American Loyalist, was to become Master of Ceremonies at the Bristol Hot Wells. He was an eccentric; Penelope was a rather foolish woman, though Anna Seward refers to 'Sophia's heart, that mine of mental wealth'. Judging from her correspondence with Mrs Piozzi, she was very subject to nerves, depression and fainting fits.
42. *Intimate Letters*, p. 69.
43. *Thraliana*, II, p. 850.
44. *Idem.*, II, p. 808.
45. *Intimate Letters*, p. 74.
46. Rylands J.R.L. Eng MS. No. 574.
47. *Intimate Letters*, p. 98.
48. Rylands J.R.L. Eng MS. No. 574.
49. *Thraliana*, II, p. 867.
50. No actor appeared on the stage as the Ghost of Banquo. Both Boaden and Campbell object to this break with tradition. It was in this production that Edmund Kean appeared as a child; see text p. 167.
51. Boaden, *Kemble*, II, pp. 101–3.
52. See Peake, *Memoirs of the Colman Family*, II, p. 219; the quotation following is at p. 226.
53. Fitzgerald, *op. cit.*, p. 307.
54. Campbell, *op. cit.*, II, pp. 183–4.
55. Fitzgerald, *op. cit.*, I, pp. 309–10.
56. *Thraliana*, II, p. 876.
57. Rylands, J.R.L. Eng. MS. No. 574.
58. Fitzgerald, *op. cit.*, I, pp. 314–15.
59. Campbell, *op. cit.*, II, pp. 190–2.
60. Rylands, J.R.L. Eng. MS. No. 574.
61. Enthoven Collection, Siddons file.

62. The letter to Mrs Pennington is in *Intimate Letters*, p. 127. For the diary entry, see *Thraliana*, II, pp. 938–9.
63. Whalley, *op. cit.*, II, p. 100.
64. Campbell, *op. cit.*, II, p. 197.
65. The facts which follow are derived from Bernard Grebanier's *The Great Shakespeare Forgery* (1966).
66. Quoted by Grebanier, pp. 125–6. The quotation which follows is at p. 119.
67. John Taylor had in 1793 proposed to write Sarah Siddons's biography. She refused as politely as possible in a letter dated 3 August 1793, quoted by Campbell, II, p. 180.
68. Quoted by Grebanier, *op. cit.*, p. 201.
69. Campbell, *op. cit.*, II, p. 198.
70. Boaden, *Kemble*, II, p. 76.
71. Farington, *Diary*, I, p. 174.
72. Campbell, *op. cit.*, II, p. 202.
73. *Idem.*, II, p. 211.
74. *Idem.*, II, p. 213.
75. Whalley, *op. cit.*, II, p. 109.
76. Campbell, *op. cit.*, II, pp. 224–5. August Friedrich Ferdinand von Kotzebue (1761–1819) wrote plays which were popular throughout Europe. He worked in Vienna, Weimar and St Petersburg. He had an adventurous life; he was for a time deported to Siberia, and was finally stabbed to death in 1819. His style was melodramatic and romantically sensational without any real depth of feeling. His most popular play was *Menschenhass und Reue* (*The Stranger*).

NOTES: 6. LAWRENCE

The main references in this chapter are to the Lawrence-Siddons-Pennington letters preserved in the Library of the University of Cambridge, and for the most part published by Oswald G. Knapp in *An Artist's Love Story* (1904). The following numbered quotations in this chapter are derived from this book:

8. pp. 13–14; 9. pp. 16–17; 10. pp. 21–3; 12. pp. 26–7; 13. p. 29; 15. pp. 41–2; 18. pp. 43–4; 19. p. 47; 20. p. 48; 21. p. 52; 22. pp. 54–5; 23. pp. 57–9; 24. pp. 66–7; 25. pp. 69–70; 26. pp. 72–3; 27. pp. 74–5; 28. pp. 76–7; 29. p. 78; 30. p. 80; 31. pp. 81–2; 32. pp. 84–5; 33. pp. 86–7; 34. pp. 90–1; 35. pp. 91–2; 36. pp. 92–4; 37. pp. 96 *et seq.*; 38. pp. 102–03; 39. p. 110; 40. p. 115; 41. p. 131 *et seq.*; 42. p. 136; 43. p. 138; 44. p. 139; 45. pp. 140–1; 46. p. 142; 48. pp. 145–7; 49. pp. 148–50; 50. pp. 151–2; 51. p. 155; 52. pp. 156–8; 53. pp. 158–60; 54. pp. 169–70; 55. p. 171; 56. pp. 172–3; 57. pp. 174–5; 58. pp. 175–6;

59. p. 177; 60. p. 189; 61. p. 193; 62. p. 195; 63. p. 196; 64. pp. 206–7; 65. pp. 207–08; 66. p. 210; 67. p. 211; 68. p. 213; 69. pp. 214–15.

The remaining notes are:

1. See Goldring, *op. cit.*, pp. 99, 109–10. Charles Greville, the some-what cynical author of the famous *Diary* and a man with a nose for a scandal, but also an acute judge of character, believed Lawrence to be a homosexual, but there appears to be no evidence to support this. It became an amusing speculation for the gossips. John Russell, in *British Portrait Painters* (1940) wrote: 'In his personal affairs he seems to have suffered from some malady of the will. So marked, in fact, is this that he seems to epitomise that *impuissance d'aimer* with which readers of *Armance* and *Adolphe* are familiar.' George Somes Layard, editor of Lawrence's correspondence in *Sir Thomas Lawrence's Letter-bag*, although he claims to be more understanding of Lawrence than Knapp, compiler of *An Artist's Love Affair* (which he calls, 'an interesting, though I maintain unfair, story'), nevertheless writes: 'The fact cannot be blinked that Lawrence was one of those men who, without dishonourable or cruel intention, find their pleasure in hanging on to the skirts of this or that woman.'

2. The portrait of Elizabeth Farren can be seen reproduced in Goldring, *op. cit.*, opposite p. 48. Now in the United States, it was for a while the property of Pierpont Morgan. One critic wrote of it: 'It is completely Miss Farren – arch and careless, spirited and engaging.' The actress was angry that he had charged Lord Derby 100 guineas for it. His charges in 1793 were 40, 60 and 160 guineas according to the size and portrait length of the picture. Elizabeth Farren's letter can be found in *Sir Thomas Lawrence's Letter-bag*, pp. 14–15.

3. This picture, now in the National Portrait Gallery, has traditionally been said to be a portrait of Mrs Siddons as Mrs Haller in *The Stranger*. According to Kenneth Garlick in *Sir Thomas Lawrence*, it was probably the portrait of her exhibited in the Royal Academy in 1797. If so, it cannot be a portrait of Mrs Siddons as Mrs Haller, since this play was first produced only in March 1798. It was customary at the Royal Academy to label portraits of actors and actresses as 'Portrait of a Lady' or 'Gentleman', since acting was still a profession outside the higher social bracket. The trouble with Miss Farren, mentioned above, had begun because Lawrence had called the picture, thoughtlessly, 'Portrait of an Actress'.

4. *Sir Thomas Lawrence's Letter-bag*, p. 28.

5. *Satan summoning up his Legions* was regarded by Lawrence as his masterpiece; he never sold it. It is in the possession of the Royal

Academy. Pasquin wrote of it: 'The figure of Satan is colossal and very ill drawn . . . a mad German sugar-baker dancing naked in a conflagration of his own treacle.'

6. By 1797 Lawrence's finances were precarious, and this was well enough known to his friends. Farington's diary entry for 9 June 1797 reads:

> We had much talk of Lawrence. He has laid out on his House in Piccadilly at least £500 – His Academy room cost £150. . . . Lawrence is very close. . . . If his mind be set on a thing, he will have it, very proud. . . . His father has gone to reside with his sister in Gloucestershire (Anne, married in 1796 to the Rev Richard Bloxam, at St Anne's, Soho). The other sister (Lucy) to set up a School with a Miss Bird (the friend of the Siddons girls) from Birmingham. Lawrence to assist her is to give her the value of his picture by Rembrandt.

Lawrence owned Rembrandt's *Rabbi*, and was eventually to own several Rembrandts. Lawrence left the house in Piccadilly (rent 250 guineas a year, plus £80 tax) late in 1897, at great financial sacrifice, and established himself in Greek St, which was within easy reach of the Siddons's house in Great Marlborough Street. His father died in October, 1797. 'He died before I could reach him' wrote Lawrence, 'but he died full of affection for us.' His mother, whom Lawrence had drawn in 1797, had died in May of that year. Lawrence wrote to Sophia Lee in Bath: 'Have you seen death often. . . . But half an hour since, I had the dear hand in mine, and the fingers seemed unwilling to part with me.'

7. Knapp drew very fully on the letters now preserved in the Cambridge University Library. Only one complete letter seems to have been omitted among those written by Sarah Siddons. It is given later in this book. See p. 252.

11. *An Artist's Love Story*, pp. 23-4. As Knapp points out, however accurate Fanny may be over the mood of the situation, she confused the object of Lawrence's love. The situation she describes results from Lawrence's reversion to Sally, not when he left her for Maria.

14. *The Intimate Letters of Hester Piozzi and Penelope Pennington*, p. 183.

16. Goldring, *Regency Portrait Painter*, pp. 137-9. This letter, and the one which follows, were not available to Knapp when he compiled his book. They first appeared in *The Nineteenth Century and After* for April 1905, presented by Lady Priestley.

17. *Regency Portrait Painter*, pp. 139-40.

47. Campbell, *op. cit.*, II, p. 230. For Mrs FitzHugh see p. 323.

70. Some significant verses written by Lawrence to Miss Upton survive:

> Urg'd by no passion, Reason only blames,
> Cold in thyself, to guide the fatal flames,
> With nice discernment touch the starting nerve,
> And every torment curiously observe;
> Affect to soothe, but to inflame the pain,
> And drive the poison faster to the brain;
> And when no more thy victim can endure,
> But raging, supplicates thy soul for cure,
> Then, act the timid unsuspecting maid,
> And wonder at the mischief thou hast play'd
> . . . ash of Heav'n in mercy to forget
> The mean ambition of the cold Coquette.

See Goldring, *op. cit.*, p. 208.
71. *The Farington Diary*, III, pp. 25–6.

Additional Note:

Greville has his own comments to make on the Lawrence-Siddons relationship. Of Maria and Sally he writes: 'one tall and very handsome (Maria), the other little, without remarkable beauty, but clever and agreeable (Sally).' Of Lawrence, he wrote: 'he lived constantly and freely in the house'. He says that he was 'remarkably gentlemanlike, with very mild manners, though rather too *doucereux*, agreeable in society, unassuming, not a great talker; his mind was highly cultivated . . . .', and adds of the change in Lawrence's affections: 'They concealed the double treachery, but one day a note which was intended for his new love fell into the hands of the old love who, never doubting it was for herself, opened it and discovered the fatal truth.'

NOTES: 7. THE DANGEROUS YEARS

The main references in this chapter are to quotations from *Mrs Galindo's Letter to Mrs Siddons* (1809). Quotations with the numbers following are derived from this book:

20. p. 7; 21. pp. 8–9; 23. pp. 17–19; 24. pp. 22–3; 25. pp. 23–5; 26. pp. 28–9; 27. pp. 32–4; 28. p. 61; 29. p. 62; 30. p. 56; 31. pp. 57–9; 32. p. 67; 33. p. 54; 34. pp. 53–4; 35. pp. 55–6; 36. p. 70; 37. p. 70; 38. pp. 12–13; 41. p. 45; 42. p. 46; 43. p. 47; 44. pp. 47–8; 45. pp. 50–1; 55. pp. 59–60; 56. pp. 76–8.

The remaining notes are:

1. Sarah Siddons was nearly burned to death while acting Hermione. She described this incident herself:

The other night had very nearly terminated *all my exertions*, for whilst I was standing for the statue . . . my drapery flew over the lamps that were placed behind the pedestal; it caught fire, and had it not been for one of the scene-men, who most humanely crept on his knees and extinguished it, without my knowing anything of the matter, I might have been burnt to death. . . . Surrounded as I was with muslin, the flame would have run like wildfire. The bottom of the train was entirely burned. . . . I have well rewarded the good man.

See Campbell, *op. cit.*, II, p. 266.
2. Fitzgerald, *op. cit.*, II, p. 26.
3. Campbell, *op. cit.*, II, pp. 262–3.
4. *Intimate Letters*, p. 224.
5. Quoted by Yvonne ffrench, *op. cit.* (1936), pp. 216–17.
6. Stephen Kemble, however, decided to stay at Drury Lane.
7. Campbell, *op. cit.*, II, p. 277.
8. He was eighty-one. He was to appear on the stage as late as 1788 in a benefit for his daughter-in-law, Mrs Stephen Kemble. See Boaden, *Kemble*, I, p. 401.
9. Campbell, *op. cit.*, II, pp. 282–3.
10. My copy, bound in hard-cover, came originally from Hookham's Circulating Library, 45 Old Bond Street, London.
11. Mrs Clement Parsons adds, very oddly for a kindly biographer, that both writer and reader 'may be allowed one passing gleam of wicked gratification at its disclosure of a sporadic vanity and obtuseness in one so generally impeccable as "S. Siddons".' (Parsons, *op. cit.*, p. 224.)
12. There is a significant entry in Mrs Piozzi's diary as late as September 1801. She was, she says, told by Penelope Pennington 'that sweet Siddons receives anonymous letters perpetually to destroy her peace – reproaching her about dead Maria'. (*Thraliana*, II, p. 1029.)
13. Whalley, *op. cit.*, II, p. 30.
14. *Thraliana*, II, p. 991.
15. *Intimate Letters*, p. 193.
16. A letter to Mrs FitzHugh survives, dated 25 May (1801) in which Sarah makes it clear she is not in very close contact with Lawrence, to whom in the summer of 1800 she had loaned one of his portraits of her (the property of William) for copying. Lawrence kept it far too long, and angered William. Now Mrs FitzHugh wanted him to make another copy for herself. William was being stubborn about a second loan of the picture. See the Morrison Collection of Autograph Letters, 1892, Vol. VI, p. 130. Mrs FitzHugh lived at Bannisters Lodge, Bannisters, near Southampton, and was the wife of the Member of Parliament for Tiverton, Devon. She was

an intimate friend, who often frequented Sarah's dressing-room. See also the additional note to Chapter 2, p. 322.

17. *Thraliana*, II, p. 1052.
18. *Thraliana*, II, p. 1070.
19. I am grateful to Miss Kathleen Barker for pointing out to me that Galindo was with the Bath company from 1793–9, though there is no record of Catherine Galindo being in the company. There was, however, a Miss Galindo who played occasional children's parts from the spring of 1798.
22. Fitzgerald, *op. cit.*, II, pp. 42–3.
39. Campbell, *op. cit.*, II, pp. 290–2.
40. *Idem.*, II, p. 293.
46. Fitzgerald, *op. cit.*, II, p. 95.
47. Farington, II, p. 198. Farington has this entry on 8 August 1805. 'Lawrence drank tea with me. He was uneasy abt. reports arising from *paragraphs*. I advised Him to disregard them and to *live against* all Calumny so as to disprove it.'
48. For the extraordinary career of Master Betty, see Giles Playfair, *The Prodigy* (1967). William Henry Best (1791–1874) took London by storm 1804–5, playing many of the great Shakespearian roles in his early teens. He eventually became a student at Cambridge; his attempts to return to the stage in adult life failed.
49. Rylands, J.R.L. Eng. MS. No. 574.
50. Ditto.
51. Boaden, *op. cit.*, p. 430.
52. Campbell, *op. cit.*, p. 315.
53. Farington, II, p. 254.
54. Rylands, J.R.L. Eng. MS. No. 574.
57. Quoted by Mrs Parsons, *op. cit.*, p. 227.
58. Campbell, *op. cit.*, II, pp. 319–20.
59. First printed in Payne Collier's *An Old Man's Diary*, and quoted by Mrs Parsons, *op. cit.*, pp. 74–5.
60. Fitzgerald, *op. cit.*, II, p. 305.
61. Quoted by Yvonne ffrench, *op. cit.* (1936), p. 246. Pictures survive of this beautiful little house, the site for which has long since been built over to make the block bounded by Woodchester Street, Harrow Road and Cirencester Street, in the Paddington area. The exact position the house occupied is known, and was described as late as 1934 by an elderly doctor who had known it as a boy: 'The house stood back from the main Harrow Road at (an) angle between it and the canal, a garden occupying a small space between it and the road. . . . I clearly see it still, the small path did not altogether pass by the side of her study, but actually *faced* it partly.' See a small undated pamphlet, *Mrs Siddons*, published by the Siddonian Housing Association Limited.

NOTES: 8. 'GRATEFUL MEMORY'

1. Campbell, *op. cit.*, II, pp. 322–3.
2. Boaden, *Kemble*, II, pp. 458–9.
3. *Catalogue of the Collection of Autograph Letters . . . formed by Alfred Morrison*, VI (1892), p. 132.
4. Letter preserved in the Folger Shakespeare Library. It is of interest to note that on 24 February 1809, Holland's Drury Lane was also gutted by fire. Dora Jordan was playing there and, like Charles Mathews, at least managed to rescue her private property. See Boaden, *Mrs Siddons*, p. 443.
5. Letter preserved in the Folger Shakespeare Library.
6. Campbell, *op. cit.*, II, pp. 325–7.
7. Boaden, *Kemble*, 11, p. 499. Boaden gives some interesting statistics on the relative distances in the theatre for the spectators when viewing the stage; see p. 491. For example, in the two-shilling gallery the back row was 100 feet from the stage door; in the upper gallery the spectator in the back row was 104 feet away. The theatre used 270 wax candles a night; 300 'patent lamps' lit the stage. The rise in seat prices which caused the riots and other disturbances was one shilling more for the boxes and sixpence for the pit, the prices becoming 7s for boxes, 4s for the pit, 2s and 1s for the remote galleries.
8. Letter in the Folger collection. Harriott Murray had been an actress at Covent Garden. I am grateful to Miss Kathleen Barker for pointing out that her mother and father had been in the company at Bristol on 15 February 1796 when Henry Siddons had played *Othello* – a single appearance; he may have met his future wife for the first time on that occasion.
9. Campbell, *op. cit.*, II, pp. 328–9.
10. *Farington Diary*, VII, p. 37. Farington also records that during September 1811, Kemble was offered £6,000 to go to the United States for a season. At Covent Garden, all he took was 12 guineas a night, while his sister received 50 guineas. Receipts at Covent Garden were reputed to be £104,000 for the previous season.
11. She also appeared in Edinburgh from 22 February to 13 March. See Dibdin, *op. cit.*, p. 266.
12. *Farington Diary*, VII, pp. 88–9.
13. Letter preserved in the Folger Shakespeare Collection.
14. A list of her reappearances is given by Campbell, *op. cit.*, II, p. 336:

> May 25, 1813, she acted gratis for the Theatrical Fund. Drury Lane, June 22, she acted for the same charity. June 11, 1813, at Covent Garden, for Charles Kemble's benefit. At Edinburgh, November 1815, ten times, for the family of her deceased son.

May 31, 1816, at Covent Garden, for the benefit of Mr and Mrs C. Kemble. June 8 and 22, 1816, by the express desire of the Princess Charlotte (Princess Charlotte and Prince Leopold of Saxe-Coburg, neither of whom had seen her act). June 29, for the Theatrical Fund. June 5, 1817, for Charles Kemble's benefit. June 9, 1819, for the benefit of Mr and Mrs C. Kemble.

She also gave readings, including, for example, one for the Royal Family at Windsor which she describes in a letter to Mrs FitzHugh; see Campbell, II, pp. 344–9. For two seasons she gave public readings in the Argyll Rooms – see Boaden, *Mrs Siddons*, p. 457 *et seq*. She earned considerable fees from these recitals, which were not confined to London. See Parsons, *op. cit.*, pp. 271–2.

15. Campbell, *op. cit.*, II, pp. 355–7.
16. See *Byron*, by Leslie Marchand, I, p. 309; II, p. 534. (See p. 342.)
17. Hazlitt, *Criticism and Dramatic Essays* (Routledge, 1851), pp. 276–7. Hazlitt saw Mrs Siddons on the occasion of her performance for Princess Charlotte in June 1816.
18. Hazlitt, in his celebrated essay on *Macbeth* in *Characters of Shakespeare's Plays*.
19. Hazlitt, *Criticism and Dramatic Essays* (Routledge, 1851), pp. 50–1.
20. Crabb Robinson, *The London Theatre 1811–1866*, p. 70.
21. *Idem.*, p. 72.
22. See Haydon, *The Autobiographical Journals* (1950), p. 350.
23. Fanny Kemble, *Record of a Girlhood*, I, pp. 15–16.
24. Haydon, *op. cit.*, p. 333.
25. See Parsons, *op. cit.*, pp. 264 and 282. In the latter year of her meeting with Washington Irving, Mrs Siddons published her only work, a selection from *Paradise Lost*, entitled *The Story of Our First Parents: selected from Milton's Paradise Lost, for the use of Young Persons, by Mrs Siddons*.
26. Campbell, *op. cit.*, II, p. 366.
27. *Idem.*, II, p. 359.
28. *Idem.*, II, p. 360.
29. *Morrison Collection*, VI, p. 133.
30. Fanny Kemble, *op. cit.*, II, p. 64.
31. *Sir Thomas Lawrence's Letter-bag*, p. 189.
32. *Idem.*, p. 209.
33. Witness her illuminating but ruthless description of her aunt, Mrs Whitlock (Sarah's sister, Elizabeth):

She was a very worthy but exceedingly ridiculous woman, in whom the strong peculiarities of her family were so exaggerated, that she really seemed like a living caricature of all the Kembles. She was a larger and taller woman than Mrs Siddons, and had a fine, commanding figure at the time I am speaking of, when she was quite an elderly person. She was like her brother Stephen in face, with handsome features, too large and strongly marked for a woman, light grey eyes, and a light auburn wig, which, I presume, represented the colour of her previous hair, and which, together with the tall cap that surmounted it, was always more or less on one side. She had the deep, sonorous voice and extremely distinct utterance of her family, and an extraordinary vehemence of gesture and expression quite unlike their quiet dignity and reserve of manner, and which made her conversation like that of people in old plays and novels; for she would slap her thigh in emphatic enforcement of her statements (which were apt to be upon an incredibly large scale), not unfrequently prefacing them with the exclamation, 'I declare to God!' or 'I wish I may die!' all which seemed to us very extraordinary, and combined with her large size and loud voice used occasionally to cause us some dismay.

For Fanny Kemble's unsympathetic and overbearing nature in later life, see the descriptions by Mrs Lynn Linton in *Sir Thomas Lawrence's Letter-bag*, pp. 223–34.

34. Fanny Kemble, *Record of a Girlhood*, pp. 43–5.
35. *Idem.*, p. 46.
36. Timbs in his *Anecdote Biography* supports this view by Lawrence, and quotes from the letter to Angerstein alluded to in the text immediately below.
37. *Sir Thomas Lawrence's Letter-bag*, p. 219.
38. *Idem.*, pp. 218–19.
39. Lawrence's letters to Fanny unfortunately appear not to have survived. Hers to him from the period October 1829 are reproduced in the *Letter-bag*.
40. *Letter-bag*, pp. 222–3.
41. Goldring, *op. cit.*, pp. 329–30.
42. Mrs Siddons was buried in the churchyard of St Mary's, Paddington; over her grave is the inscription 'Sacred to the Memory of Sarah Siddons, who departed this life June 8th, 1831, in her 76th year. Blessed are the dead that die in the Lord.' She selected the text herself. For the memorial to her in Westminster Abbey, see above Chapter 4, note 22.

Additional Notes:

i. Fanny Kemble claims (*Record of a Girlhood*, III, p. 100) that Thomas Campbell, Mrs Siddons's chosen biographer, behaved boorishly over the task, and conducted his researches as if continuously resentful of the work involved. He prevented Anna Jameson from undertaking her projected biography; as she says in her Preface to

Shakespeare's Heroines, 'When the first edition was sent to press, the author contemplated writing the Life of Mrs Siddons with a reference to her art', especially her performance as Lady Macbeth, but the task fell 'into other hands'.

Cyrus Redding, a close confidant of Campbell, gives an extraordinary picture of Campbell at work in his *Literary Reminiscences and Memoir of Thomas Campbell* (1860). 'The death of Mrs Siddons, and the request she made of the poet, that he would be her biographer, has caused him to set about the task as a reluctant duty. The style of the book is foreign to that of his former works. It is a biography on stilts.' Campbell took the work to heart 'almost ludicrously'. He 'talked of it, and wrote about it to everybody'. He put up a notice on the door of his chambers 'that he could not be disturbed, being busy about the biography of Mrs Siddons.' He told Redding it was a 'burthen he had brought upon himself. . . . "I have promised to finish it and I will; but it will knock me up".'

Redding was not very attracted to Mrs Siddons, and he quotes Byron: 'Byron said he should as soon think of going to bed with the Archbishop of Canterbury as with Mrs Siddons.'

Campbell, unlike Boaden, her other contemporary biographer, was not a man of the theatre. As Redding says, 'he had never mixed, as a matter of amusement, with the Thespian corps behind the scenes. . . . He was not versed, if it may be so termed, in the *patois* of the theatre.' After the publication of the book in 1834, Campbell took himself off for a holiday in Algiers.

ii. I am grateful to Mr Gerald Burden for drawing my attention to a letter by Sir Walter Scott written from Edinburgh on 27 March 1813 and addressed to Messrs Longman and Co., in which he refuses to support the recall of Mrs Siddons to the stage. 'Such a parting as took place between her and the public suited her genius and their gratitude,' he wrote.

. . . When Mrs Siddons was last here her health was extremely indifferent and while her performance on the stage retaind its inimitable excellence it seemed to me that her constitution was gradually becoming less able to support the fatigues of her profession. The moment of retreat to private life therefore seemed to me well-chosen while she yet enjoyed the full possession of her powers. . . . The same feeling with regard to Mrs Siddons is universal among literary persons here.

(*The Letters of Sir Walter Scott*, Vol. III, pp. 243–5; edited by H. J. C. Grierson, 1932.)

Appendices

═══════════════◦ᢒᡊᢙ◦═══════════════

NOTE GIVING THE GENERAL HISTORICAL BACKGROUND TO THE PERIOD OF SARAH SIDDONS'S ASCENDANCY IN THE THEATRE

It may be useful to summarize certain historical facts for the period of Sarah Siddons's ascendancy in the London theatre, starting in the 1780s and closing with her retirement in 1812. George III (1738–1820) of the House of Hanover reigned from 1760 to 1820; his final mental collapse came in 1811, when his eldest son, George, by Queen Charlotte (of Mecklenburg-Strelitz), became Prince Regent. The Prince (1762–1830), the future George IV, had as Prince of Wales created his own, quite different social circle, distinct from that of the Court; he had married Mrs Fitzherbert clandestinely in 1785, and Caroline of Brunswick officially in 1795. He built the Pavilion at Brighton in 1784.

Key political events during the period include the recognition in 1783 of the independence of the United States, the development of British governmental power in India, the impeachment of Warren Hastings, former Governor-General of Bengal, by Burke, Fox and R. B. Sheridan, the wars with France – first the Revolutionary war (1793–1802) and, second, the Napoleonic War (1803–15), when Napoleon threatened the invasion of England (Trafalgar, 1805; the Peninsular War, 1808–14; Wellington's successive invasions of Spain, 1809–14; Waterloo, 1815). The Younger Pitt (1759–1806), who stood for free trade, economic reform and control of public accounts, and was an advocate of Parliamentary reform, Catholic emancipation, and the abolition of the Slave Trade, was Chancellor of the Exchequer in 1882, and Prime Minister from 1783–1801 and 1804–5. At first he opposed war with revolutionary France, but finally decided that it was necessary for the security of Britain. Burke's *Reflections on the French Revolution* appeared in 1790, and Thomas Paine was prosecuted in 1792 for his response to it, *The Rights of Man*.

In literature, the period saw the romantic revival in poetry, and sentimentalism and 'Gothic' horror in the popular novel. A selection of publications of the period includes: Fanny Burney, *Cecilia* (1782); William Cowper, *Poems* (1782); William Blake, *Poetical Sketches* (1783); Thomas Crabbe, *The Village* (1783); Cowper, *John Gilpin* (1785); William Beckford, *Vathek* (1786); Robert Burns, *Poems* (1786); Blake, *Songs of Innocence* (1789); Boswell, *Life of Johnson* (1791); Blake, *Songs of Experience* (1794); Ann Radcliffe, *The Mysteries of Udolpho* (1794); Thomas Paine, *The Age of Reason* (1794–5); M. G. Lewis, *The Monk* (1795); William Wordsworth and S. T. Coleridge,

Lyrical Ballads (1798); T. R. Malthus, *Essay on the Principle of Population* (1798); Thomas Campbell, *The Pleasures of Hope* (1799); Marie Edgeworth, *Castle Rackrent* (1800); Walter Scott, *The Lay of the Last Minstrel* (1805); Wordsworth, 'The Prelude' (completed 1805) and 'Ode on Intimations of Immortality' (1807); Walter Scott, *Marmion* (1808); Lord Byron, *English Bards and Scots Reviewers* (1809); Jane Austen, *Sense and Sensibility* (1811); Byron, *Childe Harold's Pilgrimage* (1812–18).

Abroad in literature, this was the period of Schiller, Goethe (who became director of the Weimar Theatre in 1791), Chateaubriand, Anne de Staël, Benjamin Constant, Washington Irving.

In music, this was the age of Haydn, Mozart (died 1791), Beethoven, Paganini, and Rossini.

In the graphic arts, it was the time of Fuseli, Guardi, Canova, Goya, Houdon, David, Reynolds, Rowlandson, Gainsborough, Opie, Romney, de Wilde, Turner, Girtin, Raeburn. In architecture, it was a period of expansion for most cities, such as Edinburgh and London. John Nash began work on Regent Street in London in 1811.

In sport and social life, the M.C.C. moved to Lord's cricket ground, Dorset Square, Marylebone, and codified the cricket laws (1787–8); horse-racing was established at Goodwood in 1802; the Ascot Gold Cup was first given in 1807; and the 2,000 Guineas was established at Newmarket Races in 1809. The waltz was introduced into English ballrooms in 1812, the year of Mrs Siddons's retirement.

In religion, this was the period of dissent. John Wesley signed the declaration, or charter of Wesleyan Methodism in 1784; the Sunday School movement began in 1785; and the Baptist Union was formed in 1812.

For the press, John Walters founded *The Times* in 1788; *The Observer* was established in 1791, the *Edinburgh Review* in 1802, Leigh Hunt's *Examiner* in 1808, and the *Quarterly Review* in 1809.

The census of 1800–1801 showed that Great Britain had a population of 10·4 million, and Ireland 5·2 million. The population of the United States was at that time 5·3 million. London was the largest capital in Europe, with 864,000 inhabitants; New York had 60,500.

II

THE PRINCIPAL NON-SHAKESPEARIAN PLAYS IN WHICH SARAH SIDDONS PLAYED AT DRURY LANE AND COVENT GARDEN THEATRES

THE CARMELITE   Richard Cumberland. First presented at Drury Lane with Sarah Siddons as Matilda in 1784.

Romantic drama set spectacularly in Norman times. The plot turns on a long-lost husband (Saint Vallori) whose twenty-year absence is lamented by the Lady of Saint Vallori, Matilda. Matilda wrongly imagines her husband to be dead, and she raises her son by him, Montgomeri (played by John Philip Kemble) as her page without revealing his identity to him. The play has a happy end.

A typical speech is that of Matilda when the supposed murderer of her husband speaks to her of mercy:

Matilda: Mercy! – and dare thy tongue pronounce the name?
Mercy! – thou man of blood, thou hast destroy'd it.
It came from heaven to save St Vallori.
You saw the cherub messenger alight
From its descent: with outspread wings it sat
Covering his breast: you drew your cursed steel,
And through the pleading angel pierc'd his heart!

DOUGLAS   John Home. First presented in Edinburgh in 1756; Covent Garden 1757. Drury Lane 1783, with Sarah Siddons as Lady Randolph.

Another drama of mistaken identity, the story of this play is taken from the ballad *Gil Morrice*, later included in Percy's *Reliques of Ancient English Poetry*. Lady Randolph recognizes in Douglas her long-lost son by a former, secret marriage. The attention she pays him raises the jealousy of her present husband who, roused by the Iago-like Glenalvon – his heir (since he has no children by Lady Randolph) – murders Douglas. After the truth is known, Lady Randolph kills herself. The part of Lady Randolph was first created by Mrs Crawford in London. The original performance of this highly moral play in Edinburgh led to an inflated controversy in the Church of Scotland. Home, a minister of the Kirk, was forced to resign; he went to London and became tutor to the Prince of Wales. Later he returned to Scotland, where he met Mrs Siddons in his old age and saw her perform in his play.

THE EARL OF WARWICK   Thomas Franklin. First presented at Drury
Lane in 1766. Revived, with Sarah Siddons as Margaret of Anjou,
at Drury Lane in 1784.

Adapted from La Harpe's *Le Comte de Warwick* (1753), this play shows
the machinations of Margaret of Anjou, Henry VI's Queen, in relation
to the love of young Edward for Lady Elizabeth Grey.

THE FAIR PENITENT   Nathaniel Rowe, 1703. Presented at Drury Lane
in 1782, with Sarah Siddons as Calista.

Adaptation (with modifications and a change of names for certain
characters) of Massinger's *The Fatal Dowry*. The play remained in
Sarah Siddons's standard repertory at least until 1805. She played
Calista, a girl given in marriage against her will and whose husband
murders her after she has been discovered together with her former
suitor, whom he kills in a duel.

THE GAMESTER   Edward Moore. Originally produced at Drury Lane
in 1753. Revived with Sarah Siddons as Mrs Beverley at Drury
Lane in 1783.

A moral, domestic tragedy, written in prose. Beverley, a gambler, is
led astray by a false friend, Stukely, who covets Beverley's wife.
Beverley squanders his fortune and finally his wife's jewels. Lewson,
who is in love with Beverley's sister Charlotte, discovers Stukely's
villainy, whereupon Stukely attempts to have him murdered. Beverley,
in prison for debt, takes poison, only to discover too late that he has
inherited another fortune. Beverley, Garrick's old part, was taken over
by Kemble. Sarah Siddons played Beverley's long-suffering wife,
whose eyes are opened to the truth about Stukely when he makes
unwelcome advances to her. Mrs Siddons was then able to bring out
the full moral note so beloved by audiences in the late eighteenth
century.

THE GRECIAN DAUGHTER   Arthur Murphy. First presented at Drury
Lane in 1772. Revived at Drury Lane in 1782 with Sarah Siddons
as Euphrasia.

Written originally for Mrs Crawford, the play is a legendary melodrama
set in Syracuse – 'a Wild Romantick scene amidst overhanging Rocks'.
The story is that of the Grecian daughter, Euphrasia, who, having had
her baby torn from her, suckles her starving father. She proves to be
an Amazonian kind of woman. She pours scorn on Dionysius, the
usurper, her husband Phocion's enemy, and finally stabs him to death
in defence of her father. The part appealed to Sarah Siddons, who at

one point wanted to make it her first when she reappeared in London.
A typical speech by Euphrasia is:

> And dost thou then, inhuman that thou art,
> Advise a wretch like me to know repose?
> This is my last abode; these caves, these rocks,
> Shall ring for ever with Euphrasia's wrongs;
> Here will I dwell, and rave, and shriek, and giving
> These scatter'd locks to all the passing winds,
> Stand on the cliff in madness and despair!

ISABELLA, or, THE FATAL MARRIAGE   Thomas Southerne, 1694. First
presented at Drury Lane in 1757, and revived with Sarah Siddons
as Isabella in 1782.

Garrick's version of Southerne's *The Fatal Marriage*, or *The Innocent
Adultress*, was a display-piece of theatrical pathos, originally written
for Mrs Barry and Betterton. Isabella, an impoverished widow, rejects
Villeroy, her wealthy suitor, out of faithfulness to the memory of her
husband, Biron. Her father-in-law treats her cruelly, seeking to take
her child from her and disinherit her. Pressed by her creditor, Count
Baldwin, Isabella finally weds Villeroy. Her happiness is dawning in
this second marriage when Biron turns up in Act IV. Isabella spends
the rest of the play in increasing lamentation and despair. When Biron
is mortally wounded in a brawl and dies in her arms, she goes mad and
kills herself. The following lines, spoken by Isabella in her despair,
come near the end of the play:

> . . . 'tis better with me,
> Conflicting Passions have at last unhing'd
> The great Machine; the Soul itself seem'd chang'd:
> O, 'tis a happy Revolution here!
> The reas'ning Faculties are all depos'd,
> Judgment, and Understanding, common Sense,
> Driv'n out, as Traitors to the publick Peace
> Now I'm reveng'd upon my Memory,
> Her Seat dug up, where all the images
> Of a long mis-spent Life, were rising still,
> To glare a sad Reflection of my Crimes,
> And stab a Conscience thro' 'em: You are safe,
> You Monitors of Mischief! What a Change!
> Better and better still!

The final relief of madness is expressed in lines which achieve a
genuine poetry:

This is the Infant State
Of innocence, before the Birth of Care.
My Thoughts are smooth as the Elysian Plains
Without a Rub: The drowsie falling Streams
Invite me to their Slumbers.
Would I were landed there –

JANE SHORE   Nicholas Rowe (1713). Revived at Drury Lane in 1782
   with Sarah Siddons in the title role.

Jane Shore, once the mistress of Edward IV, is now in a violent condition of repentance. She is destitute and starving; pursued by her enemies, she finally dies of hunger, but not before she has challenged the tyrant Gloucester and expressed her feeling for Edward's memory. The play depends on types rather than characters, rhetoric rather than poetry, but since the pathos is exploited with considerable dramatic skill, the play remained a great favourite with both actors and audiences. Typical speeches spoken by Mrs Siddons as Jane Shore are:

In the mood of penitence –

Such is the fate unhappy women find,
And such the curse entailed upon our kind,
That man, the lawless libertine, may rove
Free and unquestioned through the wilds of love;
While woman, sense and nature's easy fool,
If poor weak woman swerve from virtue's rule,
If, strongly charmed, she leave the thorny way,
And in the softer paths of pleasure stray;
Ruin ensues, reproach and endless shame,
And one false step entirely damns her fame.
In vain with tears the loss she may deplore,
In vain look back to what she was before,
She sets, like stars that fall, to rise no more.

Dwelling on her memories of Edward –

No, though the royal Edward has undone me,
He was my king, my gracious master still;
He loved me too, though 'twas a guilty flame,
And fatal to my peace, yet still he loved me;
With fondness and with tenderness he doted,
Dwelt in my eyes, and lived but in my smiles,
And can I – Oh, my heart abhors the thought! –
Stand by and see his children robbed of right ?

Challenging her persecutors –

> No, arm thy brow with vengeance; and appear
> The minister of Heaven's inquiring justice.
> Array thyself all terrible for judgment,
> Wrath in thy eyes, and thunder in thy voice;
> Pronounce my sentence, and if yet there be
> A woe I have not felt, inflict it on me.

THE MOURNING BRIDE   William Congreve (1697). Revived at Drury
Lane in 1783 with Sarah Siddons as Zara.

Congreve's only tragedy, set in Granada. Alphonso of Valencia is
taken captive by Manuel, King of the enemy state of Granada.
Alphonso is secretly married to Almeria, Manuel's daughter. Manuel
orders Alphonso to be murdered, and then decides to impersonate him
in prison in order to confront his guilty daughter. He is, however,
murdered in Alphonso's place. Zara, a Moorish queen who is also a
captive and in love with Alphonso, assumes it is he who is dead, and
poisons herself in despair. Alphonso and Almeria are united.

PIZARRO   Freely adapted, mainly by R. B. Sheridan, from Friedrich
Ferdinand von Kotzebue's play, *Rolla's Tod*. Presented at Drury
Lane in 1799, with Sarah Siddons as Elvira.

'Carry your wonder to Mrs Siddons,' said Kemble to Boaden, 'she
has made a heroine out of a soldier's trull.' In this play, Elvira, once the
beloved of the Spanish conqueror Pizarro, conspires to make the noble
Peruvian, Rolla (played by John Philip Kemble) kill Pizarro in his
sleep; but he wakes him at the last moment, much as if Macbeth had
waked Duncan in the presence of Lady Macbeth. Elvira, claiming
responsibility for the attempt, is imprisoned, but escapes; her actions
inspire Rolla's friend, Alonzo, finally to murder Pizarro. Elvira then
devotes herself to a religious life in a cloister and expiates her guilt.
Before assuming a nun's habit, Sarah Siddons was dressed in an
Amazonian style befitting her presence in the camp. The play is written
in a curious verse-prose: this is Elvira facing the challenge of Pizarro's
wrath:

> Yes; rack me with the sharpest tortures that ever agoniz'd the human
> frame, it will be justice! Yes; bid the minions of thy fury *wrench forth*
> the *sinews* of those arms that have caress'd thee – even have defended
> thee! Bid them pour *burning metal* into the *bleeding cases* of these
> eyes, that so oft – oh, God! have hung with love and homage on thy
> looks! – then approach me bound on the abhorred wheel – there
> glut thy savage eyes with the *convulsive spasms* of that dishonoured
> bosom which was once thy pillow!

THE STRANGER   Adapted by Benjamin Thompson from Kotzebue's play, *Menschenhass und Reue*, and worked over by Sheridan. Presented at Drury Lane in 1798, with Mrs Siddons as Mrs Haller.

A play in prose, and notable as a contemporary drama, as distinct from the usual period play favoured by Kemble and Mrs Siddons. Mrs Adelaide Haller, housekeeper to the Count and Countess Wintersen, has run away from her husband and children following a love affair which has ended. She is now consumed by guilt. Meanwhile, a Stranger (played by John Philip Kemble) has arrived and taken up lodgings at the castle gates. The Countess discovers that Mrs Haller is in fact her social equal, the former Countess Waldbourg, living now under this assumed name. A further complication is that Countess Wintersen's young brother, Baron Steinfort, is in love with Mrs Haller. But the Stranger is no less than the husband she has abandoned, come back to claim her. But Mrs Haller remains determined to continue in her state of penitence until the sight of her children finally reunites the family. The dialogue was singularly stilted. Here is an exchange between the Baron, who is wooing Mrs Haller, and the lady, played by Mrs Siddons:

Mrs Haller: Oh, my lord! you cannot imagine how quickly time passes when a certain uniformity guides the minutes of our life. How often do I ask, 'Is Saturday come again so soon?' On a bright cheerful morning my books and breakfast are carried out upon the grass plot. Then is the sweet picture of reviving industry, and eager innocence, always new to me. The birds' notes so often heard, still awaken new ideas: the herds are led into the fields: the peasant bends his eye upon his plough. Every thing lives and moves; and in every creature's mind it seems as it were morning. Towards evening I begin to roam abroad: from the park into the meadows. And, sometimes, returning, I pause to look at the village boys and girls as they play. Then do I bless their innocence, and pray to Heaven those laughing thoughtless hours, could be their lot for ever.
Baron: This is excellent! – But these are summer amusements. – The winter! the winter!
Mrs Haller: Why for ever picture winter like old age, torpid, tedious, and uncheerful? Winter has its own delights: this is the time to instruct and mend the mind by reading and reflection. At this season, too, I often take my harp, and amuse myself by playing or singing the little favourite airs that remind me of the past, or solicit hope for the future.

The end of the play is remarkable for its reflection of the romanticism which sprang from eighteenth-century 'sensibility'.

Mrs Haller: Forget a wretch who never will forget you. – And when my penance shall have broken my heart – when we again meet in a better world –

Stranger: There, Adelaide, you may be mine again. (*They part, weeping, but, as they are going, she encounters the Boy, and he the Girl*)

Children: Dear father! Dear mother! (*They press the Children in their arms with speechless affection; then tear themselves away – gaze at each other – spread their arms, and rush into an embrace. The children run, and cling round their Parents.*) THE CURTAIN FALLS.

VENICE PRESERVED   Thomas Otway (1682). Presented at Drury Lane in 1782 with Sarah Siddons as Belvidera.

Jaffier (originally played by Betterton) is a noble young Venetian secretly married to Belvidera (originally played by Mrs Barry, for whom Otway suffered an unrequited love). Belvidera is the daughter of Priuli, a senator, who has disowned her. Unknown at first to Belvidera, Jaffier has become involved in a conspiracy against the state; the conspiracy is led by Renault, who tries to seduce Belvidera. When Jaffier tells her of the conspiracy, she persuades him to reveal it to the Senate, provided the conspirators' lives may be spared. They are, in fact, condemned to death. Jaffier, filled with remorse at having betrayed his companions, threatens Belvidera's life if she does not secure their reprieve though her father. She succeeds, but too late to save them. Jaffier commits suicide, and Belvidera goes mad and kills herself.

III

SARAH SIDDONS'S REPERTORY AT
DRURY LANE THEATRE

(Reproduced by courtesy of Miss Yvonne ffrench
from her book, *Mrs Siddons, Tragic Actress*)

Season	Character	Play	Author
1782–3	ISABELLA	*Isabella, or, The Fatal Marriage*	Southerne
	EUPHRASIA	*The Grecian Daughter*	Murphy
	JANE SHORE	*Jane Shore*	Rowe
	MRS MONTAGUE	*The Fatal Interview*	Hull
	CALISTA	*The Fair Penitent*	Rowe
	BELVIDERA	*Venice Preserved*	Otway
	ZARA	*The Mourning Bride*	Congreve
1783–4	ISABELLA	*Measure for Measure*	Shakespeare
	MRS BEVERLEY	*The Gamester*	Moore
	CONSTANCE	*King John*	Shakespeare
	LADY RANDOLPH	*Douglas*	Home
	COUNTESS OF SALISBURY	*The Countess of Salisbury*	Hartson
	SIGISMUNDA	*Tancred and Sigismunda*	Thomson
1784–5	MARGARET OF ANJOU	*Earl of Warwick*	Franklin
	ZARA	*Zara*	Voltaire (arr. Hill)
	MATILDA	*The Carmelite*	Cumberland
	CAMIOLA	*The Maid of Honour*	Massinger
	LADY MACBETH	*Macbeth*	Shakespeare
	DESDEMONA	*Othello*	Shakespeare
	ELFRIDA	*Elfrida*	Mason
	ROSALIND	*As You Like It*	Shakespeare
1785–6	THE DUCHESS	*Braganza*	Jephson
	MRS LOVEMORE	*The Way to Keep Him*	Murphy
	HERMIONE	*The Distressed Mother*	Racine (arr. Phillips)
	MALVINA	*The Captives*	Delap
	PORTIA	*The Merchant of Venice*	Shakespeare

Season	Character	Play	Author
	ELWINA	*Percy*	Hannah More
	OPHELIA	*Hamlet*	Shakespeare
	THE LADY	*Comus*	Milton
1786–7	CLEONE	*Cleone*	Dodsley
	IMOGEN	*Cymbeline*	Shakespeare
	COUNTESS OF NARBONNE	*The Count of Narbonne*	Jephson
	LADY RESTLESS	*All in the Wrong*	Murphy
	JULIA	*Julia; or The Italian Lover*	Jephson
	ALICIA	*Jane Shore*	Rowe
1787–8	CORDELIA	*King Lear*	Shakespeare
	CHELONICE	*The Fate of Sparta*	Mrs Cowley
	KATHARINE	*Katharine and Petruchio*	Garrick (after Shakespeare)
	DIANORA	*The Regent*	Greatheed
	CLEOPATRA	*All for Love*	Dryden
1788–9	QUEEN KATHARINE	*King Henry VIII*	Shakespeare
	VOLUMNIA	*Coriolanus*	Shakespeare
	THE PRINCESS	*The Law of Lombardy*	Jephson
	THE FINE LADY	*Lethe*	Garrick
	MARY QUEEN OF SCOTS	*Mary Queen of Scots*	St John
	JULIET	*Romeo and Juliet*	Shakespeare
1789–90	Not engaged		
1791	No new parts		
1791–2	THE QUEEN	*King Richard III*	Shakespeare
	MRS OAKLEY	*The Jealous Wife*	Colman
1792–3	ARIADNE	*The Rival Sisters*	Murphy
1793–4	No new parts		
1794–5	COUNTESS ORSINA	*Emilia Galotti*	Lessing
	HORATIA	*The Roman Father*	Whitehead
	ELGIVA	*Edwy and Elgiva*	Mme d'Arblay

Season	Character	Play	Author
	PALMIRA	*Mahomet the Imposter*	Voltaire (arr. Miller)
	EMMELINE	*Edgar and Emmeline*	Hawksworth
1795–6	ROXANA	*Alexander the Great*	Lee
	ALMEYDA	*Almeyda, Queen of Granada*	Sophia Lee
	GERTRUDE	*Hamlet*	Shakespeare
	JULIA	*Such Things Were*	Hoare
1796–7	VITELLIA	*The Conspiracy*	Jephson
	MILLWOOD	*The London Merchant*	Lillo
	ATHENAIS	*The Force of Love*	Lee (arr. Tigne)
	ARPASIA	*Tamerlane*	Rowe
	DIDO	*The Queen of Carthage*	Reed
	AGNES	*The Fatal Curiosity*	Lillo
	EMILY	*The Deuce is in Him*	Colman
1797–8	JULIA	*The Rivals*	Sheridan
	MRS HALLER	*The Stranger*	Kotzebue
1798–9	MIRANDA	*Aurelio and Miranda*	Boaden
	COUNTESS OF MONTVAL	*The Castle of Montval*	Whalley
	ELVIRA	*Pizarro*	Kotzebue(arr. Sheridan)
1799–1800	ADELAIDE	*Adelaide of Wulfingen*	Kotzebue(arr. Thomson)
	JANE	*de Montfort*	Joanna Baillie
1800–1	HELENA	*Antonio; The Soldier's Return*	Godwin
	AGNES	*Julian and Agnes*	Sotheby
1801–2	HERMIONE	*The Winter's Tale*	Shakespeare

Played at Covent Garden 1802–12, but acted no new parts.

SARAH SIDDONS AND LADY MACBETH

Her Notes on the Character, and Professor G. J. Bell's
Notes of 1809 on her performance in *Macbeth*

Lady Macbeth was to become the most celebrated of Sarah Siddons's character interpretations. It was a part she played early in her career in the provinces (see pp. 21–2), and she appeared in the role at Drury Lane for the first time in February 1785. Among the notes she gave to Campbell are those she wrote about Lady Macbeth, with their perceptive emphasis on her essential femininity, a characteristic she does not appear to have emphasized on the stage. As we have seen, she struck awe and terror into her audiences, and, in the words of Hazlitt, who saw her give one of her final performances, 'it was something above nature . . . she was tragedy personified'. Campbell reproduced her notes in full in his biography (1834, Vol. II, Chap. I), but they were not available to her critics, who only saw how she chose to enact the part. The manuscript of her notes does not appear to have survived, though the other biographical memoranda, written by her and given to Campbell, are preserved in the Harvard Theatre Collection.

Of all the parts she played, her interpretation of Lady Macbeth received the most considerable and prolonged appreciation by her contemporaries; as a result we have a close record of how she presented the character. Among these records are the annotations written in an interleaved copy of the play by Professor George Joseph Bell; they are dated 1809, and resulted from his detailed observation of a performance she gave in Edinburgh. The original notes survive and are preserved in the Folger Shakespeare Library; they were reproduced in the nineteenth century in printed form by Professor H. C. Fleeming Jenkin in his posthumously published *Papers, Literary, Scientific, etc.* (1887). It would appear that the notes were actually written in the theatre during the performance. Bell wrote:

> Mrs Siddons is not before an audience. Her mind wrought up in high conception of her part – her eyes never wandering – never for a moment idle – passion and sentiment continually betraying themselves. Her words are the accompaniments of her thoughts, scarcely necessary you would imagine to the expression, but highly raising it and giving the full force of poetical effect.

Bell also annotated in a similar style Sarah Siddons's performance as

Queen Katharine, and these notes are also given in Fleeming Jenkin's book.

A recent detailed analysis both of Sarah Siddons's notes on Lady Macbeth and of Bell's notes on her performance can be found in Dennis Bartholomeusz's *Macbeth and the Players* (1969), to which the reader is referred.

Another contemporary writer who wanted to make a special study of the performance was Mrs Anna Jameson. Prevented by Campbell from writing a biography herself, with special reference to Sarah Siddons the actress and her playing of Lady Macbeth (see Additional Note to Chapter 8), Mrs Jameson had to be content with writing about her in her book *Shakespeare's Heroines: Characteristics of Women Moral, Poetical and Historical*, from which the following quotation is taken:

> In her impersonation of the part of Lady Macbeth, Mrs Siddons adopted successively three different intonations in giving the words *we fail*. At first, as a quick, contemptuous interrogation – '*we fail?*'. Afterwards, with the note of admiration – '*we fail!*' and an accent of indignant astonishment, laying the principal emphasis on the word *we* – '*we fail.*' Lastly, she fixed on what I am convinced is the true reading – we fail, with the simple period, modulating her voice to a deep, low, resolute tone, which settled the issue at once – as though she had said, 'If we fail, why then we fail, and all is over.' This is consistent with the dark fatalism of the character and the sense of the line following, and the effect was sublime – almost awful. (1898 edition, p. 326.)

V

'THE BEAUTIES OF MRS SIDDONS'

Selections from *The Beauties of Mrs Siddons, or a Review of her Performance of the Characters of Belvidera, Zara, Isabella, Margaret of Anjou, Jane Shore and Lady Randolph, in Letters from a Lady of Distinction to her friend in the Country.*   London, 1786

Belvidera: – all that melting tenderness of voice she possesses.
- – her scream at being torn away – I could only express my feeling by tears.
- – her amazing versatility of countenance, and that she has the expression of every emotion under her absolute control.
- – But in the words – 'Murder my father', there was a horror that chill'd one's blood – It was all nature here, no declamation to dissuade her from his horrid purpose.
- – the growing madness she finely masked by the increasing wildness of her eyes, and the complete distraction manifested by striking her forehead as she exclaims – 'The air's too thin – it pierces my weak brain!'

Zara: – I think I never beheld more disdainful majesty than the fine figure of Mrs Siddons displayed in her first entrance.
- – Her features . . . assumed such a softness as added infinite beauty to her countenance.
- – Her transition from love to rage was prodigiously fine; it sparkled in her eyes; it threw a glory round her whole person; it kept dominion of her countenance, and was marked with great vivacity.
- – One perfection of Mrs Siddons's performance, even when not engaged in dialogue, she never loses sight of her character.
- – her passions seem all suspended; there is an affecting solemnity, a horrid tranquility in her whole appearance, when she orders the poison to be brought to her . . . her resolution visible on drinking the poison, at the same time the natural antipathy she shewed to it was strikingly just; but the apparent working of the deadly draught was beyond any representation I ever beheld, at that moment . . . I could only feel for the agony and torture under which a fellow-creature suffered.

Isabella: – her shriek, and immediate fall, on discovering Biron, as he throws off his disguise and exclaims 'My Isabella!' was really astonishing – to describe their effect is impossible.

– her reluctance to declare her misery, yet the dark hints she gives of it – in short, it is so full of horror, that it is impossible for description to do justice to her inimitable acting – Her start on approaching to stab Biron, – her shock when going to take a last farewell of him, – and the madness which immediately ensues; 'twas impossible not to turn away, even from her. – I recollect a thousand beauties which struck me, but recollect them with a heart chilled with horror.

Margaret of Anjou: – Mrs Siddons, in this character, displayed a species of acting which I was otherwise unacquainted with; it partakes of the dignity of tragedy, enlivened by the sharp ridicule and pointed raillery, one would suppose, the property of comedy; yet are they united in Mrs Siddons, as Margaret of Anjou, with an effect that delights us by its novelty.

Jane Shore: – her representation is so near real life, that, under that persuasion, when she appeared tottering under the weight of an apparently emaciated figure, I absolutely thought her the creature perishing through want . . . shocked at the sight, I could not avoid turning from the suffering object. . . . We wish to have something exalted in the distress to interest us, and there is nothing of that kind in the famishing Shore. . . . Her soliloquy was painfully affecting; but on discovering Alicia's door, the severe sharp hunger expressed in her looks, the ravenous flame which seemed to dart from her sunk eyes, the universal weakness which prevailed through her whole frame, the trepidation with which she knocks at the door, and the fear and terror lest she should be observed craving a relief from false friendship, altogether rendered her an object too shocking for human nature to support.

Lady Randolph: – Never shall I see an object so interesting, so affecting, as Mrs Siddons at that moment; her voice still vibrates in my ear – I see her fine figure leaning over the body of her dead son, while her eyes, illumined with despair, looked as they could reanimate.

VI

THE HARVARD LETTERS

What is probably the largest single collection of letters written by Sarah Siddons is that held by the Harvard Theatre Collection in Harvard College Library, Cambridge, Massachusetts. Through the kindness of the Curator, Miss Helen D. Willard, I am able to give below some sample extracts from these very domestic, intimate letters written for the most part to Miss Bedina Wynn, to Mrs Soame, and to the Viscountess Perceval, the godmother of Sarah's daughter Cecilia. The letters number some 200:

Writing from Hull on 15 August 1886, to the Viscountess Perceval:

I will proceed to tell you that the labours of this summer have attained for me a little comfortable independence, and that if it shoud please God in his Wisdom to afflict me with disease, it has pleased him in his infinite goodness and mercy to bestow on me the comforts, tho not the Superfluities of life. My dear friend, when I came to London – my utmost ambition was to be worth ten thousand pounds, and I have now got it, and yet I dare swear there are many who can give certain proof that I am worth forty thousand. If it shoud please God to bless me with health, my riches will be incredible, for I will go on as long as I am able, and what these good folks will bring it to in a few years more, must [–] be *immensely immense*, you know, however, just as they please, I *know* that I have *enough*, and I dont care how much more I get.

16 March 1787, to Miss Bedina Wynn:

My dear Bidini. It strikes me that the gown which I am sure your dear Aunt will not suffer you to refuse me the pleasure of seeing you wear, will be particularly becoming to your sort of Complexion with white satin Coat and trimmings. Adieu my sweet Girl, I am involved in a vast deal of Business and dont you see how I am worried with one of your vile scratching Pens – (the writing reveals this!).

2 September 1787, to Miss Bedina Wynn:

I shall be the happiest creature in the world to wait on you next Tuesday if Mr Siddons is well enough to admit of my leaving him. He has been very ill with a feverish Cold these last two days, and I have not left him except for Church this morning, and to pay my duty to my Mother, who is ill, but I hope he will be better after some medicine he is to take tonight.

18 September 1787, to Miss Bedina Wynn, concerning William's illness:

I pray that I may not be *mistaken*! for this cruel disorder has been treacherous to a great degree; about this time of the day he in general appears so much more composed that when the Evening brings an encrease of Fever and restlessness, it is impossible to describe (or to imagine) without having felt it, the bitterness of the disappointment. You would be shocked to see the devastation this Tyrant Fever has made. He is reduced to a Shaddow and is unable to sit upright five minutes – '*I* should be sick but that my resolution helps me.' I have been in bed but four nights since the commencement of this terrible illness and have never been without these wretched walls but once since I saw you.

20 October 1787, to Miss Bedina Wynn:

. . . it woud be *too* much we shoud grow too much *attachd* to this life, only a certain proportion of blessings are allowd, yet I think if I had the power of choice I woud prefer the blessing and all those *quiet* and *virtuous* joys attending on *your* situation to all the Tumult of Applause for what are calld great Talents, nay I am *sure* I woud.

13 November 1787, to Mrs Soame:

If Bidini ever walks down by the back of our House (and if She does not, I wish She woud) She woud see a fine looking woman very big with child, not knowing that She has an hour to remain out of a miserable Bed *made of Shavings* with no one comfort in her painful Situation, having a most *beautiful Boy* of a little more than a year and a half old for whose support the poor creature sits on the cold damp ground all day selling Apples and Gingerbread. She tells me her Husbands illness of three months standing has reduced her to the necessity of Selling everything She had rather than go to the Parish which She heartily resents. If you can spare a trifle from the Purse which you so constantly replenish for the *Poor* I will venture to say this is a fit object of your Charity.

18 April 1788, to Mrs Soame. She alludes to the death of Eliza Ann:

I know that you cannot be indifferent about anything you honour with your regard. I therefore take the first opportunity of telling you that Mr S. is better and that I am as well as my distress will let me be. There is no reasoner but *time* upon these subjects, and *Hope*, is the only balm for the afflicted mind. I have lately sufferd a great deal in Body *and* Mind. *But God's will be done.*

Edinburgh, July 1788, to Mrs Soame, whom her son George is visiting:

. . . he really is tho' I say it a darling Baby – O how I shoud love to see you all sitting at Breakfast, I dare say little Sauce Box makes one of the company and often assures Aunt Soame (I am delighted with the relationship he has made tho it was unnecessary to endear you *more* to me) as he usd to assure his mother that he 'wont throw down his tea no no'. I hope he wont forget me.

3 June 1789, to Miss Bedina Wynn:

. . . (I) am convincd if I coud keep clear of these dreadful Theatrical exertions which enflame my blood and exhaust my Strength that I shoud be perfectly well in a fortnight. Well, they will be over in August for some months, perhaps *years* if the Lottery answers. Heaven send it may!

26 July (1789), to Miss Bedina Wynn:

Alas my dear Girl I have waited and waited to answer your dear Letters *agreeably* if possible; but it will *not* be, for I am as great a Martyr as ever to my tormenting Complaint: the Sea which I flatterd myself was to be of use, and which I think I have tried long enough to *guess* at, is baffled by this vehement malady; which I am more convincd is not worms, but some acrimony in the blood. I now perceive very certainly, that there is corruption within the Fundament. The itching as heretofore, is *intolerable*, and it wears my Spirits night and day to a degree that overturns all my resolutions of patience. . . . Wednesday – I hope to be in better Spirits than I am this day which has been spent in weeping.

January 1795, to the Viscountess Perceval:

I have not been out of my House three times for these six weeks except to the Theatre, and in short my mornings are entirely taken up by indispensable occupation private or public. Indeed my Cold has hung about me so long, and the weather is so terribly severe that I never move from the Fireside except when I am absolutely compelld. This dreadful Winter seems to freeze ones very Heart.

24 November 1795, to the Viscountess Perceval (?):

I am now acting in a Grand *Pantomime* called Alexander the Great in which I have a very bad part and a very fine dress it is an odious thing but my brother plays very finely in it, and the Show of lighting Ladies Dancing Horses Elephants Drums Trumpets etc will *go it* several nights I suppose; well, anything is better than saying Isabella etc over and over again till one is so tired – How I do wish that Somebody woud write two or three good tragedies some wet afternoon! Apropos to new tragedies, Mr Greatheed is come to Town with his Hair cropt, out of powder and looking like – – A *Man*, and the dear soul is violent in Politicks as ever. I woud to Heaven the subject was prohibited in private society.

VII

THE KEMBLE FAMILY

(Based on the family tree in Yvonne ffrench's book, *Mrs Siddons, Tragic Actress*, with the author's kind permission.)

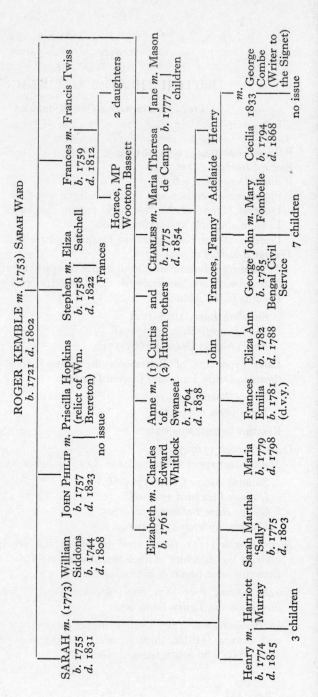

VIII

BRITISH THEATRICAL LINEAGE

From Shakespeare to Sarah Siddons

William Shakespeare 1564–1616
Richard Burbage c. 1567–1619
William Davenant 1606–68
    Shakespeare's godson and putative natural son
    Director of one of the two royal patent companies established in London after the Restoration, 1660
    Professional actresses appear in English theatres from this time
Thomas Betterton c. 1635–1710
    Trained by Davenant and head of the company by 1671
    Married to *Mary Sanderson* (d. 1712), also trained by Betterton
    Leading ladies include:

      Elizabeth Barry 1658–1713
      Anne Bracegirdle c. 1663–1748
      Anne (Nance) Oldfield 1663–1748

Later exponents of Betterton's declamatory style at the Patent theatres, Drury Lane and Covent Garden:

      Barton Booth 1681–1733
      James Quin 1693–1766

Reacting against this style:

David Garrick 1717–79
    Main career spent at Drury Lane. Leading ladies include:

      Susanna Maria Cibber 1714–66
      Hannah Pritchard 1711–68
      George Anne Bellamy 1727–1815
      Frances Abington 1737–1815

Roger Kemble (1721–1802), strolling player and provincial manager, married the daughter of an actor who had appeared as a child with Betterton, and becomes the father of:

Sarah Siddons 1755–1831, who appeared with Garrick during his final season at Drury Lane, and

John Philip Kemble 1757–1823, manager successively of Drury Lane and Covent Garden theatres, and who married *Priscilla Hopkins* 1755–1845, who had acted with Garrick

Select Bibliography

AGATE, JAMES, *These Were Actors*, London: Hutchinson. N.D.

d'ARBLAY, MADAME, *Diary and Letters of Madame d'Arblay*, edited by Charlotte Barrett, 6 vols., London: Macmillan, 1904.

BARKER, KATHLEEN, *The Theatre Royal, Bristol: The First Seventy Years*, Bristol: Bristol Branch of the Historical Association, revised edition, 1969.

BARTHOLOMEUSZ, DENNIS, *Macbeth and the Players*, Cambridge University Press, 1969.

BEATTIE, JAMES, *Day-Book 1773–98*, edited by Ralph S. Walker, Third Spalding Club, 1948.

Beauties of Mrs Siddons, The, or a Review of her Performance . . . in Letters from a Lady of Distinction to her friend in the Country, London: 1786.

BLOCH, IVAN, *Sexual Life in England*, London: Corgi, 1965.

BOADEN, JAMES, *Memoirs of Mrs Siddons*, 2 vols., London: 1827. Later edition, London: Gibbings and Co, 1896.

BOADEN, JAMES, *Memoirs of the Life of John Philip Kemble*, 2 vols., London, 1825.

BOADEN, JAMES, *The life of Mrs Jordan*, 2 vols., London, 1831.

BOADEN, JAMES, *Memoirs of Mrs Inchbald*, 2 vols., London, 1833.

BOSWELL, JAMES, *Life of Johnson*, London: 1791. Everyman Library Edition, 1906. Reprinted 1962.

BURNIM, KALMAN A., *David Garrick, Director*, University of Pittsburg Press, 1961.

BYRON, LORD, *Byron, A Self-Portrait. Letters and Diaries 1788–1824*, edited by Peter Quennell, London: John Murray 1950.

CAMPBELL, THOMAS, *Life of Mrs Siddons*, London: 1834.

CONNELL, BRIAN, *Portrait of a Whig Peer*, London: Deutsch, 1957.

DIBDEN, JAMES C., *The Annals of the Edinburgh Stage*, Edinburgh: Richard Cameron, 1888.

DOWNER, ALAN S., *The Eminent Tragedian: William Charles Macready*, Harvard University Press and Oxford University Press, 1966.

DUNBAR, JANET, *Peg Woffington and her World*, London: Heinemann, 1968.

FARINGTON, JOSEPH, *The Farington Diary*, edited by James Grieg, 8 vols., London: Hutchinson, 1923.

ffRENCH, YVONNE, *Mrs Siddons, Tragic Actress*, London: Cobden-Sanderson, 1936. Revised edition: Verschoyle, 1954.

FITZGERALD, PERCY, *The Kembles*, 2 vols., London: 1871.

GALINDO, CATHERINE, *Mrs Galindo's Letter to Mrs Siddons*, London: 1809.

GARLICK, KENNETH, *Sir Thomas Lawrence*, London: Routledge and Kegan Paul, 1954.

GARRICK, DAVID, *The Letters of David Garrick*, edited by David M. Little and George M. Kahrl, 3 vols., Oxford University Press, 1963.

GASCOIGNE, BAMBER, *World Theatre: an Illustrated History*, London: Ebury Press, 1968.

GENEST, JOHN, *Some Account of the English Stage in 1660 to 1830*, Vols. VI, VII, VIII, London: 1832.

GIBBS, LEWIS, *Sheridan*, London: Dent, 1947.

GLENBERVIE, LORD, *The Diaries of Sylvester Douglas*, edited by Francis Bickley, London: Constable, 1928.

GOLDRING, DOUGLAS, *Regency Portrait Painter: the Life of Sir Thomas Lawrence*, London: MacDonald, 1951.

GREBANIER, BERNARD, *The Great Shakespeare Forgery*, London: Heinemann, 1966.

GREVILLE, CHARLES CAVENDISH FULKE, *The Greville Diary*, edited by Philip Whitwell Wilson, London: Heinemann, 1927.

HARDIE, MARTIN, *Water-Colour Painting in Britain: I. The Eighteenth Century*, London: Batsford, 1966.

HAYDON, B. R., *The Autobiography and Journals*, edited by M. Elwin, London: MacDonald, 1950. (First published, 1853.)

HAZLITT, WILLIAM, *Characters of Shakespeare's Plays*, London: Oxford University Press; *Criticism and Dramatic Essays on the Modern Stage*, London: Routledge, 1851.

HOLCROFT, THOMAS, *Memoirs of the late Thomas Holcroft*, edited by William Hazlitt, London: 1816.

HOPKINS, MARY, *Hannah More and her Circle*, New York: Longmans, Green and Co., 1947.

HUNT, LEIGH, *The Town*, London: Oxford University Press, 1907. (First published 1848.)

JAMESON, ANNA, *Shakespeare's Heroines: Characteristics of Women, Moral, Political and Historical*, revised edition, London: Bell, 1898.

JENKIN, H. C. FLEEMING, *Papers, Literary, Scientific, Etc.*, London: 1887.

JONES, M. G., *Hannah More*, Cambridge University Press, 1952.

KELLY, MICHAEL, *Reminiscences*, London: 1826.

KEMBLE, FRANCES ANN, *Record of a Girlhood*, London: 1878.

KENNARD, A., *Mrs Siddons*, London: 1887.

KNAPP, OSWALD G., *An Artist's Love Story, Told in the Letters of Sir Thomas Lawrence, Mrs Siddons and her Daughters*, edited by Oswald G. Knapp, London: George Allen, 1904.

LATIMER, JOHN, *The Annals of Bristol in the Eighteenth Century*, printed for the Author, 1893.

LAYARD, GEORGE SOMES, *Sir Thomas Lawrence's Letter-Bag*, London: George Allen, 1906.

LEWES, CHARLES LEE, *Memoirs*, London, 1805.

MANDER, RAYMOND and MITCHENSON, JOE, *The Theatres of London*, London: Rupert Hart-Davis, 1963.

MANDER, RAYMOND and MITCHENSON, JOE, *A Picture History of the British Theatre*, London: Hulton Press, 1957.

MARCHAND, LESLIE A., *Byron: a Biography*, London: John Murray, 1957.

MATHEWS, CHARLES, *Memoirs of Charles Mathews, Comedian*, Philadelphia: Lea and Blanchard, 1839.

MAUROIS, ANDRÉ, *Meïpe: III, Portrait d'une Actrice*, Paris: Grasset, 1926.

MELVILLE, LEWIS, *More Stage Favourites of the Eighteenth Century*, London: Hutchinson, 1929.

MITCHELL, R. J. and LEYS, M. D. R., *A History of London Life*, London: Longmans, 1958.

MOORE, THOMAS, *Memoirs of the Life of the Right Honourable Richard Brinsley Sheridan*, London: 1827, fifth edition.

NICOLL, ALARDYCE, *The Development of the Theatre*, London: Harrap, 1927.

NICOLL, ALARDYCE, *A History of Late Eighteenth Century Drama, 1750–1800*, Cambridge University Press, 1927.

NICOLSON, HAROLD, *The Age of Reason*, London: Constable and Co, 1960.

ODELL, GEORGE C. D., *Shakespeare – from Betterton to Irving*, London: Constable, 1963, reprinted edition.

OMAN, CAROLA, *David Garrick*, London: Hodder and Stoughton, 1958.

PARSONS, MRS CLEMENT, *The Incomparable Siddons*, London: Methuen, 1909.

PASQUIN, ANTHONY (JOHN WILLIAMS), *The Eccentricities of John Edwin, Comedian*, London: n.d. (1791).

PEAKE, R. B., *Memoirs of the Colman Family*, London: 1841.

PENLEY, BELVILLE S., *The Bath Stage*, London and Bath: 1892.

PENLEY, BELVILLE S., *Mrs Siddons and Bath*, reprinted from *The Bath Herald*, n.d. (1922?).

PIOZZI, HESTER, *The Intimate Letters of Hester Piozzi and Penelope Pennington, 1788–1821*, edited by Oswald G. Knapp, London: John Lane, the Bodley Head, 1914.

PIOZZI, HESTER, *Piozziana or Recollections, of the Late Mrs Piozzi*, edited by N. Mangin, London: 1833.

PIOZZI, HESTER, *Thraliana: the Diary of Mrs Hester Lynch Thrale*, edited by K. C. Balderston, Oxford University Press, 1951.

PLAYFAIR, GILES, *The Prodigy: a Study of the Strange Life of Master Betty*, London: Secker and Warburg, 1967.

PLUMB, J. H., *The First Four Georges*, London: Batsford, 1956.

PRIESTLEY, J. B., *The Prince of Pleasure and his Regency 1811–20*, London: Heinemann, 1969.

REDDING, CYRUS, *Literary Reminiscences and Memoirs of Thomas Campbell*, London: 1860.

REYNOLDS, SIR JOSHUA, *Letters*, collected and edited by Frederick Whiley Hilles, Cambridge University Press, 1929.

ROBINSON, CRABB, *The London Theatre 1811–1866*, Selections from the Diary of Henry Crabb Robinson, edited by Eluned Brown, London: Society for Theatre Research, 1966.

ROBINSON, MRS MARY, *Mrs Mary Robinson, Written by Herself*, London: Grolier Society, n.d.

ROGERS, SAMUEL, *Recollections*, London: 1859.

ROYDE-SMITH, NAOMI, *The Private Life of Mrs Siddons*, London: Gollancz, 1933.

SEWARD, ANNA, *The Swan of Lichfield: Selections from the Correspondence of Anna Seward*, edited by Hesketh Pearson, London Hamish Hamilton, 1936.

SHELDON, ESTHER K., *Thomas Sheridan of Smock Alley*, Princetown University Press and Oxford University Press, 1969.

SHERIDAN, RICHARD BRINSLEY, *The Letters of Richard Brinsley Sheridan*, 3 vols., edited by Cecil Price, Oxford University Press, 1966.

SIDDONS, SARAH KEMBLE, *The Reminiscences of Sarah Kemble Siddons*, edited by William Van Lennep, Cambridge, Mass.: Widener Library, 1942. (Mrs Siddons's biographical notes supplied to Thomas Campbell.)

SIDDONIAN HOUSING ASSOCIATION LIMITED, *Mrs Siddons*, London, n.d.

SOUTHERN, RICHARD, *The Georgian Playhouse*, London: Pleiades Books, 1948.

SOUTHERN, RICHARD, *Changeable Scenery: its Origin and Development in the British Theatre*, London: Faber and Faber, 1952.

STIRLING, A. M. W., *The Hothams*, London: Jenkins, 1918.

TAYLOR, JOHN, *Records of my Life*, 2 vols., London: 1832.

THOMAS, T. C., *Sarah Siddons*, Brecon: The Brecknock Society, n.d.

THRALE, MRS HESTER LYNCH (See Piozzi, Mrs Hester).

TIMBS, JOHN, *Anecdote Biography*, London: 1860.

TREVELYAN, G. M., *Illustrated English Social History: Vol. III, The Eighteenth Century*, London: Longmans Green, 1949–52; Penguin Books, 1966.

WALPOLE, HORACE, *Letters*, edited by Paget Toynbee, 16 vols., Oxford, 1905. At present being published in the volumes of the Yale Edition, edited by W. S. Lewis.

WATERHOUSE, ELLIS, *Painting in Britain 1530–1790*, London: Penguin Books, 1953.

WHALLEY, THOMAS SEDGEWICK, *Journals and Correspondence*, edited with a Memoir and Illustrative Notes by Reverend Hill Wickham, 2 vols., London: 1863.

WHITE, T. H., *The Age of Scandal*, London: Jonathan Cape, 1950.

WILKINSON, TATE, *Memoirs of His Own Life*, Dublin: 1791.

WILKINSON, TATE, *The Wandering Patentee*, London: 1795.

WYNDHAM, H. S., *The Annals of Covent Garden Theatre from 1732 to 1897*, London: 1906.

While this book was in the press, the letters quoted in Chapters 5 and 7, and noted as being from the collection, Rylands J. R. L. Eng MS. No. 574 have been published in full as part of the complete Rylands MSS. collection of Siddons papers, with the following title: *The Letters of Sarah and William Siddons to Hester Lynch Piozzi in the John Rylands Library*. [Edited by Kalman A. Burnim, Manchester, The John Rylands Library: 1969.]

Index of Principal Plays and Parts in which Sarah Siddons Appeared

This Index cross-references the plays and parts in which Sarah Siddons appeared in London, and her principal roles in the provincial theatres.

371

General Index

This Index incorporates names and principal references except for the plays and parts in which Sarah Siddons appeared, which are listed in the preceding Index. Principal references appearing in the Notes and Appendices are included in both Indexes.